CW00549584

"LET TYRANTS TREMBLE"

The War Diary of 199 (Bomber Support) Squadron
November 1942 – July 1945

by
John Reid

Text © John Reid, 2014.
First published in the United Kingdom, 2014,
by Stenlake Publishing Ltd.
Telephone: 01290 551122
www.stenlake.co.uk

ISBN 9781840336047

Printed in China

**The publishers regret that they cannot supply
copies of any pictures featured in this book.**

Acknowledgements

My thanks go to the following: Martin Middlebrook and Chris Everitt for access to their book *The Bomber Command War Diaries* from which I gleaned details of Bomber Command raids, damage and losses; Bryce Gomersall for his assistance in correcting errors in the Squadron ORB; Mary Ghrist for her regular visits to the Public Records Office; Ann Hudson for typing the casualty lists; Ken Hartley for the many anecdotes from members of the Squadron; Cyril Bradley for locating the 199 Squadron Sortie Records at RAF Quedgeley, from which a very accurate account of the RCM role of the Squadron could be written; and Douglas Wood who first put me in touch with Stenlake Publishing.

My grateful thanks go to the following people who assisted in the removal of the Stirling Mural: Mr Maurice Hood, Mr Alan Sanders, Seamans Animal Feeds Ltd, Miss Wendy Bird, *Eastern Daily Press*, Mr W. Slater, Mr Phil Panichelli, Burralls Printers Ltd, Mr Ken Ellis, RAF Museum Hendon, Mr Colin Payne, Mr Bill Welbourne, Mr Claude Garford, Mr Michael Bowyer, Miss Pauline Plummer, Mr L. Ward-Walters, B.B.C. Look East, Mr David Reid, Mr Rod Lyons, Coleman Builders Ltd, *Flypast Magazine*, J. Lane Engineering, Mr Tony Harrold, Group Captain W.S.O. Randle MBE, AFC, DFM, Wing Commander W.G. Wood, OBE, and Seadyke Freight Systems.

Illustration Acknowledgements

Every effort has been made to confirm, acknowledge and credit the names of the individual photograph donors.

Adam Chisholm - 102
A.E. Lofthouse MBE - 224
Bert Fitchett - 73, 82
Bob Charters - 105
British Motor Industry Heritage Trust - 193, back cover (top)
Canadian Jewish Congress Charities Commission and RCAF Veterans Affairs, Canada - 137
Colin Munro - 152 (top), 156
Curly Brown - 45
Cyril Bradley - 186
Dave Lockett - 68
Dave Oddy - 48
Dorothy Allen - 223
G.M. (Jock) Duncan - 37, 39
Jim Hallas via Vivien Mathews (Keystone Press) - 192, 194
Jim Newman - 7, 49 (top)
John Reid - 219 (bottom), 220 (top), 221, 222
Keith Rankin - 36
Ken Humby - 19, 49 (bottom)

Lance Smith (199 Squadran Adjutant) Collection - 1, 6 (top), 11, 15, 27, 29, 43, 64, 75, 108, 109, 111, 113, 114, 125, 126 (both), 141, front cover (bottom), back cover (bottom)
Mathew Morton - 61, 62
MOD Crown Copyright, Defence Intellectual Property Rights - 1 (crest)
Ray Lind - 142
Reverend Peters - 190
Richard Masters - 218, 219 (top)
Roy Smith - 87, 135, 152 (bottom)
Shorts (Bombardier) - 4, 59, front cover (top)
Stan Freestone - 6 (bottom)
Stan Pallant - 138 (top), 178
Stirling Bomber Research Library - 56, 96, 138 (bottom), 145, 179, 198
Sue Whitworth - 216, 217 (both)
Tom Austin - 20
Wilf Humphries - 32, 78

Bibliography

Martin Middlebrook and Chris Everitt, *The Bomber Command War Diaries*, Penguin Books Ltd, 1985.
W.R. Chorley, *Royal Air Force Bomber Command Losses*, Midland Counties Publications.
Martin Streetly, *Confound and Destroy*, Macdonald and Jane's Publishing Co. Ltd., London, 1978.
Alfred Price, *Instruments of Darkness (History of Electronic Warfare)*, Macdonald and Jane's Publishing Co. Ltd., London, 1978.
George Millar, *The Bruneval Raid*, The Bodley Head, 1974.
R.V. Jones, *Most Secret War (British Scientific Intelligence 1939–1945)*, Hamish Hamilton Ltd, 1978.
Bryce Gomersall, *The Stirling File (Revised Edition)*, Air-Britain (Historians) Ltd, 1987.

Contents

Appendices:

No. 199 Squadron (Bomber Support) RAF

At the beginning of the First World War, a number of squadrons were formed with the sole aim of training the then fledgling air and ground crews of the Royal Flying Corps which became the Royal Air Force in 1918. For this specific purpose, 199 Squadron was formed at East Retford, Nottinghamshire as a night training squadron and continued in this role until disbanded in 1919 at RAF Harpswell, Lincolnshire, later RAF Hemswell.

Over the next twenty years, the armed forces and in particular the RAF, underwent a slow and not altogether satisfactory modernisation of its tactics and equipment. When the prospect of another war with Germany loomed in the late 1930s it was realised that the RAF was far behind in quantity and quality of aircraft compared to the Luftwaffe which had been secretly building up its numbers. To begin with, Bomber Command had to manage with only light twin-engined aircraft, mainly the Blenheim, Hampden and the Wellington and it was with these that the fight was taken to the Germans over occupied Europe. The heavy four-engined bombers were, at the start of the war, only then being tried as prototypes or were not even off the drawing board.

Expansion was all-important and, to assist with the ever-increasing numbers of men being enlisted into Bomber Command, 199 Squadron was reformed within 1 Group on 7th November 1942. The airfield chosen was at Blyton, near Gainsborough, in Lincolnshire. It was, in the words of the crews stationed there, "right out in the sticks".

1942

New beginnings – battle is joined –
mud and Wellingtons at Blyton

Wing Commander C.R. Hattersley DFC, was the Squadron C/O, responsible for getting the airfield operational, and on this first day, with a very grey and overcast sky, poor visibility, and only nine officers and 78 NCOs and other ranks to get things organised, he knew everyone would have to work extra hard.

Sergeant Stan Freestone and his crew were one of the initial six crews posted to Blyton to form the nucleus of the Squadron. He had been serving with 142 Squadron at RAF Waltham, a satellite of Binbrook; and he remembers those first days very well: *"After having completed seven Ops with 142 Squadron, we were granted seven days leave. Upon returning, we found the unit in turmoil, Wimpies [Vickers Wellington] all changing to desert camouflage and the staff getting ready to leave for the Middle East. On reporting to my Flight Commander, Squadron Leader Sands, I was informed that me and my crew were not going to the Middle East but would, the following day, meet Squadron Leader K. Humby who was to be Flight Commander of a newly formed Squadron, No.199.*

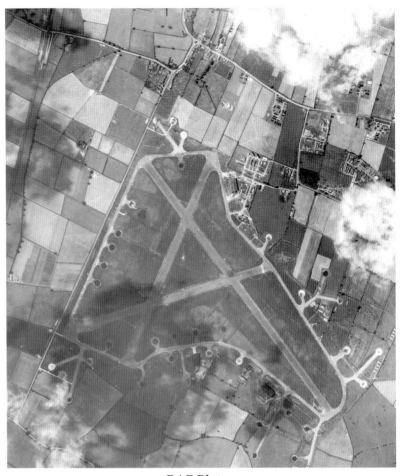

RAF Blyton

I believe six crews in all were so detailed and the new base was to be at Blyton. In a typical Lincolnshire winter Blyton was aptly named since it did on first appearances appear 'Blighted' if you will pardon the pun. Just a runway with a peri-track, very basic buildings and everyone housed in Nissen huts. It was very dispersed in every sense of the word and a bicycle was absolutely essential."

Sgt Stan Freestone and crew.

The new aircrews and ground crews did not receive their aircraft until 12th November, when three Wellington Mk III Type 423 that had been adapted to carry a 4,000lb bomb (a cookie) and five Wellington Mk III were delivered and taken over from No.12 Squadron. Flying was to be limited due to very severe weather, ice and fog restricting all but short air tests and some Bullseye exercises. The squadron spent most of the non-flying days getting settled into a routine. There were lectures for air gunners and bomb aimers on squadron discipline, practice briefings and tactics for aircrew. Navigators received instructions on air sea rescue and 'Gee' the new navigational aid that had been introduced into RAF service during August 1941. On the 20th November a representative of Bristol Engine Company, the engine manufacturer, was in attendance lecturing the pilots on engine handling.

Ground crews, as usual, bore the brunt of the cold weather as best they could, there being only three hangars for major overhauls – all other work being carried out in the open.

Corporal Mathew Morton, a fitter IIE, joined 199 at RAF Blyton and can remember those first winter days spent out on dispersals – *"Joining 199 in early November 1942 would, I suppose, class me as a founder member of the Squadron. Actually I was posted to 199 at Lindholm and arrived at Blyton a week later. I was primarily concerned with flight maintenance of the Wimpy IIIs and from my ground staff point of view I clearly recall the winter of 42/43 as being exceptionally cold, and it must also have been hell for the aircrews. Ops during this period were preceded by anti-icing precautions, which were invariably carried out by the basic trades people i.e. fitters and riggers. The hoar frost was removed by applying a liquid called Killfrost to the complete upper surface of the aircraft using a standard stirrup pump. Once this was completed, special attention had to be paid to the leading edges of the main planes, control surfaces, fins, and propellers with a compound whose trade name I have forgotten. This de-icing compound had the consistency of a modern sealing material and had a marked reluctance to spread about. Experience taught us that the best way of spreading it was to roll it on using a beer bottle full of hot water. Using other methods was dicey and there were numerous metal rulers, files, and screwdrivers truncated by the balloon cable cutters mounted in the leading edges to testify to it.*

'Anti-Glow' paint was liberally plastered over the exhaust stubs and tail pipes, but the de-icing was probably more effective than the anti-glowing.

I remember too being moved away from the aircraft when RCAF personnel carried out ground testing on the GEE and IFF sets, although with hindsight I now realise that at that juncture these devices were not as secret as we thought they were.

In early 1943 there was, I think, only one aircraft, which was capable of carrying a 4,000lb bomb, this being EX-K. One of the pilots of this Wellington was Flight Sergeant Silverman and another was a RAAF Flight Sergeant whose name I cannot remember and am ashamed to admit it. I do not know what happened to the former but I do know the Aussie pilot and his rear gunner, another Aussie, were screened after doing a tour on Wellingtons and Stirlings."

Cpl Jim Newman

Another founder member of the Squadron was Corporal Jim Newman, a flight mechanic, who joined other members of the ground crews at RAF Pocklington. He remembers – *"The ground crews arrived in dribs and drabs and were sorted out into their various trades before moving to Blyton. Here, on a very cold and overcast early November day we had our sections allocated to us within the Flights. On the next day, I think it was the 12th, about eight Wellingtons arrived and we set about servicing and checking them over as soon as the crews handed them over to us. The airfield was quite bleak and had just a few hard standings dotted about, the main runway being grass. There were two or three hangars but these were only used for major overhauls, most of the work was carried out in the open as usual. We knew time was not on our side at this point in the war and everyone got stuck in to prepare the aircraft for operations, but the weather was to hinder the Squadron's activities and over this we had no control. Equipment was slow in arriving on the flight lines and we used concrete blocks as wheel chocks and had to improvise with the few tools we had available. But, as always, we managed, perhaps being in the RAF since joining up on 9th March 1921 helped me to overcome many problems and being 38 years old upon joining 199 put me in the 'Old Sweat' division. Little by little we sorted ourselves out, attending lectures on a multitude of subjects and getting to know 'our Wimpy' and her crew and also going round scrounging sundry items we were short of".*

Jim Newman carries on with his story as the book progresses.

December 1942

The first loss and a home run

From 1st December to the 5th no flying was possible due to persistent fog, so all the Wellingtons on strength were inspected and checked. It was known that the Squadron's first operation was imminent and everyone now had to wait for the weather to clear.

On the morning of 6th December, the fog had dispersed and the visibility was fair to good, so 'A' flight sent one aircraft out on test and 'B' flight two. 'B' flight also collected Wellington Z1600 from RAF Harwarden. Many of the aircrews received a lecture that morning from the local gunnery officer Major Albreicht on the problems of flak and while this was going on, the teleprinter in the Ops room started to clatter and print out what everyone had been expecting for the past week – the Squadron's first Op was on for that night.

The target was Mannheim and eight aircraft were detailed for the raid. Crew briefings were held and the ground crews bombed up the designated Wellingtons, radios were checked and engines run up leaving only the long wait until take-off.

At 1704 hrs the aircraft began to lift off from the grass runway, but two had to abort due to engine failure and one other had to return having taken off much later than the others. The other five: BK367 EX-U, S/Ldr Davies; X3819 EX-F, Sgt Bird; BK138 EX-Z, P/O Powell; BK507 EX-E, Sgt Hockley; EJ582 EX-O, P/O Wingood, all found the target.

Mannheim was covered with 10/10 cloud and the Pathfinders had not released all their flares, so the bomb aimers dropped their loads on fires seen through the overcast. No results were observed. The city reported only 500 incendiaries had fallen on the town, together with a small quantity of leaflets. There were no German casualties and little structural damage caused to the buildings.

All the aircraft returned safely, but due to bad weather at RAF Blyton they were diverted: Sgt Bird and P/O Powell to RAF Boscombe Down, P/O Wingood to RAF Manston, Sgt Hockley to RAF Exeter, S/Ldr Davies to RAF Bourne.

The Squadron's contribution on their first raid to Germany cannot be assessed accurately due to the unfavourable weather conditions over the target. One thing was for sure, '199' was operational and would contribute in the future in ways that could be measured against the overall offensive mounted by Bomber Command.

Sgt Eric Nicholas was posted to RAF Blyton in December 1942 and recalls – *"I first joined the W/T section at Blyton just before Christmas and the Squadron was still getting itself sorted out. Little did I know at that point in time that I would remain with the Squadron until the end of the war."*

J.G. Nixon, Rear Gunner was another of the aircrew stationed at RAF Blyton – *"I joined 199 at Blyton in December 1942 and remained with them until the end of '43. I was very much an 'old boy' of the Squadron having been a "Tail End Charlie" [rear gunner] who had finished his tour. During my Ops I had three skippers – F/Lt Wingood, S/Ldr Humby and S/Ldr Pettit."*

Keith Rankin, a Canadian, arrived at RAF Blyton on 11th November just a few days after the Squadron officially took over the airfield. He had arrived from Canada after completing his training as an air gunner and now takes up his story: *"On completing my training in Canada I was posted overseas in May 1942. Our transportation was a freighter, which could accommodate twenty-five passengers. We took fourteen days to cross the Atlantic from Halifax to Liverpool. Our crossing was not without its periods of danger, especially when the engine broke down and the rest of the convoy proceeded without us. It took twenty-four harrowing hours for the crew to repair the fault and get underway again and eventually we arrived safely in Liverpool. Almost immediately we were marched off to board a train for Bournemouth on the South Coast. Upon arrival, we were billeted in the Bath Hill Court, and, while there, had my first taste of war when three German fighters attacked one evening. One bomb just missed our quarters while another bomb hit the Officers hotel killing seven Canadians and a third hit the train yard. One German fighter was shot down and crashed into the English Channel.*

On July 23rd 1942 I was transferred to 7 Air Gunnery Scool at Stormy Downs, Wales for a refresher course and I remained there until Sept. 1942. During the training, we flew in Whitleys and Defiants and then, upon completion, I was posted to 28 Operational Training Unit. I met the other crew members: Sgt. Len Waldorf, Pilot; Sgt. Hughes, Nav; F/O Cook, W/Op; Sgt. Wilson, Bomb Aimer.

Our pilot instructor on these training flights was F/Sgt Williams. He remained with us until Sept. 10th, 1942 and then we were on our own, except for the occasional flight check carried out by F/Sgt Williams. This training carried on until Nov. 11th, 1942 at which time we were transferred to Blyton to form 199 Squadron.

During our training at OTU two incidents stand out in my memory. The first incident happened when we were out on a fighter affiliation exercise when the turret jammed, which meant if we had to bail out I was stuck in the turret as there was no way to reach my parachute. The second incident happened during night circuits. On our last circuit a Petrol Bowser started across the runway just as we were touching down. We hit the Bowser with our left wing tip and then ran into the tractor pulling the Bowser. Fortunately the airman driving the tractor saw us coming and he jumped clear, however the tractor was a mess, in fact they never found the steering wheel and the radiator cap was found buried in the aircraft just below the pilots seat. Our aircraft received substantial damage overall.

Our first operational flight was planned for Dec. 31st, 1942 as we had carried out our Air Test in the morning, which was the routine prior to an operational flight. We had been assigned "R" for Robert for our first operational flight, but due to engine failure as we proceeded down the grass runway the pilot aborted the take-off, we ground looped and the undercarriage collapsed and we ended up well off the runway in the mud. I received a bang on the head from the guns and the turret doors were jammed, however I was able to force the door open, and I fell out on my back in the mud. I remember getting up and running to the front of the aircraft and Len the pilot had opened the escape hatch above the cockpit, and I remember asking him if all was ok and he replied that he had just a few bruises. As he turned to get the rest of the crew out I must have fainted as they found me lying in the mud. I was taken to hospital for observation where I spent the night.

We were back on Ops on Jan 2nd 1943. Our first trip was to St Nazaire and others included La Rochelle, Lorient, Mannheim and Air/Sea Searches. I continued flying Ops until May 1943 when I was grounded for a severe case of sinus and bronchitis and finally declared unfit for any further flying duties.

My position on the crew was taken over by Sgt Wharmby and on May 13th 1943 they were shot down and crashed in Holland. My crew were all killed and buried in the Harderwijk General Cemetery, Netherlands.

It comes to mind that during one of my trips, as we were climbing for altitude, the bomb aimer saw a Lancaster coming straight at us and called for the pilot to dive, which he did just in time. From my rear turret I remember seeing the Lancaster for a fleeting moment and then it ran into another Lancaster and they both crashed near Waddington. I often wondered why there were not more mid-air collisions with so many bombers in a confined area.

People I personally remember on the Squadron are: W/Cdr Bloomfield, W/Cdr Howard, S/Ldr Powell, P/O Hagues, W/O Palmer, S/Ldr Davis, F/O Wingood.

If I am correct, W/Cdr Bloomfield was a prisoner of war and his bomb aimer Sgt Bradshaw escaped and returned to England.

On my return to Canada I took my discharge and joined the Department of Transport as an Air traffic controller. I remained with the Department until December 1976."

9th December 1942

The Squadron was detailed for a raid on Turin. Overall the raid was disappointing and the target was poorly marked, resulting in scattered bombing. Turin reported 73 people killed and 99 injured. Wellington BK514 EX-T failed to return. This was the first loss on the Squadron and to make matters worse, the pilot was Wing Commander Hattersley DFC, the Squadron Commander. An engine failed over France and then the aircraft was hit by flak, causing a fire in the port engine that spread to the wing tanks. The crew was ordered to bale out just South of Paris, but W/Cdr Hattersley, DFC; Sgt Prescott, 2nd Pilot; Sgt Jarman, Nav; Sgt Fijal, W/Op, and Sgt Lindsay, R/G, were captured by the Germans.

The bomb aimer, Sgt J.G. Dawson, managed to keep clear of the search parties and evaded capture. Part of Sgt Dawson's report to MI9 reads:

"Our aircraft took off from Blyton on 9th Dec 42 to bomb Turin. Before we reached the Alps we had engine trouble and turned back. As the aircraft would not maintain height on the one engine, we were ordered to bale out over France. I believe the other members of my crew were captured. There was also in the aircraft a Wing Commander (name unknown). I do not know exactly where I came down, though I think it was in the region of Moret, on the SE edge of the forest of Fontainebleau. I hid my parachute, Mae West, Irvin Jacket, etc under some hay (where they were later found by the Germans). I waited around for about twenty minutes and then went south across fields for about two or three hours. I slept in a thicket for a few hours and then continued walking until daybreak (10th Dec). I was out of sight of any farms so I hid in a ditch for the day.

At nightfall I began walking, trying to head south. I slept again by day in the fields. About dusk on the 11th Dec I got bread and water but no other help at a farm, the people being frightened. That night a dog discovered me after I had been sleeping near a house. I told the owner of the dog I was English and she fetched an old man who suggested I give myself up to the police. When I did not agree he brought me food and cider. I slept all day in a ditch, the old man bringing me more food. Next morning another man came to my hiding place bringing me a beret, coat and dungarees and food and coffee. He indicated that I should be moving. I stayed in the ditch till dark, no one coming near me.

Deciding to continue, I walked south for one and a half to two hours. Suddenly I thought I should go back to where I had been and I retraced my steps to the same place. I had no sooner got back than the man who had brought me civilian clothes came for me. This man took me to his garage at Villemarechal and hid me there for one or two nights. He then took me by lorry to Lorrez-le-Bocage. I stayed at a farm near Villemarechal for about a week and in a house at Lorrez for one night. I was then handed over to an organisation."

Sgt Dawson's report ends here, but he reached Gibraltar on 4th April 1943 after crossing France and Spain to the coast, arriving back in England on 11th April 1943. He had joined the RAF on 31st May 1941 having been a clerk in civilian life while living in West Hartlepool, Co. Durham.

For the remainder of December, flying was curtailed due to very bad weather, but some mine-laying details were successfully carried out. The rest of the time was taken up with lectures, mainly on incendiaries, for the aircrews, whilst the wireless operators were shown the correct procedure for deploying the dinghy kite aerial.

Flying was cancelled on Christmas Day and a football match was organised. The Squadron records show that there were also running exercises laid on for the aircrews. How popular this was I leave to one's imagination considering the winter months of '42 – '43 were some of the hardest on record. On Boxing Day the wireless operators received a lecture on IFF (Identification Friend or Foe) and how to destroy this equipment in the event of an emergency over enemy territory. There was also clay pigeon shooting for all ranks.

31st December 1942

A mine-laying operation was laid on and six Wellingtons were readied. All completed their mission to drop mines off the Biscay ports, except P/O Bell who was attacked by enemy night fighters in the Mont Saint Michel area. He jettisoned the mines live and managed to evade the fighters, but on the return journey he noticed another enemy aircraft with its navigation lights on flying about 1,000 yards away which was flying parallel with another fighter without lights. The lights on the first aircraft were doused and then an attack came in from the starboard beam. Taking evasive action, P/O Bell shook off both fighters and managed to get back to make an emergency landing at RAF Ford two miles south west of Arundel, West Sussex, due to lack of fuel.

The Squadron was involved in many minelaying operations and perhaps a brief description of the types of weapons employed would be of benefit. The initial use of sea mines sown by ships was seen as a defensive weapon, but the development of aerial mines quickly made them a useful offensive weapon. It fell to the Admiralty to place the first order for a small quantity of magnetic mines and these were delivered in mid 1939. Due to the lack of suitable aircraft capable of dropping mines it was suggested that the Beaufort or Swordfish aircraft of the Fleet Air Arm could be modified. However the poor range and load carrying capabilities of these aircraft quickly became apparent and so Bomber Command's Handley Page Hampden was tested and eventually approved for the first sea mining trials. The trials were successful and manufacture of the 1,500lb "A" (Airborne) Mk I bomb was set in motion, which became available in increasing numbers.

During 1940, approximately 1,500 mines were laid from aircraft – the main areas sown were the Baltic, Kattegat and along the coastal waters of Holland and France. The Wellingtons flown by '199' could carry two mines and later, once converted to the Stirling, a total of six could be carried. Mines were the subject of much scientific research and the engineers involved devised several means of detonating the weapon for optimum results. In the early stages of development the trigger was a magnetic sensing device to detect the magnetic field surrounding a large steel plated ship. Later an acoustic sensor was fitted which was actuated by the noise of a ship's engines or propellers and for certain operational requirements both types were fitted.

Further trials and modifications resulted in there being two main types of mine that were used until the end of the war – the 1,500lb A Mk I – IV and the 1,000lb A Mk V. In 1940 the recommended height for releasing the mines was in the region of 1,500ft but by 1943 through strengthening the casing, and other modifications, the mines could be dropped from 12,000ft. This higher altitude gave a measure of safety from flak ships and coastal batteries that had taken an ever-increasing toll of the lower flying minelayers.

The areas designated for mine-laying were given code names to prevent their location becoming known to the enemy and names of trees, fish and flowers were used. Typical code names were Sweet Pea (Baltic), Beech (St Nazaire), Nectarines (Frisian Islands) and Jellyfish (Brest). The code names were taken a stage further and mining operations became known as "Gardening" and the mines were called "Vegetables". For example, a sortie over enemy waters might have been recorded as – 'Gardening at Hyacinth, Stirling 'N' planted six vegetables as detailed' – enough to confuse anyone!

Loading sea mines.

1943

The pace of activity quickens – a change of scenery to RAF Ingham and RAF Lakenheath –
conversion from the Wellington to the Stirling four-engined heavy bomber

January
Mining and bad weather mark the beginning of a New Year

A new year dawned and with it came more bad weather with persistent rain, fog, snow and low cloud. A mining operation was flown on the 2nd January with seven crews briefed to drop mines at 4708N 0224W, a pinpoint a few miles west of the mouth of the River Loire and the entrance to the port of St Nazaire. This was one of the most important German naval installations from which a large number of U-boats launched their attacks on the Atlantic convoys sailing to and from America. Of the seven Wellingtons, one was forced to return early due to icing and landed at RAF Hurn, four miles north of Christchurch, Dorset, at 0050 hrs. Sgt Waldorf was also forced to land at Hurn, touching down at 0325 hrs, Sgt Burton landed at RAF Warmwell, five miles south east of Dorchester, Dorset, and Sgts Moses and Barnard landed at RAF Tangmere, three miles east of Chichester, West Sussex. Sgt Moses was forced to bring back his mines due to the bomb doors being iced up. Crews reported heavy and light flak over Granville and St Nazaire.

9th January 1943

Four crews were detailed for a mining trip of the East Frisian Island of Spiekeroog. Sgt Waldorf had two close encounters with German night fighters when his crew first saw a single engine aircraft, believed to be a Fw190, on the starboard beam and ten minutes later a twin engined Ju88 coming in from the same direction. No contact was made and the pilot continued to complete his sortie.

14th January 1943

Seven crews were detailed for mining and four crews to bomb Lorient. Pinpoints for the mining operation were given between 4748N 0344W and 4745N 0335W, the first is a small inlet leading to Port Manech and Le Pouldu a small town on the Brittany Coast slightly WNW of Lorient, the bombing target. The bombing attack on Lorient was carried out just after 0100 hrs and the Pathfinders had dropped markers on the docks and surrounding area, but Sgt Bird had bad icing and, although he descended from 14,000ft to 8,000ft, he could not find any gaps in the cloud, so jettisoned his bombs and turned back. Of these four Wellingtons, three landed at RAF Hurn and the other one at RAF Exeter.**

One of the aircraft Wellington BK541 EX-N, flown by Sgt Moses, was attacked by a Ju88 as he approached the Isle de Batz, but his rear gunner, Sgt H. Read, fired off two 150 round bursts and the Junkers broke off and was not seen again. Sgt Harlem, Z1602 EX-B, also reported a night fighter in close proximity in the same area and at almost the same time, which could have been the aircraft Sgt Moses had fended off.

15th January 1943

Target was again Lorient with seven crews detailed, but only four crews took part, and technical problems with two of these aircraft forced early returns. Three pilots aborted the mission before take-off due to various malfunctions and of those that did leave, Sgt Pinchin, BK509 EX-J, took off at 1710 hrs, but had gyro instrument problems and landed back at base at 2025 hrs.

P/O Bell, BK367 EX-U, also aborted his mission at 1920 hrs just before reaching the target and jettisoned his bombs on the turn. He reported a loss of power on the port engine for being unable to continue his attack.

Only Sgt Burton and Sgt Dennis reached the target, reporting good marking by PFF and good concentrations of bombing. The town was hit hard overall and over 800 buildings were destroyed in the raid in which 157 aircraft took part.

**Authors Note*: The mining pinpoints mentioned above are approximately 30kms from Lorient, but Sgt Stan Freestone, flying Wellington BK158 EX-G, reports they mined Lorient and pinpoints used for navigation were at Pont Aven and the Island of Groix. This island is just SSE off the entrance to Lorient Docks and would be an excellent area to mine as all shipping traffic would get confined to a narrow approach to the coast. Having examined the other crew de-briefs, I think they were given specific primary dropping positions all along the Brittany Coast and that the general purpose was to harass German coastal shipping close in.

26th January 1943

Lorient was once again selected for attack with fourteen crews detailed. Two aircraft had to return early: Sgt Waldorf, Z1600 EX-C, had technical failures and landed at RAF Babdown Farm, and Sgt Harlem's Wellington BJ819 EX-A had a complete electrical failure and was forced to land at RAF Hemswell. All the aircraft were hindered in the raid by poor visibility.

A mining sortie was carried out on 27th January by Sgt Prangle and Sgt Harlem who dropped their mines in the waters on the east end of the Frisian Island of Schiermonnikoog. Sgt Harlem flying BJ960 EX-M was hit by flak and the port tail plane was damaged.

28th January 1943

Nine Wellingtons were detailed for operations, but again the weather clamped down and at 2040 hrs the order to stand down was given. The next day was no better with heavy snow for a time, but later in the day some circuits and landings were carried out. The wireless operators and bomb aimers were given a lecture on flash flare launching and its inherent dangers.

29th January 1943

The Squadron was ordered to prepare for another raid on Lorient, if the weather cleared, and twelve aircraft were bombed up in readiness. As the snow eased off and conditions improved the order was given to proceed with this raid on a target pounded remorselessly by Bomber Command. The docks were the prime area for attention as this had become one of the main bases for the German U-boats that operated in packs all over the North and South Atlantic. Some aircraft were allotted targets in the town area on these raids as it was felt that the maximum disruption to those people repairing any bomb damage and involved in reconstruction work would slow down servicing of the submarines.

Twelve Wellingtons took off, but Sgt Dennis, BK541 EX-N encountered severe icing and was forced to turn back. The remaining aircraft pressed on and ten reached the target.

F/Lt Powell, BK507 EX-E could not find the target and brought his bomb load home. Those who found the target were faced with 10/10 cloud cover, icing conditions and no PFF marking. Coupled with heavy flak and searchlights, the raid was not very successful and bombing was scattered over a large area.

BJ582 EX-O (F/O Wingood) was hit by flak that resulted in a large hole in the starboard inner main plane.

Sgt Waldorf, X3413 EX-Q also had some slight damage to the fuselage caused by flak bursts. He reported difficulty locating the target due to cloud but did get a fix when the bomb aimer caught a glimpse of the river. Most of the bombs were dropped on fixes obtained in a similar manner. All the aircraft returned to base safely.

January 30th and 31st 1943

No flying due to adverse weather conditions.

February
Stark reality – the Squadron's first fatalities – Lorient reduced to rubble

In accordance with the Movement Order received during the latter part of January, the Squadron started the move to RAF Ingham on 2nd February 1943 with the advance party proceeding early in the morning with F/O Smith in charge. The next day the whole Squadron moved by road to the new airfield and set about getting the buildings ready and bringing the unit up to operational status. 'A' Flight flew in six Wellingtons and 'B' Flight a further eleven, which the ground crews immediately started to check over. There was to be no time to spare before these aircraft were required for operations.

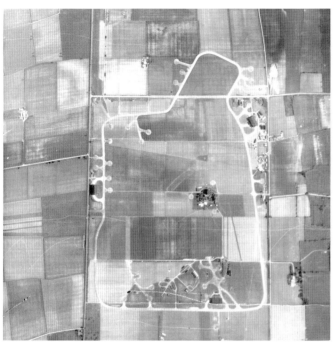

An aerial photo of RAF Ingham airfield taken after the war. Note the farmhouse and buildings in the centre.

By the 3rd of February all of the stores and equipment had arrived and most of the aircraft had been delivered and checked as serviceable. In the late afternoon the bomb aimers attended lectures on bombing photography, the use of bomb panel (a number of switches to activate the release mechanism in the bomb bay) and the manual release of bombs, whilst some of the wireless operators honed their Morse code skills.

Another attack on Lorient was planned for 4th February and nine aircraft and crews were detailed. This would be a two-stage attack, with one flight dropping incendiaries and the other high explosives. The incendiary attack appeared scattered but the high explosive element was much more concentrated and it was agreed there was a definite gap in the two types of bombing. Large areas of the town were set on fire and six large fires were seen in the docks area. There was no PFF marking.

6th February 1943

Sgt Moses was reported missing on a mining operation. There are no comments or entries in the ORB relating to this incident and a further line of enquiry was required to get the necessary details of the crew. They are listed as lost without trace and were as follows – Wellington Mk III, BK367, EX-U, Crew: Sgt George Moses, Pilot, RAFVR, age 30, from Bangor, Caernarvonshire; Sgt Ronald Stevens Guy, Nav, RAFVR, age 29, Weymouth, Dorset; Sgt Derek Wilfrid Turner, B/A, RAFVR, age 20, Gloucester; Sgt Leonard James Sweitzer, W/Op, RCAF, age 21, Sundre, Alberta, Canada; Sgt Howard Jack Read, R/G, RAFVR, age 22, Ringwood, Hampshire. All are commemorated on the Runnymede Memorial.

Of the other three aircraft detailed, Sgt Joseph and Sgt Brough were forced to bring their mines back due to severe icing conditions. The only pilot to complete his mission was Sgt Barnard who dropped his mines at 4707N 0227W and reported his Wellington suffered very bad icing over France. He also encountered a lot of flak near St. Nazaire but managed to avoid it.

7th February 1943

Pressure was again put on Lorient when six Wellingtons attacked the U-boat pens. Crews saw many large fires and heavy smoke on both sides of Port Militair and Sgt Holt, BK138 EX-Z, reported huge fires at the aiming points A and B. Bomber Command sent a total of 323 aircraft on this raid, which was accurately marked by PFF and resulted in a devastating attack. The Squadron suffered another loss when Sgt K. Powell was hit by flak and crashed on the outskirts of the target.

Wellington Mk III. BK507, EX-E, Crew: Sgt Kenneth Powell, Pilot, RAFVR, age 24, Llanilltern, Glamorgan; Sgt Anthony Edward Keeton, 2nd Pilot, RAFVR, age 20, Mapperley, Notts; Sgt Morris John Norgate, Nav, RAFVR, age 22, Ropley, Hampshire; Sgt David Coventry Pennycook, B/A, RAFVR, age 21, Dundee; Sgt Charles Barry Sullivan, W/Op A/G, RAAF, age 21, Elwood, Victoria, Australia; Sgt Ronald Valentine Baker, W/Op A/G, RAFVR, age 21, Whitchurch, Glamorgan. All the crew were killed and are buried in Guidel Communal Cemetery, north of Lorient, France.

13th February 1943

Ten of the squadron's aircraft completed a Bomber Command force of 466 aircraft in an attack against Lorient and its docks.

The crews reported good visibility but a considerable amount of smoke from many fires around the town. During this raid over 1,000 tons of bombs were dropped on one single target for the first time.

F/O Bell and his crew were lost on this raid, when X3870, EX-S, crashed near Lorient. They were: F/O John Morling Bell, Pilot, RAFVR; Sgt Elwyn Knowles Jones, Navigator, RAFVR, age 29, Bangor, Caernarvonshire; Sgt Harold Eunson Woodruff, W/Op, RAFVR, age 24, Alvaston, Derby; F/O Robert Joseph Keyes, B/A, RCAF, age 24, Regina, Saskatchewan, Canada; Sgt George Easey, A/G, RAFVR, age 20, Laxfield, Suffolk; F/Lt Arthur Cowie, DFM, A/G, RAF, age 25, married to Margaret of Low Fell, Gateshead, Co. Durham. They were buried in Guidel Communal Cemetery, France. F/Lt Cowie was the Squadron Gunnery Leader and won his DFM while flying with 10 Squadron, Royal Air Force (*London Gazette*, 9th May 1941).

Matthew Morton, Fitter, IIE: *"Memories of Ingham are rather scant, though I have vague notions that at this time some 'specials' were carried out by 199 Wellingtons. There was the day when we heard an enormous explosion coming from Scampton. It was said a photo-flash had ignited in a Lancaster and the mines it was loaded with all went up. Another incident at Ingham occurred during the ground testing of one of 'B' Flight's Wimpies when they discovered that a propeller would not change pitch. This aircraft was down to leave on operations in 20 minutes after this snag was found and it was decided to change the prop. From this decision being taken, a spare propeller was found and brought to the dispersal, the u/s item removed and the new prop fitted and tested – all in 16 minutes. Cpl. Chick Henderson-Smith carried out this work with his ground crew and, if my memory serves me right, he received no official recognition. The operation that night was a 'maximum effort' and personally I considered Chick should have a least got a 'Mentioned in Despatches' for his wonderful effort".*

14th February 1943

A 243 aircraft raid on Cologne involving four crews from '199': Sgt Joseph, F/Sgt Bird, Sgt Shortle and Sgt Dennis. Unfortunately F/Sgt Bird encountered a complete electrical failure soon after he took off at 1825 hrs, and landed back at 1900 hrs. The other three aircraft bombed the target, but results were poor, only about fifty of the main force hitting the target but only the western district of the city. Fifty civilians were killed and 25 French workers died when their accommodation in an old fort took a direct hit.

From the 12th to the 16th of the month high winds, with gusts up to 45mph, made servicing the aircraft a nightmare for ground crews working outside in temperatures barely above freezing, and pilots taking off and landing in crosswinds.

16th February 1943

The weather finally moderated and the Squadron mounted its last raid on Lorient, when seven aircraft and crews took off for what, to most, was a familiar routine. The cloud had broken and mostly cleared by mid afternoon and the pilots now found conditions much more favourable. The raid by 377 aircraft dropped mainly incendiaries in clear visibility. This was the culmination of 1,853 sorties in eight main area raids on the town and docks. The Air Ministry had seen the danger posed by the U-boat pens and dealt with the target accordingly. Bomber Command dropped 4,000 tons of bombs in these raids and reports show that the town itself was almost completely destroyed with most of the inhabitants living elsewhere.

From contemporary local records it is possible to get some idea of the effect of the German occupation and the Allied bombing campaign on the local population. Many French naval and merchant vessels were using Lorient prior to the German's arrival on June 21st 1940 and over fifty ships left the base. The French registered merchantman *Victor-Schoelcher*, loaded more than 6,000 crates of Belgian & Polish gold and the future Resistance fighter Colonel Remy (Gilbert Renault 1904-1984), whilst money from the Bank of France left aboard *The Barbut*. Any un-seaworthy ship was scuttled and oil depots were set on fire. Once the Germans took charge of the town and docks they started to restrict people's movements and curfews were set from 11pm to 6am. Strong drink was banned, as were private cars, unless you were a priest, mid-wife or doctor. Resistance or acts of sabotage would not be tolerated and "would result in severe repression if they occurred". If a German soldier was killed, ten French citizens would be shot. Anyone caught listening to British radio broadcasts could face the death penalty and newspapers were censored. Shops could only open for business from 8am to 7pm. German flags and posters were everywhere.

The commander of the German submarines, Admiral Karl Donitz (1891-1980), arrived in Lorient on 23rd June and by 7th July U-boats had started to use the base to refuel. The dockyard was ready to make repairs and refits by 2nd August. Donitz moved his main headquarters to a large manor house in Kernevel, a short distance from Lorient, to enable him to oversee the base and be near his naval staff at all times. At this time the submarines were refuelled in the open and tied up alongside the various wharves and jetties used by normal shipping. This situation was to prove much too vulnerable and a decision was made to build 'Pens', as the Allies were to name them, to house the U-boats and afford them maximum protection from air attack. It was this decision that was to seal the fate of Lorient and the town and 199 Squadron and Bomber Command would eventually become inextricably linked to the Battle of the Atlantic.

The construction of the Keroman Submarine Base began in early February 1941 and over 10,000 workers were used by the Todt Organisation (a civil & military engineering group founded by Fritz Todt) to pour thousands of tons of concrete in its construction. In the first 'bunker' (using the German terminology) to be built, known as Keroman 1, only a limited number and type of U-boat could be housed, so work began on "K2" in May 1941. A third, known as K3, was completed in 1943. Once the building work was completed, 40 U-boats could be sheltered or repaired in these or other facilities at a time. K1 was 199.5m long, 85m wide and 18.5m high. The roof was 3.5m (almost 10ft) thick. It could take five U-boats. K2 was 128m long, 138m wide and 18.5m high. Again, the roof was 3.5m thick. This could house seven U-boats. K3 was 138m long, 170m wide and 20m high. The roof was 6.4m thick (17'6") and could house seven U-boats. This last building covered 24,000 sq metres.

Also built in conjunction with these massive fortifications were two 'Dombunkers' that were erected in the early phase of the construction work. These were known as 'East' and 'West' Bunkers, but could only house one U-boat each. Each of these pens were shaped like a pointed Gothic arch 25m high, 16m wide and 81m long. To the north west of the main pens a further six reinforced bunkers were built to house the vast stocks of torpedoes.

Building the U-boat base brought many problems to the townspeople of Lorient, the main one being getting enough food to live on. The German garrison had first priority over everything and in 1940 it was hard to obtain staple things like butter, cheese and eggs. During August 1940 it had become necessary to obtain special tickets to be able to buy coal and by December sugar, bread, rice, milk and oil, together with soap products, were all rationed. People in the surrounding country were also affected and had to obtain permits for fertilizer and seed for their fields. Many farmers' horses were requisitioned by the German army and, together with restrictions on obtaining any kind of fuel, they were left without the means to cultivate the land, which subsequently led to shortages of grain, potatoes, carrots and beet. Some people were forced to look

Bomber Command's Answer to a U-boat's Activities

U-107, under Kptlt. Günther Hessler, put out from Lorient, France at 19:30 on 29th March 1941 for what would become the most successful patrol of the entire war against allied merchant shipping. It left the base along with U-94 commanded by Kptlt. Kuppisch but then U-107 headed southwards.

U107's operational area was around the Canary Islands and nearby Freetown where she sank 14 ships for a total of 86,699 tons, starting with the British merchant SS Eskdene, *which required some two torpedoes and 104 rounds from the heavy 105mm fast firing deck cannon. The largest ship sunk during that patrol was the* British Calchas *of 10,305 tons. On 1st June, 1941 they sank the British merchantman* Alfred Jones *of 5,013 tons.*

On 3rd and 4th of May, U-107 refuelled from the German support ship Nordmark. *There they also met U-105. Five days later they took on board 14 torpedoes and some food, fuel and water from the support ship* Egerland. *The boat returned to Lorient on 2nd July 1941.*

Kptlt. Hessler had married Karl Dönitz's daughter, Ursula, in November 1937. At that time Hessler was serving on the torpedo boats, but in April 1940, he joined the U-boat force. Because Hessler was his son-in-law Donitz had trouble giving Hessler his deserved Knights Cross and eventually Grand Admiral Raeder signed the papers.

for alternatives for the commodities. Coffee was substituted with ground acorns and sweetened with saccharin. Another method used was to wash, peel and thinly slice carrots, roasting them in the oven until brown. They were then ground and crushed and some people even went as far as saying this 'ersatz' tasted good with a small amount of milk and a dash of sugar if it was available. By the end of 1941 a typical ration allocation for an adult was down to 10 ounces of bread per day, a weekly ration of 2 ounces of cheese and a monthly ration of 1lb of sugar, 8lbs of potatoes, 10 ounces of fat and 4 litres of wine. Many people chanced taking clandestine trips out into the countryside to obtain food and other essentials on the black market where butter, flour and pork fat were at times available. Some of these items could be purchased for high prices in the town which was perhaps a safer way of obtaining goods. People stood more chance of being stopped and searched returning from out of town and if any black market items were found being smuggled in they were always confiscated. During the early months of 1942 there were no potatoes and other foods also became unobtainable, although green vegetables were in good supply. Supplies of fish dried up due to the fishing boats being unable to obtain fuel and the few catches that were brought in were mostly sold on the black market. Further regulations imposed restrictions on the sale of clothing and shoes. A special order laid down by the Germans meant that all the leather produced in France had to be sent to Germany. Shoes started to appear with wooden soles. With U-boats leaving Lorient from September 1940 to May 1943, this base was a major contributor to the Battle of the Atlantic and was therefore marked out for intense bombing by Bomber Command. By the end of 1942, the Americans had also began a campaign against the port. At the meeting of Churchill, Roosevelt and Stalin in Casablanca in January 1943 the decision to destroy everything around Lorient was taken. By this time, the construction of the U-boat pens had been completed, as had installations in Brest, St. Nazaire, Le Pallice and other ports in Germany. Photographic evidence of the bombing suggested that these buildings were virtually indestructable, so Churchill decreed that the towns and surrounding infrastructure be destroyed. Previous attacks on the town and port were nothing compared to the ones on 14th and 15th January 1943 when 200 aircraft of Bomber Command took part in the night attacks and the USAAF sent 200 Flying Fortresses that bombed the town in daylight. The British raids caused over 80 large fires with 120 buildings and two churches destroyed and the dockyard suffering some damage to plant and equipment outside the main pens. The American raid is reported to have lasted for two hours and 400 fires were burning in the town that took three days to put out. In total 800 buildings were destroyed and 100 people died.

On January 23rd, the virtual end of the town began with a series of unrelenting raids by the RAF and USAAF, when the post office was destroyed in the afternoon and the mayor's office took a direct hit in the evening. The telephone systems, gas and water were cut off in many parts of town. The naval dockyard was also extensively damaged. Another 500 buildings were reduced to rubble and 25 people were killed. This type of attack carried on, with further raids on 29th January, 4th, 7th, 13th and 16th February. It became necessary to start evacuating people on 26th January as conditions were then very bad, but as the raids built up, more and more civilians were affected and the authorities tried to get as many people out of the town and into the surrounding countryside with the limited means available.

From 14th January to 17 February 1943 60,000 people were evacuated from the town, and by the end of February, three quarters of the town had been destroyed. Bombing continued on a lesser scale into May and the town was left with over 90% of its buildings reduced to rubble. Thanks to the construction of large numbers of reinforced concrete bomb shelters, many people survived the raids. It is reported that 353 civilians were killed and this low number was a direct consequence of the sturdily built shelters.

The labour force of the Todt Organisation carried on unhindered inside the U-boat pens, but outside it was a different matter as bombing knocked down building work as fast as it was put up. The German army also suffered much damage to its stores and equipment with many artillery pieces destroyed.

Due to its importance, the Germans carried on holding the port and its facilities right up to the end of the war, only relinquishing their hold on VE Day. Over 26,000 troops had formed a pocket in late August 1944 and nothing could dislodge them. Reconstruction of the town and surrounding areas was begun in earnest on 19th December 1946.

After the campaign against Lorient, the Squadron was now to begin taking part in raids mainly set against targets in Germany, but when called upon they would also carry out minelaying duties.

19th February 1943

Still operating against the seaborne threat, the Squadron was detailed to attack Wilhelmshaven. Sgt Austin was forced to return early when Sgt Bartlett was taken ill. The remainder of the crews encountered 7/10 cloud over the target, and although the PFF claimed to have marked accurately in clear visibility, the majority of the bombs fell in open countryside well outside Wilhelmshaven. Some buildings were hit, but casualties were light with five people killed and 47 injured.

During the daytime, lectures were given to the Squadron's wireless operators and on 23rd February the first mention of Mandrel is made, along with the use of Tinsel. More on Mandrel later, but a brief explanation as to what Tinsel was used for can be made here. This device entered service on 3rd December 1942 and was a measure used against the German high frequency (HF) radio transmission (RT) links where, in the past few months, most jamming had been aimed at the enemy radar. A German-speaking crew member using the bomber's normal wireless receiver would scan for enemy control RT transmissions to its fighter aircraft. Once a voice communication signal was picked up, the frequency was noted and a Marconi T1154 transmitter tuned to it and using a microphone mounted in a metal box in an engine nacelle it would broadcast the engine noise and swamp the German transmission. This equipment was modified several times and during the summer of 1943 it was re-designated Special Tinsel with the search facility moved to a land base at Kingsdown, where German-speaking operators searched for the frequencies used by the enemy. Once found, they would broadcast these to the bombers who would all tune their jammers to the frequency and switch on. This was a much better method as the bombers did not have to carry a German-speaking operator and all the aircraft could carry a jamming set that was easy to set up and use.

25th February 1943

A mining sortie was carried out by six aircraft over the Pont-Aven area. Sgt Waller, BK541 EX-N, was caught in several coastal flak bursts and came back to base with panels in the rear turret smashed and a large hole in the port wing. The remaining aircraft reached their allotted areas and returned unscathed.

26th February 1943

A large raid of 427 aircraft was mounted against Cologne, with 199 Squadron contributing nine Wellingtons. This raid was to prove far from satisfactory from the point of view of aircraft serviceability. P/O Waterfield, Z1600 EX-C, abandoned his sortie on take off due to technical problems. Another aircraft, BJ647 EX-V, crashed on take-off and Sgt Clifford and his crew were lucky to escape uninjured. Sgt Burton took off at 1900 hrs, but returned early (the explanation given was that the aircraft was unserviceable) and landed at 2100 hrs. Sgt Austin had lifted off at 1905 hrs, but due to problems with the starboard engine, was forced to turn back and landed at 2345 hrs. Another early return was by Sgt Dolan. He was back at base at 2150 hrs. S/Ldr Humby, F/O Wingood, W/O Palmer and Sgt Barnard reached the target and dropped their bombs. Sgt Barnard reported that the target was covered with incendiary fires. From German records it appears that only parts of the south west of the city were hit, but caused enough damage for over 6,000 people to be classed as bombed out. 109 people died and 150 were injured in the raid.

S/Ldr Ken Humby and crew.

Sgt Tom Austin and his regular crew. Not in order: Sgt Tom Austin, Pilot; Sgt W. Overbury, Nav; Sgt L. Laurence, B/A; Sgt T. Greenhaulgh, W/Op; Sgt G. Murray, R/G.

28th February 1943

St. Nazaire was the target for Bomber Command and was a continuation of the list of French U-boat bases ordered to be destroyed. Eight Wellingtons took off from RAF Ingham but only five reached the target and bombed on PFF red and green TIs (Target Indicators). Sgt Coupar, Z1748 EX-P, stated in his report that the whole town was well alight as they came in on their bombing run, with two large concentrated fires to the west of the town and one to the north.

W/Cdr Blomfield, BK507 EX-E, took off at 1830 hrs and released his bombs at 2124 hrs onto a target well alight and with large fires all around the docks. He landed safely back at base at 2400 hrs. F/Sgt Birt, BJ960 EX-M, left the runway at RAF Ingham at 1805 hrs and arrived over the target at 2125 hrs. His bomb aimer reported that their bombs fell in the north west area of the docks. The crew also saw several high explosive bombs go off in the target area. This aircraft landed at 0040 hrs. Again, there were problems with aircraft requiring early returns to base. Sgt Weller, BJ916 EX-T, took off at 1815 hrs, but was forced to turn back due to the port engine failing. He landed at 2230 hrs. Sgt Clifford, BK138 EX-Z, left RAF Ingham at 1805 hrs and a short time later his rear gunner reported his turret was not functioning, so returned and landed at 1925 hrs. Intercom problems caused Sgt Joseph to turn back in BK345 EX-Y and he landed at 2215 hrs. The raid, pressed home by 437 aircraft, caused a huge amount of damage to the town and dock area. A large proportion of the bombs fell in the port and at least 60% of the town was destroyed. It seems that a large number of the population had evacuated the town, perhaps in the knowledge of what had been meted out to Lorient.

March
The Squadron joins the Battle of the Ruhr – a close encounter with 'Bomber Harris'

1st March 1943

Five crews were detailed for mining in the 'Artichoke' (Lorient) area of the Bay of Biscay on 1st March; all completed their operation and returned to land at RAF Ingham.

3rd March 1943

417 aircraft attacked Hamburg in clear visibility, with ten Wellingtons being despatched by 199 Squadron. It appears that PFF mistakenly thought the echoes on their H2s sets were the dock area, when in fact they were the mud banks in the River Elbe showing up at low tide. Consequently they marked 13 miles downstream from the centre of the city on the small town of Wedel, which suffered large areas of destruction including several industrial plants, and a large naval stores, which was completely burnt out. Some aircraft did bomb Hamburg and the city reported over 100 fires that took some time to control and before the fire services could offer any assistance to the town of Wedel. Even though the wrong target was hit, it appears that much damage was caused to the German war effort in other areas.

Again there were mixed fortunes for the crews taking part in this raid. One aircraft was declared u/s before take-off. Sgt Coupar, BK158 EX-G, took off at 1840 hrs, but found that his starboard engine was overheating after two hours into the trip. Various attempts were made to rectify the fault, but nothing could be done to reduce the temperature below 300°F. He could not gain sufficient height for the attack and as his Gee set was also not working, the decision was made to abort and turn back at 5400N 0920E, the time recorded as 2103 hrs. The bombs were released at 5359N 0907E on an area the crew noted as being Michaelis Denn (sic). Many incendiary fires were seen as a result. Sgt Pinchen, BK509 EX-J, took off at 1850 hrs, but had problems with both engines and could not gain height. He arrived at the enemy coast too late to proceed to the main target, so at position 5420N 0920E he turned for base and released his bomb load on flak positions five miles south of Husum. W/O Palmer, Z1748 EX-Z, took off at 1850 hrs and arrived over the target at 2151 hrs, having struggled with having the port engine revs fluctuating all the time. The bombs were released on the green TIs and the docks could be clearly seen. The crew saw many concentrated fires and classed the raid as highly successful. They landed back at RAF Ingham at 0045 hrs. Sgt Austin, BJ960 EX-M, lifted off at 1840 hrs and had a non-eventful trip dropping his bombs at 2136 hrs onto a target that was well alight with many large fires. He reported several large concentrated fires one mile west of Außenalster Lake. F/O Wingood, HZ259 EX-W, released brakes and lifted off at 1850 hrs and appears to have had some problems arriving on time and stated that there were no TIs to be seen as a result. The crew observed many large fires in the dock area and north of the river in the town and claimed a satisfactory trip.** Sgt Harlem, BJ819 EX-A, took off at 1840 hrs and reported that there was good visibility over the target and very little cloud. Bombs dropped at 2128 hrs and stated that his own bursts were observed. Many good size fires going all over the city, particularly large one to east and another one on west side. *"PFF did an excellent job"*. He landed back at RAF Ingham at 0025 hrs. Sgt Bolton, HZ263 EX-E, took off at 1900 hrs and released his bomb load on red and green TIs, with the markers in the bombsight. He reported *"many young incendiary fires seen but that they had not yet taken hold. PFF technique excellent"*. Sgt Hockley, BJ991 lifted off at 1845 hrs, but only got as far as Mablethorpe, when he was forced to turn back to base. It was found that the rear turret doors would not remain closed when it was being rotated. The Wellington landed at 2040 hrs. Sgt Dennis BJ916 was also in trouble, just after two hours into his mission, when Sgt Johnson, his navigator, found there was a problem with the plot. On investigation, it appeared that the compass was inaccurate and there was now insufficient time to make good the error and arrive on time over the target. The bombs were jettisoned live at 5330N 0550E at 2115 hrs, and were seen to explode. This pinpoint is just off the North Frisian Islands.

4th March 1943

The day dawned fair with a light east-southeast wind and good visibility. Three aircraft and crews were readied for a mining operation off 'Nectarines', the Frisian Islands. F/Lt King, F/O Archer (on his first operation) and Sgt Hockley took off at 1900 hrs and after successfully completing their allotted tasks returned to base landing between 2300 hrs and 0030 hrs.

**Author's Note: F/O Wingood was not late on the target if compared to other crew reports, but he may have felt this was the reason for no target indicators burning on the ground. However, it must be remembered that the PFF had wrongly marked the target and the TIs had been dropped 13 miles away. His navigator had plotted the correct course and arrived over the target and visually identified the docks and city correctly. F/O Wingood landed back at base at 0045 hrs.

The Battle of the Ruhr
5th March to 24th July 1943

5th March 1943

Another fine day with light winds from the north west saw ten aircraft being readied by the ground crews for a raid on Essen. Loading containers of 4lb incendiaries into some aircraft and 4,000lb 'cookies' in others, all were ready for the evening take off times. At 1900 hrs all the crews were at their allotted aircraft and most of the pre-flight checks had been carried out as the fully-laden Wellingtons left their dispersals and headed in line for take-off. By 1915 hrs, all the engines had been run up and final checks made as BK354 EX-X, with Sgt Couper at the controls, lifted off first and set course for the target. In short order, all the remaining aircraft were airborne in little more than 15 minutes. However, Sgt Hockley, BK509 EX-J, who took off at 1920 hrs, was faced with the problem of an over revving starboard engine, so at 1930 hrs, made the decision to return to base. He made several circuits of the airfield until all the other aircraft were safely away and landed with all his bombs on board at 2005 hrs much to everyone's relief. Sgt Pinchin, BK509 EX-J, was another pilot forced to make an early return, when his starboard engine failed at position 5301N 0119E. He jettisoned his bombs at 2006 hrs and made it back to RAF Ingham on one engine.

Sgt Coupar, who had been the lead aircraft for the raid, had a good outward journey and approached the target on a heading of 175° magnetic. He observed good marking by PFF with red and green TIs visible. The crew reported that the whole city appeared to be on fire and several large explosions were seen. He released his bombs at 2125 hrs from 15,000ft but did not see the results due to the fires and smoke. On the return trip, near the Dutch coast, his aircraft was attacked by a German night fighter and was hit by machine gun fire that caused some damage to the fuselage. Sgt Davy, the wireless operator, and Sgt Barkwell the rear gunner were both wounded but not seriously.

Sgt Waldorf, X3413 EX-R, was next to take off at 1916 hrs and arrived over the target area that was well alight. He ran in onto the red and green TIs on a heading of 188° at 12,000ft and dropped his bombs at 2122 hrs; no results were seen due to smoke. The crew reported many large fires in the west of the city and one very large explosion, to the east of target area, which produced large clouds of blue-black smoke rising to 4,000ft. The rear gunner, Sgt Wharmby, saw another extremely large explosion in the same area about one minute later and said that there was an orange flash and large volumes of smoke. The crew claimed a very successful trip.

Sgt Harlem, BJ819 EX-A, approached Essen on 170° at 15,000ft and encountered lots of smoke haze. The bomb aimer released the load at 2116 hrs onto the red TIs. Sgt Harlem reported that there seemed to be many square miles of the city in flames and saw one enormous explosion unlike anything he had ever seen before. On the return journey a night fighter attacked their aircraft, causing damage to the port side of the fuselage, holes in the port engine cowling and the port tyre. Evasive action was taken and the enemy fighter shaken off. The crew made it back to base and landed safely at 0020 hrs.

Sgt Holt, BK138 EX-Z, lifted off at 1920 hrs and had an uneventful trip to the target. His bomb aimer identified the aiming point by the red and green TIs and they made their attack run on 190°, at 15,000ft dropping the bomb load at 2123 hrs. Their report states that their own bursts were not observed due to fires and smoke, but one huge concentration of fire around the aiming point was seen. Sgt Holt stated at the debrief *that if the Pathfinders had put their markers in the right place, Krupps* (major steel producers and armament manufacturers) *should be finished".* The glow of fires could still be seen after crossing the coast on the way back.

Sgt Shorttle, BJ960 EX-M, took off at 1922 hrs and arrived on time at the target on a heading of 090°, at 13,000ft, releasing the bombs at 2122 hrs. He reported no cloud and very good horizontal visibility, heavy smoke from target area but identified aiming point by red and green TIs. The crew counted fifteen very large fires within a two square mile area, and said it was the best concentration seen so far. They landed at 0010 hrs.

Sgt Dennis, BJ916 EX-J, was airborne at 1925 hrs and had no problems on the way to the target. The aiming point was seen clearly on the run in on 194° at 15,000ft and the crew saw their own bombs explode in the centre of the red indicators. There was a huge concentration of fire around the aiming point, and Sgt Dennis reported, *"if PFF were accurate target was severely damaged"*. He landed back at base at 2355 hrs.

S/Ldr Humby took off at 1925 hrs and arrived over Essen at 12,000ft on a heading of 180°, reporting no cloud but very hazy, with thick smoke. He picked up the red TIs at 2058 hrs about 35 miles ahead. The bomb aimer had the aircraft lined up and released the load on the green TIs that were surrounded by a mass of flames and enormous explosions. S/Ldr Humby was of the same opinion as his other crews when he reported, *"if PFF were on target then Krupps is non-existent"*. The fires were visible from 145 miles away on the trip home. Landed at RAF Ingham at 2355 hrs.

P/O Wingood and his crew, aboard HZ259 EX-U, were the last to get aloft, leaving the runway at 1930 hrs. They made their approach to Essen on 180° at 15,000ft and dropped their bombs at 2122 hrs. P/O Wingood encountered poor visibility and 8/10th cloud. The bomb aimer identified the target by the red and green TIs and, the concentration of fires. Bombs were released on the centre of the concentration. P/O Wingood reported *"Very concentrated attack and if PFF were accurate the target certainly got it"*.

Of the 442 aircraft that took part in the raid – 157 Lancasters, 131 Wellingtons, 94 Halifaxes, 52 Stirlings and eight Mosquitoes – at least 56 were forced to abort and turn back due to a range of technical difficulties. Of the eight 'Oboe' Mosquitoes taking part, three returned early. This could have had serious consequences as much reliance was placed on these primary Pathfinders to mark the target. However, the remaining five arrived on time and accurately marked the aiming point. Following Pathfinder 'backers-up' also carried out their marking on time and kept the target supplied with red and green indicators throughout the raid. The main force attacked in three waves, with the Halifaxes in the first wave, Wellingtons and Stirlings in the second and the Lancasters in the last. A large percentage of the bomb loads were incendiary, but many of the high explosive bombs dropped had long delay fuses, causing disruption to the fire-fighters and utility workers attempting to restore services, as they could go off at any time after the raid, and the all clear sounded. Some of these bombs went off several days after being dropped and slowed up repair work. Post raid photographic reconnaissance showed that 160 acres of the city had been destroyed and within the main Krupps industrial plant 53 buildings had been hit. German records from Essen show that 3,018 houses were destroyed and 2,166 seriously damaged. Ten firemen and up to 480 civilians were killed.

During this period of intense activity, LAC Jack Richardson, a Fitter 2E, and his friend LAC Haydock applied for aircrew selection, but heard nothing for several weeks. Richardson recalls:

"One evening while standing at the top of Hemswell Hill trying to thumb a lift into Gainsborough, we were picked up by none other than the C in C himself, Air Chief Marshall Sir Arthur Harris. He asked us where we were stationed and we also informed him that we had offered to join aircrew, upon which he took all our particulars. After a very interesting talk he dropped us in Gainsborough and went on his way. The very next morning the Tannoy system went berserk – 'Hear this, Hear this – LACs Richards and Haydock report to the CO at once. After a lengthy interrogation of – 'What did he say'? 'What did you say' – we were told to pack at once and report to the Aircrew Selection Board at Doncaster. Doug Haydock passed and was posted for training. Returning from his first operation as Flight Engineer in a Lancaster, the aircraft crashed into a hill at Lakenheath and all the crew perished in the flames. Me, I failed my medical examination – colour blind".

Also at RAF Ingham was LAC Ken Hartley who had a 'testing' time:

"I was testing the I.F.F. circuits in a 'Wimpey' in the early days at Ingham. Pressing the detonator button by mistake resulted in a loud explosion towards the rear of the aircraft, a ruined I.F.F. set and me being put on a charge for this costly mistake".

9th March 1943

Started as a fine day with a slight haze and light winds from the north west. During the day seven Wellingtons were prepared for a sea mining sortie, each loaded with two 1,500lb mines. Those not on Ops attended lectures and the newly arrived crews received instructions on the use of the photo flash and how it should be launched. All the new navigators were shown recent developments in navigational aids. Experienced crews did not escape these lectures and there was one on the techniques to be employed on Bullseye exercises, the wireless operators were given Morse practise and there was a film about fighter affiliation.

In the evening, S/Ld Wynne-Powell, Sgt Waldorf, Sgt Hockley, Sgt Pinchin, Sgt Harlem, Sgt Holt and W/O Palmer all took off with no problems. Sgt Harlem, HZ263 EX-E, who got airborne at 1850 hrs, found his compass was not working correctly and at 1938 hrs turned back for base at 5330N 0140E, which is a few miles east of Mablethorpe. His two mines were brought back and he landed at 2130 hrs. W/O Palmer, Z1748 EX-P, was hit by flak, after being coned by six searchlights near Esbjerg in Denmark. The aircraft was hit aft of the front turret on the port side and the port engine sustained some damage that caused an oil leak. The crew sustained no injuries and they completed their mission successfully. The remaining five aircraft also completed their tasks.

12th March 1943

The fog of the early morning, dispersed to become fine, with good visibility and light and variable winds from the south. Ground crews loaded up the thirteen Wellingtons detailed for the evening's raid. Ground staff were not told the target, for security reasons, but this did not stop speculation and the odd side bet of where their charges were being sent. Using the fuel and the bombs loaded they could calculate the range of the raid and the possible targets.

During the day, lectures were given for aircrew, and wireless operators had their usual morse code practice. The navigators had a lecture on the use of 'Gee', and bomb aimers were instructed in the finer points of the fuses used on photo flash flares. 'A' Flight sent two aircraft on fighter affiliation details and two test flights were carried out. Briefings were held for all the crews during the afternoon and "the target for tonight" was announced as another raid on Essen.

One Wellington was unserviceable shortly before take-off started at 1925 hrs, when Sgt Hockley, BK158 EX-G, lifted off, followed in quick succession by the other eleven crews. Of these, two more succumbed to technical problems: P/O Waterfield, BJ960 EX-M, returned with a faulty air speed indicator and F/O Wingood, HE634 EX-S, due to problems with the R/T set. Both pilots jettisoned their bomb load before landing.

When Sgt Hockley arrived over the target, there was no cloud and good visibility. The target was identified by red and green TIs, with the latter well scattered. Many fires were burning in the centre of the concentration, but their own incendiaries, dropped by 2130 hrs on a heading of 210°, were not seen to ignite due to smoke. A very large explosion was followed immediately by a vivid red glow and thick black smoke to 2,000ft. Landed at 0015 hrs.

Sgt Dennis, BK541 EX-N, left at 1930 hrs and had no problems until shortly before the bombing run began, when a night fighter appeared to be shadowing him. He ordered Sgt Kettle, the bomb aimer, to leave his position and man the front turret in case the night fighter put in an attack. The bombing run continued on a heading of 191° and Sgt Dennis toggled the jettison button himself to drop the bomb load on the red TIs. This was claimed as a successful trip, but both markers and bombing appeared scattered compared with the previous raid, and the crew also stated they were somewhat suspicious of a few (about six) red TIs which were scattered singly a good distance from the main concentration. These were seen to drop, but went out much more quickly than regular TIs. Returned to RAF Ingham at 2350 hrs.

Sgt Holt, BK138 EX-Z, also took off at 1930 hrs, reported no cloud, good visibility, but much smoke rising from Essen. Attacked and dropped bomb load at 2141 hrs on a heading of 210°, but the results were not observed due to evasive action to avoid heavy flak. The crew reported two bright yellow-orange explosions, which appeared larger than a 4,000lb 'cookie' (high capacity blast bomb) and lit up the aircraft. One of the explosions appeared to be east of the Krupps works. In their de-brief they considered the PFF had laid their markers well, but the attack was not so concentrated as the last raid. Some of the bombs were noted as falling two to three miles west and north of the aiming point and many well outside area of defence. Returned at 0015 hrs.

Sgt Humphries, BJ991 EX-H, took off at 1935 hrs and picked up the preliminary markers en route. Visibility was good and the target identified by white TIs and one large red explosion among incendiaries. Bombs dropped at 2133 hrs on 150°. A large fire was developing just to the south west of the red TIs. Landed at 0030 hrs.

Sgt Shorttle, HZ262 EX-K, lifted off at 1940 hrs and reported good visibility, but smoke haze was a problem. He made his bombing run on 190° and released the load of incendiaries at 2134 hrs, with green TIs in the bombsight. The crew reported many scattered fires to the east of the aiming point in the town area. The conclusion was that the raid was disappointing in comparison with the previous attack on this target. Landed 0010 hrs. Sgt Waller, X3413 EX-R, is also listed as leaving at 1940 hrs and arrived over Essen on a heading of 192°. The route was marked and the target identified by white TIs at Dorsten, north of Essen. Red and green markers on the aiming point with many fires in the target area. Bombs dropped at 2140 hrs. One very large explosion observed in centre of target. Landed back at base at 0020 hrs.

F/O Archer, Z1748 EX-P, lifted off at 1945 hrs on his first operation with the Squadron and had an uneventful trip. He reported visibility good with some industrial haze on the approach to Essen and identified the target by the red and green TIs. Bombs were dropped at 2131 hrs on 180° magnetic, but no results observed by the crew due to the many fires already burning. It was deemed a very successful operation and the area marked appeared to be a shambles. Glow from fires seen 80 miles away on return to base. Landed 0040 hrs.

Sgt Burton was the last to leave the runway at 1950 hrs, but made good time to the target and bombed at 2134 hrs on a heading of 150°. He saw many fires and one very large explosion, giving off an orange coloured flame that caused a large area to flare up and burn. He claimed a very successful and effective trip. On landing back at RAF Ingham at 2350 hrs it was found that 4 x 30lb incendiaries had failed to release.

Two aircraft were lost. Sgt Clifford and F/Lt King had both taken off at around 1930 hrs, but nothing more was heard from them. It appears that Sgt Clifford, HE519 EX-X, was hit by flak at 2203 hrs over the Dutch coast and crashed into the North Sea about 5 kms west of Camperduin. Crew: Sgt Dennis John Clifford, Pilot, RAFVR, age 20, Gravesend, Kent; F/O C.M. Kitson, Nav; Sgt Leslie Morgan Jones, B/A, RAFVR, Chepstow, Monmouthshire; F/Sgt Jack Graydon Richardson, W/Op, RCAF, age 20, Manitoba, Canada; Sgt Raymond Lambert, R/G, RAFVR, age 19, Whitworth, Manchester. F/O Kitson survived but was captured; he was later promoted to Flight Lieutenant. The remainder of the crew have no known grave and are commemorated on the Runnymede Memorial.

The other aircraft, HZ263 EX-E, is presumed lost over the North Sea off the coast of Holland. Crew: F/Lt William John King, Pilot, RAF; Sgt Douglas Arthur Nunn, Nav, RAFVR, age 21; Sgt Charles Richard Townsend, RAAF, B/A, age 24, from Bassendean, W. Australia; Sgt Cyril Frank White, W/Op, RAFVR, age 22, Thame, Oxfordshire. Sgt Russell Irwin Edwards, A/G, RCAF. Only one body, that of Sgt Edwards, was recovered from the sea and is buried in Bergen General Cemetery, Netherlands. The remainder of the crew are commemorated on the Runnymede Memorial.

Overall, the raid on Essen was successful, with 457 aircraft taking part. Mosquitoes using 'Oboe' accurately marked the target area, which included the giant Krupps works. The bombing later drifted onto the north-western areas of the city. Later assessments of the Krupps factory calculated that 30% more damage was caused in this raid than the one of 5th March. Almost 500 houses were destroyed and approximately 198 people were killed. From contemporary German records, it appears that up to one third of the bombs fell on other towns close to Essen, with Bottrop bearing the brunt.

The morning following the Essen raid broke fair, with a light wind from the east and 'A' and 'B' flights carried out air tests and local flying. Nine Wellingtons were detailed for night mining operations and the ground crews fueled and armed the aircraft. Navigators were given a lecture on navigational aids and tactics and the wireless operators their usual practise and tests on the morse key. Several of the less experienced crews received a lecture on the techniques required for a 'Gardening' operation.

Two crews carried out an unsuccessful sea search for the two missing crews.

In the afternoon Wellington BK158 EX-G broke up in mid-air near Skellingthorpe, three miles west of Lincoln, with the loss of all the crew whilst on an air test. Later investigations found the dinghy had broken from its housing and fouled the elevators. Crew: Sgt Terence Frederick Hockley, Pilot, RAFVR, age 26, from Ilford, Essex; Sgt Leonard George Vaughan, Nav, RAFVR, age 29, married to Eleanor Vaughan; Sgt Leslie Joisce, B/A, RAF, age 24; Sgt Albert George Shorten, W/Op, RCAF, age 20, Regina, Saskatchewan, Canada; Sgt Archibald McKay Cormack, A/G, RAFVR, Glasgow. The crew members were buried in their home towns, except Sgt Shorten, from Saskatchewan, Canada, who was laid to rest in Newport Cemetery, Lincoln. His promotion to Warrant Officer Class II came through a few days later. On the 18th, P/O Reid and six squadron personnel attended the funeral of Sgt Shorten, acting as pallbearers and guard of honour.

The weather curtailed activities with widespread fog and haze, and there were no operations between the 14th and 26th March – only limited local flying and air tests being carried out.

At RAF Ingham, there were lectures on the use of 'Gee', bombing and mining techniques, morse, gunnery and navigation. Some football games were played and PT was included wherever possible, especially for the aircrews. In all, this was a very frustrating time. Orders were still arriving by teleprinter for operations to be mounted, and then cancelled at the last minute. This occurred every day from the 18th to the 25th and meant eight days of preparing up to seventeen aircraft for missions, with the armourers hard pressed loading bombs for a particular target and then having to unload them when the mission was scrubbed.

The 25th saw the fog beginning to clear, but was replaced with continuous heavy rain and the cloud base down to 600ft. Sixteen aircraft and crews had been detailed for operations, but were stood down.

Early next morning, the fog was back, and at first it seemed that no operations would be possible, but a light wind of 10 mph from the WNW dispersed the mist and with moderate visibility and variable cloud forecast, an attack on Duisburg by fourteen aircraft was ordered. However, conditions would change later in the day and cloud was forecast over the target, so Bomber Command detailed nine Oboe equipped Mosquitoes to drop sky markers on the aiming points. Things went badly from the start, with five Mosquitoes forced to return early with various technical difficulties and one forced to ditch in the North Sea. The pilot, F/Lt L.J. Ackland was never found, but his navigator, W/O F.S. Sprouts survived. Due to the lack of marking, this attack was deemed a failure by Bomber Command. The markers were scattered over a wide area and only fifteen houses were destroyed. Three crews from '199' had to return early. W/O Palmer had only just taken off, at 1940 hrs, when it was found the hydraulic system had developed a serious leak. He abandoned the mission and flew out over the North Sea and jettisoned the bomb load together with several packages of 'Nickels', landing back at RAF Ingham at 2036 hrs. Sgt Waldorf reached 5255N 0240E and turned back at 2043 hrs due to an overheating port engine that was showing a temperature in excess of 300°F. Sgt Barnard was only 90 minutes into his flight when the rear gunner and navigator reported their oxygen supply had failed. As they were above 14,000ft the aircraft was brought down to 10,000ft and course set for base.

The remainder of the Squadron found the target, but the bomb aimers had great difficulty in acquiring the correct aiming points. Almost all the crews stated in their de-brief that the markers were too widely scattered, and Sgt Austin even went so far as to say that the sky markers were dropped too high to be of use to the Wellington crews. Sgt Shorttle was also critical of the marking and said that the marker flares were, in fact, immediately above his aircraft when the bombs were released, and at times no flares were visible. His Wellington sustained some damage from flak, with several large holes in the rear fuselage. All the crews that reached Duisburg returned safely to base.

27th March 1943

Started off cloudy with poor visibility, but twelve aircraft were put on standby for operations. During the afternoon five were cancelled and the remaining seven ordered to load with sea mines for a 'Gardening' trip to the Frisian Islands, off the Dutch coast.

The following pilots all successfully dropped their 'Veg': F/Sgt Ivary, BK366 EX-D; Sgt Odgers, BJ991 EX-H; P/O Waterfield, X3819 EX-F; Sgt Sinclair, BK509 EX-J; Sgt Fisher, HE495 EX-L; F/Lt Hawkins, BK541 EX-N.

Sgt Fisher was ordered to drop flame floats on the position coinciding with the co-ordinates given for release of the mines – 5240N 0400E. He made this observation at his debrief; *"We dropped the flame floats as ordered and they were visible for 15 miles and three to four minutes after. A fact which would point to their being of good value for 'Gardening Ops' provided they do not form a guide to the enemy defences"*. His other comments regarding the mission are mentioned here as they are fairly typical of most mining operations carried out by the Squadron: *"Target area approached at 2201 hrs at 750ft. Small amount of cloud, very dark with moderate visibility. Timed run of 7 minutes on course 064° magnetic, ground speed 180mph from dead reckoning position of 5240N 0400E obtained from a Gee fix at 5242N 0352E one minute previously. Both parachutes seen to open"*.

Preparing sea mines for loading.

28th March 1943

The Squadron was detailed to raid St. Nazaire. Thirteen Wellingtons were bombed up with a mixture of high explosives and incendiaries. During the evening, the weather was set fine with very good visibility – recorded at midnight as being 10 miles. All the aircraft took off successfully, but Sgt Austin, X3819 EX-F, who took off at 1905 hrs, experienced problems with his aircraft as he found it unstable and tending to dive, so at 1935 hrs he aborted the mission. He jettisoned the bomb load in the North Sea and landed back at base at 2045 hrs. The remaining aircraft all made an uneventful journey to the target and found it accurately marked by the PFF 'Oboe' equipped Mosquitoes and Main Force 'backers up'.

Of those that made the target, Sgt Waldorf, BJ582 EX-G, was the first to lift off, leaving at 1855 hrs. He reported no cloud and good visibility over St. Nazaire and his bomb aimer Sgt Wilson dropped their bomb load on the red and green TIs. He saw two very large fires in the target area and the crew could still see the fire glow from at least 110 miles on the return leg. The other pilots followed Sgt Waldorf in quick time and all the Wellingtons except one were airborne by 1910 hrs, only Sgt Dennis was slightly delayed leaving the runway at 1922 hrs.

S/Ldr Humby, DFC, took off at 1908 hrs and made good time to the target area. The bomb aimer reported he could see the green target indicators a good 10 minutes before setting up the bombing run. The load was released, with the red TIs in the bomb sight, and the crew saw that several fires had already taken hold in the dock area, with some scattered fires up to two miles north of the town. One big explosion was seen in the dock area. S/Ldr Humby was of the opinion that *"The first wave of bombers seemed to have made a good concentrated attack on the position marked by the PFF"*. Returned to base and landed at 0110 hrs.

P/O Archer, BJ960 EX-M, lifted off at 1900 hrs and arrived over St. Nazaire at 2200 hrs, identifying the target by green TIs and visually identifying the docks. He approached on the bomb run at 15,000ft and dropped his load at 2207 hrs on the greens, but no results were seen. Later he reported *"easy and successful trip, good fires were already started and could still be seen 100 miles away, defences were poor"*.

Sgt Harlem was away at 1910 hrs and had a quiet trip to the target. The bomb aimer, Sgt McLaren, set up the bomb run, reporting good visibility having identified the docks and the red and green markers. Flying at 13,500ft they crossed the docks on 175° magnetic and, with the green TIs in the bomb sight, Sgt McLaren released the load. At debriefing Sgt Harlem explained *"We saw a huge explosion and sheet of flame resembling burning oil right in the target area. Photo flash burst, but the camera indicator lamps did not function"*. No problems encountered on the return trip and landed at 0110 hrs.

The other crews taking part in this raid were captained by: Sgt Burton, HE490 EX-C; F/Lt Hankins, HE159 EX-U; Sgt Waldorf, BJ582 EX-O; W/O Palmer, HE470 EX-P; Sgt Waller, X3812 EX-Q; Sgt Barnard, BJ916 EX-T; P/O Haques, BK366 EX-D; Sgt Holt, BK138 EX-Z.

They all reached and bombed the target and their reports are very similar to those mentioned above. From the debriefings it appears that all the crews agreed that the PFF marking was well timed and accurate, with only Sgt Barnard commenting that the first green TIs dropped were not on the target, but that the second green markers were spot on. Most of the pilots saw the massive explosion in the middle of the dock area. All the aircraft returned to RAF Ingham and no flak damage was reported. The 13 Wellingtons of the Squadron were part of a force of 323 aircraft detailed for the raid on St. Nazaire, which in the main was concentrated on the port area. Of this number only two aircraft failed to return.

The last two days of the month saw the weather turn for the worse, with low, heavy, cloud at 2,000ft and the wind increasing from 15mph on the morning of the 30th to gale force in the afternoon. During the evening of the 31st the cloud base was down to 1,000ft, but the wind did back off slightly. No operations were ordered and crews were given the usual lectures, with the pilots receiving instructions on bombing procedures and on jettisoning a bomb load. Wireless operators had a series of lectures on the correct dinghy radio procedures and the gunners did not escape, as they were required to attend talks on maintenance of the Browning .303 machine gun. The last requirement of all the crews during the afternoon of the 31st was to attend a conference aimed at discussing tactics, passing on intelligence information and generally involving everyone in the progress being made by the Squadron.

April
Not for the faint hearted – low level over Mannheim

2nd April 1943

Two crews were ordered to conduct an air sea rescue search over the English Channel. The plan was for both aircraft to fly to the south of England, refuel, and spend as much time on the search as possible.

Sgt Humphries, BK138 EX-Z, left RAF Ingham at 0640 hrs and reached RAF St. Eval in Cornwall at 0840 hrs. He took off again at 1240 hrs and, having completed his search, returned to RAF Ingham at 1900 hrs. Nothing was seen of the dinghy they hoped to find, but they did come across a convoy of 12 ships, which was noted in the navigation log. F/Sgt Odgers, Z1602 EX-B, took off at 0655 hrs and landed at RAF St. Eval in Cornwall at 0855 hrs. He took off again at 1235 hrs to conduct an extensive search, but he too failed to spot anything. Both returned to base at 1900 hrs.

During the morning, while the other two aircraft were off on the ASR mission, eight crews were detailed for operations later in the evening. While checking these day's activities I found that one crew had been ordered to attack St. Nazaire, while the others were to conduct a mining operation in the "Beech" area, between Lorient and St Nazaire. It is strange why only one crew was given the task of going to bomb a target, as in almost all operations mounted by Bomber Command, the available aircraft of a Squadron were sent together for maximum effect. Perhaps the answer lies in the fact that only 55 aircraft from various units took part in the raid on the port, with a further 47 sent to attack Lorient. Three days after these raids took place, Bomber Command was released from their obligation for further attacks on the ports. The towns were by now mostly deserted, with the civilian population living in the outlying districts.

P/O Hagues' aircraft, BK541 EX-N, was the lone Wellington detailed for the bombing raid on St Nazaire and he took off at 1930 hrs. However, as he made his way over France, severe icing conditions were encountered and he reported he could not maintain height or sufficient airspeed, so the mission was aborted near the town of Mohon in Brittany. The bombs were jettisoned in the Channel at 2205 hrs and the crew landed back at RAF Ingham at 0040 hrs. The remaining seven crews had completed their checks by 1900 hrs and, loaded with two 1,500lb sea mines each, began to taxi round to the end of the runway. A technical fault was found in one of the aircraft and it was forced to abort the mission.

The remaining six proceeded to their allotted 'gardening' areas and all successfully dropped their mines, with the exception of Sgt Waldorf, who had a temporary electrical fault for a few seconds, which delayed the second mine from leaving the bomb bay. He said afterwards that he felt the mine was dropped safe as the safety fork was not found in the aircraft on return to base. Sgt Fisher, HZ281 EX-E, reported in his debrief that he could see the fires burning in St. Nazaire. Sgt Pinchin, Sgt Dennis, Sgt Burton and Sgt Shorttle all returned safely to base, the last aircraft landing at 0210 hrs.

Loading sea mines.

The next day, the 3rd, another sea mining operation was ordered, with five crews detailed to drop mines in the same area as the previous day. All aircraft took off between 1915 hrs and 1930 hrs, with Sgt Harlem returning early with a fault in the hydraulics to the rear turret of HE495 EX-L. The remaining four crews pinpointed the area with fixes taken from La Calabasse (Britanny), Du Feur Point and Belle Island in the Bay of Biscay. Sgt Austin, Sgt Ivery and Sgt Hagues all landed back at base between 0100 hrs and 0140 hrs, but Sgt Barnard was forced to land at RAF Swinderby as his navigator, P/O Plunkett, was unsure of their position and they were short of fuel. The crew landed at 0218 hrs.

4th April 1943

The morning began rather cloudy, but visibility improved to moderate, late in the afternoon with a southwest wind blowing at 10-15 mph. Bomber Command had picked out Kiel as the next target and decided on a maximum effort, with double the number of aircraft previously sent to the port. '199' detailed 14 aircraft for this raid but only 13 were able to take off on time. There were the usual gremlins at work, which meant the early return of three crews.

F/Lt Hawkins took off at 2030 hrs, but had trouble with the constant speed unit on the starboard engine of HE424 EX-X and was only airborne for a matter minutes before he turned back for the airfield. He remained in a circuit while the other aircraft got away and landed at 2100 hrs.

Sgt Waller, BJ916 EX-T, took off at 2030 hrs loaded with a 4,000lb 'cookie' and was nearing the target, having just crossed the west coast of Denmark near the town of Ribe, when the oxygen supply failed to the navigator. Sgt Waller instructed Sgt Couper to jettison the bomb, which was seen to explode, by the resulting flash, but the bomb aimer was unsure if it had hit anything on the shore line or if it had come down in the sea due to the heavy cloud cover. The pilot made the following report *"The oxygen failed and this seriously effected the navigator Sgt Pym. A very disappointing trip after having gone so far but I had no alternative but to abort the task in view of the condition of the navigator"*. Sgt Austin, BK366 EX-D, had almost reached the same position at 2225 hrs when he turned back due to instability of the aircraft caused by problems with the trimmer box.

Another aircraft to return early was that of Sgt Burton, BK509 EX-J, due to the starboard engine failing over the Danish town of Nordborg, on the Island of Als, and only a few minutes from the target. He reported: *"The engine was emitting sparks and we were losing altitude from the 12,000ft we had been flying at. The bombs were jettisoned live but no results were seen due to the cloud. The engine vibrated considerably during the whole of the return journey. This was a very disappointing trip having reached a position where considerable activity could be seen over the target area"*.

The remaining nine crews reached the target area but found it covered with dense cloud. As a result the Pathfinders had great difficulty marking and there were reports of decoy fires drawing off some of the bomb loads. The 199 Squadron Wellingtons crossed the target between 12,000 and 14,000ft and Sgt Fisher reported TIs cascading down from above 15,000ft. The bomb aimer, Sgt Nairn, released the load with green sky marker TIs in the sight. The crew's debrief report also mentions the use of Mandrel, although there are no further details as to why it was used or how the equipment performed.

Sgt Shorttle, HZ262 EX-K, was critical of some of the route markers and said *"We approached the target on a heading of 180° at 13,000ft with cloud of 10/10 and tops at 7,000ft. Bombed on green TIs seen through cloud. Yellow markers on points A and B. These would seem to be inadvisable with 10/10 cloud as they tend to silhouette the aircraft against the cloud and advertise the route. No results of own bombing seen."*

Sgt Waldorf, BJ582 EX-C, was hit by flak over the target, damaging the bomb doors and rendering the Gee equipment unserviceable. He was able to drop his bomb load, but was unable to observe any results. The crew made it back to base without further mishap and landed at 0235 hrs.

The Commanding Officer, W/Cdr Howard, was on this trip, flying HE259 EX-U. He also observed the yellow markers on points A and B, but made no other comments about them. He stated after the raid *"Rather disappointing show owing to 10/10 cloud. Our bomb bursts not seen owing to cloud cover"*.

The other pilots – W/O Palmer, Sgt Humphries, Sgt Dennis, Sgt Pinchin and P/O Wingood – all reported similar attack runs and results, with the main emphasis on the cloud cover restricting accuracy and observation. Generally it was felt that the markers and the bombs were widely scattered and no one thought the raid was successful. In fact, reports from Kiel show that hardly any bombs fell on the town or installations, with only 11 buildings destroyed. As previously mentioned, with 577 aircraft sent to this target, this was the largest raid on Kiel and with twelve of those aircraft lost it was later classed as a failure. The next three days saw the weather deteriorate, with the wind on the 6th reaching 80mph from the northwest. Rain showers and heavy squalls with a continuing gale force wind followed on into the afternoon of the 7th and then started to back off.

On the 8th, twelve crews were detailed for mining operations off St Nazaire and the aircraft were loaded with two mines each. During the morning, lectures were held for the bomb aimers on bombing errors and fuses, with a questionnaire on bombing apparatus. The wireless operators had a lecture on the inter-com systems fitted to the aircraft. Of the twelve Wellingtons detailed, two were found to have problems and taken off the Battle Order. At 2000 hrs the remaining ten prepared to take off for the 'Beeches' region where the Squadron had been operating a few days before. By 2030 hrs all had taken off and after reaching their allotted positions, all but two completed their task. Sgt Pinchin, HE495 EX-L, failed to return. Crew: Sgt Kenneth Albert Pinchin, Pilot, RAFVR, age 20, from Newport, Monmouthshire; P/O Lionel Cottrell Wheeker, Nav, RAFVR; P/O Leslie Robert Townsend, B/A, RCAF, age 24, Calgary, Alberta, Canada; Sgt Joseph Hector Paquin, W/Op, RCAF, age 33, Rouyn Noranda, Quebec, Canada; Sgt James William Green, R/G, RAFVR, age 22, Grimsby, Lincolnshire. Only Sgt Green's body was recovered from the sea and he was buried two days later in the French coastal town of Guidel. The remainder of the crew are commemorated on the Runnymede Memorial.

Sgt Barnard was unable to place his mines in the correct position, as he reported later: *"I believe the mines fell short of the allotted position owing to us being intercepted by a night fighter, evasive action taken and no damage sustained."* Sgt Holt had some problems with light flak from a coastal battery and returned with damage to the tail plane of his aircraft. Sgt Harlem, P/O Waterfield, Sgt Burton, W/O Palmer, Sgt Humphries, P/O Archer, Sgt Waller and P/O Hagues all dropped their mines, observing the parachutes opening, and reported a successful trip.

10th April 1943

Eleven aircraft were detailed for a raid on Frankfurt, but only ten took off for a raid that would be dogged by bad weather and 10/10 cloud over the target. Of the ten Wellingtons converging on Frankfurt, two of them experienced problems and turned back early. After being airborne for approximately 90 minutes, Sgt Hallem's rear gunner, Sgt Finlayson, was taken ill and the mission was aborted. The bomb load was dropped in the North Sea before landing back at RAF Ingham at 0310 hrs. Sgt Barnard had just reached the French coast and was crossing Abbeville when the oxygen supply to the rear turret failed and the decision was made to return to base. The remaining eight aircraft used yellow track markers laid by the PFF to navigate to the target, but the dense cloud up to 9,000ft obscured the whole area. F/Sgt Fisher arrived at 0239 hrs, but seeing no sky markers, circled for five minutes before releasing on red TIs seen in the bomb sight.

Another pilot, P/O Wingood, was also faced with no visible markers and orbited for eight minutes before his bomb aimer was able to release the load. He commented *"Marking seemed very poor and we had no wireless as it went u/s at 0016 hrs until we landed. We landed at [RAF] Downham Market at 0645 hrs and having no R/T we fired a Very cartridge, which set fire to the felt lining underneath the outer fabric. This continued to smoulder in spite of efforts to put it out with an extinguisher".*

S/Ldr Wynne Powell was at 14,300ft when he reached the target and saw the sky markers going down into the cloud cover. His bomb aimer, P/O Bevington, set up his bomb run and released on the reds, but no results were seen. This pilot was also critical of the marking and considered it very poor. He also made the following comment *"Marker method considered dangerous with 10/10 cloud because with markers in the cloud then aircraft become clearly silhouetted against cloud tops".* He also said he thought the searchlight at Dungeness was extremely useful.

The remaining pilots – Sgt Holt, Sgt Waller, Sgt Humphries, Sgt Burton and P/O Waterfield – all had similar difficulties bombing the target due to the cloud. Bomber Command classed this raid as another failure; the city reported only a few bombs falling in the suburbs and no casualties. Of the 502 aircraft taking part in the raid 21 failed to return.

11th April 1943

Six crews detailed for another mining sortie to the Bay of Biscay, this time slightly further south than any previous operations. The area designated was 4626N 0139W, an inlet leading to Le Poiroux. P/O Hagues, Sgt Harlem, Sgt Austin, F/Sgt Oggers and F/O Archer all laid their mines in their allotted area and returned safely to base. S/Ldr Humby at his debrief said *"We had an exciting trip on the return journey due to getting off course and numerous attempts to cross the enemy coast resulted in much opposition".*

14th April 1943

The day started with rain and low cloud, but conditions improved as the day wore on. Bomber Command ordered a major raid on Stuttgart and eleven aircraft and crews were put on the Battle Order. The detailed aircraft started taking off at 2110 hrs and by 2125 hrs all were airborne, but Sgt Harlem, HE281 turned back at 2254 hrs with a complete failure of the intercom system. He had just reached the French coast near Dieppe, but returned and dropped his bomb load in the water at 0014 hrs east of Hull (as directed). The remaining crews reached the target and reported excellent visibility, no cloud, and just a slight ground haze, which was a complete change to the previous two raids.

F/O Wingood bombed on the green TIs, *"We saw a huge pall of black smoke rising up to 8,000ft that came from the southern part of the town, fires were still visible 60 miles away on the return leg"*. Both Sgt Dennis and Sgt Humphries observed a large blue coloured explosion in the west section of the target, with smoke rising to 2,000ft. Sgt Humphries reported, *"This explosion was so brilliant it lit up several aircraft in the sky"*. On this raid, Sgt Burton was accompanied by Group Captain Wray and they reported a successful trip. The remaining crews – F/Lt Hawkins, F/O Archer, Sgt Holt, F/Sgt Odgers, F/Sgt Fisher and F/O Waterfield – all bombed on red and green TIs and returned to base.

Sgt Wilf Humphries and crew.

Several pilots claimed good marking and results, but the later evaluation obtained from bombing photographs and photo-reconnaissance, plus post-war reports from Stuttgart, show otherwise. There was considerable 'creepback' due to the marking and main bombing developing in the north east of the town along the line of approach of the main force. If the PFF backers-up did not press right into the target area, but dropped their markers on the earliest markers visible, and the main force also dropped their bomb loads early, this creepback could mean the intended target could be missed altogether. It was found that this creepback went as far as an area known as Bad Cannstatt, that was in itself largely industrialised and contained a large railway repair facility which received substantial damage.

Two other outlying districts, Muhlhaüsen and Münster also received a large proportion of the bombs intended for Stuttgart with 393 buildings destroyed, 942 damaged and over 200 casualties. Of the few bombs that did fall in the centre of the town, one destroyed the Gedachtnis Church and a direct hit on an air-raid shelter killed 257 French and 143 Russian prisoners of war. Of the 462 aircraft taking part in this raid 23 failed to return.

15th April 1943

Five aircraft were sent on a mining operation to plant 'veg' in the Lorient area in the Bay of Biscay. All the aircraft ran in on a timed run from the Isle de Groix. Sgt Freestone, HE470 EX-P, had dropped his mines but was hit by flak, which splintered the starboard engine propeller; some damage was also caused to the fabric in the wing. He was able to return to base without further mishap and landed at 0220 hrs.

16th April 1943

The target selected for the Squadron was Mannheim, with Main Force sending a total of 271 aircraft on this raid and also 327 to Pilsen, where the Skoda Works was the intended aiming point. Eleven Wellingtons were detailed for the Mannheim raid and all lifted off with no problems between 2115 hrs and 2120 hrs. On approaching the Lincoln area at 2155 hrs F/Lt Hankins had serious problems, his report stated – *"The starboard engine cut out on three occasions due to fuel starvation when using the overload tank, we set course three times, but finally aborted for the above technical reasons"*. He jettisoned the bomb load safe in the North Sea and landed at 2350 hrs. P/O Hagues took off at 2125 hrs and initially made good progress towards the target, but at 2138 hrs the port constant speed unit started to give problems and the revs and boost on the engine started to fluctuate. He decided to abort the mission and dropped the bomb load of incendiaries on a runway at 'Rosieres' (sic) that was well lighted and saw the bombs clearly ignite on runway. F/O Wingood and S/Ldr Wynne-Powell both reported that the PFF were late marking and that the first markers seen were after they had bombed visually and left the target area. S/Ldr Wynne-Powell saw several aircraft coned by searchlights over the target, but made it back without any problems. He landed at RAF Newmarket at 0420 hrs to avoid problems with fuel shortage. F/O Waterfield, F/Sgt Odgers, Sgt Humphries, F/O Archer, Sgt Holt and Sgt Dennis reached and bombed the target successfully and all the crews returned safely to base, the last aircraft touching down at 0520 hrs.

F/Sgt Bryant, DFM, wrote later regarding this raid: *"The Squadron took part in the first ever 'Massed Attack Low Level' taking advantage of bright moonlight. Mannheim was the target for Wellingtons and Stirlings and Halifaxes, with a large number of Lancasters and Halifaxes going on to a further target (The Skoda Works at Pilsen). The height across enemy territory was 300ft, climbing to 3,000ft just before Mannheim to bomb. This was a terrible raid and of the 271 aircraft despatched to Mannheim 18 were shot down, plus a further 36 on the Pilsen operation. I personally put out four searchlights that night plus another from F/O Bell in the front turret. On return we also got mixed up with three Fw190s but sustained no damage."*

The raid on Mannheim was quite effective, with the PFF marking the target accurately, and reports show that 130 buildings were destroyed, and a further 3,000 suffering varying degrees of damage. 41 factories had their production halted or seriously reduced. Almost 7,000 civilians were bombed out of their homes. Of the 609 aircraft taking part in the two raids 54 were lost, which was the highest proportion so far in the war, exceeding the 50 lost on the 1,000-bomber raid on Bremen on 25th June 1942. Fourteen of the aircraft that failed to return came down in the sea and a large proportion of the crews were rescued.

20th April 1943

Another mining operation was launched against the French coastal waters in the Bay of Biscay. Twelve aircraft took off, but two were forced to abort the mission. Sgt Humphries took off at 2045 hrs, but then discovered that the port engine nacelle cover was missing, and with the port nacelle cock and port wing tanks closed the engine cut out. He dropped his two mines safely into the North Sea, 60 miles east of Grimsby. S/Ldr Humby was just approaching the French coast and having navigational difficulties due to his navigator, W/O Dick, feeling ill. He could not get a correct pinpoint, so jettisoned his mines mid-Channel and returned to base. The remaining ten aircraft successfully dropped their mines in the shipping lanes between Lorient and the Gironde estuary. As he was turning for home, F/O Archer was attacked by a Ju88. The rear gunner, Sgt Donnahay, returned fire claiming he had hit the Junkers. F/O Archer evaded further attacks, which was as well because the rear gunner reported damage to the hydraulics to his turret and the emergency hydraulic system was also unserviceable. They and the other crews all landed safely back at RAF Ingham.

Between 21st and 25th April no operational sorties were flown, mainly due to bad weather. Although a raid had been planned for the 24th it was cancelled shortly before the fourteen aircraft detailed took off. These few days of respite were put to good use with everyone attending lectures and demonstrations relating to their roles.

Duisburg was the target on 26th April and '199' prepared twelve aircraft and crews for the raid. All took off between 0030 hrs and 0050 hrs and reached the target without problem. The attack commenced at approximately 0230 hrs, with F/Lt Wingood, HE281 EX-E, running in at 12,000ft. He was hit by flak, just after dropping the bomb load, which damaged the starboard main plane, stripped the fabric off part of the fuselage and smashed the bomb sight and bomb selector panel. He was carrying two extra crew as passengers – Fl/Lt Newsome and a person named Ross, who is not identified further in the records. If they were flying with this crew to get first hand knowledge of a bombing mission, they probably got more that they bargained for. Sgt Shorttle, HE462 EX-F, had the pitot head damaged and the starboard main plane and aileron holed by heavy flak. Sgt Dennis, HE702 EX-Y, had the port propeller and tailplane slightly damaged as he ran in on his bombing run. Sqd/Ldr Wynne Powell also received damage to his aircraft from a burst of heavy flak and later counted eight large holes in the starboard fuselage and wing.

Many 4,000lb cookies were observed by Sgt Humphries to undershoot the aiming point, although he felt the raid was a success. Both Sgt Waller and Sgt Dennis reported that they thought a large number of bombs appeared to be directed at the north east of the target area. These comments tie in with the raid report prepared later by Bomber Command. Although receiving varying degrees of damage, all '199' aircraft and crews returned safely to RAF Ingham, the last touching down at 0535 hrs.

 The raid on Duisburg was not the success initially thought by many of the returning crews. The PFF claimed to have marked accurately, but later photographic reconnaissance proved that the majority of the bombs from the 561 aircraft assigned to the target had fallen to the north east of the town – which corroborates several of the '199' crews' debriefing statements. It was apparent that the main force had bombed too early or been drawn away by early fires started short of the target. Although the raid was deemed a partial failure, in fact over 300 buildings were destroyed in Duisburg itself, and there were reports of bombs falling on at least six other towns in the area. Seventeen aircraft failed to return.

27th April 1943

Seven aircraft, led by W/Cdr Howard, took off at 2145 hrs for a mining sortie to the Bay of Biscay. Sgt Sinclair aborted his mission when it was found that both the Gee and radio equipment were not working and brought both mines back to base. Sgt Barnard had a successful trip and dropped both mines, but on returning to base found there was a hydraulic system failure. He was forced to make a flapless landing at RAF Fiskerton, as the runway at RAF Ingham was considered too short. F/Sgt Odgers also found his pinpoint and the bomb aimer released the mines, but only one was seen to deploy its parachute. A short time after release, the other mine was seen to explode in the sea. He also landed away from base, at RAF New Zealand Farm in Wiltshire. The remaining crews were able to lay their mines and return to base. Interestingly there were no bombing details ordered on this date, but Bomber Command launched the biggest mine laying operation so far in the war. 160 aircraft took part and laid 458 mines in the Bay of Biscay, the Brittany Ports and off the Frisian Islands. Another point of interest is that the Squadron ORB simply mentions Sgt Sinclair having problems with his radio and Gee equipment and returning to base. A note I received from the Rear Gunner F/Sgt C. Bryant, DFM, paints a slightly different picture: *"The Squadron on this occasion was flying from Ingham in Lincolnshire, a grass field with Scampton on one side and Hemswell on the other. The aircraft were Wellingtons, all the very latest, which in itself was a blessing. I was actually a 166 Squadron man, but had no crew and Sgt Sinclair had no rear gunner at 199, so I was loaned to the Squadron.*

On the night of 27th April 1943, we were detailed to lay mines at Lorient and this happened to be my birthday, so no party that night. At briefing there was a "Boffin" present and he was rubbing his hands with glee, for these mines now being loaded could not be 'swept up' like the old type we had been using. Everything went fine, on course, ETA correct etc. But when the time came to release, the mines failed to drop and after several runs we tried to shake them off, but they would not budge. Nothing for it but to head for home and ask for instructions. Base informed us to wait out over the sea off Mablethorpe, but be sure not to try and drop the mines. We heard nothing for twenty minutes, so back to base. After much discussion and a further wait we received the following instruction. 'Climb to 3,000ft, head 090 and put "George" in and bale out'. While climbing over base we received another message, cancelling the last order and proceed to land. Relief was expressed by all aboard, but of course we didn't know how the aircraft would stand up to landing with a load aboard, or if the mines would drop off on impact with the ground. Sgt Sinclair made probably his best ever landing and the old 'Wimpy' held on in one piece. Very quickly ground staff and the fire section surrounded us. Out came the sandbags stacked up under the bomb doors and that's how it remained until next day when the mines were defused. What a birthday, one to remember and all this for a D.N.C.O. (Did not complete operation), we thought we would get a D.C.O. (Did complete operation) just for the effort, still that was life under Bomber Command. Our C.O at that time was G/Capt. 'Hoppy' Wray. Only one of our crew failed to finish the war F/O Peter Bell, who was shot down over Berlin 16th March 1944 on his second tour while with 103 Squadron at Elsham."

May
More casualties but not all of them inflicted by the enemy

2nd May 1943

The Squadron was ordered to stand by for operations and 15 aircraft were readied, but in the late afternoon all the crews were stood down.

4th May 1943

Fifteen aircraft were detailed for a raid on Dortmund, but the end result was far from satisfactory. Before taking off at 2245 hrs a total of four aircraft had been forced to abort due to sickness, and eleven aircraft did get away, but Sgt T. Austin turned back due to his rear gunner being ill. Sgt Burton, the pilot of HE490, was himself too sick to continue and turned back for base. Sgt Barnard's wireless operator and rear gunner were likewise stricken with sickness and he was forced to abandon his mission. F/O Hagues' rear gunner, Sgt Benfell, reported that his oxygen supply had failed, so this aircraft also returned early. The remaining seven aircraft were flown by: F/O Archer, Sgt Dennis, Sgt Shorttle, F/Sgt Fisher, F/O Waterfield, F/Sgt Harlem, and F/Lt Hankins. All reached the target and dropped their bombs in the centre of the town. F/O Waterfield was the only pilot to report any damage – his aircraft HE787 EX-Z, suffered several small holes in the fuselage due to light flak.

F/Lt Hankins' report is a fair summing up on the raid for all the crews who made it to the target: *"We bombed from 14,000ft, visibility was good with no cloud. Target identified by green TI's and our bombs fell in the centre of the concentration. Large fires observed in centre and north area of the town. Fire glow could be seen from 150 miles away on return trip. If PFF were accurate raid was a success".*

F/Sgt Harlem, flying HE428, EX-L, reported at de-brief that *"Mandrel was used effectively"* but there is no mention in the ORB of his aircraft being in a combat with a German night-fighter on the homeward run. However, a combat report was filed at Group Headquarters and reads: *"Night 4/5 May 1943. Homeward bound from Dortmund at 0100 hrs, on a heading of 125 degrees, our rear gunner saw a single engined enemy aircraft on his port quarter, about 800 yards away and slightly below. While watching this aircraft, a searchlight appeared from the nose of a second enemy aircraft at about the same range and on the starboard beam. Our rear gunner concentrated on the E/A approaching from the port quarter that closed to about 250 yards. The rear gunner told the pilot to turn to port and opened fire at the same time and fired a four second burst, and then as our aircraft was turning, the rear gunner fired a further two second burst. The E/A was seen to hover with the nose pointing up, as though stalling, and was lost to sight by the rear gunner. The front gunner then saw an aircraft diving in flames to the ground. It hit the ground and continued burning and this is claimed as the E/A at which our gunner fired. While the encounter was going on the second aircraft with the searchlight continued to fly in approximately the same position, but its tactics could not be observed by the rear gunner whose attention was concentrated on the first aircraft. After our aircraft turned to port and continued to take evasive action, by weaving, the E/A with the searchlight continued to shadow our aircraft with searchlight extinguished, but did not make an attack and was lost to sight at 0115 hrs. There were no searchlights (other than the one on the E/A) or flares observed. Our rear gunner Sgt Finlayson, RAAF, fired a total of 500 rounds. The E/A didn't fire at all".*

The mystery of the large number of aircrew taken ill prior to and just after take-off for Dortmund, may have been severe food poisoning but was never resolved.

The raid on Dortmund by 596 aircraft was the largest to date, excluding the '1,000' raids, and the first full scale attack on the city. PFF marking was accurate, although some later backing up fell short. The Germans were able to light a large decoy fire that attracted several bomb loads. About half of the force bombed within three miles of the aiming point and severe damage was caused to the centre and northern suburbs of the City. The German reports prepared after the raid show that 1,218 buildings were totally destroyed and 2,141 damaged. The Hoesch and Dortmunder steel factories, and a large number of installations in the dock area, were severely damaged.

Over the next few days, operations were somewhat curtailed. On the 9th, twelve aircraft were detailed for operations and then cancelled, and the same happened on 11th when thirteen crews were detailed and then had the operation scrubbed. From the 5th May to 11th May only limited flying training was carried out, although the usual lectures were held for all roles. The weather was a governing factor from the 7th to the 10th with a WSW gale, accompanied by heavy rain and hail.

12th May 1943

Rain and drizzle persisted for most of the day and into the late evening. Orders were received for a raid on Duisburg and fourteen Wellingtons were fuelled and bombed up during the afternoon. Just before 2300 hrs one of the aircraft was found to have technical problems and was taken off the battle order. At midnight the remaining thirteen aircraft started to lift off and in fifteen minutes all were airborne and setting course for the target. At 0030 hrs, Sgt Freestone was crossing the coast at Skegness when both the Gee set and the IFF transmitter had the explosive charges fitted to them blow up, causing much consternation among the crew. These charges were only meant to be used in the event of a crash landing, to prevent the equipment falling into enemy hands, but as it later turned out, a fault had occurred in the wiring causing the charges to go off. Luckily there was no fire, only a large amount of smoke, and Sgt Freestone was able to jettison the bomb load and return to RAF Ingham, landing at 0155 hrs. The remaining crews all reached Duisburg and bombed the target within a period of ten minutes of one another.

Sgt Austin had problems with the oxygen system in his aircraft, but still completed his trip and reported:

"We had clear visibility over the target although the ground was obscured by a considerable amount of smoke. The target was identified by a timed run from the yellow TI's and a concentration of greens were in the bomb sight when the load was released. No results observed but fires well concentrated around markers although some bombs were observed bursting west of the main aiming point. Quite a good raid".

Back: **F/O Cook, W/Op; Sgt Wilson, B/A; Sgt Hughes, Nav.**
Front: **Sgt K. Rankin, A/G; Sgt Waldorf, Pilot.**

The other pilots taking part in this operation were: F/Lt Wingood, Sgt Burton, F/Sgt Harlem, F/Sgt Fisher, F/Sgt Odgers, F/O Hagues, Sgt Humphries, Sgt Waller, Sgt Barnard, and F/O Archer.

Sgt Waldorf and his crew were shot down on this raid and their aircraft came down near Harderwijk, Holland. They were all killed. Wellington Mk X, HE702, EX-Y, Crew: Sgt Leonard Waldorf, Pilot, RAFVR, age 20, from Stamford Hill, London; Sgt Ronald Hughes, Nav, RAFVR, age 20, Shotton, Flintshire; Sgt John Guyie Wilson, B/A, RAFVR; F/O Ronald Hermond Downes Cook, W/Op, RAFVR, age 30, married, Walton-on-Thames, Surrey; Sgt Tom Wharmby, R/G, RAFVR, age 21, married, Walkden, Lancashire. The crew are buried in Harderwijk General Cemetery, Holland. It will be remembered from the earlier story by Keith Rankin, who was the regular rear gunner of this crew, that he had been replaced by Sgt Wharmby as, due to medical problems, he was no longer fit for flying duties.

The reports from the crews taking part in this raid all give a clear indication that they felt that the PFF had marked the target area very accurately and that there was a good concentration of bombing. Bomber Command and local German reports all appear to back up the claims made by the various crews – the Pathfinders were, in fact, spot on with their marking and German reports show that the port area on the River Rhine was severely damaged, with a total of 1,596 buildings in the port and surrounding area totally destroyed. 21 Barges and thirteen ships were sunk at their moorings and at least 60 other ships of various tonnage were damaged. Four important steel works were also hit with the subsequent loss of production. The planning committee of Bomber Command issued a statement that they felt it was not necessary, in the short term, to attack Duisburg again.

13th May 1943

A raid on Bochum was ordered, with thirteen Wellingtons and crews briefed. Bochum was a choke point for many of the main railway lines serving the Ruhr and thus any damage to the tracks and marshalling yards would cause major disruption to the movement of essential war supplies. With persistent regularity, there was the one rogue aircraft that refused to check out serviceable and only twelve took off for the target just before midnight. Mechanical faults soon forced Sgt Humphries to return to base. *"We had just reached the enemy coast when the rear gunner Sgt Gore reported that the turret rotation was slow and it gradually worsened, until it failed to respond to the controls altogether. We jettisoned the bombs at 5200N 0240E and returned to base"*. The fault was later diagnosed as a leak in the rotation service joint. Sgt Harlem had a more difficult situation to contend with when he encountered an enemy night fighter. *"It became necessary to abort the mission due to persistent interception by a Ju88. Constant evasive action for 30 minutes made it impossible to reach the target in the allotted time. Bombs and 'nickels'* (bundles of propaganda leaflets) *jettisoned together in the North Sea"*. As the remaining crews reached the target area, one in particular, Sgt Burton, had arrived slightly early and there were only a few green markers to be seen. He pressed on with his attack using these markers and stated *"The attack had only just started on our arrival, but the TIs appeared to be going down in a good concentration by the time we left the target. Consider route was not very favourable, search lights were most troublesome and confusing to early arrivals"*.

Bomb damage at Bochum, photographed by W/Cdr G.M. (Jock) Duncan of 608 Squadron in the summer of 1945.

F/O Archer and F/Sgt Fisher were also critical of the planned route to the target that took them between Dusseldorf and Cologne, following yellow ground markers, stating that the searchlights were very active and appeared to be working in large cones.

All the crews commented on the intense and heavy flak on the approach to the target, with Sgt Barnard's aircraft sustaining three large holes in the starboard wing. No other damage or injuries were reported and the general feeling was that the raid had been a success. However, later intelligence photographs and reports show that the raid caused most damage to an area two miles from the aiming point and five miles south of the town itself. Although the first bombs dropped fell on the target the Germans managed to get several decoy fires alight which drew some of the bombers away from the town. The main marking of the aiming point by 109 Squadron Mosquitoes ran into trouble as five of the ten aircraft detailed had major technical difficulties and only two main red TIs were placed in the correct position. The backing up became spread out and short of the target, some by as much as two miles, and with no further 'reds' the 'greens' continued to creep back. Of the 442 aircraft taking part in this operation, 24 were shot down.

14th to 22nd May 1943

There were no operations detailed for the Squadron, mainly due to the preparation and execution of 'Operation Chastise', the attack on the Mohne, Eder, Sorpe and Ennepe Dams by 617 Squadron. This, however, did not prevent a concerted effort on everyone's part to attend the many training lectures laid on for all aircrews, plus a varied flying training program. Many air tests were carried out with a large number of crews taking part in Bullseye cross country and fighter affiliation exercises. All new members of the Squadron were subjected to intensive lectures aimed at preparing them for the continuing 'Battle of the Ruhr'. The air gunners were given several hours of clay pigeon shooting to improve their skills at giving a moving target sufficient 'lead'. A naval staff officer, based at Group HQ, gave a lecture on mining coastal waters. All the crew members, with the exception of the rear gunners, attended lectures on the use of 'Gee'. This was another attempt at cross-referencing skills amongst the crew. Many pilots saw this type of lecture as a good way of getting everyone to be able to carry out different tasks if the need arose and also extended the learning curve to teaching the bomb aimer, navigator or wireless operator to fly the aircraft. In many cases during combat, this extensive training paid dividends when a crew member was seriously wounded and their role was taken over.

On May 21st, Sgt A.D. Finlayson was awarded the DFM for shooting down a German night fighter on 4th May.

23rd May 1943

The day dawned clear with good visibility and a brisk westerly wind. Eighteen aircraft were detailed for an operation to Dortmund. The bomb loads for fourteen aircraft were to be mainly 4lb and 30lb incendiaries, with four to carry 9 x 500lb medium case bombs. All eighteen Wellingtons took off for the raid, starting at 2300 hrs and the last leaving the runway at 2317 hrs. The only aircraft to return early was that of Sgt Freestone, HE487 EX-J, who was forced to turn back at 0009 hrs. He landed back at RAF Ingham at 0115 hrs and reported, *"The port engine cut out twice, once over base and again before reaching the coast. The engine continued to cause anxiety and, after a further cut with revs very spasmodic, it was decided to abort the mission and return to base"*. The remaining aircraft reached the target, but one pilot was again critical of the yellow TIs used for marking the correct track. Sgt Burton stated in his de-brief that *"I consider the Yellow TIs should have been placed earlier on track owing to the search light belt."*

F/Lt Wingood was over the target at 0115 hrs and received considerable damage to his aircraft. The port engine, port and starboard tail plane, the fin, fuselage and bomb doors were hit by flak and all the electrical circuits were cut. He managed to keep the aircraft flying and landed back at RAF Ingham at 0330 hrs. Sgt Tom Austin was also to get a hot reception. As he dropped his bombs at 0125 hrs the flak was intensifying and soon his aircraft, HE921 EX-A, was hit, causing a large hole near the starboard bomb door, and the wireless operator, F/Sgt Greenhaulgh, was wounded. *"We were coned by many searchlights and found the air speed indicator was u/s, also the starboard cylinder temperature gauge was not working indicating possible engine damage"*. The final major problem was found to be the undercarriage, which would not lock down, and Sgt Austin was forced to make a crash landing at RAF Mildenhall. Apart from the W/Op, there were no other injuries to the crew.

F/O Makin, HE277 EX-M, dropped his bomb load of 450 x 4lb and 32 x 30lb incendiaries at 0124 hrs and was then hit by flak. The rear turret vision slide was broken and the wireless operator, Sgt Martin, was wounded in the hand as he tried to close the escape hatch that had been blown open by the blast.

The other pilots carrying out the raid were: W/Cdr Howard, S/Ldr Wynne-Powell, F/O Archer, Sgt Spring, F/Lt Hankins, Sgt Dennis, P/O Hagues, Sgt Humphries, F/Sgt Harlem, F/Sgt Odgers, and P/O Waterfield.

All the crews reported large fires and much smoke in the target area, with good concentrations of TIs and bombs. Several large explosions were observed and most crews logged a very satisfactory operation. Sgt Anderson and his crew could still see the glow of the fires 70 miles away on the return journey.

One aircraft, HZ 582 EX-R, piloted by Sgt H.W. Austin, failed to return, having been shot down at 0215 hrs over Schaijk, 7kms ESE of Oss, Netherlands. Three crewmen were killed: Sgt Horace William Austin, Pilot, RAFVR, age 20, from West Norwood, London; Sgt Arthur Herbert, W/Op, RAFVR, age 22, Darlaston, Staffs; W/O Ralph Matthew Costello, R/G, RCAF, age 25, married to Marie Costello. All were buried at Uden War Cemetery, Netherlands. Sgt D.R. Keevers, Nav, RAAF, baled out, was taken prisoner, and interned at Camp 357 (Stalag Kopernikus), and given the POW number 185; Sgt J.P.E. Last, B/A, RAFVR, baled out, was taken prisoner, interned at Camp 9B (Stalag Wegschlelde), and given POW number 24779.

Bomber Command recorded the raid on Dortmund, by a total of 826 aircraft, as very successful. The north and east of the city were devastated after accurate marking by the PFF in clear weather. Almost 2,000 buildings were completely destroyed, with a large number of industrial factories and warehouses hit. The Hoesch steelworks was put out of action completely. 599 people were killed and 1,275 injured. 38 aircraft were lost on this raid.

An incident occurred during this raid that bears out the policy of training aircrew to take over someone's position, should the need arise. 199 Squadron, as already stated, was going through this course of action previous to the raid on Dortmund. Although it does not concern a '199' crew, it is worth relating.

A Wellington of 431 Squadron was coned by searchlights and had been hit by flak just after leaving the target. The rear gunner reported the aircraft on fire and, during some confusion regarding the order to bale out, the pilot and rear gunner took to their parachutes. The bomb aimer, Sgt Sloan, took over the controls of the bomber and successfully shook off the searchlights. With the aid of the navigator and wireless operator, who were still on board, they flew the

Bomb damage at Dortmund, photographed in the summer of 1945 by W/Cdr G.M. Duncan.

aircraft back to England and made a perfect landing at RAF Cranwell. Sgt Sloan was awarded the CGM, the navigator Sgt Parslow received the DFM and the wireless operator F/O Bailey, the DFC. This incident highlighted the benefits of all aspects of crew training.

25th May 1943

Dusseldorf was again to be the target, and fourteen Wellingtons were placed on the battle order and each bombed up with an all incendiary load. One aircraft was declared unserviceable before the raid commenced. Between 2345 hrs and 0010 hrs the thirteen Wellingtons took off for the target, but again, Sgt Freestone, flying HE487 EX-J, was to have the same problem with the port engine as on the 23rd. He took off at 2355 hrs and started to climb away from the base, but at 0007 hrs, the engine cut out completely. He carried on out over the North Sea, jettisoned the bomb load and landed safely at 0100 hrs. Sgt Sinclair also returned early. He took off at 2400 hrs, but crossing the coast at Southwold, he became ill and returned to base, landing with his bomb load still on board. All but one of the remaining aircraft arrived over the target and dropped their bombs. F/O Waterfield found the target and released on the green TIs, but said afterwards: *"Many fires seen, but they appeared scattered, The raid did not appear to be concentrated and it was my impression that most crews undershot the target"*. F/O Hagues and Sgt Spring both bombed the target and saw two large explosions, one of which appeared to be in the Neuss area. Sgt Dennis also reported a colossal explosion in the Neuss area and reported in his de-brief: *"The defences were comparatively weak with search lights operating singly with no big cones seen"*. S/Ldr Humby, DFC, dropped his bombs at 0146 hrs and reported: *"We identified the target by the docks and river and bombed the green TIs. The reds seemed to be widely dispersed in about five different places. Target appeared to be burning well, although there was evidence of a considerable amount of scattered bombing. Mandrel operated"*. F/O Archer was the last '199' aircraft to bomb, at 0200 hrs, and reported: *"Concentrated fires appearing around the green TIs, but also a lot of scattered fires seen some 50 miles away"*.

One aircraft, HF 488 (EX-U), was shot down when it was intercepted outbound by a German night fighter at 15,000ft and crashed at 0140 hrs at Caberg, 3kms NW of Maastricht, Netherlands. All but one of the crew were killed. Crew: F/O Dennis Makin, Pilot, RAFVR, age 29, from Ashton-under-Lyne, Lancs, married to Doris Constance Makin; F/O Ronald Thomas Douglas, B/A, RAFVR, age 23, from Marton, Blackpool, Lancs; Sgt William Henry Thomson, W/Op, RAFVR, age 32, married to Norah Thomson of Hornsey Rise, North London; Sgt Thomas Mackie Scott, A/G, RAFVR, age 20, from Thankerton, Lanarkshire. F/O F.S. Reade survived, was captured, and taken to Stalag Luft Sagan and Balaria, and given the Pow number 1453.

Those who were killed were initially buried in a military cemetery at Venlo, but their remains were later removed to the Jonkerbos War Cemetery.

According to Bomber Command records, the raid on Dusseldorf was classed as a failure. The Pathfinders had great difficulty marking the target due to a double layer of cloud. The German ground defences were also able to deploy many decoy fires and markers that resulted in bombs being dropped over a wide area. Dusseldorf recorded between 50 and 100 buildings destroyed. Of the 759 aircraft taking part in this raid 27 were lost.

26th May 1943

After preparing ten aircraft for operations, the order was given to cancel the raid.

27th May 1943

During the morning, the navigators received a lecture on tactics and the bomb aimers a course on map reading, and orders were received for ten aircraft to be prepared for a raid on Essen. Arming of the Wellingtons proceeded with incendiaries for all the aircraft except one, which was to have a high explosive load. Prior to take-off three aircraft were withdrawn due to technical difficulties and the remaining seven took off for the target between 2300 hrs and 2305 hrs.

Sgt Freestone, flying a different aircraft on this sortie, HE490 EX-C , had a trouble free trip to the target and released his bombs consisting of 360 x 4lb, including 30 Type 'X' and 40 x 30lb incendiaries from 15,800ft. He later reported: *"We identified the target by the red and green markers with the green TIs in the bomb sight on release. There was a large explosion believed to be a 'cookie' seen through a break in the clouds in the NW of the town".*

The breaks in the cloud allowed F/Lt Wingood to observe many large fires in the target area and his crew stated that they could still see the fire glow 80 miles away on their return leg. Sgt Dennis was the only pilot carrying a high explosive load, consisting of 7 x 500lb MC and 2 x 500lb GP bombs which his bomb aimer, Sgt Kettle, dropped at 0105 hrs from 16,500ft. Sgt Shorttle and F/Lt Hankins both had successful trips and remarked on the large number of fires seen through the cloud cover, but thought some of the loads dropped were widely scattered, probably, due to undershooting.

S/Ldr Wynne-Powell HE741 EX-N had problems on his approach to the target: *"As we made our bomb run at 0105, at 16,500ft the bomb aimer, P/O Bevington, had the release flares in the sight, but reported that he could not open the bomb doors. It was suspected the release lever was frozen, although a burst of heavy flak immediately below the fuselage may have caused the failure. Repeated efforts to open the doors was finally successful at 6,000ft and we dropped the bombs at 5330N 0330E (this position is approximately midway between Den Helder on the Dutch coast and Grimsby) on the homeward track. A very disappointing raid".*

Sgt Waller and his crew were lost on this raid and the entire crew killed. Flying HE634 EX-S they had taken off at 2300 hrs, but were intercepted by a night fighter flown by Lt Karl-Heinz Vollkopf, III./NJG1 at 0130 hrs. As the other aircraft on this raid had all dropped their bombs between 0105 hrs and 0110 hrs it might be assumed that Sgt Waller had bombed the target and was on his way back to base. The Wellington came down on Plantlunne Flugplatz, 17 kms NNW of Rheine. Crew: Sgt John Roland Smith Waller, Pilot, RAFVR, age 21, from Norwich; Sgt Frederick Reginald Pym, Nav, RAFVR; F/Sgt Harold Coupe, B/A, RAFVR, age 29, married to Beatrice Rushforth Coupe of Heywood, Lancashire; Sgt Davis William Glover, W/Op, RAFVR, age 22, from Leeds, Yorkshire; Sgt Richard Taylor Anthony Hudson, A/G, RAFVR, age 20, from Grimsby, Lincolnshire.

The crew were initially buried at Lingen, on 31st May 1943, but their bodies have since been moved and laid to rest in the Reichswald Forest Cemetery.

A total of 518 aircraft were detailed for this raid including twelve PFF Mosquitoes. Due to a blanket of cloud over the target, sky markers were used. The result was limited to damage in the central and northern areas of Essen with bombs reported falling in ten surrounding Ruhr towns. 23 aircraft were shot down.

29th May 1943

Bomber Command detailed the first raid on Wuppertal, with seven aircraft from '199' on the Battle Orders. All took off between 2255 hrs and 2300 hrs with incendiary loads in the bomb bays. F/Sgt Fisher was the first to arrive over the target and dropped his bombs at 0057 hrs, but had 24 of the total of 40 x 30lb incendiaries hang up. The remaining 360 x 4lb incendiaries dropped satisfactorily. Sgt Freestone came in on his bomb run at 0112 hrs and the bomb aimer, Sgt Whittington, had the green TIs in his sight when he released the bombs. The crew reported: *"We saw many large extensive fires in the target area, with much smoke, and one column reaching up to 6,000ft. Hit by flak. Damage to glycol tank, bomb door jacks, overload oil tank and general fabric holed. The hydraulics were effected and the emergency system was used to lower the undercart. PFF very good. Wizard prang. Landed at Scampton".*

The other pilots – F/Sgt Fisher, F/Sgt Odgers, F/Lt Hankins, Sgt Barnard, P/O Waterfield and F/O Archer – all commented on the excellent marking carried out by the PFF and were able to drop their bomb loads on the target. Sgt Barnard reported seeing at least six large explosions caused by 4,000lb cookies hitting the target area and F/O Archer spotted another smoke column at 10,000ft. F/Lt Hankins perhaps summed up the raid when he reported in his de-brief after the raid – *"Wuppertal has had it".*

The Bomber Command raid report stated that 719 aircraft had taken part in the raid and classed it as the outstanding success of the Battle of the Ruhr. The PFF marked the target accurately and Main Force delivered a devastating attack on the town. Large fires developed to almost 'firestorm proportions' in some parts of the narrow streets and, because the raid was delivered on a Saturday night, many of the fire and town officials were away in their country homes for the weekend. German reports state that the firefighters, who were dealing with their first raid, could not cope with the fires which steadily got more and more out of control. Over 1,000 acres of the built up area was destroyed. Five large industrial factories plus 211 other important manufacturing premises and 4,000 homes were totally destroyed. There was also serious damage to a further 71 industrial and 1,800 civilian buildings. Approximately 3,300 people were killed.

Bomber Command's loss of 33 aircraft reflects the intensity of the German defences over the Ruhr.

30th May 1943

The weather was at first very unsettled, with heavy continuous rain followed by a heavy thunderstorm. Later in the afternoon the storm cleared, leaving just a light drizzle to annoy the ground crews readying four Wellingtons with sea mines. The target area was off the French coast at Lorient, code named "Artichokes". Each aircraft was loaded with two 1,500lb mines and the four crews took off at 2150 hrs and reached their designated area without any problems.

The pilots – F/Lt Wingood, Sgt Austin, Sgt Stevenson and Sgt Andrews – all dropped their mines within ten minutes of each other using a pinpoint at Pont Aven. They flew from this position on a timed run on a course of 141° magnetic. All the mines were successfully planted, but on the return leg, Sgt Andrews found his port engine was causing problems and eventually it failed and he was forced to make a one engined landing at RAF Middle Wallop, Hampshire.

31st May 1943

No operations, but as an example of the activity that kept everyone on their toes, I have listed the work carried out on a typical non-Ops day. This is taken directly from the account written up in the Squadron office by an admin WAAF, whose job was to keep records up to date. It must be said that, without their diligence, many of the things that occurred within a Squadron would be lost.

A Typical Non Ops Day

Weather report issued, stating – winds SE light and variable, later 10 mph veering SW 10-15 mph. Weather fair, becoming cloudy. Visibility moderate 6-8 miles.

"A" Flight – 2 flying training, 1 air test, 1 cross country, 1 air test after engine change, 1 air test for flaps, 1 night dual solo landing.

"B" Flight – 1 airframe and engine test, 1 SBA Hemswell and air firing, 1 low level cross country and 1 flying training.

Synthetic map reading for bomb aimers.

GEE' training for navigators.

Morse practise for wireless operators and turret training for air gunners.

The list gives a clear idea what was required to keep the squadron operational. There were some days when Bomber Command detailed most of the aircraft for a raid and then most, if not more of the tasks mentioned, would have to be carried out in conjunction with fuelling and arming for the mission.

June

Packing up and moving on again – destination Lakenheath – four engined heavies

199 Squadron "doing a spot of crop spraying".

Operations were suspended from the 1st to the 6th of June, but on the 7th, thirteen aircraft and crews were detailed for a raid, which was eventually cancelled. It was not until the 11th that the squadron was called on for a maximum effort.

11th June 1943

A raid on Dusseldorf was planned and sixteen Wellingtons and crews were detailed. All the aircraft were bombed and fuelled up in readiness awaiting the scheduled take off beginning at 2300 hrs. After several days of non-operational activities and plenty of time for testing it was hoped this raid would not be plagued by any difficulties, but this was not be the case. First to experience problems was Sgt Erickson, who aborted at 2320 hrs, just four minutes after lifting off: *"We had a detonation in the Gee set. The cathode ray tube blew up immediately after take-off and the mission was abandoned. All bombs jettisoned safe in the sea."* He landed back at RAF Ingham at 0037 hrs. Next to have problems was Sgt Burton, who took off at 2313 hrs and was soon informed by his rear gunner, Sgt Wells, that his turret would not function correctly and the sortie was abandoned at 2335 hrs. The bomb load was jettisoned and the crew landed back at 0031 hrs. The fault in the turret was traced to a broken ball race. As the rest of the aircraft made their way to the target, icing became a major problem and two more crews were forced to turn back early. Sgt Tom Austin, flying at 8,000ft, reached a point just north of Thetford at 0050 hrs when icing forced him to return to base, landing at 0212 hrs. A second Wellington flown by F/O Hagues, who took off at 2310 hrs, was similarly affected just as it had passed over Great Yarmouth at 16,000ft. He decided to abort his mission and at 0052 hrs the aircraft turned back to base. However, the ORB states that F/O Hagues did not jettison his bombs into the North Sea until 0238 hrs and then only part of the load was dropped, as he brought back 16 x 30lb and 270 x 4lb incendiaries. The crew landed back at RAF Ingham at 0315 hrs, just over four hours after taking off.

After these early problems, the remainder of the aircraft arrived over Dusseldorf and proceeded to bomb the target indicators that had been accurately laid by the PFF. Sgt Freestone, Sgt Shorttle, Sgt Dennis, F/O Archer, F/O Waterfield, S/Ldr Wynne-Powell, F/Sgt Harlem, P/O Hardy, Sgt Stevenson, Sgt Barnard, and F/Lt Hankins, all reported bombing on the green TIs.

This was a very well executed raid by the squadron, with all the pilots arriving and bombing between 0150 hrs and 0157 hrs from heights of 14,000 to 18,000ft. The staggering in height allowing some element of protection by confusing the German gun laying predictors. F/O Archer, who bombed from 18,000ft, reported smoke columns at that height as he made his run in and also saw a large explosion to the east of the last turning point. Sgt Barnard reported: *"The whole of the main part of the town appeared covered by concentrated and large fires, the glow of which could still be seen as we passed over the Dutch coast on the way back. We were hit by heavy flak near the target, but suffered no serious damage"*. F/Lt Hankins also reported being hit by flak in the port wing but, again, there were no subsequent problems and he was able to return safely to base. F/Sgt Hyde, the rear gunner on S/Ldr Wynn-Powell's crew, said: *"We had just bombed the target and at 0200 hrs I saw a vivid blue flash on the south side of the target followed by a bright red glow"*. Some of the other crews also saw this explosion.

Sadly, another crew was fated to go missing, nothing being heard from Sgt Andrews and his crew after taking off at 2312 hrs. Later investigations did not shed any light on their fate and they were officially listed as lost without trace: (HE277 EX-Q) Crew: F/Sgt Clifford Raymond Andrews, Pilot, RCAF; Sgt William Henry Bellhouse, Navigator, RAFVR; Sgt Patrick Edward Kevin Daly Merry, Bomb Aimer, RAFVR, age 21, from Morden, Surrey; Sgt William Edward Jackson, W/Op, RAFVR, age 20, Anstey, Leicestershire; Sgt Leonard Richard Barrow, Rear Gunner, RAFVR, age 21, from Dagenham, Essex.

This raid caused very serious damage to the town, but at a high price; of the 783 aircraft taking part, 38 were shot down. The Pathfinders dropped their initial markers with great accuracy and Main Force were bombing on these, until an 'Oboe' Mosquito mistakenly dropped its load of indicators fourteen miles to the north east. These drew part of the bomber stream away, dropping their bombs in open country. However, the main bombing effort caused considerable damage to the centre of the town, where 130 acres were claimed as destroyed and was the most devastating attack on the city so far in the war.

A report prepared by the authorities in Dusseldorf stated that the fires covered an area 8 km by 5 km covering the city centre, including both old and new parts, the south of the city and the Derendorf district. 8,882 separate fire incidents were recorded with 1,444 classified as large. 1,292 people were killed and 140,000 bombed out. 42 industrial factories suffered complete stoppages and a further 35 partial stoppages. Twenty military buildings were hit and eight ships in the port were sunk.

The Squadron was informed that it was moving again, this time to RAF Lakenheath, and being re-equipped with the four-engined Stirling heavy bomber.

Sgt Stan Freestone describes the imminent change: *"Whilst still on Wellingtons with Main Force as late as mid 1943, there were rumblings amongst us that we should get four engined aircraft now that the Bomber Command offensive against Germany was intensifying. It was 'put about', probably from Group, that over the next few weeks the performance of the remaining Wellington Squadrons in 1 Group would be monitored and the pecking order established for those to go first onto four engined aircraft. This must have produced some enthusiasm, since I remember a certain keenness in the air. It so happened that 199 had a pretty good record and we became top of the list. Everyone imagined that it would be Lancasters, since we were in No 1 Group. I think I can honestly say that the announcement that we were to convert to Stirlings and transfer to No 3 Group was received with mixed feelings"*.

One more operation was to be flown from RAF Ingham and six crews were ordered to prepare for a mining sortie to the Biscay ports on 13th June. All the aircraft took off, heading for French coastal waters, but P/O Hagues was unable to find the pin-point and abandoned the operation at 0128 hrs. Sgt Freestone, Sgt Ericson, F/O Archer and Sgt Stevenson all reached their target areas and dropped two mines each.

F/O Sawdy and his crew aboard HF597 EX-Y, lifted off at 2213 hrs, on only their second operational mission, but nothing was heard from them after take-off. It is not known what caused them to crash. All the bodies were found and buried at Guidel Communal Cemetery, about 10 kms from Lorient. The crew consisted of: F/O William Ernest Sawdy, Pilot, RAFVR; Sgt E. Burton, Nav, RAFVR, age 22, from Mansfield, Notts; F/O Stuart Quentin Robinson, B/A, RAFVR, age 22, from Broadstairs, Kent; Sgt Claude Stephen Bell, W/Op, RAFVR, age 35, married, from Edgware, Middlesex; Sgt John Charles William Stevens, A/G, RAFVR, age 22, from Lower Edmonton, Middlesex.

From the 14th to the 16th June, all operations were cancelled and the Squadron prepared for the move to RAF Lakenheath. Not only was the Squadron changing to a new airfield, it was also being moved out of 1 Group into 3 Group for operational purposes.

On the 17th, the advance party moved to RAF Lakenheath and the following pilots, plus their crews, were posted for transfer to heavy conversion units: S/Ldr Humby, DFC; F/O Waterfield; F/Sgt Freestone; Sgt Hathaway. Their crews were instructed to report to 1651 HCU; S/Ldr Wynne-Powell, F/Sgt Barnard, P/O Hagues, F/O Archer, and Sgt Hodson, to 1665 HCU.

Sergeants Mess at RAF Lakenheath, 1943.

Author's Note: It seems fitting at this point to include some first hand accounts written by F/O Geoff Archer, covering some of the previous Wellington operations. This will be concluded when he finished his flying on Stirlings and includes details relating to his navigator, 2nd Lt Carl Carlson, USAAF, who flew with him on sixteen Wellington and three Stirling missions.

"I arrived at Ingham sometime in early February 1943; in fact I was 20 years old on February 8th 1943 with the grand total of 360 flying hours in the log book and just 36 of those on Wellingtons. The latter hours gained at 28 OTU Wymswold. So, as you can see, a real 'Sprog'.

My first memory was walking – with trepidation – into the mess on the first day, and seeing in the entrance what appeared to be a giant of a man, with red hair and a large bushy moustache, but a cheerful countenance. He was playing a record on the gramophone; I well recall it, the 'Ink Spots' singing 'Don't get around much any more'. This chap was F/Lt Newsome from Canada and was the Squadron gunnery leader. Any other thoughts escape me, though I vaguely recall thinking what an odd aerodrome – being all grass and with a farm complex in the middle of the three runways. For night flying we flew off on the original 'T' configuration of 'goose-neck flares' – no luxury, like the Lancaster boys up the road at Scampton.

My first operation was as co-pilot to Sgt Holt, a cool customer if I recall correctly, on 19th February 1943 to Wilhelmshaven with a 4,000lb cookie. To carry this beast in a Wimpy called for major modifications to the original bomb beams, plus the inner bomb doors were removed. The bomb itself partially hung out of the bomb bay and appeared to give scant clearance with the uneven grass runway. You can imagine bouncing about on take-off with a bloody great 4,000lb bomb kissing the grass at irregular intervals – a great incentive to get airborne as quickly as possible.

My first impression of the target area, not greatly feared I will admit, was how pretty all the lights were, fires on the ground and various coloured balls like roman candles climbing skywards and whooshing past our aircraft. I did not feel a panic, Sgt Holt being calm and doing his job well, I think I was more amazed and entranced than anything else. I think it eventually penetrated my thick skull that the 'roman candles' were actually bullets and that the natives down below did not welcome our presence and were intent on killing us. Damned unsporting really!

My second Op was as co-pilot to another distinctive personage – F/O 'Smokey' Wingood – a Colonial from Bermuda and another 'cool cookie'. He was tall with thinning blond hair and a roman nose and slightly protruding front teeth. A great smile and a great guy and of course the American accent. This time we went to Cologne with a load of incendiaries, but I do not recall the trip at all. Must have been a "Ho Hum" – no warning of the days to come!!

My first solo Op was a mining sortie to settle in the crew, that was the same except for a change in the bomb aimer's position on all my Wellington sorties."

F/O Archer's crew was: Sgt C. Carlson, Nav, then with the RCAF; Sgt O. Bagshot, B/A, replaced 28th March by Sgt C.J. Lywood; Sgt J. Livingstone, W/Op; Sgt W.E. Donnahey, R/G.

"Then it was in at the deep end – the Ruhr. In 1943, Bomber Command was "doing" the Ruhr and it was no picnic.

On March 12, 1943, we went to Essen with incendiaries and the trip started in spectacular fashion. After crossing the enemy coast outbound the bomb aimer said: "Skipper there is a red light out to port following us", yes – true there was. Later, "Skip, there is a green light off to starboard also keeping pace". Yes, true there was. Then the penny dropped, I'd forgotten to turn my navigation lights off and was blithely flying across enemy territory lit up like a Christmas tree. I grabbed the switch and turned them off – then all hell broke loose – the German flak gunners, thinking we were 'one of them' returning home, realised otherwise and then opened up. This was not pleasant and I had a brilliant idea, I switched the nav lights back on again, and voila, or achtung, or whatever, peace and quiet!! True! Eventually we switched them off again well away from peeking eyes.

The Ruhr was ringed with searchlights, hundreds of them, and amongst them all the most brilliant blue master searchlights. If one of these picked you up all the others followed it and to put it mildly, all hell again broke loose. In amongst the searchlights and all over the sky of the Ruhr the flak bursts were continuous and terrifying. I fully admit that I was terrified – I all but stood up at the controls, my knees literally banging on each side of the control column and flew transfixed by fear and awe. You knew you had to penetrate the ring of searchlights and fly through the flak and knew the chance of coming out was pretty slim. But in we went and everywhere the searchlights waved back and forth – searching – searching. Occasionally one saw another aircraft caught and blow up in an orange ball of flame. The noise of the flak and smell of cordite was everywhere. We dropped our bombs and then it happened, a brilliant blue light lit up the cockpit and the whole aircraft, then the others joined in – it was like bloody daylight, in fact brighter than daylight. We were 'coned'!! I knew what was to follow, all the guns concentrated on the plane at the apex of the cone, altitude now known, also direction and speed. There was only one way out: 'down'. I did a wing over (in a Wimpy?) and keeping my eyes inside the cockpit to avoid the glare, shoved the stick forward, and down we went.

Apart from giving me a feeling of doing something positive in an impossible situation, it also offered maximum deflection to the guns – one hoped. We just headed earthwards, like a black bullet, with the bomb aimer keeping an eye out for terra firma.

Now you may not believe the following, but it is the gospel truth, the bomb aimer in all the chaos, called up "quick Skip, pull up, pull up, there's a gate ahead!!" Naturally we pulled up and continued blindly across the pitch dark countryside, engines screaming and the wind howling past the windscreen, the odd dark shape of a chimney or building flashed past. How we hit nothing remains in the Good Book above. But, we were out of the cone. Then I checked the instruments to see all was well and then, consternation, the airspeed needle was remorselessly falling back round the dial. How could this be, with the noise going on around us and the engines flat out, temperatures and pressures ok and yet the instrument was telling me we were slowing down? This couldn't be true, the mind went blank, what the hell is going on.

Then, as the needle passed '0' and continued on doing so, finally settling at about 140, I realised what had happened. In our dive, the air speed indicator had gone round twice – twice mind you – in a fabric covered aircraft and we were still flying!!

The angels were with us that night to be sure. Can't recall any more details except that the wimpy **(Z1748 EX-P) had to be recovered with fabric. Since then, my love affair with the Wellington blossomed with an obsession.

The other Ops came and went and I can't now remember any salient features, but I was once grimly amused when mining at Lorient, France, when the flak was coming down on us, not up.

I was becoming an old hand by now and it was after one such mining trip, quietly coming home across France – a moonlit night – close to the ground, that we were jumped by a Ju88. Having crossed the coast, I had stupidly decided on low altitude over the water and was on my gradual way up, when a stream of tracer passed through the plane from low and behind. The instrument panel disintegrated, the rear gunner was hit in the leg, the hydraulics buggered, so the wheels came down and the flaps went to trail and we were in a sorry state, with the Ju88 off to the starboard silhouetted against the moon waiting to finish us off.

To keep the machine in the air, I went to full boost and fine pitch. Then, as he turned in for the kill, I turned towards him to make the target small. He missed, and then he flew back alongside parallel, waiting. I then became very cross – the bastard – he's not going to get us, if he is I will get him as well! I was livid, we could not operate any guns due to the hydraulic failure, so I decided, right you bastard, I am going to ram you, and each time he turned in for an attack I did the same and aimed the Wimpy straight at him. Needless to say he didn't even fire a shot, but after a few goes he went home. I don't think he realised that a Wimpy makes a bloody big Spitfire when the pilot is very cross!!

As we flew home at full bore, the sweet notes of those Bristol Hercules were music to the ears, not a falter the whole way. We crash landed at Exeter and funny as it was, my bomb aimer, who had always nursed his thermos flask through thick and thin, feeling relieved to be back, placed it on the runway beside the aircraft – and the fire engine ran over it. The faithful wimpy had once again come out on top.

I recall one raid, no doubt over the Ruhr, hearing over the W/T on the way home, near our base, the Canadian voice of F/Lt Newsome saying they had been damaged and as far as he was concerned he was on the "outside". Looking at his aircraft when they landed, we saw it had a huge hole blown in the starboard side aft of the trailing edge of the wings and yet she still held together and flew."

Geoff Archer's story will continue later when he converted to Stirlings.

On the 18th June 1943 major preparations were made for moving the Squadron, with all equipment being packed and loaded.

RAF Lakenheath

By the dawn of the 20th, all was ready and the senior officers of the Squadron held a marching out parade and inspection. The move was then initiated with part of the equipment and personnel travelling by road and the remainder sent by rail. During the late afternoon a marching in parade was held at Lakenheath, followed by the immediate unloading of equipment. On the following day the unloading was carried on with urgency and the Squadron administration staff started finding suitable buildings to turn into offices and stores. At this point there were no aircraft on charge, so all the ground staff were involved in setting up and checking over their spares and getting them racked for use. Once this duty was completed, all the available ground staff were themselves sent on conversion courses to be instructed in the maintenance and engineering skills required to keep the Stirling in the air.

On 23rd, W/Cdr Howard, DFC and F/Lt Newsome were posted to 1651 HCU and F/Lt Kerr was posted to 1657 HCU.

At the end of June, it appears that only a skeleton staff was left at Lakenheath and there were no aircraft on Squadron strength. Leave was granted, but the majority of personnel were away on training courses.

Frank Gymer, Electrician: *"When I arrived at Lakenheath, 199 Squadron was in the throes of changing over from Wellingtons to Stirlings and possessed only one ageing Wimpy and no personnel. On arrival I was sent to a 'Thorn' hut near the armoury, the only building allotted to the Squadron during the following two or three weeks as personnel were posted in or returned from leave. As soon as these chaps found there were no aircraft they realised they had more leave to come and they obtained a pass, which I would sign, and off they would go again. It became so obvious that on one occasion, I was called before the SWO and told not to sign any more passes".*

199 Squadron inspection at RAF Lakenheath. W/Cdr Bray (pointing) conducts the Duke of Kent, on a visit to Lakenheath.

July
Enter the Stirling – more training and its initial operations

Stirlings started to arrive on July 5th and were parked up on their allotted hard standings. The first to come were EF455 EX-B, EF926 EX-T, EH927 EX-E, EE943 EX-X, EE946 EX-P, EE947 EX-D with others following over the next two weeks. Ground crews were now returning from the courses, and a programme of checking and maintenance was put into action to prepare the aircraft for operations.

Frank Gymer, Electrician: *"In due course, the aircraft and personnel arrived at Lakenheath and an exceedingly happy Squadron was formed in which I found myself in charge of 'B' Flight Electrical Section. Most of the electricians together with some wireless mechanics were billeted in huts 7 and 9 on Site 5, a few hundred yards from the pub on the way in to the village".*

Doris Lefeuve (now Appleton) ACW Electrician: *"I was in the Electrical Section, first at Lakenheath and later at North Creake. I can only remember the names of a few electricians – Cpl George Meadows, LAC Stan Clayton, LACW Elsie Watts and George Leaman. My best friend was Pauline Kenning, who was one of the parachute packers".*

On the 9th, six aircrews returned and air tests were immediately carried out, coupled with an intense flying training program. This program was carried on in tandem with lectures and drills for all. The Stirling was proving to be more of a challenge than the Wellington.

RAF Lakenheath, 1943. Engine fitters on the starboard wing of a Stirling.

By the 27th the bulk of the Stirlings had been flown in and serviced, and to get some of the aircrews doing something practical, they were detailed for an air sea search. During the afternoon of the 27th, five aircraft were readied and fuelled up and Sgt Austin, P/O Fisher, Sgt Humphries, F/Sgt Barnard and F/O Archer took off between 1755 hrs and 1810 hrs. The records do not reveal where the actual search took place, but nothing was found and all were back at Lakenheath by 2145 hrs.

30th July 1943

Their first operational mission was to sow mines off the Frisian Islands: six aircraft and crews were detailed.

F/O Archer flying Stirling EH926 EX-T was the first to lift off at 2307 hrs loaded with four mines, closely followed by W/Cdr Howard, DFC, Sgt Humphries, F/Sgt Freestone, P/O Fisher and S/Ldr Humby, DFC. A textbook operation, all the crews successfully laid their mines in the allotted areas and returned safely to base, with W/Cdr Howard the last to touch down at 0233 hrs.

Most of the pilots and crews were now back from their courses, with other personnel being drafted in to make up the numbers to the required Squadron strength. To the Wellington's five strong crew was added, a flight engineer and mid upper gunner. The Stirling was a more sophisticated aircraft and it was essential that everyone knew the controls and switches at their stations and how to deal with an emergency with little or no light to guide them. Circuits and landings were carried out to familiarise the pilots with the Stirling's tendency to swing on take off. There was a problem with the difference in the pilot's eye-line – 12 feet in the Wellington – 21 feet in the Stirling.

S/Ldr Ken Humby with Air and Ground Crew.

August
First bombing sorties using the Stirling – flight engineers in the news – a 'Jump' take-off to rival any modern Harrier

1st August 1943

A mining operation to the mouth of the Gironde, in the Bay of Biscay, taking off between 2130 hrs and 2150 hrs was detailed for seven crews. The navigators and bomb aimers picked up a pinpoint on the centre of Lake Hourtin and each Stirling dropped four mines in the allotted areas. All the aircraft returned safely to RAF Lakenheath, with no reports of enemy activity, the last landing at 0548 hrs. The pilots on this mission were: F/Sgt Odgers, F/Lt Hankins, F/O Waterfield, Sgt Austin, F/O Hauges, S/Ldr Wynn-Powell, and F/Sgt Barnard.

7th August 1943

Armourer LAC Ronald Bottomley was killed in an accident involving a motor vehicle whilst cycling along the Brandon to Newmarket Road.

8th August 1943

Four aircraft and crews were detailed for an operation, which was later cancelled.

9th August 1943

A mining operation was ordered for four crews, targeting the area 15 kms NNW of the West Frisian island of Terschelling. Sgt Hodson, F/Sgt Harlem, F/O Pettit and P/O Widdecombe were all airborne by 2210 hrs and sowed their mines with the aid of Gee fixes. Each rear gunner reported seeing the parachutes open as their respective mines were dropped from approximately 1,000ft. All returned, touching down within 15 minutes of each other, the last, Sgt Hodson landing at 0115 hrs.

10th August 1943

Ten crews were detailed to attack Nuremberg, the squadron's first major bombing mission using the Stirling. From the records it appears that a policy of giving as many pilots as much combat experience as possible was in place and several flew on this operation as second pilots: W/Cdr Howard with F/Sgt Davey; S/Ldr Humby and F/O Pettit; F/O Fisher and F/O Widdecombe; W/O Odgers and Sgt Allson; F/O Hauges and Sgt Hodson. The remaining pilots were: F/Sgt Freestone, F/Sgt Austin, F/O Waterfield, Sgt Humphries, and F/O Archer, who each flew a normal crew of seven.

F/Sgt Austin led the squadron's contingent, taking off at 2150 hrs, with the last, F/O Hagues, lifting off at 2219 hrs. There were no problems on the outward leg and each crew reached Nuremberg dropping their ordinance from between 11,000 and 15,000ft on the green TIs or fires seen through breaks in the dense cloud covering the target. Most crews stated in their de-brief that the raid appeared scattered, with one or two large explosions, and S/Ldr Howard reported that the flak was spasmodic and the searchlights un-coordinated and wavering.

F/Sgt Freestone saw an area near Mannheim burning what he thought to be decoy TIs, but after raid reports do not mention the Main Force being drawn from the intended target. There is no mention in the ORB relating to Sgt Freestone's encounter with a night fighter on his return journey, but '199' combat reports held in the Public Records Office show that his aircraft had reached a point in the English Channel midway between Le Treport and Hastings when the Stirling EE948 was attacked by a Fw190 at 0428 hrs. His debrief reads – *"The wireless operator, Sgt Weeks, who was in the astrodome, reported to the rear gunner Sgt Barkwell, that an enemy aircraft was on the starboard quarter. As soon as the fighter was reported, both the rear and mid upper gunners spotted the aircraft and the rear gunner gave the pilot instructions to corkscrew to starboard. The enemy aircraft came in very fast and the gunners identified it as a Fw190.*

Both gunners opened fire simultaneously when the E/A was approximately 250 yards away and claimed hits as it broke away to port and disappeared into cloud and was not seen again. The E/A did not fire at our aircraft. Our rear gunner fired 200 rounds and our mid upper gunner, Sgt Slevens, fired 100 rounds in the encounter".

The crews returned to RAF Lakenheath and landed safely, with Sgt Humphries touching down first at 0517 hrs and the others coming back over the next hour or so. W/O Odgers was the last to land at 0625 hrs much to everyone's relief, especially his ground crew.

This raid on Nuremberg was a large one consisting of 653 aircraft and, with 199 Squadron's contribution, a total of 119 Stirlings took part. Sixteen aircraft were lost. PFF ground marked the city and it was only because of gaps in the cloud that several crews were able to bomb accurately. This, however, led to a concentrated attack on the central and southern areas of Nuremberg, resulting in a large 'fire area' in the Wohrd district. Reports from Nuremberg show that serious damage was caused to both industrial areas and housing in the city with 577 people killed.

On a historical note, it is perhaps worth mentioning that seven months later, a similar raid was mounted against Nuremberg in moonlit conditions, when 95 aircraft were shot down. If 199 Squadron had participated in a raid similar to this, with the high number of second pilots flying, it would probably have lost almost the whole of its flying capability.

12th August 1943

Eight crews were briefed for a raid on Turin in northern Italy. This being a long range target, the aircraft carried maximum fuel and a slightly lighter bomb load. The ground crews had the Stirlings ready and tested by the late evening and at 2100 hrs the crews were running up the engines and going through the final checks. F/O Hauges was the first away at 2110 hrs followed by F/Sgt Barnard, F/Sgt Freestone, F/Lt Hankins, S/Ldr Humby, P/O Fisher, F/O Waterfield and last at 2135 hrs F/O Archer, on his last operation with '199' before being posted. As he approached the coast, F/O Archer was forced to shut down one of his engines, but carried on to the target. Over Turin, the weather was fine with some ground haze and the PFF had marked the aiming points with red and green TIs. F/O Waterfield led the attack, dropping his bombs at 0117 hrs, closely followed over the next ten minutes by the other seven crews. By 0127 hrs the attack was over and courses set for the return leg. The crews reported a good concentration of bombing with several large fires taking hold as they were leaving.

F/Sgt Freestone was attacked by a night fighter over Cabourg on the outward journey. The Stirling EE948 EX-G was flying at 9500ft over Cabourg on the French coast, 30 km SSW of Le Harve when Sgt Barkwell, the rear gunner, spotted a Fw190 on the port quarter down at a range of 400 yards. The crew's report states: *"The rear gunner reported a fighter and instructed the pilot to corkscrew port and he opened fire at the same time. The mid upper gunner, Sgt Stevens, also opened fire at the same time and fired about 100 rounds. The E/A came around dead astern and the rear gunner continued to fire, but the mid upper could not see the E/A because it was below his range of vision. The E/A closed in to about 250 yards and our rear gunner continued firing, until it broke away in a steep dive to starboard and was not seen again. Our rear gunner fired in all about 600 rounds and the mid upper 100 rounds. The rear gunner claimed hits on the enemy aircraft, but was not seen to crash so is just claimed as damaged".*

The raid on Turin was not large, with 152 aircraft, but Bomber Command had also detailed 504 aircraft to attack Milan, so overall this was classed as a maximum effort. By and large the majority of the crews reported a heavy and concentrated raid, but Turin records show that only eighteen people were killed and 83 injured. Two Stirlings were lost.

A Stirling pilot was awarded the Victoria Cross for his actions during this raid. He was F/Sgt Arthur Louis Aaron, serving with 218 Squadron, stationed at RAF Downham Market, Norfolk and is worthy of mention. It was many years before the true story of what happened to Stirling EF452 and her crew came to be told. The official story at the time of Aaron's death and citation was that the aircraft had been attacked and hit by a night fighter as they approached Turin, their target for that night. In fact, they had been fired on by the rear gunner of another Stirling off to the starboard side and slightly in front. The gunner had raked Aaron's aircraft from wingtip to wingtip and back again. Bill Brennan, the navigator, was killed instantly with a bullet through the heart. Aaron was wounded in the jaw with part of his face torn away, a lung was perforated and his right arm almost severed. The instruments and the pilot's windscreen were shattered and two other members of the crew wounded. F/Eng Sgt Mitchem's right ankle was hit, but he succeeded in regaining some control as the Stirling dived towards the ground at over 250 mph. Bomb aimer, F/Sgt Larden, although wounded by two bullets in the right buttock, took over and levelled out at about 4,000 feet. Astonishingly, Aaron had remained conscious despite his wounds and scratched a message out on the dead navigator's pad, asking the crew's intentions to get the bomber to safety. Once satisfied that they were in control of the situation he allowed himself to be carried to the rest bunk in the rear fuselage and to be given a shot of morphine.

As the Stirling crossed the Italian coast, F/Sgt Larden released the bomb load on Spezia Harbour, and a little later, Sgt Jimmy Guy, the wireless operator, sent out a plain language message to Bone airfield in Algeria, and they instructed him to try to make a landing there, although this meant flying across the Mediterranean.

Although weak from loss of blood and shock, Aaron kept asking how things were by writing messages on his pad. Alternating the task of piloting the aircraft, Sgt Mitchem, F/Sgt Larden and Sgt Richmond, the mid upper gunner, together with the help of Sgt Tom McCabe, the rear gunner, assisting as flight engineer, made landfall after four hours flying. F/Sgt Larden took the controls and decided on a wheels up landing. Aaron regained consciousness and asked what was happening; Sgt Guy told him they were about to land. Although in terrible pain, Aaron crawled up to the cockpit to take over, in an attempt to get his crew down safely. F/Sgt Larden took the co-pilot's seat and Mitchem went to his flight engineer's position. With only his left arm to operate the controls and, being unable to talk, he could only indicate his wishes by nodding his head.

The airfield instructed them that there was a crashed Wellington at the end of the runway. Aaron, unaware of this, lined the Stirling up for a normal landing. He seemed to sense that something was wrong and ordered F/Sgt Larden to open up the throttles to go round again. On the second approach Sgt Mitchem indicated that the fuel state was almost zero, but Aaron still instructed F/Sgt Larden to open up and go round again. As they came in for the third time at 500 feet and, just entering the runway threshold, Aaron gave the order to abort yet again. F/Sgt Larden knew there was not sufficient fuel for another circuit and wrestled the controls away from Aaron and, with the bomber almost at stalling point, he pushed the control column forward and just before they hit the sand, pulled up sharply and the Stirling hit the ground hard and slid along on its belly coming to rest in a huge cloud of dust.

Arthur Aaron was quickly transferred to the base hospital where he was operated on. The rest of the crew were treated for their minor wounds and released. They all prayed that their skipper might survive, and at first it seemed he would pull through, but at 3pm on Friday 13th, Aaron finally succumbed to his injuries. He was buried with full military honours in Bone War Cemetery, Annaba, Algeria. Sgt Guy and Sgt Mitcham were both awarded the DFM and F/Sgt Larden the CGM.

This is another example of crews training for any eventuality. Those choosing not to often paying the price in full.

Another consequence of this raid was an immediate DFC awarded to F/O Geoff Archer who, as previously mentioned, flew his Stirling to Turin on three engines. His citation (listed in his full name Geoffrey Ernest Charles Archer), gazetted on 31st August 1943 reads: *'One night in August 1943, this Officer was the pilot of an aircraft detailed to attack Turin. When nearing the Alps on the outward flight one of the bomber's engines failed. Despite this, F/O Archer continued to the target which he bombed successfully. Shortly afterwards, F/O Archer succeeded in starting the defective engine, but soon after crossing the Alps on the return flight the engine again failed. Nevertheless, F/O Archer succeeded in flying the bomber back to base. This Officer displayed outstanding skill and determination, setting a commendable example'.*

As this was F/O Archer's last Op with 199, it is a good point to add the last account from his correspondence that describes his experiences a few weeks before and shortly after the trip to Turin. This encapsulates his brief, but eventful time flying the Stirling: *"At the end of June, we heard that we were going onto Stirlings – what no Lancs! – news not greatly welcomed, though eventually I came to love the Stirling as much as I had the Wimpy."*

"We were posted to 1665 Conversion Unit at Woolfox Lodge and, since it was staffed mostly by 'Operational Types', the conversion was clouded greatly by alcoholic fumes. After 28 hours, we or at least I, was considered fit to fly the bomber and I rejoined the Squadron at Lakenheath. All I can recall of the airfield is the acres and acres of mud and the odd Stirling with

its gear folded up. Being a bit short, I had to fly with the bomb aimers couch cushion folded up behind me, even with the pedals fully back. I liked the Stirling as an aeroplane and being so high in the air sitting in the cockpit gave one a feeling of awe. Also having four engines was beaut!

Life settled down, until the evening of August the 13th, being a Friday and Ops to Turin. You have no doubt heard in recent years about the carrier 'Ski Slope' jump jet take-offs by the Royal Navy Harriers and what a big deal they are. Well, I have news for them – on 12th August 1943 I did a 'Jump' take-off in a fully-loaded Stirling and survived!

It happened like this. The lever for the autopilot "engage" was on the left hand side of the cockpit wall, roughly level with one's leg calf. When warming up prior to taking off one selected "spin" on the autopilot to get it warmed up for use when airborne, or else it performed erratically for some time. Once airborne I would usually select "engage" and relax. As one also realises, with no great heating in British bombers one dressed for the occasion, not least large fur-lined boots inside which were beaut, long thick white woolly socks from Australia, (thanks OZ). These were turned down over the tops of the boots making them a really warm, but bulky arrangement. And so, as we started off along the runway, and working the pedals to keep straight, my left boot moved the autopilot lever to "engage". Not being trimmed it took command, and the aircraft, now tail up swerved to the right and took off across the airfield towards the control tower and the bomb dump.

I briefly noted a rapid abandonment of the tower and my bomb aimer Sgt Lynwood's hand going for full power on the throttles, when there was an almighty bump which jerked my head down onto the control column. We were apparently, and I thought momentarily, temporarily airborne. I recollected that I was completely calm in my mind and I thought my last moments had come and I was not the least bit afraid. However, I continued to fly the aircraft – complete the take-off drill and set a course for the target.

Shortly a voice from the tower asked if we were alright, and I replied yes and I'm heading for Turin. My navigator 2nd Lt Carlson USAAF had banged his head on the chart table and was bleeding profusely from the nose. Being the first class guy he was he made some cryptic remarks about the standard of my flying and then continued with his job.

Crossing the Alps we suffered an engine failure. I was down the back relieving myself at the "Elsan" (a portable toilet situated near the rear door – it was a glorified bucket with a seat and lid attached) when my co-pilot informed me that the starboard engine was on fire. I exhorted him to keep the aircraft flying till I got back to the cockpit, then set about re-dressing myself in the 101 items I had shed earlier. We got the fire out, but fully laden with only three engines, we began to lose altitude. This over the Alps is not recommended and eventually we were flying down the valleys. We tried to ditch ammo and extra cargo, but lack of tools made this exercise unproductive. By luck we took all the right turnings and came out over Italy. The target was almost like a rest cure after the Ruhr and we were able to get a photo of the aiming point – a plus for the bomb aimer and the crew.

Now I was presented with the problem of getting us home on three engines "through" the Alps. We had been told that the Allies had landed in Sicily and if trouble was met we could land there. I put this idea to the crew and it was voted 'No', we were due for leave on our return and no way were they going to spend it in Sicily. Anyhow, people were fighting down there and it would be dangerous – even fatal!! So I suggested to Sgt Rawlings, our flight engineer – try the dead engine, maybe it will work long enough to get us over the Alps. He tried it and it started up, picking up as we gained altitude, but this time being lighter we maintained height. There was one thing that was very strange about this however. Although the engine was running and giving power, none of the instruments indicated any activity. OK, so the electrics may have been burned through during the fire that caused the initial shut down. But added to this, the exhaust ring which always glowed red on an operating engine, the other three did, remained black and presumably cold. We shall never know – but maybe the angels were working overtime again that night.

We went on leave and on waking the next morning at my fiancée's home, I was handed a telegram from Bomber Harris congratulating me on the immediate award of the DFC. I have never been so proud in my life, but I was only sorry that my crew did not receive any awards as well. I can only thank them all for the great team spirit we had and now unhappily we have lost contact over the years. We had been through a lot together and yet, once split up, we were like ships that pass in the night. I salute them all".

The Turin crew, Stirling EE926 EX-T: F/O G. Archer, RAAF, Pilot; Sgt Dodsworth, 2nd Pilot; 2nd Lt Carlson, USAAF; Nav, "Carl" (killed on operations 1st Dec 1943); Sgt "Johnnie" Lynwood, B/A; Sgt "Jimmy" Livingstone, W/Op; Sgt "Bill" Donnahay, R/G; Sgt "Smithy" Smith, M/U; Sgt "George" Rawlings, F/Eng.

Coincidently, 40 years after the war, Geoff Archer was sitting in an office in Aviation House, Brisbane, Australia, when he realised the person sitting next to him was Sgt Dodsworth, his co-pilot from that last fateful trip to Turin. After all those years they were still sitting side by side.

15th August 1943

A mining detail was ordered for three crews in the Gironde area of the Bay of Biscay. This was successfully carried out by two of the crews, Sgt Hodson's two mines exploding on contact with the sea.

16th August 1943

Orders received for another attack on Turin and ten crews were briefed for this last raid on the city – the first having been in June 1940. Ground crews readied the aircraft, checking fuel and bomb loads for another long trip, and the electrical systems double-checked for faults. The aircraft relied on its electrics to operate the undercarriage, bomb bay doors, flaps and the tail wheel units. Without power the only way of operating each was by engaging hand cranks on the various gearboxes.

The first, P/O Hagues, lifted off at 1955 hrs, and the last was airborne at 2005 hrs. On these long hauls no one wanted to spend time on the ground wasting fuel and the crews were now getting their take-off drills almost to perfection. After an uneventful trip to the target the crews dropped their bomb loads with the aid of the yellow and green TIs and also the larger red spot fires. Most comments after the raid, spoke of a scattered effort and some pilots felt the raid was not as successful as the previous one. Turin, in fact, reported only five deaths and 56 injured, with no mention of damage of any worth.

17th August 1943

Two Stirlings and crews were detailed for a raid on Peenemünde, the German research establishment on the Baltic coast, where they were carrying out the building and testing of the V-2 rockets. S/Ldr Humby, DFC and Sgt Hodson were selected for this important raid and took off from RAF Lakenheath at 2050 hrs to join the other 594 aircraft from 1, 3, 4, and 5 Groups. Both crews had the housing estate area of the site as their targets, which had been allocated to 3 and 4 Group aircraft in the first of three waves, and bombed the target at 0028 hrs, which PFF had marked with red and green TIs. The second wave of 1 Group aircraft commenced at 0031 hrs after the Pathfinders had moved the markers onto the production works, followed by time and distance bombing by 5 Group, which attacked at 0043 hrs aiming for the experimental works. It had been decided during the planning stages that, for accuracy, this was to be a moderately low level attack with the upper limit between 6,000 and 10,000ft and the lower limit at 4,000ft. S/Ldr Humby chose to bomb from 7,500ft and Sgt Hodson from 6,000ft. One quote from a Stirling crew after the raid said that it had been *"nice to have been bombing at the same height as the Lancs for a change"*.

There was little opposition during the initial stages of the operation as a 'spoof raid' on Berlin by eight Mosquitoes drew the majority of the German night fighters to the capital. A 'Master Bomber', Group Captain Searby, the OC of 83 Squadron, was employed to control the whole attack on Peenemünde, which overall was very successful. The two '199' crews reported after the raid that they *saw several large fires among groups of buildings and one large explosion with black smoke billowing up from the same area"*. Mid-way through the raid, the ground defences got over their initial slow reaction and got their light flak firing, though with limited results. As the last wave of bombers came in, they were subjected to a long and harrying attack by German fighters which had been diverted to Peenemünde, having spent a fruitless search for the expected attack on Berlin. It was during this last phase that the majority of the 40 bombers lost were shot down. This was the first night the Germans employed "Schrage Music", twin, upward firing, cannons fitted to the Me110. Two of these fighters found the returning bomber stream and shot down six of them.

Many estimates made after the raid state that the German rocket program was set back by as much as two months and had a significant effect on the final numbers launched against England. Approximately 1,800 tons of mainly high explosive bombs were dropped on Peenemünde, 180 Germans were killed, mostly those caught in the workers' housing estate, but sadly as many as 600 foreign labourers, mostly Polish, were killed in the workers' camp where they were housed in wooden huts and had no air raid shelters.

The two '199' crews returned safely to RAF Lakenheath and touched down at 0430 hrs.

On the 19th and 20th of the month, detailed operations were cancelled, but maintenance and checks carried on.

Matthew Morton, Fitter 2E: *"I can remember a 'B' Flight Stirling which, when loaded with a perfectly distributed bomb load, flew left wing low and yawed to the right. Yet it would fly straight and level 'hands off' without bombs".*

22nd August 1943

Four aircraft were detailed to mine the waters off the Frisian Islands. All reached the allotted area, but only P/O Gilbert and F/Sgt Davey were successful. Sgt Allan and Sgt Drayton both had failures with their Gee sets and were unable to pinpoint the target area.

23rd August 1943

Berlin was to be targeted, and twelve crews were placed on the Battle Orders. During the afternoon checks, one Stirling was found to have technical problems and was scrubbed. The remaining eleven aircraft all took off and were well on their way when icing became a problem. F/O Hagues was the first to experience difficulties when his aircraft stalled, due to the heavy build up of ice, so he jettisoned his bomb load and returned to base. F/Sgt Freestone was also forced to turn back, faced with the same problem. He too jettisoned his bombs live into the North Sea and landed at RAF Lakenheath at 0055 hrs.

The others reached Berlin and bombed the target, but events took a turn for the worse. On the return trip, Sgt Humphries' Stirling, EH926 EX-T, was flying at 14,600ft in good visibility with a quarter moon on the starboard quarter when: *"Our rear gunner spotted an enemy fighter coming in from the starboard quarter fine at about 500 yards range and as he came dead astern, it was recognised as an Me110. Our rear gunner, Sgt Gore, immediately gave me the order to corkscrew starboard just as the fighter opened fire and our rear gunner also opened up, firing a six second burst and hits were observed by both the gunner and the wireless operator, Sgt Christopher, who was in the astro-dome. The fighter broke away up on the port beam and then the mid upper, Sgt Whitbread, caught sight of it and opened up, firing 500 rounds observing more strikes. The enemy aircraft disappeared from sight about one minute later and then a twin engined fighter appeared on fire on the port quarter up, at about 300 yards range. The aircraft broke into three separate pieces and fell burning to the ground. As no other combats were observed, our gunners feel sure this is the aircraft that attacked us and claimed it as destroyed. The rounds from the fighter holed one of the port petrol tanks and caused damage to the port aileron and the rudder. The gunners fired 1,500 rounds in the encounter".*

Sgt Humphries maintained altitude and reached base at 0425 hrs.

The following account comes from two reports filed by F/O Pettit and his crew after the raid.

F/O Pettit, EE948 EX-G, had just bombed on the green TIs at 0020 hrs when he was coned by approximately 30 searchlights, and at 0027 hrs, was attacked by a night fighter – *"We were flying in good visibility when we were coned and then the rear gunner, Sgt Phipp, reported a Ju88 night fighter on the starboard quarter up at a range of 400 yards. Just as the fighter came in we were taking evasive action in an endeavour to evade the searchlights, but he made his attack, opening fire at about 300 yards. Our rear gunner returned fire, but after 50 rounds, the hydraulic system was hit and he was unable to operate his guns. The mid upper gunner, Sgt Tye, did not fire as he was blinded by the searchlights. As the enemy fighter broke away on the port bow he dropped two flares, one white, the other red. We were not attacked further and having broken the searchlight cone, tried to assess the damage. It was found that we had been hit 20 to 30 times on the top of the port mainplane and damage caused to both inboard engines, all the electrical circuits had failed except the flaps and radio and some hydraulic systems were out. Both starboard rev counters and the two inner boost gauges had failed. The hydraulic oil pipe feeding the rear turret was damaged and the cables of No1 and 4 fuel tanks had been cut by a burst of flak. Our flight engineer, Sgt Currie, using the emergency axe cut his way through the fuselage skin into the port wing, crawled through and repaired the damaged petrol cables".*

The crew were able to bring their aircraft back to base and landed at 0520 hrs, having presumably wound down the undercarriage by hand, as there is no mention of an emergency landing being made.

Two awards were made to members of the crew as a result of this night's action. The first was the Distinguished Flying Cross to F/O W.R. Pettit, the pilot of EE948. His citation was promulgated in the *London Gazette* on 15th October 1943. It reads: *"As Pilot, this Officer has participated in many attacks on important targets and has displayed great skill and determination. On a recent occasion whilst over Berlin, his aircraft was hit by fire from ground defences, but he continued his bombing run to execute a successful attack. Shortly afterwards, the bomber was again hit, this time by fire from an enemy fighter. The rear turret was rendered unserviceable, most of the electrical system was shot away, while the control wires of two petrol tanks were severed. Coolly and skilfully, F/Lt Pettit* [He had been promoted when this citation was published] *evaded the attacker and afterwards flew the bomber to base. This Officer displayed great courage and determination throughout".*

Sgt Robert Currie, DFM, Flight Engineer

The second award for his action this night was made to Sgt Robert Currie, who received the Distinguished Flying Medal. His citation, gazetted on Wednesday, 15th September 1943, reads: *"This airman was the Flight Engineer of an aircraft detailed to attack Berlin one night in August 1943. Whilst over the target area the aircraft was hit by anti-aircraft fire, and whilst illuminated by searchlights, was attacked by a night fighter. The controls which regulated the petrol supply from 2 of the tanks were severed. Sgt Currie, displaying much resource, cut an aperture in the fuselage by means of an axe and then crawled into the wing to turn on the petrol supply so essential for the completion of the return flight. His coolness and resource set a very fine example".*

Sgt Currie was born in Ayr and at the time of his service with '199' lived in East Lothian. He was a motor engineer before enlisting in the RAFVR in 1941.

One of the ground crew working on returning Stirlings was armourer Sgt Ross Clark, i/c 'B' Flight, who remembered this incident – *"Early one summer morning at Lakenheath I was checking aircraft on return from Ops for bomb hang-ups etc when I saw a Stirling touch down and within seconds all four engines cut. On being towed to dispersal I talked to the Stirling's NCO flight engineer, a big curly haired Scot, who said that the aircraft was shot up and the fuel pipes severed – this engineer hacked his way through the wing root and connected the pipes with rubber tubing. I went into the aircraft and saw the jagged hole and was amazed how he had got into the wing. His action was superb and deserved a high honour – I don't know what they gave the lad, but his good airmanship has always been with me".*

Of the other returning aircraft, two were forced to bring back part of their bomb load due to hang-ups. Sgt Hodson had 90 x 4lb incendiaries still on board when he landed and F/Sgt Harlem jettisoned 8 x 30lb and 90 x 4lb incendiaries into the North Sea just before landing back at base. From the raid on Berlin, two of 199 Squadron's crews failed to return: Stirling, EH927 EX-E, Crew: F/O Ronald James Widdecombe, Pilot, RAFVR, age 22, from Saltash, Cornwall; Sgt Ivor George Williams, F/Eng, RAFVR; F/O Robert John Massie, Nav, RAFVR, age 24, from Oldmeldrum, Aberdeenshire; Sgt Mark Sidney Baras, B/A, RAFVR, age 19, from Higher Broughton, Salford, Lancs (all commemorated on Runnymede Memorial); F/Sgt Philip Francis Stanley, W/Op, RAFVR, married to Lois Nellie Stanley of Southall, Middlesex; Sgt Norman James Calcraft, M/U, RAFVR, from Winchmore Hill, Middlesex, both were buried in the Berlin 1939–1945 War Cemetery; The rear gunner, Sgt A.E. Nixon, survived the crash, was captured and held at Stalag 4B Muhlberg-Elbe with the POW number 222754. The Stirling crashed near Doberitz, approximately 40 km west of Berlin. It is believed that the two crew members buried in the Berlin cemetery were initially buried at Doberitz, but moved after the war ended.

Stirling, EH934 EX-K, Crew: F/O Russel Gardiner Fisher, Pilot, RAAF, age 29, from Brunswick West, Victoria, Australia; Sgt Edward Harold Cuff, W/Op, RAFVR, age 20, from Witchhampton, Dorset; P/O Clifford Morton Nairn, B/A, RAAF, age 22, from Cronulla, New South Wales, Australia; F/Sgt Norman Kendall, Nav, RAFVR, age 24, from Boythorpe, Chesterfield, Derbyshire; F/Sgt Henry Cecil Elsley, R/G, RAAF, age 26, from Coogee, New South Wales, Australia; Sgt Jeffery Cyril Bert Parkinson, F/Eng, RAFVR; Sgt Robert George Cameron Forbes, M/U, RAFVR, age 23, married to Mary Florence Forbes of Addlestone, Surrey, all were buried in Berlin 1939–1945 War Cemetery. The Stirling crashed at Ruhlsdorf 30 km north of Berlin and the crew were first buried there, but were moved after the war to the Berlin cemetery.

This raid cost Bomber Command 58 aircraft from the 727 detailed and was the biggest loss to date, due to fierce resistance by night fighters and flak defences. The resulting casualties are summarised as follows:

297 killed,
107 captured and taken prisoner,
Nine injured, of whom three died later of their wounds,
Nine interned in Sweden and one Canadian pilot from 428 Squadron evaded capture.

The bombing photographs, and later reconnaissance photographs, show that the raid was not altogether successful, many of the bombs falling outside Berlin. This was mainly due to PFF being unable to identify the centre of the city with their H2S radar and consequently marking the southern outskirts.

The main bomber stream arrived late and several approached from the SW instead of from the SSE, resulting in a large proportion of their loads falling in open country. Many villages in the surrounding area reported bombing around them, but only light casualties. Had the bombing been more accurate, the city would have had a very serious problem. As it was, although many bombs were misdirected, Berlin suffered its most serious raid of the war. Many houses were destroyed in the Lankwitz and Lichterfelde districts and factories and associated facilities hit in the Tempelhof, Mariendorf and Marienfelde areas. A total of 2,611 buildings were destroyed or damaged and several ships were sunk in the canals serving the city. The total death toll was put at 854, with 83 classed as missing – mainly caused by civilians not using their allocated shelters, as ordered.

24th August 1943

Sgt Drayton and his crew aboard Stirling EE953 EX-E, were detailed for an 'air sea search' which was logged as successful with a dinghy sighted at 1135 hrs. Stirling EH953 EX-E took off at 0955 hrs, they returned to base at 1745 hrs. The records give no further details.

25th August 1943

A mining detail was ordered for three crews to the La Rochelle area and Sgt Drayton EH909 EX-Z (who had flown a successful ASR the previous day aboard EE953 EX-E), F/Sgt Dodsworth EE943 EX-X and F/Sgt Davey EE946 EX-P all sowed their mines in the designated areas.

26th August 1943

Another 'Gardening' operation called for two crews to mine the Gironde estuary off the French coast. Sgt Allson, BK772 EX-A had a successful trip and planted his mines as ordered, having taken off at 2000 hrs and landed back at 0030 hrs. Sgt Lumsdain EH909 EX-Z was unable to find his pinpoint due to his navigator's watch developing a fault, and upsetting the plots. The crew did not get back to RAF Lakenheath until 0235 hrs, two hours after Sgt Allson had landed, perhaps as a consequence that their course was in error due to the faulty watch used by Sgt White the navigator.

27th August 1943

A raid on Nuremberg was planned and twelve aircraft were prepared during the day. One of the Stirlings developed mechanical problems during testing and was cancelled from the operation. The remaining eleven

Stirlings and crews started to take off at 2110 hrs with F/Sgt Harlem first away and within ten minutes, all the aircraft had cleared the airfield. This was another maximum effort by Bomber Command, but the raid did not go exactly to plan.

In his post-raid report, S/Ldr Humby, DFC, EE953 EX-E, who had F/Sgt Moore as 2nd pilot, wrote: *"I was on the run in to the target when a message from the 'Master of Ceremonies' was heard directing the PFF to ignore the green TIs to the west. The visibility was very good and streets could be made out in the bomb bursts and one large explosion was seen"*.

F/O Pettit, EE911 EX-G, also had instructions from the M/C as to the aiming point and he bombed a group of green TIs as ordered. He described the attack as scattered. Other pilots recorded scattered fires, with F/Sgt Freestone and F/Sgt Harlem reporting that the photo flash flares had illuminated the target so well that buildings could easily be made out from between 14,000 and 15,000ft.

From other post-raid reports, this raid on Nuremberg appears to have been far from successful. Although the first PFF over the target accurately marked the aiming points, a creepback developed which could not be corrected. The creepback was blamed on the fact that a very limited number of crews could hear the 'Master Bomber's instructions, and coupled with this, some Pathfinder H2S sets were not working correctly. As a result only the southeastern suburbs of the city were hit and relatively little damage was caused.

Having completed their missions, '199' crews started to land back at RAF Lakenheath, with F/O Hagues the first to touch down at 0425 hrs, followed by eight other crews – F/Sgt Dodsworth being the last to arrive back at 0520 hrs.

It soon became apparent that two crews were missing and checks were made to see if they had landed at another airfield. Once the time ran out for the aircraft to make it back, everyone realised another fourteen of their comrades would have to be listed as missing in action. Later, confirmation came in that both Sgt Drayton and W/O Odgers had gone down, with only one survivor.

Stirling BK806 EX-S, Crew: Sgt Victor Alfred Drayton, Pilot, RAFVR, age 33, married to Lily Drayton of Clapham, London; Sgt David Skinner, F/Eng, RAFVR, age 20, from Inverurie, Aberdeenshire; Sgt William Madine Dalzell, Nav, RAF, age 20, from Whitehaven, Cumberland; Sgt Herbert Thomas Hathaway, B/A, RAFVR, age 19, from Oxford; Sgt John Leigh Kemp, W/Op, RAFVR, age 20, from Wavertree, Liverpool; Sgt Eric George Shepherd, M/U, RAFVR, from Wandsworth, London, all buried in Durnbach War Cemetery. The Stirling had crashed near Ansbach, 40 km SSW of Nuremberg. Only the rear gunner, Sgt D.R. McAllister, RCAF, survived and he was captured and sent to Stalag 4B (Muhlberg-Elbe) and given the POW number 222622.

Stirling EE913 EX-F, Crew: P/O Thomas Rex Odgers, Pilot, RAAF, age 29, married to Marjorie Odgers of Castlemaine, Australia; F/Sgt Cyril Elvett Gregory, F/Eng, RAF, age 20, from Pontygwaith, Glamorgan; F/Sgt Roland Ernest James Rees, Nav, RAFVR, age 35, married to Ivy Rees of West Bromwich, Staffordshire; Sgt Lancelot Walter Davies, B/A, RAFVR, age 21, from Bury St Edmunds, Suffolk; Sgt Benjamin Joseph Barton, W/Op, AG, RAFVR, age 23, married to Beryl Barton from Colchester, Essex; Sgt Thomas William Albert Wilkes, M/U, RAFVR, age 19, from Aldershot, Hampshire; F/Sgt Barton Thomas Eric Parker, A/G, RNZAF, age 30, from Lower Hutt, Wellington, New Zealand, all buried in Durnbach War Cemetery. They had come down at Futtersee, 13 km NNE of Scheinfeld.

On 29th August two crews were detailed for a mining operation, but this was cancelled prior to take-off.

30th August 1943

A raid on Munchen Gladbach appeared on the Battle Orders and eleven crews were detailed for the raid. The usual preparations ensued, with fuel and bombs loaded during the morning, guns checked, wireless sets warmed up and tested, compasses swung and all other necessary checks carried out.

A mechanical fault grounded one of the Stirlings, but the remaining ten were classed as serviceable and at 0015 hrs Sgt Dodsworth lifted off, followed by the other nine.

All went well until F/O Pettit's flight engineer, Sgt Currie, reported a 50 Mag drop on both port engines. He later reported: *"The aircraft attempted a slow roll, coupled with an engine power fall off. The loss of control was not due to slipstream. Mission abandoned, bombs jettisoned live and returned to base landing at 0240 hrs"*.

Over the target, stiff opposition was encountered from flak and fighters.

Sgt Hodson EE910 EX-Q was attacked by a night fighter, just after dropping his bomb load from 13,000ft at 0218 hrs. He confirmed later that: *"We had just bombed the target and were silhouetted by the fires, when we were attacked. The mid upper gunner Sgt Quar saw an enemy fighter coming in from the starboard beam at a range of 900 yards and called for a corkscrew to starboard. The mid upper turret was not working due to an electrical fault, so the guns could not be used. As the enemy aircraft closed, it was positively identified as a Ju88. As we continued to corkscrew, the enemy pilot opened fire and hits were made on our aircraft. He broke away under us and came up again on the starboard quarter and opened fire again from about 200 yards, hitting us hard in the starboard inner engine which caught fire. This engine was shut down by Sgt Taylor, the flight engineer, who also feathered the prop.*

After the second attack, the fighter broke away to port and came in for a third time from the port beam. He opened fire and again hit our aircraft, then broke away underneath and came up on the starboard beam and flew along parallel to us at about 600 yards range.

All the time, during the three attacks, our aircraft was doing violent corkscrews, but flew straight and level when the fighter was flying parallel. After about three minutes the enemy fighter crossed underneath us and continued on the same track for about another minute. It was thought that, as the fighter crossed underneath, he was going to make another attack, so the mid upper ordered another corkscrew, after which the enemy aircraft disappeared from sight and was not seen again.

Refuelling prior to an operation, with the bomb doors open awaiting loading.

Our aircraft was badly shot up and both the starboard and port inner engines were hit and damaged. The starboard tyre punctured, the dinghy was destroyed and the IFF aerial broken. No reply to our SOS received from MF/DF, although replies could be heard to other emergency calls from other aircraft".

Unfortunately, Sgt Hodson did not elaborate any further and the ORB does not give details regarding the landing with one tyre burst. It must be assumed that the pilot landed the Stirling without wrecking the undercarriage, as EE910 was flying Ops again on 15th September.

One other aircraft, that of F/Sgt Freestone, BK762 EX-C, flying at 13,000ft, was also attacked over the target at 0200 hrs.

"Our aircraft was not illuminated by searchlights at the time of the attack, but we were silhouetted over the fires burning in the target area. The bomb aimer, F/Sgt Whittington had just started to drop the bombs when our rear gunner, Sgt Barkwell, identified a Fw190, attacking from the starboard quarter up at 750 yards and immediately ordered a corkscrew to starboard and opened fire at the same time. The mid upper, Sgt Slevens, also opened fire. The enemy fighter returned fire as soon as our gunners opened up. The fighter closed in dead astern but as we were doing a violent corkscrew, no hits were made on our aircraft. Our gunners felt that they had hit the enemy fighter in this attack. After making just one attack, the fighter broke away at about 200 yards to the port quarter down and was not seen again.

After ensuring the entire bomb load had been released, F/Sgt Freestone turned onto the homeward track, but eleven minutes later, Sgt Barkwell spotted another night fighter bearing in from the starboard quarter down at a range of 300 yards. The fighter was identified as an Fw190. The rear gunner ordered a corkscrew to starboard and he and the mid upper opened fire at once. No return fire from the enemy was observed. Both gunners fired a two second burst and the engine of the fighter appeared to catch fire, it broke away to port and dived down toward the cloud. Just as it entered the cloud it was seen to explode and our gunners claim the enemy fighter as destroyed. Both gunners fired a total of 1,700 rounds in the engagement and no damage was sustained to our aircraft".

S/Ldr Wynne-Powell had 8 x 30lb incendiary bombs hung up and he was forced to bring these back to RAF Lakenheath.

The other pilots and crews – Sgt Allson, F/Sgt Davey, F/Sgt Austin and F/O Hagues – all had successful trips and felt the attack was a success, with good concentrations of fires around the aiming point.

Unfortunately, F/Sgt Harlem and his crew failed to return from this raid. Their aircraft was shot down by a night fighter and crashed near Eind north of Eindhoven, Holland at 0356 hrs. From German combat reports, it appears that the Stirling may have been shot down by Ofw Bruno Eickmeir, 2./NJG1; his claim matches the aircraft type, time and location. All the crew were killed in the crash.

As the remainder of the Squadron bombed the target between 0218 hrs and 0229 hrs, it can be assumed that F/Sgt Harlem had dropped his bomb load before being shot down.

Stirling EE917 EX-L, Crew: F/Sgt Athol Asher Harlem, Pilot, RAAF, age 21, from Melbourne, Victoria, Australia; Sgt John Thomas Smith, F/Eng, RAFVR, age 27, married to Ellen Smith of Virley, Essex; F/Sgt William Bailes Julian, Nav, RAFVR, age 21, married to Marjorie Julian of Ripon, Yorkshire; F/Sgt Ian Nichol McLaren, B/A, RAFVR, age 24, from Keith, Banffshire; F/Sgt Frank Ernest Gee, W/Op, RAAF, age 25, from Forbes, New South Wales, Australia; Sgt Harry Eli Elphick, W/Op, A/G, RAFVR, age 34, married to Vera Elphick of Torquay, Devon; Sgt Royston Hazeldine George Ellis, A/G, RAFVR, age 27, married to Doreen Ellis of Kensington, London; W/O Alexander Douglas Finlayson, DFM, M/U, RAAF, age 29, from Yerong Creek, New South Wales, Australia. All were buried in Woensel General Cemetery, Eindhoven.

W/O Findlayson had gained his DFM on 4th June 1943 for destroying a night fighter while on a raid to Dortmund in May 1943. Sgt Elphick was flying with this crew as an extra wireless operator/air gunner and had accompanied them on at least two raids.

Bomber Command records show that a total of 660 aircraft took part in this raid, losing 25 to flak and fighters. The raid was, in fact, a double attack on Münchengladbach (North Rhine-Westphalia) and the town of Rheydt. 199

Squadron's primary was Münchengladbach and overall, the individual reports of the crews match those of the command as a whole. 'Oboe'-equipped Mosquitoes accurately marked Münchengladbach, which resulted in a concentrated raid with hardly any creepback. A few minutes after the attack began, more 'Oboe' Mosquitoes arrived and moved the target indicators over to Rheydt, that again resulted in some very accurate bombing from Main Force. Over half the buildings in each town were reported to have been destroyed. German records show that 1,059 buildings in München and 1,280 in Rheydt were totally destroyed with 370 people killed and over 2,000 injured.

31st August 1943

The last target for August would again be Berlin, with its hundreds of flak guns and scores of night fighters positioned at airfields around the city. Ten crews were detailed to join the raid, but mechanical failures in one of the Stirlings meant only nine took off from RAF Lakenheath for the German capital.

Problems soon started to appear, and F/Sgt Barnard, EE943 EX-X, who took off at 2233 hrs, was informed that the navigator, F/O Plunkett, had been taken ill and was unable to perform his duties. The mission was abandoned between Skegness and Den Helder, on the Dutch coast, with all the bombs jettisoned into the sea. The 1,000 pounder was dropped safe and all the incendiaries dropped live. The crew landed back at RAF Lakenheath. Next to turn back was Sgt Hodson, EH926 EX-T when the port outer engine failed completely due to overheating. He had almost reached the Dutch coast when it became clear that the Stirling was not maintaining height on three engines. The bombs were jettisoned into the sea and the crew returned to base, landing safely at 0318 hrs. F/Sgt Freestone, Sgt Humphries, F/Sgt Austin and Sgt Allson all reached the target dropped their bombs within a few minutes either side of midnight and reported successful missions.

Sgt Dodsworth and crew.
Back: Sgt J. French, W/Op; Sgt S. Brooks, M/U; Sgt J. Carr, F/E; Sgt. F. Fenwick, R/G.
Front: Sgt H. Todd, DFM, Nav; F/Sgt W. Dodsworth, DFM, Pilot; Sgt. A. Cheese, B/A.

F/Sgt Dodsworth was hit by flak approaching the target and the aircraft suffered damage to the starboard bomb doors and hydraulic lines. He later reported: *"The bomb aimer Sgt Cheese dropped the bombs at 0002 hrs from 14,000ft and then went to man the front turret. He had only just settled into his new position when, at 0006 hrs, the rear gunner, F/Sgt Fenwick, called for a corkscrew to port as he had spotted a German night fighter fire on the port quarter. He positively identified the enemy aircraft as an Me110 at a range of 150 yards. As our aircraft started to dive, the enemy fighter opened fire, by which time he was dead astern and, at 100 yards, our rear gunner opened up at point blank range and observed hits on the enemy.*

The fighter passed us on the starboard side at a range of 75 yards and the mid upper gunner Sgt Brooks then opened fire and more hits were observed. The fighter then passed round the front of our aircraft and hung on the port wing tip at about 100 yards and all three gunners opened fire, observing more hits and the wireless operator, Sgt French, who was in the astro-dome, also saw hits register on the enemy aircraft. The fighter then broke away to the port beam and was not seen again. The crew claim the enemy aircraft as damaged, but it was not seen to catch fire or crash. The gunners fired a total of 1,100 rounds in the engagement".

Another pilot to encounter a night fighter was F/O Pettit, EE911 EX-G, who had reached a point just south of Salzgitter-Bad in Germany on the outward journey, when, at 2247 hrs flying at 12,000ft, he came under attack from a night fighter: *"Our rear gunner, Sgt Phipp, reported an unidentified twin engined aircraft attacking from the port quarter up at 1,000 yards and immediately gave the order to corkscrew port. The fighter followed our aircraft round and closed in to attack, the rear gunner and mid upper, Sgt Tye, opened fire when the enemy fighter was at a range of 300 yards. Our aircraft continued to corkscrew and the fighter overshot to the starboard and then dived below and was not seen again. The gunners fired a total of 450 rounds and observed strikes and a break in their tracer pattern and claim the enemy as damaged, our gunners also said that the enemy was high winged twin engined aircraft and may have been a Dornier 217".*

After the attack, F/O Pettit carried on to the target and dropped his bomb load at 2358 hrs and saw several concentrated fires. The return journey was uneventful and the crew landed at RAF Lakenheath at 0345 hrs.

This raid and the month of August was to end with the loss of another crew when F/Sgt Davey failed to return. The Stirling was shot down by a night fighter at Schlalach, 50 kms SSW of Berlin killing all the crew. They were initially buried in Schlalach, but after the war, their bodies were laid to rest in the Berlin 1939–1945 War Cemetery. Stirling EE946 EX-P, Crew: F/Sgt Allan John Davey, Pilot, RAAF, age 24, married to Peggy Davey of Croydon, New South Wales, Australia; Sgt William Arthur Crawford, F/Eng, RAFVR, age 19, from Dün Laoghaire, Co Dublin, Republic of Ireland; F/Sgt Russell Edwin Adam, Nav, RCAF, age 27, married to Betty Adam of Toronto, Ontario, Canada; Sgt Brian James Kennell, B/A, RAFVR, age 21, from Ipswich, Suffolk; F/Sgt Leslie Edwin Short, W/Op, RAFVR, age 21, from Thornton Heath, Surrey; F/Sgt David Scott, M/U, RCAF, age 20, from Toronto, Ontario, Canada; F/Sgt Kevin John Wilkes, R/G, RAAF, age 20, from Yarraman, Queensland, Australia.

The raid on Berlin by 622 aircraft was deemed a failure as 47 were shot down, including seventeen Stirlings of the 106 detailed, making a loss rate of 16%. The majority of the bombers shot down fell to night fighters, who used 'fighter flares' for the first time to mark the routes in and out of the target. Cloud over the target hindered the PFF Mosquitoes and also the backing up aircraft

199 Squadron Wireless Operators, Lakenheath, August 1943.

which were still having problems with their H2S radar sets. The defences around the city were reported as putting up a wall of steel and this, coupled with the tenacious night fighter attacks, resulted in the TIs being dropped south of the aiming points. Main Force came in and started dropping their bombs well short of the TIs and the resulting creepback extended almost 30 miles back along the inward track.

Berlin records show minimal damage, with no industrial premises hit to any great extent and 68 people killed. After this raid, all non-essential civilians and children were ordered out of the city to safer locations in the countryside.

September
A close encounter with an incendiary –
the USAAF begin experimental night bombing operations

1st September 1943

Three crews briefed for a mining operation, which was later cancelled.

2nd September 1943

Three crews were again briefed for a mining operation and, this time, they all took off for their allotted areas. First away were F/Sgt Moore and P/O Gilbert, who lifted off at 1955 hrs en route for La Rochelle, on the west coast of France, followed half an hour later by Sgt Lumsdaine tasked to mine an area off the Frisian Islands.

Sgt Lumsdaine reported a successful trip, as did F/Sgt Moore, but again, the Squadron was dealt a blow when P/O Gilbert and his crew failed to return. Their Stirling, EE911 EX-G, crashed in the sea north of Rochefort.

Stirling EE911, EX-G, Crew: F/O Reginald Campbell Gilbert, Pilot, RCAF, from St. Vital, Manitoba, Canada, buried in Pornic War Cemetery; Sgt William Connell Mitchell, F/Eng, RAFVR, buried in Yves Communal Cemetery; F/O Macdonald Stuart Gordon, Nav, RCAF, age 23, from Selkirk, Manitoba, Canada, remembered at Runnymede Memorial; F/Sgt Clifford Charles Maw, B/A, RCAF, remembered on Runnymede Memorial; Sgt Francis William Watts, W/Op, RAFVR, age 21, remembered on Runnymede Memorial; Sgt George Ezard, M/U, RAFVR, age 31, married to Dorothy Ezard of Whalley Range, Manchester, buried in Pornic War Cemetery; Sgt Arthur Thomas Newton, R/G, RAFVR, married to Joan Newton of Manor Park, Essex, remembered on Runnymede Memorial.

3rd September 1943

Four crews were detailed for two separate mining sorties. Two aircraft took off at 2030 hrs for the Frisian Islands and both had successful trips dropping their mines in good visibility. Both aircraft were back by 2319 hrs.

F/Sgt Freestone and Sgt Humphries had a much more difficult mission, having been detailed to mine an area off the west coast of Denmark. They took off just before the other two crews, at 2018 hrs, but their round trip took them almost eight hours to complete. The target area was located and the mines sown as ordered. F/Sgt Freestone reported that he was able to pick up a pinpoint on Vorsaa and also Anholt Island. Both aircraft returned to RAF Lakenheath and landed between 0404 hrs and 0411 hrs.

4th September 1943

Two more crews were on orders for mining, F/O O'Conner to the SW coast of France and Sgt Chappell to the Frisian Islands. Both completed their tasks.

5th September 1943

The Squadron was back to bombing operations, with Mannheim selected as the target. Nine aircraft and crews were placed on the battle order, but as the day wore on, one of the Stirlings developed serious faults while being

Loading 250lb GP Bombs into the narrow bomb cells.

tested by the ground crew and was withdrawn. The forecast was for clear weather and good visibility, with some icing conditions possible on the outward trip. The eight serviceable Stirlings took off between 1920 and 1945 hrs, but two were soon in difficulties –

F/Sgt Moore, BF481 EX-W, was informed by his flight engineer, Sgt Southgate, at 2124 hrs that the starboard outer oil pressure had dropped below 65 psi and the temperature had reached unacceptable levels. It was decided to abort the mission and return to base dropping the bombs safe on Rushford Range near Thetford, Norfolk. Sgt Hodson, EH909 EX-Z, was informed of a similar problem, but this time it was low oil pressure in the starboard inner engine. Again the decision was made to abort and the bombs were jettisoned live into the sea. Both these aircraft were back at Lakenheath by 2255 hrs.

The target was reached by the remaining crews, although F/Sgt Dodsworth EF450 EX-N had problems 40 miles out from base when his 'Gee' set went unserviceable. He pressed on with his attack bombing Mannheim at 2318, but shortly after, F/Sgt Dodsworth reported:

"We encountered severe icing and the Stirling went into a spin, which we found out later had damaged the bomb doors. The aircraft was recovered and straight and level flying was achieved, but I was informed that Sgt Cheese, our bomb aimer, had sustained a broken ankle, so he was made as comfortable as possible and checks made on the remainder of the crew. No one else had received anything worse than a few bruises, but many items of equipment and instruments had suffered as a consequence of the violent spin we had successfully recovered from. Upon landing, Sgt Cheese was taken to the base hospital for treatment".

The other crews flying the mission all reached and bombed the target between 2118 hrs and 2324 hrs – Sgt Humphries, F/Sgt Barnard, F/Sgt Austin, F/O Pettit and F/Sgt Freestone all claimed to have hit the target area and reported large concentrated fires burning, with some large explosions.

Bomber Command records show that 605 aircraft took part in this raid, which was split into two parts. The main initial target was Mannheim, with PFF re-marking Ludwigshafen so that Main Force could approach from the west, sweep over Mannheim, and then onto Ludwigshafen. Both targets were hit severely, with a great deal of damage caused to civilian and industrial premises. 34 aircraft failed to return.

The Squadron spent the next two days attending to maintenance of the aircraft and crews attended the usual lectures and drills.

Ted Coppen, FME: *"Initially, I worked on 'G' George with Johnny Wagstaff, Jimmy Kelly, Vic Greenwood and Sgt Bob Jones. Then I transferred to 'B' Beer with Vic Greenwood, Percy Stell, Harry Foster and Sgt Hartley. I have a photo of 'B' with all the aircrew and ground staff. I also have a photo of Halifax 'J' taken at North Creake. I was known as Ted, with a nickname of 'Pickles'. Vic and Perce used to call me 'Ike'. I then went on to 'H' Harry with Cpl Niemen, Jimmy Kelly and Hugh McGrory. Some of us were then left on the station as rear party to repair a Stirling that was in the graveyard prior to moving to North Creake".*

8th September 1943

The target selected by Bomber Command for this night's raid was the heavy gun position on the French coast at Boulogne. Eight Stirlings and crews were briefed for the raid and all took off without problems. Sgt Allson, F/Sgt Dodsworth, F/Sgt Hodson, F/O Hagues, F/Sgt Freestone, Sgt Lumsdaine, F/O O'Conner and Sgt Chappell all dropped their bombs on the red and green TIs, but reported thick ground haze. The marking, however, was not accurate and the raid was not deemed a success, with no damage inflicted on the battery. Sgt Chappell, EF455, carried on to the target, although the rear turret of his Stirling was not functioning. It was fortunate that two Ju88s spotted by the gunner did not attack. However, another Ju88 did attack from the starboard bow up and the bomb aimer, Sgt Higgins, who was manning the front turret at the time, fired off a long burst at about 600 yards range. No hits were observed and the enemy fighter passed beneath the Stirling on the port side.

On this mission, five American B-17s flew the first night raid of the USAAF, joining up with 257 aircraft of Bomber Command. There were no losses.

From the 9th to the 14th the Squadron was stood down from operations due to bad weather and the time was spent on checking and testing the Stirlings, with several air tests carried out.

15th September 1943

The Dunlop rubber factory, located at Montluçon in central France, was selected as the target, as it was reported to be producing large quantities of tyres and other war materials for the Germans. Twelve Stirlings and crews were detailed for the raid and the aircraft loaded, mainly, with incendiaries.

Twelve Stirlings took off between 2031 hrs and 2040 hrs, with F/Sgt Hodson first away. All reached Montluçon without mishap. The defences around the target were found to be weak and did not interfere greatly with the attack. A thick layer of cloud was encountered over Montluçon and most of the crews decided to keep to 6,000ft and fly below it on the bomb runs.

Sgt Hodson stated: *"We flew in higher than the other crews, bombing from 8,500ft, aiming through gaps in the clouds and saw thick black smoke rising to a height of 10,000ft above the cloud tops"*.

F/Sgt Barnard reported: *"We identified the target by the green TIs and the master bomber, Wing Commander Deane, confirmed that the greens were 'bang on the aiming point', several large fires and thick smoke observed"*.

Sqd/Ldr Humby, DFC, also saw a very good fire in the target area but he had to bring back 16 x 30lb incendiaries due to one failing to release. All crews had completed the bombing within seven minutes, Sgt Catterall arriving first at 2342 hrs and Sgt Winters last at 2349 hrs. F/Sgt Guthrie, EH995 EX-L, who completed his attack at 2348 hrs had done remarkably well as his starboard outer had failed 80 miles short of the target. There are no reports of fighter attacks and the crews made it back to base unscathed with everyone on the ground by 0302 hrs. Again the Americans contributed five B17s to the total of 369 aircraft detailed for the raid which was classed as very successful. The Pathfinders had marked the target accurately and every building in the Dunlop factory was hit and damaged. It appears that this was the last time a master bomber was used until the following spring of 1944. Three aircraft failed to return.

16th September 1943

The French railway system was next in line for Bomber Command to attack, with the marshalling yards at Modane chosen as the primary target. The yards were situated in a steep Alpine valley on the main route, midway between Grenoble in France and Turin in Italy, and the railway carried large amounts of war materials between the two countries. The target proved very difficult for accurate marking and as a consequence very little damage was caused.

There were eleven crews detailed from '199', all of whom took off, but Sgt Austin, BK772 EX-A, was nearing Dieppe, on the French coast, when he found his Stirling unstable and difficult to fly, so he returned to base, dropping his bombs into the Channel. Also having problems was Sgt Allson, EE947 EX-D, who was just east of Le Havre, when the starboard outer engine closed down and he also jettisoned his bomb load into the sea and returned to RAF Lakenheath. Another crew having an eventful trip was that of F/Sgt Moore, EF453 EX-F, who is reported to have hit a balloon cable over London. He said in his de-brief: *"The aircraft appeared to hit a balloon cable over London at 6,000ft at 2051 hrs and went into a spin to port. We recovered, after losing about 1,000ft. Carried on to the target and bombed the green TIs at 0016 hrs and landed back at base at 0350 hrs"*.

All the remaining crews reached the target and reported having bombed on the green markers which had not been dropped in the correct position. Had they been, it must be assumed from the raid debrief, that the Squadron would have caused some considerable damage as all the bomb aimers claim that the target was identified by the greens when the loads were released.

The next five days saw a general lull in operations by Bomber Command, with only one air sea rescue flown by 199 Squadron on the 20th. Sgt Robinson, EF453 EX-F, was detailed for this sortie, but there is no indication that anything was found.

22nd September 1943

It had been decided at Bomber Command that Hanover was to be attacked on a large scale, having not been a major target for two years. '199' was instructed of this directive and, for the first raid, twelve aircraft and crew were detailed to take part.

No technical difficulties were encountered during the pre-flight testing and the full complement of Stirlings took off without incident and reached the target. The crews reported the weather very clear as they approached Hanover and the target identified by markers laid down by PFF. It appears that winds stronger than forecast caused the markers to be dropped between two and five miles SSE of the city centre, but with no Master Bomber now being used, the crews were unaware of the discrepancy. Within twelve minutes all the '199' crews had dropped their bombs onto the markers and turned for home.

F/Sgt Chappell EF505 EX-K said after the raid *"The weather was clear and we bombed on the green TIs, large fires observed which could still be seen 200 miles away as we crossed the coast on the way back"*.

Members of this crew also observed two aircraft coned in searchlights. Both were shot down. They also saw a bomber explode on the outward leg of the sortie at about 1915 hrs. This was a 90 Squadron Stirling flown by Sgt E. Hayman that had just taken off from Wratting Common. The starboard engine had developed a major problem and caught fire and quickly spread to the fuel tanks in the wing. The aircraft blew up at 500ft and scattered wreckage over a wide area near Brockley Green in Suffolk. All but one of the crew were killed, but F/Sgt Duffy, who survived the crash, died later from his injuries.

S/Ldr Humby, DFC, EE947 EX-D, also reported that the fire glow could be seen from the coast. F/Sgt Austin, BK762 EX-C, released his bombs at 2139 hrs from 15,000ft and saw smoke from several large fires reaching up to 12,000ft. The crew also said the glow over Hanover was still visible for one hour after leaving the target. Sgt Hodson, EH909 EX-Z, approached the target at 13,500ft, low enough to observe individual buildings, including one large one lit up by the bomb burst flashes. The crew also saw one considerable explosion, which illuminated the surrounding area. Another 90 Squadron Stirling was lost when it crash landed at RAF Lakenheath and has been recorded by '199' crews in personal notes, but was not mentioned in the Squadron ORB. This aircraft had been hit severely by cannon fire from a night fighter and, as a consequence, two of the crew had baled out over enemy territory. For conspicuous airmanship and courage of the highest order, Sgt O.N. Jones was awarded the CGM; W/O R.F. Denton, pilot, was awarded the DFC and Sgt R.W.C. Suddens the DFM. One of the crew, Sgt Morgan R/G, was killed.

The Americans sent five B17s from the 422nd Squadron in the first night bombing operation mounted by the USAAF. On board one of these was Brigadier-General Fred Anderson, who was in charge of the American 8th Air Force, was keen to learn how the allies operated and flew to gain first hand experience.

However, the Americans did not pursue a night bombing role and instead concentrated on daylight operations.

There are no German reports available to enable damage details on Hanover to be listed. Of the 711 aircraft taking part in this attack 27 were shot down.

23rd September 1943

Sgt Winter, EE943 EX-X, detailed for an air sea rescue, took off from RAF Lakenheath at 0825 hrs and returned at 1115 hrs, without making a sighting.

Earlier in the month, Mannheim had been attacked, but later reconnaissance photographs showed that the northern district had not been damaged as it should. It was decided to launch a raid on the unaffected area and 199 Squadron was detailed to send eleven aircraft. F/O Hagues, EF450 EX-N, returned early when the inter-com failed. The remaining crews reached the target and dropped their bomb loads between 2157 hrs and 2207 hrs. Sgt Hodson, EH909 EX-Z, was the first to approach the target, but just as he was lining up for the bomb run, the flight engineer, Sgt Taylor, informed him that the port inner engine had failed. He reported later: *"Owing to the failure of the port inner, the bomb load was dropped early on a built-up area to the north west of the aiming point".* On leaving the target F/Sgt Moore, EF450 EX-B, observed two large explosions and fires taking hold, with smoke up to 8,000ft. Sgt Lumsdaine, EE943 EX-X: *"The weather was very clear and the target was identified by fires and five TI markers in a semi-circle, large fires observed to the west of the river".* F/Sgt Dodsworth and F/Sgt Guthrie both commented that they felt the bombing was insufficiently concentrated, but it appears that overall this was not the case. F/Sgt Chappell, EF505 EX-K, reported as many searchlights as Hanover, but twice the amount of flak. At the de-brief he said that just after releasing his bombs, the aircraft was struck by a flak burst that punched a hole four feet long by one foot wide in the starboard wing. This prevented the flaps from being used and cut the power to the undercarriage that had to be lowered by hand when he returned to base.

Back: **Sgt Lumsdaine, Pilot; F/Sgt Murray, F/E; Sgt Lockett, R/G; F/O Brooks, M/U; F/O White, Nav.**
Front: **P/O Ward, B/A; P/O Townsend, W/Op.**

Reports from Mannheim show that the PFF plan did get the markers down on the intended aiming point and a good concentration of bombs fell within the designated area. Towards the latter part of the raid some 'creepback' did occur and several bombs fell on the northern edge of Ludwigshafen and into open countryside. In Mannheim 927 houses and twenty industrial premises were destroyed, plus a large number of other buildings damaged. 25,000 people were bombed out of their homes. 102 were killed and 418 injured. The fire service reported over 2,000 fires and the I.G. Farben factory was severely damaged, killing 47 people and injuring 260. In Ludwigshafen over 8,000 people were bombed out, many of these being foreign workers. The small towns of Oppau and Frankenthal were hit, the latter having the centre completely burned out. The raid consisted of 628 aircraft, of which 32 were lost. The USAAF contributed five B17s.

After the raid, F/Sgt Chappell's Stirling was examined to assess the damage caused by the "flak burst". It was found that the 4ft x 1ft hole was eight inches from the control cables and three feet from the starboard inner petrol tank; fifteen inches from the oil tank and two inches from the main petrol pipe. As one of the crew commented at the time: *"It couldn't have hit in a better place".* But that was not the end of the story, as later on, during a closer inspection, the so-called flak burst wasn't flak after all. It was a large unexploded target indicator dropped from one of our own aircraft, flying directly above the Stirling. This was removed with extreme care and the hole patched up.

24th September 1943

One aircraft was required for a minelaying mission to the Frisian Islands and Sgt Robinson and crew, EE947 EX-D, were put on standby. The order came through and the aircraft took off from RAF Lakenheath at 1915 hrs.

Midway between the English and Dutch coasts, the 'Gee' set failed and the mission was aborted at 2040 hrs, and three of the five mines were jettisoned into the sea. On approach to Lakenheath, about one mile from touchdown, they came too low and crashed through some trees, causing the wing tanks to explode. F/Sgt W.H. Morrison, the bomb aimer, was killed and the other members of the crew injured.

Shortly after the crash, the two mines still on board exploded, injuring F/O Cubby (W/Op) and F/Lt Banahan (bomb aimer) who served on F/Lt Noble's crew. They and other members of their crew had been cycling back from a pub in Brandon. Cubby and Banahan managed to get close to the burning aircraft and saw flames coming out of the mid upper turret, which was empty. They went to the rear turret and were standing close by when the mines exploded. They were first taken to the sick quarters at Lakenheath and later transferred to Ely Hospital, for treatment. Both made good recoveries.

F/Sgt William Hugh Morrison, RAAF, Bomb Aimer, age 31, was a New Zealander and married to Beryl Morrison of Hamilton, Auckland, New Zealand. He was buried in St John's Churchyard, Beck Row, Suffolk.

25th September 1943

Another solo mining operation was detailed for F/Sgt Robertson and his crew. The target area was again the waters off the Frisian Islands. Sgt Robertson, flying BK762 EX-O, took off at 1902 hrs and completed a successful trip, sowing five mines at the allotted pin point, and landing back at RAF Lakenheath at 2142 hrs.

27th September 1943

Another major raid on Hanover and again five B17s of the USAAF joined the 678 Bomber Command aircraft. 199 Squadron was detailed for twelve aircraft and crews to be placed on the Battle Order for the night's operations.

All twelve Stirlings took off on time, with Sgt Winter, EE943 EX-X away first at 1935 hrs. Problems for one crew, however, would force them to abort.

Sgt Dodsworth, EH926 EX-T, was midway between Lowestoft and the Dutch coast, when the starboard outer engine caught fire. The flight engineer, Sgt Carr, and the pilot, working together, shut down the engine and feathered the propeller, after which Sgt Dodsworth hit the appropriate nacelle fire extinguisher down by his left knee and everyone was relieved to see the flames go out. The bomb aimer, Sgt Gardner, jettisoned the bomb load live into the sea and the flight engineer dumped 200 gallons of petrol from the number 4 fuel tank. A course was set for base and almost an hour later, they touched down safely at RAF Lakenheath.

The Squadron's other aircraft had uneventful trips and reached the target, spotting the target indicators in good time, but, as later reports unfolded, the TIs were, in fact, in the wrong place. The error was due to the Pathfinders being given the wrong information on wind directions and strength and dropping their markers five miles north of the city centre. The main stream of bombers including those of '199' dropped a very concentrated pattern of bombs directly on the markers, but the majority of them dropped on outlying villages or onto open countryside.

From the crew de-briefings it appears that some large fires were in evidence and Sgt Lumsdaine, BK762 EX-C, F/Sgt Austin, EE953 EX-E, and F/Sgt Guthrie, EH995 EX-L all logged seeing a huge orange coloured explosion in the target area at 2210 hrs. In view of the misplaced markers it seems slightly ironic that Sgt Catterall went round again, when his bomb doors would not open on the first run. He also had problems with the starboard undercarriage, which would not lower on the landing approach to base. The faulty unit was wound down by hand under the emergency procedure.

P/O Humphries, EE957 EX-Q, said in his report that the crew had observed the fires from the target as they crossed over the Zuider Zee on the way home.

P/O Hodson, who had been one of the mainstay members of the squadron, and his crew aboard EF118 EX-O was shot down and crashed at Ramlingen, west of the main road between Celle and Hanover. Crew: P/O Maurice Albert Nicholas Hodson, Pilot, RAFVR, age 21, from Sheffield; F/O Leonard Douglas Clay, 2nd Pilot, RAFVR, age 26, from Chadwell Heath, Essex; Sgt Jack Taylor, B/A, RAFVR, age 19, from Newton, Hyde, Cheshire; F/Sgt Brian Purdy Higginson, Nav, RNZAF, age 22, from Auckland, New Zealand; Sgt Dugald Gillies Wood, W/Op, RAFVR, age 23, from Clarkston, Renfrewshire; Sgt Alfred John Quar, M/U, RAFVR, age 21, from Fulham, London; Sgt William Henry Boyden, R/G, RAFVR, age 33, married to Irene Boyden of Barkingside, Ilford, Essex. All were buried in Hanover War Cemetery.

Only the flight engineer Sgt R. Taylor survived and was taken prisoner. Sent to Stalag Kopernikus he was given the POW number 609. F/O Clay, the 2nd Pilot, had only joined the Squadron on 18th September, having been posted in from 1657 HCU and was on his first operational flight to gain experience. A total of 38 RAF aircraft were lost on the raid, plus one of the American B17s.

The next day at one o'clock, the BBC Home Service broadcast the following news report: *"Last night, a strong force of our home based bombers made a ferocious attack on Hitler's industrial stronghold of Hannover. This was the second hammering given to the city in a week. Fierce sky battles took place along the route. High flying German aircraft would release flares, which in turn would light the sky as though it were day. The night fighters would swoop in on our bombers and great battles would ensue. 38 of our bombers are missing".*

29th September 1943

An air sea search was carried out by Sgt Catterall, BF481 EX-W from 0950 hrs to 1640 hrs, but no outcome was recorded.

Operations for the night were scrubbed due to bad weather.

During the month of September, F/Sgt Burton, Pilot, was awarded the DFC. This was gazetted on 10th September and his citation reads: *"This airman has invariably displayed a fine fighting spirit, skilful captaincy and airmanship and has pressed home attacks against many of the enemy's important industrial centres. These sorties have frequently been accomplished in the face of heavy opposition. He has also participated in mine laying sorties. F/Sgt Burton has achieved a splendid operational record, always setting his mind fearlessly on the task in hand".*

*F/Sgt Burton was born in Fulham and was a local government clerk in civilian life. He initially joined the Army Dental Corps, but transferred to the RAF in 1941.

October
The arrival of Wing Commander Bray

1st October 1943

Ten aircraft and crews detailed for operations (Stuttgart) but all were subsequently cancelled.

2nd October 1943

Only one crew required for a mining operation to the Frisian Islands. F/Sgt Kyle was detailed for the mission and EF453, EX-F was prepared and loaded with five mines. The aircraft took off at 1900 hrs and proceeded to the designated area. The navigator P/O Humphreys obtained a Gee fix at 5332N 0434E NNW of Vlieland and the Stirling made a DR run in and dropped the mines on target. All the chutes were seen to open but one was believed to have exploded on impact with the sea.

3rd October 1943

Target selected for this raid was Kassel and eleven aircraft and crews were placed on the Battle Order. The precise aiming points were detailed as the Focke-Wulf works and the heavily populated SE part of the town. The crews had been briefed that a dummy attack was to be mounted by twenty Mosquitoes on Hanover and that Main Force would set a course as though they were heading for this target. Short of Hanover they would then swing south and head for Kassel.

All 199 Squadron aircraft detailed took off between 1835 hrs and 1845 hrs and proceeded to settle on a heading for the target. One Stirling, that of Sgt Lumsdaine, EH909 EX-Z, was just two hours into the flight when problems started with one of the engines and he aborted the mission. He reported later: *"We had just reached a point 15km west of Vechta in Germany, on course for Kassel, when the starboard outer failed at 2036 hrs. The starboard outer would not re-feather, so it was decided to return to base. Part of the bomb load was immediately jettisoned after setting course for home and the remainder a few minutes later at 2047 hrs. On approach to base, we overshot the runway and while attempting to go round again, the starboard inner cut out and the aircraft crashed at 2306 hrs behind the watch tower".*

There are no reported injuries and Sgt Lumsdaine and his crew were soon back on Ops, none the worse for their experience.

The remaining ten crews experienced flak as they crossed the Frisians and searchlights started to point their track to the waiting fighters. They executed the change in direction from Hanover to Kassel at the correct co-ordinates and reached Kassel to find a ring of at least 50 searchlights and an intense flak barrage waiting for them.

According to the crew de-briefs, they all identified and bombed the target indicators. The horizontal visibility at the time was described as very clear and P/O O'Conner, EF450 EX-N, saw many well concentrated fires around the green TIs. F/Sgt Dodsworth, EE957 EX-Q reported that his bomb aimer had difficulty due to the dense smoke almost obscuring the target indicators. F/Sgt Chappell, EE910 EX-K, saw four very large fires and much dense smoke as they bombed the target. The incendiary load would not release in a stick, so Sgt Higgins B/A jettisoned them all together; he also commented on the two large decoy fires just outside the city.

F/Sgt Austin appears to be the only one to have had any problems releasing the bomb load, as he was forced to bring back 8 x 30lb incendiaries that had hung up due to an electrical fault.

All the crews again put in a good attack with navigation and timing, bringing them all over the target at 15,500 to 16,000ft within six minutes of each other. The first to bomb was P/O Allson, EF453 EX-F and F/Lt Pettit, EF508 EX-G, who arrived and attacked simultaneously at 2125 hrs, and the last to arrive flying at 16,000ft was Sgt Catterall, EF138 EX-S at 2131 hrs.

This raid was led in by H2S equipped 'blind markers' who relied on their radar to pinpoint the target, but the aiming point was overshot by a considerable distance and the first markers dropped were well off the AP. Again, as a consequence of not having a master bomber, the backing up 'visual markers' hampered by thick haze could not correct the problem and coupled with German decoy markers, the raid was well off target. Most of the attack ended up concentrating on the western district of Kassel and the outlying towns and villages. Two important industrial installations were hit and considerable damage was caused to the Henschel and Fieseler aircraft factories. From German reports, it appears that parts of Wolfshanger was utterly destroyed and a large ammunition dump was blown up. The city suffered 118 dead and 304 injured. Bomber Command sent 547 aircraft on this raid of which 24 failed to return.

4th October 1943

A raid on Frankfurt was ordered and ten Stirlings were detailed. However, three were unserviceable and withdrawn from the operation.

The seven remaining aircraft and crews took off from Lakenheath with the first, Sgt Catterall away at 1835 hrs and, after some delay, finally F/Lt Waterfield lifted off at 1905 hrs. F/Sgt Dodsworth, EE957 EX-Q, with Sgt Noble as 2nd pilot had navigational problems en-route and reported *"Primary not reached due to a compass failure so attacked Darmstadt instead"*. This town is situated about 30 km south of Frankfurt. P/O Allson, EF153 EX-D, and F/Lt Pettit, EE953 EX-E, visually identified the target by the River Main and also red and green TIs. They both saw several large explosions and heavy smoke.

All the Squadron aircraft returned safely to base, with F/Lt Waterfield the last to land at 0125 hrs. This raid, by a total of 406 aircraft, was the most successful on Frankfurt with a large amount of damage caused to the eastern side of the city. The inland dock area was also extensively damaged. Unfortunately an underground shelter in a hospital that was being used as an orphanage was hit and fourteen nuns and 90 children were killed. The USAAF again participated in this night raid, sending three B-17s to Frankfurt. One was shot down, but this was the last time they would be involved in attacking targets in the dark. Bomber Command lost ten aircraft.

6th October 1943

No operations ordered.

Wing Commander N.A.N. Bray was posted to the Squadron, from 1657 Conversion Unit, as Squadron Commander. This was a very popular assignment with all the personnel on the camp, and W/Cdr Bray has been described as *"a real swell guy"* by one of the Americans serving with the Squadron and sums up the feeling of high esteem bestowed upon him by all who knew and served under him.

Before his posting to 1657 CU, W/Cdr Bray had been attached to No.12 Operational Training Unit, at Chipping Warden, and while serving there, he and his crew had a remarkable escape when their aircraft, Wellington, BJ702, was shot down on 13th July 1943. They had been detailed for a 'Nickel' sortie to drop leaflets over the Rennes area of France, but were hit by flak in the port engine and mainplane while flying over the River Orne. The damage was too severe to carry on with the operation and W/Cdr Bray turned back and set a course for base. Losing altitude, he was re-crossing the French coast, when several searchlights started to probe for the Wellington and he was forced to take evasive action to avoid them. This lost more valuable height and the 'Nickels' were jettisoned over the sea. The wireless operator sent out an SOS after W/Cdr Bray had decided that he was no longer able to keep control of the aircraft and that he would have to ditch it in the sea. This he did, putting the Wellington down using his considerable skill and the entire crew were able to take to their dinghy. No serious injuries were reported, apart from W/Cdr Bray who sustained a broken nose.

The crew were in danger of being carried onto the French coast by the tide and, by paddling against the current for upwards of thirty hours, they kept seaward and were eventually spotted by a Spitfire pilot. A message was broadcast and soon after, a Hudson, equipped with an airborne lifeboat, was despatched, escorted by a number of Typhoons. The lifeboat was successfully dropped near the dinghy and the six crew scrambled aboard and, lost no time in reading the various instructions attached to the boat and organised themselves to prepare the boat and get underway. The engine was started and the navigator set up the compass and obtained a heading on which to steer.

However, the Germans had spotted the Hudson and Typhoons flying close to the coastline and sent several Fw190s to investigate. A terrific scrap took place as the Typhoon pilots threw themselves into a dogfight to prevent the Germans from strafing the helpless crew in the lifeboat. They beat off all the German fighters and continued to give air cover and an hour later were rewarded to see a high speed rescue launch approach from England and pick up the survivors from the lifeboat. By now the Typhoons' fuel was running low and they were replaced by a flight of Spitfires, who covered the remainder of the journey home by a very lucky bomber crew.

Of note, is the fact that by the time W/Cdr Bray and his crew were picked up, the Air Sea Rescue organisation had, from its founding in 1941, saved 3,306 Allied airmen.

W/Cdr Bray, Pilot, centre front, with his crew: consisting of (but cannot be individually named) P/O Wilde, Nav; F/O Parkinson, B/A; P/O Stokes, RG; Sgt Perkins, M/U, and F/Sgt Fitchett, W/Op. This photograph was taken immediately after their rescue and W/Cdr Bray can be seen with the dressing covering his broken nose sustained in the ditching.

7th October 1943

The Squadron was back to mining operations, with seven crews detailed although the pre-flight tests found one aircraft to be unserviceable. The aircraft were split into two sorties with five aircraft going to the Kattegat and one to the Frisian Islands.

F/Sgt Chappell, EE910 EX-K, reached the Kattegat area, but his navigator, Sgt Crossman, reported he had taken a pinpoint from the wrong position on the east coast of Denmark, resulting in the mines being planted almost 30 miles from the intended target area. They did not get off lightly being so far off track as they were fired on by flak batteries on the Danish coast and almost shot down. Later five large holes were found in the fuselage.

The other crews successfully completed their missions, including the one to the Frisian Islands, flown by F/O Barson. The east coast of Denmark was also liberally sprinkled with propaganda leaflets as each of the Kattegat bound aircraft carried seven bundles of 'nickels'.

8th October 1943

A diversionary raid on Bremen was ordered to cover the main attack on Hanover and 199 Squadron detailed nine crews for the mission. This diversion was a larger scale raid than normal with 119 aircraft taking part. The majority of the pilots reported 7/10 to 9/10 cloud cover over Bremen and were forced to make dead reckoning timed bomb runs from the yellow route markers placed by the PFF. Once again, the navigation and timing of all the crews was spot on with all the aircraft bombing the target within six minutes of each other.

F/Sgt Barnard, EF138 EX-S, stated after the raid – *"We made a dead reckoning run from the yellow TIs and ground detail. The bombs were released at 0114 hrs on the red TIs. Green TIs were probably dummies seen well away from the recognised built up area. Flashes seen from our own 1,000 pounders. 8 x 4lb incendiaries hung up and brought back"*. Following in closely, F/Sgt Moore, EF453 EX-F, dropped his bombs at 0115 hrs from 15,000ft and reported – *"The weather was 7/10 cloud with cumulus at 5,000ft. The target was identified by scattered red TIs. Green TIs seen and later reds were more concentrated. Two bomb burst flashes seen when bombs released"*. The scattered effect of the target markers was also remarked upon by Sgt Lumsdaine, EJ111 EX-P – *"The weather was hazy with low cloud and the target was identified by a DR run from the route markers. There seemed to be very few fires visible. 90 x 4lb incendiaries hung up. The TIs were far more dispersed than usual"*. F/Sgt Guthrie, EH995 EX-L, dropped his bombs on the target at 0115 hrs from 15,000ft and was almost immediately attacked by a night fighter. (See combat report at end of narrative for this raid.) All nine crews, including Sgt Winter, F/O O'Conner, F/Sgt Kyle, P/O Allson, and F/O Robertson, returned safely to Lakenheath.

One other crew was also on operations, having been ordered to fly a mining mission to the south west coast of France. This detail fell to F/O Barson, EF508 EX-G, and he successfully planted five mines in the allocated area. The aircraft was hit by light flak near the dropping zone and the bomb doors were slightly damaged, but the crew made it back to base. without any further problems. As stated, the main target for this night was Hanover and Bomber Command sent 504 aircraft to attack the city. PFF accurately marked the city centre and a very concentrated attack followed with considerable damage to buildings and services. The electricity and telephone systems were knocked out and a large number of water mains fractured. A total of 3,932 buildings were destroyed and 30,000 damaged. 1,200 people were killed and 3,345 injured. As many as 8,000 received eye injuries caused by the heat and smoke. The Continental rubber factory and Hanomag machine works were also hit and badly damaged.

This was the last time that the Wellington Bomber was used in a night time bombing raid on Germany, with 26 of this type used in the attack on Hanover coming from 300 (Polish) and 432 (Canadian) Squadrons.

Combat Report for F/Sgt Guthrie, EH995

Position; Target area. Time: 0115½. Course: 035 True. Height: 15,000ft. Speed: 190. Visibility good with 7/10 cloud underneath.

"Our aircraft was not coned in searchlights at the time of the attack, but the target area was well lit up. On the run up to the target our engineer (Sgt Duroe) sighted a Me109 from the astrodome. He immediately told the rear gunner (Sgt Morgan) who swung his turret round and sighted the enemy aircraft at 150 yards dead astern. The enemy aircraft fires a short burst at about 100 yards and missed. The fighter broke away up to port of our aircraft. As he broke away our rear gunner fired a burst of about 200 rounds but did not observe any hits. The Me109 was not seen again. A few minutes later our aircraft had a short attack from a Ju88 identified by the bomb aimer (P/O Perry) in the bombing panel. The Ju88 attacked from below our aircraft, fired a short burst and went on ahead to attack another Stirling in front of our aircraft. We were not hit in either attack. Our rear gunner was handicapped because he had a bad leak in the RSJ (Rotating Service Joint) and oil was all over the perspex of his turret".

From 9th to the 18th October only minor operations were conducted by Bomber Command, these mainly being nuisance raids by Mosquitoes to Berlin, Cologne and Dortmund with 199 Squadron being detailed for mining operations on the 17th. Some trials were carried out with a new navigation aid called G-H during this period which to all intents and purposes were successful. During this stand down an air sea rescue was conducted on the 10th October with Sgt Noble, EF138 EX-S, spending four hours on a search, but no results are recorded.

9th October to 16th October 1943

No operational flying possible due to dense fog, lasting all day in many cases. The ground crews carried out maintenance work putting this lull in activities to good use. Only a limited number of local test flights were possible. At some point in this period there was news that .5 machine guns were to be installed in the Stirling rear turrets, although as it later transpired, this did not take place. The aircrews did not like these long periods of inactivity; many felt the need to get on with the job in hand. The USAAF did mount some attacks and one important one to the ball bearing factory at Schweinfurt was mounted on 14th. This would go down in the annals of the American Air Force as "Black Thursday". A total of 291 aircraft were despatched and 60 were shot down, mainly by fighters. A further five crashed in England and twelve more had to be written off due to the severity of the damage inflicted on them. This was the greatest loss suffered by the USAAF so far in the war.

Squadron Armourers

17th October 1943

Two separate mining operations were carried out, with W/Cdr Bray, DFC, EF138 EX-S going to an area off the Frisian Islands having lifted off at 1810 hrs. Five mines were dropped and all the parachutes were seen to open. He landed back at base at 2115 hrs. The other mission was flown by F/O Barson, EF154 EX-V, who mined an area in the Bay of Biscay, picking up a pinpoint from the north tip of Lake Hourtin. This flight also required the crew to drop a load of 'nickels' over the coastal towns of France.

20th October 1943

Sgt Knowles, BF481 EX-W, detailed to mine an area 40km off the west Frisian Islands. This was successful with four chutes seen after release. Due to the lack of flying, it was thought that the Stirling was to be taken off long range operations into Germany (these rumours had in fact much substance to them).

21st October 1943

Two aircraft detailed for an air sea rescue mission. F/Sgt Chappell and F/Sgt Kyle completed this search, but there are no details in the ORB if it was successful. F/Sgt Chappell did have problems at the very end of the search when all the engines cut out. Some quick checks by the flight engineer, Sgt Oxley made him realise he had forgotten to switch over the petrol tanks. Crew comments are unprintable!

22nd October 1943

Sgt Noble, EE943 EX-X, on a solo mission to sow mines off the Frisian Islands. Five mines released and all deployed.

24th October 1943

Again, only one crew was required for a mining trip to the Kattegat, but this time Sgt Knowles, EF154 EX-V, was forced to abandon the mission when the 'Gee' set failed. All the mines were brought back to base.

25th October 1943

Two crews detailed for mining in the Kattegat. W/Cdr 'Nan' Bray, the Squadron Commander, EE910 EX-E, and Sgt Noble, EE943 EX-X, both reached their allotted positions and sowed a total of ten mines. Both aircraft landed 2322 hrs at RAF Lossiemouth.

The Squadron carried out no further operations until the beginning of November, mainly due to dense fog over Norfolk. At around this time, a request went out to all aircrew on the Squadron for volunteers to join a special force know as "Airborne Cigar" This unit was to be equipped with jamming equipment fitted in modified B-17 Flying Fortress and used to disrupt the German R/T channels controlling their fighter aircraft. Some aircrew did, in fact, volunteer, but nothing more was heard from the Air Ministry about the posting.

November
The Battle of Berlin commences – fundamental changes ordered for the Stirling

3rd November 1943

F/O Button and Sgt Bennett carried out a mining operation to the Frisian Islands, which was successful and uneventful.

4th November 1943

Two crews detailed for mining the Kattegat off the coast of Denmark. Sgt Catterall dropped his mines in the target area and reported seeing three chutes open satisfactorily and then went on to drop one package, but there are no specific details as to what the package contained, nor where it was dropped. The other Stirling, EF453 EX-F, piloted by P/O Moore, failed to return from this mission and was lost without trace. EF453 Crew: P/O Donald Francis Moore, Pilot, RAAF, age 26, married to Patricia Moore of Double Bay, New South Wales, Australia; Sgt Victor Jack Southgate, F/Eng, RAFVR, age 21, from Bury St Edmunds, Suffolk; F/O Douglas Clement Welch, Nav, RAFVR, age 20, from Musbury, Devon; Sgt Walter Jones, B/A, RAFVR, age 20, from Conisbrough, Yorkshire; Sgt Arthur Richmond, W/Op, RAFVR, age 20, from Bowling, Yorkshire; F/Sgt Douglas Menere, M/U, RAAF, age 20, remembered on Runnymede Memorial, panel 193; F/Sgt Peter Watson, R/G, RCAF. All are remembered on Runnymede Memorial.

F/Sgt Moore had his promotion to pilot officer promulgated just before he was killed, but it had not been recorded in the ORB.

11th November 1943

Four crews were detailed for mine laying to the mouth of the River Gironde on the west coast of France. Technical problems forced one aircraft off the mission. The remaining three Stirlings flown by F/Sgt Knowles, EE957 EX-Q, Sgt Bennett, EF154 EX-V and Sgt Turner, BK762 EX-C reached the target areas and dropped their mines. Sgt Turner reported after the operation that the rear turret of his aircraft went u/s, as did the D/R compass, but he completed his mission successfully.

14th November 1943

F/O Eddy, EH995 EX-L, took off at 0835 hrs for an air sea rescue search. There are no details as to the outcome of the search and he landed back at base at 1245 hrs.

15th November 1943

Another air sea rescue, and F/O Button, EF450 EX-N, took off at 0950 hrs returning at 1405 hrs. Nothing was reported, so it must be assumed there were no sightings of a dinghy in the sea.

16th November 1943

Two awards were made to members of 199 Squadron. P/O Stan Freestone was awarded the DFC and S/Ldr Ken Humby the DSO.

The Battle of Berlin

18th November 1943

This night marked the beginning of the main effort against the German capital. The attack called for two separate raids, one to Berlin, consisting of 440 aircraft and the second to Mannheim, with 395 aircraft. 199 Squadron was detailed for the Mannheim raid and prepared thirteen Stirlings, but mechanical and electrical problems with four aircraft meant they were withdrawn from operations. Of the nine Stirlings that did take off between 1715 hrs and 1745 hrs, it soon became apparent to the crews that the weather was a cause for concern.

F/Sgt Noble had taken off at 1730 hrs, and was in trouble an hour later as he reported: *"Coring* on three engines and the starboard outer had to be feathered due to a fall in oil pressure. Experienced coring at 15,000ft and severe icing in cloud tops at 12,000ft. Losing height and mission abandoned at 1830 hrs. Bombs jettisoned in the sea"*.

P/O Humphries, EE957 EX-Q, also had problems when the crew reported an oxygen leak that could not be traced and repaired. The operation was abandoned and the bombs jettisoned in the sea to bring the all up weight to the required landing requirements.

One other aircraft was forced to return early, that of P/O Barson EF192 EX-J. The aircraft had started to cross Belgium, when his flight engineer, Sgt Wild, found that the starboard outer oil pressure dropping. The pilot stated later: *"Coring was experienced in all engines as the aircraft crossed the English Channel and the S/O oil pressure continued to drop and it was decided to abandon the mission at 5026N 0443E (east of Charleroi, Belgium). It was also impossible to feather the engine, so the bombs were jettisoned and returned to base"*.

Over the target, P/O Chappell, EE910 EX-K, was forced to deviate from his planned bomb run when the port outer engine failed and the bomb aimer, F/Sgt Higgins, released the load to the left of the green TIs. The engine was feathered and the crew returned on three engines. He stated that no red spot markers were seen over the target and a large explosion was observed by the crew SW of the green TIs. F/Sgt Kyle, W/O Barnard, P/O Guthrie, F/Sgt Knowles and P/O Robertson also reached Mannheim, but most had problems to deal with as they ran into, or away from, the target. A compass error meant F/Sgt Knowles was north of his intended track as he approached the target, but was still able to get his load away.

P/O Robertson, EF455 EX-B, said in his de-brief: *"Weather clear, target identified by bend in river. Small concentration of green TIs seen with many yellow markers among them. Concentration of green TIs was very poor and yellow TIs at same spot not understood. [These could have been route markers mistakenly dropped over the target. Ed.]. Some yellow route markers at last turning point before 'D'. No red spot flares seen. Starboard outer gave out over 'A' and was feathered on circuit 12 miles north of Nach coming home"*.

---

*Coring was the result of excessive cooliing of the engine lubricating oil as it passed through the radiator causing the oil to congeal leading to overheating.

Wilf Humphries and crew with EE957 EX-Q.

P/O Guthrie, EE953 EX-E, reached Mannheim at 2023 hrs and, at 2039 hrs, the bomb aimer, F/O Perry, dropped his bombs on a cluster of green TIs from 16,500ft. He stated: *"I saw the 2,000lb bomb burst to the right of the greens and there were scattered fires in that area"*. The crew also saw yellow route markers at the last turning point before reaching Mannheim. On the return journey they saw two large explosions in the target area, one at 60 miles at 2107 hrs and the second at 2125 hrs. Landed at base at 2345 hrs.

W/O Barnard, EE943 EX-X, lifted off from RAF Lakenheath at 1730 hrs and reached Mannheim at 2025 hrs. Approaching the city, the target area was identified by a bend in the river and F/Sgt Kirkbright dropped the bomb load at 2031 hrs from 13,500ft. He reported later: *"The 2,000lb bomb burst north of the railway marshalling yards to the south of the actual target area"*. 34 x 30lb incendiaries hung up and were brought back to base.

It appears that at least four of the nine Stirlings flew all or part of the return journey on three engines and almost all the crews were at one time or another having to deal with some form of setback.

From some accounts it would appear that all the aircraft on this raid were subjected to a great many searchlights and flak all the way in from Frankfurt to Mannheim. The raid in general was scattered over a wide area with most of the damage caused in the north of the city. The Daimler-Benz factory was severely damaged and 325 other buildings totally destroyed with a further 335 seriously damaged. The scattered bombing around the perimeter of Mannheim caused much damage to farms. Of 884 aircraft sent to Berlin and Mannheim (a new record of sorties flown) 32 were lost.

19th November 1943

A raid on Leverkusen, north of Cologne, was planned but bad weather over England and Germany, plus 'Oboe' equipment failures in several of the PFF Mosquitoes, hampered the attack to the extent that it was deemed a failure. The Squadron Operational Record Book states that eleven Stirlings were placed on the battle order and that nine took part in the raid, however, subsequent research by Bryce Gomersall (*The Stirling File*) shows that in fact ten aircraft took off from Lakenheath and the sortie flown by F/Sgt Winter EF154 EX-V has been completely omitted from the ORB.

Take-off from RAF Lakenheath started at 1658 hrs, but it was not long before the gremlins, once again, started to show up, with a complete oxygen failure in W/O Barnard's Stirling, EF505 EX-R. He aborted the mission at 1810 hrs, jettisoned his fuel load, and returned to base, landing at 1850 hrs.

Next to turn back early was P/O Humphries, DFC, EE957 EX-Q, who had F/O Craw, with him as 2nd pilot. They had lifted off at 1705 hrs, but an hour and a half later, the pilot's and the D/R compasses went u/s and the decision was made to abandon the mission at 5150N 0400E. P/O Humphries reported *"The pilot's and D/R compass went u/s at 1828 hrs, and, as we flew over the tip of Overflakkee Island, we were very hotly engaged by accurate flak. Fired off colours of the day at Southwold at 1918 hrs flying at 2,000ft – best route to base. Landed at 2000 hrs"*.

The first crew over the target, at 1918 hrs, was F/Sgt Kyl, EJ115 EX-H, who had difficulty identifying the target due to 10/10ths cloud. His report states: *"Two greens seen behind, so turned and bombed on new cluster of greens, clouds lit up by search lights and plenty of flak bursts. Our aircraft hit by flak. Route to target as ordered, then returned Zeebrugge, Beachy Head, landed Thorney Island. Aircraft u/s owing to damage by flak and trouble with two outer engines."*

F/O Robertson, with F/O Button as 2nd pilot, EE953 EX-E, commented after the raid: *"We bombed on the green TIs cascading through the clouds. Heavy flak over the target. PFF was late. Diverted to Tangmere and then to Ford due to weather"*.

P/O Allson, with F/Sgt Turner as 2nd pilot, EF153 EX-D, who took off at 1656 hrs, recorded: *"A poor show, PFF markers very scattered. No reds seen and camera may have been u/s"*.

An interesting inclusion in his report are some map references noted by the navigator Sgt Sanderson, which gives a route away from the target and pin points on the way home. It shows the aircraft flew away from Leverkusen eastwards to avoid Cologne out to a small town called Thien, then turned south and west to pass between Cologne and Frankfurt to cross the river Rhine at a point near Rheinbrohl. If any aircraft was forced to fly out northwards it would have brought them over the most heavily defended areas of Dusseldorf, Essen and Duisburg. The route taken brought them over Belgium and over the coast at Bergen-op-Zoom and Vlissinggen (Zeeland). The final pinpoint given, put them about 55kms from the English coast, heading for Clacton-on-Sea and base, landing at 2220 hrs.

F/Sgt Knowles, LK381 EX-Z, arrived over the target at 1922 hrs carrying a typical bomb load for this particular operation of 1 x 2000lb, 1x 1,000lb, 10 x 4lb inc and 5 x 30lb inc. Due to the cloud, he bombed on an approximate position of the markers. This crew landed at RAF Ford at 2235 hrs with the rear turret, radio transmitter and navigation lights all unserviceable.

One pilot, P/O Guthrie, managed to coax his aircraft, BK762 EX-C, up to 17,000ft for his attack and reached the target at 1929 hrs having had no problems on the outward journey. However, things soon changed and in his de-brief report stated: *"PFF late and TIs scattered. Aircraft damaged by flak and the throttle controls became disconnected during flight, at cruising boost engines failed to cut out when switches were thrown. Return route home Ostend, Ramsgate, Ford and while landing at Ford, swung the aircraft to port to avoid obstacles and undercarriage collapsed. The bomb aimer, F/O Perry, cut port engine switches first and then starboard to assist swing"*. This Stirling was eventually repaired but never flew operationally again.

As can be seen, the German flak was intense over the target and F/Sgt Dodsworth, EE948 EX-T, was only a short distance from his aiming point when he too was hit. *"Two minutes from the primary target at 15,000ft noted pale green TIs six or seven miles to port and at same time we were hit by flak. Inter-com and all three turrets put out of action. Fire broke out near the flare chute, probably oil from the damaged feed to the rear turret. Bombs jettisoned immediately by Sgt Edwards. The Flight Engineer Sgt Carr was wounded, but carried on with his duties. Fire broke out again, but was quickly extinguished by the wireless operator Sgt French and the mid upper gunner Sgt Brooks. Diversion signal received and aircraft crashed on landing at Ford, due to tyre being punctured by flak, but it did not catch fire"*.

The raid was a complete failure and Leverkusen records only one high explosive bomb falling on the town. It appears that there were many small towns around the primary target that received a load due to the complete cloud cover and inaccurate marking. But, because of the bad weather, it kept most of the German night fighters grounded and there were much smaller losses to Main Force, with five aircraft lost from a total of 266 detailed for the raid.

As a consequence of his actions during this raid, F/Sgt William Walter Dodsworth, RAAF, was awarded the DFM and was promulgated in the *London Gazette* 17th December 1943.

22nd November 1943

The target of the night's raid was Berlin, and the last raid that Bomber Command would use Stirlings to bomb targets in Germany, although some squadrons were occasionally detailed for targets in France and the Low Countries. The operation was only partially successful for '199' because, of the five aircraft ordered, one was withdrawn before take-off and the remaining four all had serious problems on the mission.

After taking off at 1710 hrs, W/O Barnard and P/O Chilcott, flying EF138 EX-S, were forced to turn back at 1816 hrs when Flight Engineer Sgt Rawlings was taken ill, and landed at 1910 hrs.

Shortly afterwards, F/O Allson, with F/O Eddy as second pilot, EE957 EX-Q, who had taken off at 1708 hrs, was plagued with engine trouble and a partial failure of the oxygen system, and aborted the mission at 1837 hrs. The bombs were jettisoned in the North Sea and he was back at base at 1956 hrs.

The remaining two crews – F/Sgt Noble and P/O Lumsdain reached the target area over Berlin, but neither was able to bomb the aiming point accurately.

F/Sgt Noble reported in his de-brief that: *"We identified the target by red TIs seen going down 30 miles from the aiming point and saw reds bursting into greens at 2016 hrs. Another red burst to port at 2018 hrs. No route markers seen. As we settled into the bombing run TIs were bursting around the aircraft so decided to dive sharply to avoid them"*.

In his report, P/O Lumsdaine, EJ111 EX-P, also said that there were no route markers on the way in to the target. He said after the raid: *"There was 10/10ths cloud cover in stratus layer over the target, which was identified by sky markers. The bomb aimer, Sgt Ward, centred the bombsight on three cascading sky markers and also observed that other TIs formed three points of a triangle, which were accurately backed up. On the point of bombing it was found that the bomb panel was u/s through freezing, so we jettisoned the load".*

This was a very disappointing result in view of the fact that this was to be the last bombing mission using the Stirling; the only positive result was that no crews were lost.

Fate was to deal another blow, next morning, when the returned aircraft were checked. That flown by P/O Lumsdaine, EJ111 EX-P, had problems with its bomb release panel and the armourers had to check the systems.

One of the ground staff, Sgt Norman Timms (Timmo), was checking for bomb hang-ups. This was quite common with 2lb incendiary loads. The procedure was to open the bomb doors slowly to about an inch gap allowing the silver coloured incendiaries straddling the doors to be seen. The next stage was to erect steps under the bomb doors and climb up so that as the doors opened, the small bombs could be grasped and removed safely.

Sgt Ross Clark takes up the story: *"On the morning of the 23rd November 1943 we were cycling to the mess for breakfast and noticed a pall of smoke above the dispersal area and jokingly remarked that Timmo must have set an aircraft on fire. Later on arrival at dispersal this exact joke had materialised. When the bomb doors were being opened and just as Timmo was about to get hold of the incendiary it slid back and fell to the ground. Normally this would not be a problem but this particular bomb was one of about four packed in each container that held explosive pellets. The incendiary went off and set fire to the Stirling that resulted in the complete nose end being burnt off back to the wing leading edge, it certainly looked an ugly duckling. Fortunately Sgt Timms was only slightly burned and he had his head bandaged for about three days and it was the usual topic of our conversation when we met again overseas – on two different tours and again when I was at Coltishall and he at Swanton Morley, we met by chance in Norwich. For the record I served with (1). 214 Squadron, Wellingtons, Stradishall. (2). 7 Squadron, Stirlings, Oakington. (3). 199 Squadron, Wellingtons at Blyton and Ingham and Stirlings at Lakenheath and moved to North Creake on Stirlings and Halifaxes".*

It was not uncommon for Stirling crews to experience bombs and target indicators falling close by or even onto their aircraft, sometimes with fatal results. Due to its poor maximum ceiling, many aircraft returned with incendiary bombs, dropped by high altitude Lancasters and Halifaxes, protruding from wings and fuselage and some of these actually caused fires that were difficult to deal with. Larger high explosive bombs that fell onto a Stirling usually meant catastrophic damage from which there was no hope of recovery. In a few rare instances the rear turret of the Stirling was shorn off completely by a 500lb or larger bomb and the aircraft was able to make it back to base minus the unfortunate gunner but, in the main, a direct hit like this was usually the end of aircraft and crew.

The Stirling squadrons were now to see a fundamental change in their operating brief; some would adopt an almost exclusive minelaying role, whilst other aircraft were modified to tow gliders or drop paratroops and were re-located to specialised units.

23rd November 1943

F/Sgt Kyle and Sgt Bennett conducted an air sea rescue search from 0835 hrs to 1330 hrs; but there is no report of anything being seen. Nine aircrew, including the bombing leader, visited 467 Squadron, giving some credence to rumours that '199' were to convert to Lancasters. They were given some flying time and all were very impressed with the Lancaster's capabilities. Speculation and rumour were rife as to the timing of the changeover, with 20th January being hedged as a safe bet. But as time would tell, the conversion never took place.

24th November 1943

Another air sea search by W/O Barnard and F/Sgt Catterall, but again nothing was found.

25th November 1943

Three aircraft and crews were detailed for a mining operation to the south west coast of France. Bad weather and mechanical problems again had a significant part to play in this mission. F/Sgt Sturrock, EE910 EX-K, had the starboard inner fail, having reached a point at 13 miles NNE of the Cherbourg Peninsular. He jettisoned the mines and returned to base on three engines. F/O Button reported 10/10ths cloud and he also jettisoned his mines and returned to RAF Lakenheath. F/O Eddy, EF508 EX-G, reached his target area and dropped six mines, using a pinpoint at 4626N 0047W, but owing to the poor weather conditions no parachutes were seen to open.

"A" Flight crew, Lakenheath, 1943.

Front row, left to right: F/O G. Wilde, Nav; F/Lt H. Sturrock, Pilot; P/O R. Stokes, M/U. *Back row, left to right*: Sgt A. Howe, F/Eng; F/Sgt W. Matthews, B/A; F/Sgt H. Fitchett, W/Op; Sgt L. Perkins, R/G.

26th November 1943

Mining operation ordered for the Frisian Islands and three aircraft and crews were detailed. One of the aircraft developed technical problems and was removed from the mission. Low cloud was again a problem, with the base sometimes down to 2,000ft.

F/O Eddy, EF508 EX-G, reached his target area and dropped six mines from 1,200ft. Due to the poor conditions no chutes were observed. The other crew, with F/Sgt Sturrock at the controls, had a lucky escape soon after crossing the coast. He reported: *"About 15 miles from the English Coast we spotted four aircraft testing their guns over the sea. Tracer passed above from an aircraft at aprox 5255N 0155E at 1745 hrs at 1,000ft"*. He laid the six mines as ordered, with all the parachutes seen to open and the crew returned to base, none the worse for their encounter.

28th November 1943

Two crews detailed for mining in the Le Havre area.

Sgt Bennett, LK381 EX-Z, successfully dropped 6 x 1,500lb mines in the target area. Soon after the mines were released the DR compass went u/s. The aircraft flew around the Le Havre and Seine Estuary area for ten minutes before the navigator F/Sgt Thorneycroft was able to get a visual sighting of the Pole Star and set course for home using the P4 compass.

F/O Chilcott, EF505 EX-R, released five of the six mines carried and was forced to bring one back due to a technical fault on No 4 station. He claimed a successful trip.

30th November 1943

On this last operation of the month, three aircraft and crews were detailed to mine waters off the west coast of France. The technical problems, that always seemed to be present during the daily checks, prevented one of the aircraft from taking off. The remaining two, flown by F/O Chilcott and F/Sgt Turner, flew a successful mission, dropping a total of twelve mines using Lake Hourtin as a pinpoint.

December 1943

The Squadron loses 'Mr Cool' – world record for lowering a Stirling undercarriage by hand

1st December 1943

The beginning of a new month and another mining operation was ordered to the 'Silverthorn 10' area of the Kattegat, off the east coast of the very top of Jutland. Five Stirlings and crews were detailed for the long haul, but technical faults put two of them out of commission and only three took off at 1523 hrs carrying six mines each.

F/O Eddy, EF508 EX-G, reached the general dropping area, but was prevented from completing his mission due to the weather. His report stated: *"We were unable to pinpoint in mining area due to 10/10ths cloud cover, tops at 8,000 down to a base of 1,500ft. West coast of Denmark identified on route in and we were seven miles off track owing to increase in cloud to 10/10. Approaching the garden area it was found impossible to pinpoint and the primary mining was abandoned owing to loss of time in searching for pinpoints. It was impossible to get accurate DR. Course was set for base, route as given, all the mines were brought back".*

The crew landed back at RAF Lakenheath at 2327 hrs.

Only one other crew reached the mining area, that of F/O Button, EF153 EX-D. He also reported 10/10ths cloud, but dropped the mines from 2,000ft – no parachutes were observed. One mine hung up, possibly due to icing, and was brought back to base.

In the crew's de-brief, they claimed to have seen a Stirling shot down at 5607N 0815E by heavy flak, timed at 1752 hrs. They estimated the height of the Stirling when it was hit as 10,000ft. From papers received from my friend and fellow researcher Ole Kraul, who lives in Denmark, I have been able to confirm that the Stirling shot down was EF191 WP-H of 90 Squadron. It crashed at Hemmet near the south shore of Ringkøbing Fjord on the west coast of Jutland. All the crew were killed and are buried in Esbjerg Cemetery. Times and map references given from Denmark all agree with those given by F/O Button.

The third Stirling despatched by 199 Squadron, EF154 EX-V flown by F/Sgt Knowles was also shot down. It was hit by flak at 2000 hrs and came down, according to Danish sources, at 5730N 1035E, near the tiny island of Hirsholmene, three miles NE of Frederikshavn; and on the border of the 'Silverthorn 10' and 'Yewtree' mining areas. All the crew were killed, but sadly only three bodies, those of F/Sgt Knowles, Sgt Robotham and 2nd Lt

Carlson, USAAF, were recovered and were buried in Frederikshavn Cemetery. EF154 Crew: F/Sgt Jon Alfred Knowles, Pilot, RAF, age 23, from Guildford, Surrey; 2nd Lt Carl Carlson, Navigator, USAAF, initially buried in Frederikshavn Cemetery, but subsequently exhumed and reburied in the U.S. Military Cemetery, Neuville-en-Condroz, Belgium (Note: Because it was unusual for an American to be serving in the RAF, I took some time to investigate the background to 2nd Lt Carlson's involvement with the Squadron. He initially joined the Royal Canadian Air Force as a way of entering the war and was given the rank of sergeant. When the Americans entered the conflict, most of their people who had joined other forces were, over a period of time, re-absorbed back into their own fighting units, be it airforce, navy or army. However, Carl Carlson had other ideas when he was finally tracked down and given the rank of 2nd Lieutenant, he avoided his own people, determined to stay with the RAF.); Sgt Frederick William Barrie, F/Eng, RAFVR, age 22, from Colney, Norfolk; Sgt Charles Stanley Stockwell, B/A, RAFVR, age 27, from Twickenham, Middlesex; F/Sgt Gordon Strachan Cunningham, W/Op, RAFVR; Sgt Harry Victor Dawe, M/U, RAFVR, are all remembered on the Runnymede Memorial; Sgt Kenneth James Robotham, R/G, RAFVR, buried in Frederikshavn Cemetery.

The funeral of the three crew members was conducted by the Rev Bender, but without the usual German turn out of band and guard of honour. This procedure had been discontinued on orders from Berlin after the firestorm raids over Germany, especially that on Hamburg during August 1943. However the German naval chaplain, Rev Bender, would quietly turn up, more or less secretly, to perform the Christian internment, whenever more than one Allied airman was buried. The Danish undertaker, Harding Qvesehl, provided a Union Jack to decorate the edge of the grave and for which he charged the Germans a rent. As the Germans no longer participated in any funeral proceedings, the coffins were placed in the grave by people employed by the cemetery which was left open for half an hour while other local Danes paid their respects and laid flowers on the coffins. Since August the German authorities had tried to keep all local people away from any burial service as they said it was a demonstration in favour of the enemy – which of course it was. The Danes were adamant that they would pay all due respect to anyone killed and buried in their country and dozens of cases of confrontation took place between them and the Germans when they were not permitted to attend a burial of an Allied serviceman.

His pilot, F/O Geoff Archer, has written an epitaph: *"To start with, 'Carl' can only be called by our general name for him and that is "Mr Cool". Never did I find him anything but cool calm and collected, doing his navigating job to perfection, and always getting us there and back without a problem.*

However, I jump the gun. To be perfectly honest, I cannot recall when and how Carl found our crew. I went through 28 OTU at Wymswold, near Loughborough, and since we all crewed up at OTU, I can only presume Carl joined us there. He was at that time a sergeant with Canada flashes up, that I can recall, and he also wore his side cap in the most ghastly American way, he was never the epitome of satirical elegance. Sadly I cannot remember any outings with him, but we must have shared the odd pot of beer together – some time some place.

He was a very quiet and private person and not given to discussing his life and fortunes. I can recall him saying that for some reason or the other he wanted to 'get with the war' when hostilities first broke out, and as the USA had not then experienced their "Day of Infamy" the Royal Canadian Air Force was the only way. The Canadian Navigator Schools then operating may have some record of him passing through.

I'm not sure of the exact moment in time when he became a 2nd Lieutenant, it could have been when the USAAF first arrived in the UK, but I think he commenced Ops with us as a Sergeant RCAF. I can remember when he did get his commission he took his hat and dumped it in the bath – bashed it around a bit and then sat it on the bedside lamp to dry. The net result was a 'real' operational hat.

In spite of the fact that he now resided in the officers' mess, I still cannot recall any great association with him. I have read through my diary for 1943, but notice that most of it was devoted to time spent with my fiancée in Leicester, with whom I apparently spent a lot of time. Incidentally we parted company (she and I – not Carl) soon after my epic vertical take-off as previously mentioned. Throughout the whole time at Ingham my diary doesn't mention any sorties with Carl at all, alas – oh for a decent memory.

Regarding his navigation, as I have said, he was the master of his craft. I can remember returning from an Op and, low on fuel, saying 'how long to base Carl? – I think we should divert as we are low on fuel'. He would reply with his American drawl 'no, no skipper, keep on course, only a few miles to go, and we'll make it ok, keep on this heading.' And we always made it, usually with the gauges showing almost zero. When we got 'Gee' he'd repeat the dose, but do a 'Gee' course right back to the runway end and once he remarked 'keep on skipper, I'll take you to the end of the runway with this thing', and he did. On another occasion, I think it may have been after we had been coned over Essen, when our subsequent aerobatics got us 'orribly lost en-route home. Most of the navigation gear had been shaken round in the Wellington and Carl had a job restarting everything from scratch. We eventually ended up crossing the coast 'somewhere over Europe'. Not to be perturbed, Carl took out the sextant and Mr Cool shoots a few stars, dives into his office and comes up with a course to steer for home.

I have alas no more memories of him during operational trips, probably because he just sat there at his nav table doing his job quietly and efficiently – no fuss and consequently unnoticed.

I can recall from the back of my mind talking to him at some stage, probably trying to form some picture, and he mentioned something about having some estate or property in Italy. What it was I don't know. Maybe a family thing pre-war, but the idea sticks. He also had scant regard for authority, after he obtained his commission he really went for the warrant officer (Dicip), who had continually harassed him as an NCO for his complete lack of dress sense. I also heard, through the post op grapevine, that he had got into a lot of trouble through slugging some senior USAAF officer because he didn't agree with something he said. This could be only a rumour, but was like Carl, a real sleeping dragon, cool most of the time but hell when aroused.

I must say, he was a 100% good guy and friend, and an asset to any crew and a great pity he was killed after completing 27 operations with the Squadron."

Another of 2nd Lt Carlson's pilots, F/Sgt Tom Austin with whom he flew four operations, also remembers Carlson as an extremely efficient navigator, unperturbed by any crisis. He also commented on his total disregard for regulation dress and always being in hot water for his attitude to discipline. From conversations with F/Sgt Austin, he confirms the stories of Carlson disappearing whenever any American personnel appeared at Lakenheath, such was his determination to remain with 199 Squadron to the end of his tour.

2nd December 1943

Two crews were detailed for mining operations, but these were subsequently cancelled.

4th December 1943

A mining operation to the Frisian Islands was ordered and four aircraft and crew were detailed for the mission. One aircraft was unserviceable, but the remaining three took off at 2305 hrs. F/Sgt Harrison, EJ115 EX-H, F/Sgt Turner, LK385 EX-A and F/O Craw LK397 EX-P successfully completed their tasks and landed back at Lakenheath by 0310 hrs.

11th and 14th December 1943

Two mining operations ordered, but both cancelled.

15th December 1943

An air sea rescue sortie was undertaken by F/O Craw, EF505 EX-R and Sgt Cutler, EF138 EX-S. Sgt Cutler completed his search, but reported not seeing anything. Sgt Craw was forced to abort his mission when, shortly after taking off, all the electrical circuits went dead.

16th December 1943

The target selected for this night's raid was the flying bomb (V1) site at Abbeville in France. Initially, ten Stirlings and crews were placed on the Battle Order but, due to many technical factors, only four aircraft were cleared to fly. Later in the day one of the crews was ordered to take part in a mining operation off the south west coast of France leaving three crews for the Abbeville mission.

The raid undertaken by the '199' aircraft was centred on the Tilley-le-Haut site and W/Cdr Bray, LK385 EX-A dropped his bombs on a group of six red TIs, noting that the greens were two to three miles east of the reds. His bombs burst close to the red TIs and more reds were observed falling on the site of earlier markers. F/O Chilcott, EE957 EX-Q also bombed on the red TIs, observing several white flashes on the ground. Sgt Bennett was on the outward leg of the mission when the port inner engine failed and, shortly after that, both starboard engines cut out but quickly recovered. The bombs were jettisoned into the sea, but as this was being carried out, the majority of the electrical equipment failed. Seriously burdened by all the problems, the crew eventually managed to set course for base, but were forced to land at RAF Tempsford as their fuel was running dangerously low.

The raid on Abbeville was not a success overall. The 'Oboe' Mosquitoes markers could not get close to such a small target and most of the bombs fell wide of the mark.

20th December 1943

Five crews, comprising Sgt Clifton, F/Sgt Robinson, Sgt Cutler, F/O Craw and Sgt Derbyshire, were detailed for mining ops off the Frisian Islands. F/O Craw had one mine hang up and, shortly after dropping the remaining load, was fired on by medium flak guns from flak ships, with the shells bursting above and below the aircraft. No damage was reported. Sgt Derbyshire had navigational problems and aborted the mission when it became clear that their true position was uncertain. All the mines were brought back to base.

22nd December 1943

The target for this night, was again, flying bomb sites around the Abbeville and Amiens area and eleven aircraft were detailed for the attack. This was the largest number of crews ordered for a raid for some time and, to everyone's credit, all the aircraft were checked out, bombed up and fuelled ready for take-off with no withdrawals. A slight deviation to the plan was ordered and two of the aircraft were assigned to go mining in the Bay of Biscay, the remaining nine took off for Abbeville as planned.

F/O Craw, with Sgt Johnson as 2nd pilot, took off at 2107 hrs but at 2125 hrs, the starboard engine caught fire. This was extinguished, but the engine was now u/s and height could not be maintained. The mission was aborted and the bomb load dropped safe at Rushford before landing at 2210 hrs. Sgt Bennett arrived over the target and, seeing no markers, did an extra orbit before bombing. F/O Chappell likewise flew two extra orbits as he too was early and then had one 500lb bomb hang up, but otherwise completed his sortie with no other problems. The remaining crews F/Lt O'Conner, F/Sgt Derbyshire, F/O Chillcott, F/Sgt Turner, F/O Eddy and F/Sgt Harrison all bombed accurately and returned to base.

The Stirlings flown by Sgt Cutler and Sgt Clifton assigned for the mining operation both reached their pinpoints and dropped their loads in good visibility. The bombing panel in Sgt Clifton's aircraft was found to be u/s so the mines were delivered using the jettison switch.

29th December 1943

The poor weather conditions on this day were responsible for the failure of the mining operations ordered for the five crews detailed. Four crews were allocated target pinpoints off the west coast of France and one crew off the Frisian Islands.

F/Sgt Harrison, EE953 EX-E, returned with all his mines, after encountering 8/10 cloud and finding it impossible to pinpoint the dropping zone. F/Sgt Robinson and F/Sgt Derbyshire found 9/10 cloud and ground haze over the French coast and aborted their missions. Engine problems forced P/O Noble, EE957 EX-Q to return early when the port inner failed completely and the other three engines were overheating. He could not maintain height, so jettisoned fuel south of Selsey Bill and after reaching the 30 mile limit off the English coast all the mines were dropped safely into the sea. Due to lack of fuel he put down at RAF Dunsfold at 1945 hrs.

The navigator, P/O Roy Smith remembers this incident and later recorded what happened: *"We were flying out on track for Selsey but, prior to reaching the coast, we lost an engine and one of the remaining three was not functioning too well. Our pilot decided that the only chance of getting back was to continue on to clear the coast, drop the mines (I think they could be dropped safe) and let as much fuel go, just saving enough to get back to base. We did this, but having done so we were still losing height and there was no chance of getting back to Lakenheath. It was decided that we would try and get in at Dunsfold, between Horsham and Haslemere.*

As we approached the runway, there appeared to be a large black cloud about a mile before the beginning of the runway. Allen Noble was not sure if he could get over the top or whether he should try and get underneath, but height was precious and a decision was made to go over the top. This decision was supported by the fact that the electrics which controlled the undercarriage were dependent on the generator powered by the engine that had failed and the undercarriage had to be wound down by hand. Each side had to be fitted with a cranked handle and four of us – two each side – had to wind at maximum speed changing over with our partner every 30 to 60 seconds. The official time to complete the operation was 5½ minutes – I don't think we took longer than three minutes. We just managed to lock each undercarriage in the down position two or three seconds before the wheels touched the runway. What a relief, but not such a big relief as we experienced after getting out and looking back to see that we had not skimmed the top of a black cloud but a forest of tall trees.

We celebrated our good fortune by going to Brighton, having a good night out, sleeping on the floor of Chess Chessell, our rear gunner's house and returning to Dunsfold the next morning.

After the war, I was on a ramblers group walk about 1995 when we took a path along the crest of that same hill overlooking Dunsfold runway. The trees were still there and I remembered what a near miss we had experienced in 1943. I took Allen Noble, my pilot, back there in 1997 and we both relived this incident before going off to the pub and once again celebrating our very narrow escape".

The single aircraft detailed for the Frisians was flown by F/Lt Betts, but he too was unable to complete his mission. When approaching the eastern area of the target all the navigational aids failed and he aborted. He reported that the failure of the navigation equipment was due to 'jamming'. It's unclear if the jamming was of a German or British source. Two mines were jettisoned and two brought back to base.

30 December 1943

The final operation for 1943 fell to F/Lt Betts, EF138 EX-S, who was detailed to lay six mines off the south west coast of France. He encountered 8/10 strato-cumulus cloud on the outbound trip, but found the pinpoint clear and in good visibility, sowed all six mines and recorded a successful operation.

Right: Sgt H. "Chess" Chessell, Rear Gunner.

Attached to the rear of the Stirling under the turrett is an aerial known as 'Monica'. This was developed to warn the crew of an approaching German night fighter by giving off audible beeps, However, the Germans soon used the Monica transmissions to their advantage by homing in on them. Many bombers were lost through using this equipment.

1944

Transfer from Bomber Command operations to 100 Group Bomber Support –
a new role for the Squadron – RAF North Creake, Norfolk

January
A reminder not to fly over London's AA defences –
V1 sites 'visited' – farewell to 'Killer Dodsworth'

2nd January 1944

The new year started as the old one had finished with mining operations. F/O Craw was detailed to mine an area off the south west coast of France and, although he encountered 10/10 cloud, he found the base at 3,500ft and, keeping below this, in clear visibility, sowed six mines on the allotted pinpoint. Sgt Bowering, EE910 EX-Q, was assigned an area off the Frisians which he reached successfully. He reported: *"the bomb aimer found that there was a technical problem with the release mechanism and the mines would not drop. Later he tried to jettison the load, but this also failed and the mines were brought back to base".*

4th January 1944

The flying bomb sites in France were still high on Bomber Command's agenda and would receive its attention on several occasions during the month of January. Eight aircraft were prepared for this raid, with one being scrubbed early in the morning due to mechanical problems. The remaining seven took off in the afternoon and bombed targets around the Abbeville area. The marking was reported as being very concentrated, with many red spot fires, although some green markers were also used. Large numbers of bombs were seen bursting on and around the ground markers with P/O Sturrock, LK385 EX-A, counting sixteen bombs bursting on the target. Most crews bombed from between 9,000 and 10,000ft and encountered little ground opposition. The attack was compressed to a matter of minutes, once more, demonstrating the excellent airmanship of everyone taking part. The post raid report stated that the raid had been most effective.

6th January 1944

The mining operations for the night were for three areas. F/Sgt Cattell, EF153 EX-D and Sgt Bladon, EE943 EX-X were assigned to pinpoints just off the coast adjacent to Amsterdam, in a shallow lake known as the Markermeer.

F/Sgt Cattell returned to base with one of the mines hung up, although the bombing panel indicated that the complete load of six mines had dropped. Hang-ups were an armourer's nightmare and to find ordnance still in the bomb bay required care and teamwork. It was not unusual to see piles of old mattresses and other soft material within easy reach of the dispersals that could be placed under an aircraft suspected of not releasing its full load. The worst scenario was if the rogue bomb or mine had released itself during the flight home and was lying on the unopened bomb doors. From experience, the armourers would open the bomb bay doors just a fraction and check that nothing was waiting to fall out.

Two crews were detailed for a new target area given as San Sebastian, off Spain's Bay of Biscay coast – codenamed 'Furze'. This seems unusual, given that Spain was supposed to be neutral, but research has shown that they were assisting the Germans. There is mention of this happening in various publications that I have consulted and some go so far as to say that direct aid was offered to the Kriegsmarine and the Luftwaffe. This took the form of allowing U-boats port facilities for repairs and replenishment of stores plus lying up in territorial waters to recharge batteries and exchange crews. The Luftwaffe were given the use of airfields and a United Nations Security Council investigation after the war found that long-range German aircraft had been operating from Spanish facilities against Allied shipping. It is also claimed that German aircraft forced down in Spain were repaired by Spanish technicians and returned to the Luftwaffe. Any Allied aircraft forced down was allowed to be inspected by the Germans, allowing them to check for new or additional items of equipment or innovations. The port of San Sebastian is only a few kilometres from the French land and sea border and it can be assumed that, had there been any objection from the Spanish about sowing mines in their waters, the British would have apologised and claimed a navigational error.

The two crews detailed for this mission were F/Sgt Dodsworth and F/Sgt Winter, LK397 EX-P, who reported a successful trip in excellent weather conditions, cloudless and clear for most of the time. However, F/Sgt Dodsworth, EJ115 EX-H had quite a hot reception soon after dropping his six mines. He later reported: *"We had clear weather with extremely good visibility. At 2358 hrs a U-boat fired cannon shells directly below. Five hits sustained and the navigator Sgt Todd was injured in the knee. The rear turret was made unserviceable due to damage to the hydraulics. The moon was behind the aircraft and it was impossible to pick up the U-Boat until it was astern of us"*.

Sgt Derbyshire, EF505 EX-R, Sgt Clifton, EF138 EX-S and F/Sgt Bowering, EF455 EX-B, who all had successful and uneventful trips, carried out a mining operation to the south west coast of France. The crews reported very good weather with excellent visibility.

No more operations were ordered for the Squadron until 14th January, allowing the ground staff time for maintenance and repairs and some well-earned leave for those who could be spared.

Ron Shaw, radar mechanic from Herne Bay: *"One thing I remember in particular about Lakenheath was the good food we had there. But I can't remember for sure the name of the flight sergeant responsible, but I think it was Chiefy Dines [it was:Ed]. I seem to also remember that when he was posted many 'Erks' asked to be posted to the same camp."*

14th January 1944

Another raid on 'special targets' (V1 rocket sites) around Ailly, Bonneton and Bristillerie was ordered and eight Stirlings and crews were despatched. One crew was detailed to mine waters off the Frisians. Those taking part in this raid were: F/Sgt Robinson, EE953 EX-E; F/Lt Lumsdaine, LK397 EX-P; P/O Noble, EF505 EX-K; P/O Guthrie, EF455 EX-B; F/Lt Betts, EF138 EX-S; Sgt Cutler, EE943 EX-X; F/O Kyle, EH995 EX-H; F/Sgt Bowering, LK385 EX-A.

P/O Guthrie saw several sticks of bombs fall over the red spot fires in the target area and also reported being fired on by our own defences while the aircraft was orbiting over Beachy Head at 9,000ft. The other crews reported successful missions with no opposition.

F/O Chillcott, EE930 EX-N, detailed for the mining operation to the Frisian Islands, also had a successful trip with clear weather and good pinpoints.

20th January 1944

A large operation was initially planned against the V1 sites and thirteen crews were detailed, but during the course of the day ten were stood down leaving three ordered to lay mines off the Frisians. F/Sgt Cattell, EF153, Sgt Clifton, EF161 and Sgt Cutler, EE941, delivered six mines each to their allotted pinpoints and reported fine weather with good visibility.

21st January 1944

Six V1 sites near Abbeville were selected for this raid by 111 aircraft including 15 from 199 Squadron. Take-offs began at 1850 hrs.

Shortly after lifting off from RAF Lakenheath at 1928 hrs, F/Sgt Derbyshire, EF138 EX-S collided with another Stirling, flying on a reciprocal course eight miles south of base at 9,000ft. Both starboard engines were damaged and after he jettisoned the bomb load at Rushford it was decided to land at RAF Woodbridge. This was an emergency landing airfield and was specially equipped to cope with damaged aircraft. F/Sgt Derbyshire later told investigators that he had his navigation lights on at the time of the collision but the other aircraft had no lights. It appears from records available that the Stirling F/Sgt Derbyshire collided with was EH958, of 90 Squadron.

The remaining aircraft attacked the target with some crews noting accurate medium flak, making things interesting. As in previous raids, it seems that red spot indicators predominated in the marking.

The crews taking part were: P/O Harrison, LK385 EX-A, who reported: *"Identified target by red TIs, our own stick of bombs were seen bursting in the centre of spot flares. Several flashes seen before and after the attack"*; F/O Button, EF455 EX-B, also observed two loads of bombs burst on the red spot fires; P/O Turner, EF192 EX-J; F/Lt Allson, EF153 EX-D; P/O Sturrock, EF508 EX-G; P/O Guthrie, EH995 EX-H; P/O Chappell, LK382 OJ-W (a 149 Squadron Stirling assigned to '199' for this raid); F/Lt Lumsdaine, EF459 EX-X; P/O Noble EF505 EX-R; F/O Craw, EH930 EX-N; P/O Winter, EE943 EX-V; Sgt Clifton, EF161 EX-Z; F/Lt Betts, EE957 EX-Q, who all reached and bombed the construction sites associated with the German rocket programme.

Generally they spoke of a good concentration of markers and many bomb flashes around the target area. All the aircraft carried 23 x 500lb GP bombs for maximum blast effect. The journey home over England was to prove, for some crews, almost as hazardous as the journey over enemy territory. P/O Sturrock was flying near London when the crew observed a number of the anti-aircraft balloon barrage at close quarters. At the time he was flying at 8,500ft and the balloons were above them at 9,000ft. F/Lt Lumsdaine and his crew decided to come home on a route west of London because they could see flak bursts on the briefed course.

Sgt Clifton was not quite so lucky, as his aircraft was hit by flak over London at 2125 hrs and, although he turned on his navigation lights, it made no difference. The navigator also fired the colours of the day, but this did not curb those firing at them until they were out of range. Luckily no one hit a balloon cable nor was anyone shot down. London anti-aircraft gunners like those in Royal Navy ships around the coast always fired on any aircraft with a kind of shoot first and find out if it's friendly afterwards attitude. Not much comfort to returning bomber crews who must sometimes have wondered whose side they were on.

One member of F/Lt Lumsdaine's crew, rear gunner F/Sgt Dave Lockett, relates his experience of flying near the London defences that night: *"On the night of 21st January 1944 we were on a bombing Op to France. It was rather a quiet trip but our return route was over London. At the same time we arrived near the City there were some German aircraft dropping bombs and we were of course caught up in this. The AA batteries let us have everything they could throw at us and it was worse than being over a German target and any second I expected a direct hit as the shells were bursting all around. I rotated my turret around and I fitted my chute on ready to drop out if the worst happened. The wireless operator, P/O Townshend, fired off all the very cartridges with the colours of the day but to no avail, we eventually came through unscathed and returned to Lakenheath intact. F/Lt Noble was also caught in the barrage and it was reported that one of his crew had mistakenly baled out over London."*

Such an incident did happen, occurring in similar circumstances, when three '199' Stirlings were caught by the London barrage on 13th February. *"I would also like to add a comment here about our pilot F/Lt Jack Lumsdaine who was later promoted to squadron leader and became our flight commander. He was a fine example of the qualities required to be a crew captain. He was an inspiration, with his courage, coolness and kindness. It was our privilege to fly with him. We flew on operations from August 1943 to September 1944 and upon completion of our tour Jack Lumsdaine immediately transferred to a Mosquito squadron and completed another tour. He served many years with the RAF and then transferred to the Canadian Air Force in 1955. In 1966, on a jet trainer flight, he met an untimely end to his life when the jet crashed in the Quebec Mountains".*

The next day the *Daily Sketch* (London Edition) reported big air battles over London and the south east of England. It also stated that possibly German and English bombers were over London at the same time. In fact, the Luftwaffe had launched their heaviest raid on London since the Blitz in 1940-41 and the defences shot down eight German bombers.

25th January 1944

Further V1 sites around Pas de Calais and Cherbourg were singled out for attention and a total of 76 aircraft drawn from various squadrons were detailed to attack them. '199' briefed ten crews for the operation and a further two were put on orders for a mining sortie, but this was subsequently cancelled. This raid, again using high explosive 500lb HC and 500lb MC bombs, followed the pattern of previous raids.

The weather in general was very poor and P/O Harrison EE910 EX-Kwas forced to make five orbits of the target area in a bid to identify the aiming point, but abandoned his mission and turned back to base having jettisoned 15 x 500lb bombs in the sea and brought eight back to base.

F/O Craw, LK397 EX-P, also made several orbits of the target trying to locate the markers – but he too was unsuccessful and returned to Lakenheath having seen no markers in the estimated target area.

F/Lt O'Connor, EE957 EX-Q, was the third pilot to encounter the problem when he could not identify his aiming point due to dense cloud. He dropped 4 x 500lb bombs safe in the sea at 5014N 0115E and brought the remaining nineteen back to base.

The other crews did drop their bombs on and around the target but there was no clear indication as to the overall success of the raid. P/O Kyle, EH995 EX-H, and P/O Noble, EF505 EX-R, and W/Cdr Bray could only observe bomb bursts reflecting in the clouds. F/Lt Betts reported seeing two orange explosions at the time his aircraft bombed and P/O Turner, EF192 EX-J, F/Sgt Cutler, EF161 EX-Z, F/O Button, EF455 EX-B observed sticks of bombs exploding, but were unable to say if they were accurately placed. No aircraft were lost during the raid.

F/Sgt Dodsworth, DFM, RAAF, one of the Squadron's most experienced pilots, was screened on this day. He had flown fifteen operations, but had been assessed as having a tough tour since joining the Squadron. He was affectionately known by his fellow aircrew as "Killer Dodsworth the Crack up Kid" and was just 20 years old when he left Lakenheath for the Gunnery School at Newmarket. He remained in the Australian Airforce until 8th March 1946 and was discharged with the rank of flight lieutenant. His most noteworthy exploit was pulling his Stirling out of a spin after a raid on Mannheim, from 15,000ft he only regained control by some exceptional airmanship at 5,000ft. It was the first time, to anyone's knowledge on the Squadron, of a Stirling being successfully pulled out of a spin. He and his crew were shot up over Berlin and Leverkusen and again over Frankfurt that resulted in a crash landing. Another crash landing was made as the result of being hit by cannon fire from a German U-boat. In all a very eventful tour and worthy of his DFM (Distinguished Flying Medal).

27th January 1944

The Squadron was back to mining coastal waters and twelve crews were detailed – two for waters in the Kattegat and ten to the Heligoland area.

P/O Guthrie and P/O Noble were selected for the Kattegat operation and both planted their mines in the allotted area, reporting excellent visibility all the way. The ten Heligoland crews who took off were soon depleted when oil pressure problems on F/O Eddy's aircraft, EF153 EX-D, caused the port inner to fail. F/Sgt Derbyshire, EE941 EX-U, also returned early when the crew reported a defective airframe and all four engines overheating. All the mines were dropped successfully. F/Sgt Robinson, EE910 EX-K, had to abort his mission, when the starboard inner engine's temperature went off the clock. F/Sgt Clifton, F/Lt Betts, F/O Chillcott, F/O Button, F/Sgt Cattell, P/O Bonnett and F/Sgt Bowering had successful trips and reported excellent weather conditions all the way to the mining areas.

At about this time, word filtered through to the Squadron that the conversion to Lancasters was well and truly off. A number of Stirling units were to retain their aircraft and concentrate on 'Special Targets', namely low-level flights supplying the French Resistance fighter, known as the Marquis, mining and support of the army once the second front (D-day) got under way.

28th January 1944

Mining off the south east coast of Denmark was ordered for nine aircraft and crews, all of whom took off. This mining operation was part of concerted diversionary tactics, employed to draw off the German night fighter defences prior to a Main Force raid on Berlin. A total of 63 Stirlings and four Pathfinder Halifaxes took part and was the first time Pathfinders assisted in minelaying. The TIs were dropped on the Danish island of AerØ and all the aircraft made a six minute run to their release point in Kiel Bay.

P/O Chappell, EF153 EX-D, dropped six mines in the correct position, but commented that he had difficulty seeing anything, owing to severe icing on all the windows of the aircraft. He reported that his compass was u/s for a short time, but one of the crew managed to repair it. The crew also saw a Stirling coned by searchlights and taking a pounding from the flak batteries on the Island of Sylt. F/Lt Betts, EF192 EX-J, P/O Sturrock, EH995 EX-H and F/Sgt Cutler, EE943 EX-V also encountered heavy icing conditions in the higher cloud up to 15,000ft and the latter was forced to descend to 3,000ft on the return journey to find safer conditions. S/Ldr Pettit, DFC, EE953 EX-E, F/O Craw, EE941 EX-U, F/O Button, EF455 EX-B and P/O Bonnett, LK397 EX-P did not report any difficulties and laid their mines as ordered. On the return trip some crews spotted fighter flares being dropped but they were too far back to be a problem.

Sadly, F/Sgt Clifton and his crew failed to return from this operation; they had taken off from Lakenheath at 1846 hrs and set course for the Kiel Bay area as ordered, but were intercepted by a night fighter on approach to the Danish coast. The Stirling, EF505 EX-R, which had completed eleven operational sorties, was shot down and crashed onto Juure Sand between the island of Romo and the mainland. All seven crew were killed in the crash and six buried in the Kirkeby Churchyard on Romo Island. The seventh member of the crew, Sgt Atherton, was not immediately found and was later washed up on the shore of the Danish mainland at Vester Vedsted on the 10th February 1944. He was buried at Fourfelt Cemetery, Esbjerg.

Details of the crew are as follows: P/O Charles Clifton, pilot, RAFVR, age 22, married to Joan Clifton of West Mersea, Essex; Sgt Leslie Gordon Rush, F/Eng, RAFVR; P/O Thomas Edward Ord, Nav, RAF; F/Sgt Albert Edward Sealy, B/A, RCAF; Sgt Walter Newman, W/Op, RAFVR, age 22, from Kettering, Northants; Sgt Andrew Johnston, A/G, RAFVR, age 20, from Campbeltown, Argyllshire; Sgt Cyril Atherton, A/G, RAFVR, age 31, married to Beatrice Atherton of Hay Mills, Birmingham.

30th January 1944

An air sea rescue sortie flown by F/O Chillcott and F/O Eddy. Nothing was seen by either crew after a search lasting four hours.

31st January 1944

The month ended with a single air sea rescue flown by F/Sgt Bowering and his crew, but they failed to locate anything during a search of almost four hours duration.

February
Special Operations in support of Resistance fighters – bad weather

This month saw another change in the use of the Squadron and the Stirling aircraft in particular. It will be remembered that the Stirling squadrons had been withdrawn from bombing operations over Germany due to its limitations of operating height and bomb load capacity and the aircraft was being used more and more in a minelaying capacity with additional short sorties over France to bomb V1 sites. Now, at the beginning of February, 199 Squadron was to be used in another role – that of delivering arms, ammunition and supplies to the Resistance fighters in occupied Europe. These were termed "Special Operations" and very little information was entered in the Squadron Record Book as it was felt that the less people knew about these missions the better. However, there are some other accounts of these supply operations available, but they are by no means a full account of what took place on a particular date. The following sorties mounted under the general term 'SOE' (Special Operations Executive) have, if available, the codename of the operation, the container load and if the drop was successful or not. While the main thrust of the Squadron's efforts was to be aimed at SOE supply runs, they were also called upon to occasionally contribute to the ongoing mining program.

4th February 1944

Fourteen aircraft and crews were detailed for the first 'Special' operation dropping supplies to the Resistance, but two were cancelled due to the usual technical faults. The remaining ten took off, but only W/Cdr Bray, EF459, EX-X ("Paul 30"), F/Sgt Cutler, EE941 EX-U ("Wheelwright 61") and F/Sgt Bowering, EF192 EX-J ("Marc 11A") completed their missions successfully.

5th February 1944

Special operations were again detailed, with eleven aircraft taking off for various destinations over Europe. Bad weather conditions and poor visibility prevented seven crews from finding their dropping zones and only P/O Catterall, EF161 EX-Z ("Bob 113"), F/O Craw, EF138 EX-S ("Bob 144") (dropped on alternative) and F/Lt Lumsdaine, LK397 EX-P ("Bob 81A") were able to get the necessary recognition signals from the ground and deliver the containers. F/O Craw could not locate his primary and reported that he dropped seventeen containers and one package on a reception located at 4737N 0440E. P/O Harrison found DZ lights, but at his de-brief said: *"The correct lights were on, but then we saw a train pull into a nearby station and thought it scared off the reception. Lights were switched off and did not appear again, so the drop was abandoned".* The remaining aircraft brought their loads back to Lakenheath.

Matthew Morton, Fitter, IIE: *"The move to Lakenheath and conversion to the Stirling was accomplished with apparent ease – things were just bigger and much more prone to mechanical failures – particularly the seemingly ever presence of negative earths, which when traced were in inaccessible areas such as behind the inboard oil tanks. In retrospect though I think our serviceability record was comparable with the Lancs and Halifaxes of that era.*

I saw 199 aircraft being used to transport supplies to Resistance fighters in occupied Europe and on one occasion saw a young woman, who clearly didn't want to board a 199 Stirling, put unceremoniously on the aircraft, – she did not return with the crew.

One or two aircraft were sent to Tempsford for covert operations, but this incident happened at Lakenheath. We sent only two aircraft on the Peenemunde raid, all our other Stirlings were unable to return to base due to heavy fog at the airfield to which they had been diverted from the previous night's operations.

My sojourn with 199 lasted from November 1942 to February 1944 and had I not had an altercation with the squadron engineering officer about a piece of carburettor supercharging equipment, (which in theory was workable, but in practical terms was useless) I would have gone to North Creake. In the event I finished up at Base Major Servicing at Mildenhall to ponder over the fact that in any difference of opinion between a flying officer and a corporal there is only one winner, and he doesn't wear stripes!!"

6th February 1944

Due to the continuing poor weather, the ten crews detailed for 'Special Operations' were stood down at 1530 hrs and the following day the same conditions again prevented any flying and all Ops were scrubbed.

8th February 1944

Only a slight improvement in the weather was forecast, but thirteen crews and aircraft were readied in case there was a chance of better conditions later in the day. At 1745 hrs, ten were cancelled but three did manage to get airborne and proceeded to their allotted drop zones.

F/Sgt Cotterall, EE953 EX-E ("Pimento 57") and F/Lt O'Conner, EE957 EX-Q ("Pimento 58") both found their pinpoints and delivered their loads of fifteen containers and one package. The poor visibility prevented F/Sgt Derbyshire, EE943 EX-V ("Pimento 56") from completing his drop and he was forced to bring his load back to base. He had spent 38 minutes in the area but could not see any reception lights.

9th February 1944

All operations were cancelled at 1620 hrs due to very bad weather conditions.

10th February 1944

The weather continued to remain poor with snow forecast during the day, but the Squadron prepared thirteen aircraft for more drops to the Resistance forces. The conditions improved enough for all thirteen crews to go through the briefings and receive their allotted pinpoints and at 2041 hrs W/Cdr Bray lifted off first.

The remaining aircraft followed over the next hour without any problems until F/Lt Allson, EF153 EX-D, took off at 2230 hrs and was soon experiencing difficulties. Due to low batteries the undercarriage was being wound up by hand and it is believed the weather had deteriorated with a heavy snowstorm over the airfield that compounded the problem. Unable to maintain height and flying speed the Stirling came down at Shakers Road, Lakenheath, 10 minutes after taking off, with the undercarriage only two thirds retracted and the flaps half out. In the resulting crash four of the crew were killed and three seriously injured.

EF153 crew: F/Lt Alan Ernest Allson, Pilot, RAFVR, age 21, from Lyminge, Kent, buried in Ss Mary and Ethelburga Churchyard, Lyminge, Kent; Sgt George Herbert Royston, F/Eng, RAFVR, age 20, from Hammersmith, London, buried in Cambridge City Cemetery; P/O Bertram William Miles, Nav, RAFVR, age 22, from Weybridge, Surrey, buried in Walton and Weybridge Cemetery; P/O Robert Louis Sanderson, B/A, RCAF, age 21, from Elstow, Saskatchewan, Canada, buried in Cambridge City Cemetery. The seriously injured members of the crew – Sgt Hall-Brooks; W/OP Sgt Challis; M/U Sgt Davis, R/G – were immediately taken to hospital.

This crew had been assigned to drop their containers in France at a site codenamed "Wheelwright 51".

W/O Ken Hall-Brooks later wrote of this incident: *"I was a W/Op A/G with 199 and joined at Lakenheath in August 1943, later going to North Creake until December 1944. I flew with F/Lt Allson's crew until we crashed in the fir woods, just off the local bombing range, about three miles from the airfield on the night of February 10th, 1944, in Stirling EF153 EX-D. I was one of the three lucky ones that managed to get out alive, the other two being the rear and mid-upper gunners, the other four however, died in the crash. Our aircraft had a painting of "Donald Duck" on the nose that was done by Sergeant Bill Hartley who was I/C of the ground crew."*

Corporal Ken Hartley serving in the radar section witnessed the crash: *"At work in the radar section at Lakenheath one morning when a Stirling coming in to land crashed beyond the section near the Brandon Road. We all rushed across to do what we could, but were told there were only two or three survivors, and even they were seriously injured. This was my first real introduction to the horrors of war".*

Due to the weather and other problems at the drop sites, only five crews reached and successfully dropped their containers to the waiting reception parties. These were: P/O Turner, EE953 EX-E ("Wheel 44A"), P/O Noble, BK816 EX-R ("Wheel 55"), F/Lt Chilcott, EH930 EX-N ("Paul 33"), F/Lt Eddy, LJ501 EX-H ("Wheel 54"), and F/Lt Betts, LK397 EX-P ("Wheel 48").

One crew, P/O Catterall, EF161 EX-Z ("Footman 5"), who had an unsuccessful trip, was nonetheless airborne from 2040 hrs to 0605 hrs – a total of 9 hours 25 minutes in most difficult and trying flying conditions.

11th February 1944

'Special Missions' to France were again the order of the day, with eleven Stirlings and crews readied for operations. All the aircraft took off between 2020 hrs and 2044 hrs, but again poor visibility prevented seven of the crews from locating the drop zones and were forced to bring their containers back to base.

F/Lt Betts, LK397 EX-P ("Peter 47"), F/Lt Button, EF455 EX-B ("Marc 12"), S/Ldr Pettit, EE953 EX-E ("Paul 52") and F/Sgt Cattell, EF192 EX-J ("Trainer 111") did locate their DZs or the alternatives and released the containers to those waiting on the ground. F/Sgt Cattell reported that he released on alternative DZ "Trainer 133". F/Lt Betts dropped his containers on alternative "Peter 22", although the lights from his primary "Peter 47" were seen as they were leaving. F/Sgt Derbyshire, EF161 EX-Z ("Paul 32") was one of those who could not find the target due to the appalling weather conditions, but logged a flight of 9 hours 32 minutes. Several other crews were airborne for over eight hours, each of which must have been extremely taxing on everyone.

12th February 1944

Ten Crews were detailed for another 'Special Mission', but at 1200 hrs the operation was called off due to bad weather.

13th February 1944

The weather lifted enough for twelve crews to take off, loaded with containers, but trigger happy anti-aircraft gunners near London fired on three of the aircraft and they were forced to turn back. The three pilots, F/Sgt Bowering, EF192 EX-J ("Trainer 114"), P/O Turner, EE910 EX-K ("Marksman 7") and P/O Noble, EE941 EX-U ("Marksman 7") all made safe landings back at Lakenheath. As a consequence of P/O Noble's aircraft getting more than its fair share of the anti-aircraft barrage, one of the crew baled out over the city.

P/O Noble's navigator P/O Roy Smith relates what happened: *"We were routed over north west London, but it seems the ground defences were not informed and we were subjected to some anti-aircraft fire. Our wireless operator, F/O George Cubby, fired off the colours of the day to no avail. As a precaution, someone (I think it was Sgt McGarrigle the flight engineer) opened the hatch in case we had to make an emergency escape. Our mid-upper gunner, Sgt Sanders, bent down from his turret to see what was going on and, seeing the hatch was open, switched on his intercom to contact the pilot. However, when bending down he must have pulled his intercom plug slightly out of the socket, so there was no connection to the other crew members. Having seen the open hatch and being unable to contact anyone, he assumed that we had all jumped and quickly followed suit. It is understood that he landed in Walthamstow and his parachute caught on some railings leaving him suspended a foot or two above the ground. He was arrested by the Home Guard, but after establishing his identity, was returned to the station".*

There are no further details available, so it is not possible to assess the damage inflicted by the 'friendly fire'.

Sammy McGarrigle, Flight Engineer (F/Lt Noble's crew at Lakenheath), with his engine fitter.

Although down to nine aircraft, six of them did find the drop zones and delivered their loads, while the remaining three brought their containers back to base due to no receptions and fuel shortages. The successful crews were: F/Lt Guthrie, EF455 EX-B ("Marksman 16"), F/Lt Eddy, EF262 EX-D ("Marksman 7"), F/Lt O'Connor, EE957 EX-Q ("Marksman 7"), P/O Winter, EE943 EX-V ("Peter 38"), F/Sgt Robinson, EF271 EX-F ("Trainer 115"), and P/O Harrison, LK385 EX-A ("Trainer 116").

14th February 1944

Although twelve crews had been detailed for SOE Ops and the aircraft loaded, the order to cancel the missions was received at 1700 hrs.

15th February 1944

The previous twelve crews were again detailed for SOE container dropping operations in France. During the afternoon, the aircraft to be flown by F/Lt Craw was found to be unserviceable due to problems with the port inner engine. Of the remaining eleven, four reached their drop zones and two reached the assigned areas, but failed to locate the receptions and brought their loads back. Four crews were forced to return early due to bad weather conditions.

W/Cdr Bray, LK385 EX-A ("Mongrel 3") took off at 2303 hrs and dropped fifteen containers and one package at 0224 hrs from 3,000ft after making a dead reckoning run from a Gee fix at 4610N 0420E. This pinpoint is situated at the NW tip of the Rhone Alps near the town of Belmont de la Loire. F/Sgt Bowering, EF 192 EX-J ("Pitcher 26") made a dead reckoning run from a Gee fix on Lake Bourget and delivered fifteen containers and one packet from 7,000ft. F/Sgt Cattell EF262 EX-D was also successful dropping fifteen containers and one package to the same DZ. P/O Noble, EE957 EX-Q ("Peter 47") reported that they had dropped seventeen containers "On the Lights". F/Lt Betts, EF161 EX-Z ("Paul 32") took off at 2300 hrs, but was forced to turn back after crossing the English coast due to instrument failure. He landed back at base at 0135 hrs. P/O Winter, EE943 EX-V ("Trainer 113") returned early due to a compass failure. F/Sgt Cutler, EE941 EX-U ("Peter 23") made a dead reckoning run in to his appointed DZ, but reported that no reception lights were seen and returned with his load of 24 containers and one package. F/Lt Button, LJ501 EX-H ("Mongrel 3"), P/O Turner, EE910 EX-K ("Trainer 114") and F/Lt Chilcott, EF459 EX-X ("Mongrel 3") all encountered 10/10 cloud over their DZs and were unable to drop their loads.

F/Lt Butler and F/Lt Chillcott were assigned the same DZ as W/Cdr Bray, but had taken off half an hour earlier and encountered 10/10 cloud cover and both were unable to locate the pinpoint. Weather conditions such as these had a major bearing on the success of a drop, as can be seen W/Cdr Bray arrived a short time later over the same area and was able to complete his mission with no problems.

Sadly, F/Sgt Robinson EF271 EX-F ("Wheelwright 44B") crashed at Vergt in the Dordogne, France and all the crew were killed. It is unclear if the aircraft was shot down or if it succumbed to the severe weather conditions that had earlier made several of their comrades turn back.

EF271 crew: P/O Kevin Alphonsus Robinson, Pilot, RAAF, age 28, from Port Pirie, South Australia; Sgt Reginald Alfred Williams, F/Eng, RAF, age 28, married to Irene Williams of Tottenham, north London; Sgt Ronald Stubbings, Nav, RAFVR, age 20, married to Gwendoline Stubbings of Bentley, Doncaster, Yorkshire; Sgt Gerrard Caine, B/A, RAFVR, age 22, from Barrow-in-Furness, Lancashire; F/Sgt Henry Edward Lambourne, W/Op, RAAF, age 21, from Hurstville, New South Wales, Australia; P/O James Alexander Jackson, A/G, RAFVR; Sgt Arnold Whimpenny, A/G, RAFVR, age 21, from Ardwick, Manchester, Lancs. All were buried in Mazargues War Cemetery, Marseilles.

16th and 17th February 1944

The weather precluded all flying apart from some short local air tests.

18th February 1944

A mining operation was ordered for the Kiel Bay area and three aircraft were prepared and crews briefed, but at 1610 hrs the mission was scrubbed owing to heavy snow.

19th February 1944

The mining detail was re-issued for the Kiel Bay area and F/Sgt Cattell, EF262 EX-D, F/Lt Chappell, LJ501 EX-H and F/Lt Lumsdaine, LK397 EX-P all took off in slightly better conditions than the previous two days. The Stirlings had each been loaded with 4 x 1,500lb mines and also a stack of 'Window' to dispense on the inward journey. The operation was designed to draw off the German night fighters from Bomber Command's planned attack on Leipzig.

F/Lt Lumsdaine reported that the weather improved and cleared over the west coast of Denmark, but that it clamped down over the target area with 10/10 cloud cover. F/Lt Chappell and F/Sgt Catterall also encountered 10/10 cloud over the target, but stated that the visibility was quite good once over the tops. F/Lt Chappell had a lucky escape during the outbound trip when the crew spotted a Ju88 flying almost in formation a 100 yards off the starboard wingtip. A gentle alteration in course was made and the fighter disappeared, much to the relief of everyone on board. All the mines were laid in an area close to 5030N – 1025E and the three aircraft landed back at Lakenheath between 0448 hrs and 0511 hrs. The crews reported that this was one of the coldest missions they had ever flown.

Although the 'Windowing' along the route was intended to draw the German fighters away, the German controllers only sent a small number to intercept the Kiel diversionary raid. As main force, consisting of 823 aircraft, crossed the Dutch coast they were met by a considerable number of fighters. Those that had been sent to attack the Kiel raid turned back and soon found the bomber stream and a running battle ensued all the way to the target at Leipzig. An incorrect wind forecast had been given and several aircraft had to orbit the target waiting for the Pathfinders to arrive and in the ensuing mêlée four aircraft collided. In total, Bomber Command lost 79 aircraft on this raid, with approximately twenty shot down by flak and the remainder falling to night fighters.

20th February 1944

No flying possible due to the poor weather conditions.

21st February 1944

Two separate mining details were ordered – one, of three aircraft, for the west coast of France and the other, of two aircraft, for the Frisian Islands.

P/O Catterall, LJ480 EX-S, F/Lt Eddy, EF262 and F/O Harrison, EF459 EX-X all managed to get away on the French coast assignment, but F/Lt Eddy was forced to abort at 4520N – 0140W when the aircraft became badly iced up at 5,000ft and he experienced problems with oil temperatures on both starboard engines. The load of 3 x 1,500lb mines were brought back.

F/O Harrison was also forced to turn back at 2241 hrs having overshot the Spanish coast, which was not seen owing to cloud cover. Icing was also a problem on the outbound flight. He brought his mines back to base. P/O Catterall was allotted an area off the San Sebastian coast and, although having difficulties with icing in cloud over the target, was able to plant all his mines successfully. P/O Winter, EF161 EX-Z and P/O Turner, LJ501 EX-H took off at 1810 hrs for the Frisians and arrived at their pinpoints within two minutes of each other. They found the target area clear with only a slight haze and dropped all the mines claiming later a 'good trip'.

22nd February 1944

'Special Operations' were ordered for six crews, but owing to very dense fog over the airfield and en route to the targets, they were called off at 1410 hrs.

24th February 1944

Kiel Bay was again on the target list and five aircraft took off, flown by P/O Sturrock, EF262 EX-D, P/O Turner, EE953 EX-E, P/O Noble, LK397 EX-P, P/O Catterall, LJ480 EX-S and P/O Winter, EE943 EX-V. The crews reported 10/10 cloud, with tops to 9,000ft with only occasional gaps. Apart from P/O Sturrock, the remaining aircraft each had a mine hang up.

Ken Derbyshire. Electrician: *"During my service with 199 Squadron, I gained the reputation as being immortal, having dropped a two-ton parachute mine 15ft off a Stirling onto the concrete dispersal point and lived to tell the tale".*

25th February 1944

Areas in the Baltic were selected for mining operations and six crews were put on standby. During the final ground tests, one was found to have a defective flap motor and on another the rear turret was unserviceable. The other four took off for pinpoints north of Copenhagen.

F/Lt Lumsdaine returned early due to the rear turret being u/s. Later investigations put the problem down to a defective gun. F/Lt Button, EE953 EX-E, F/Lt Chappell, EE943 EX-V and F/Lt Betts, BK816 EX-R all found the drop zone and in good clear weather dropped their mines at 5523N – 1223E, and returned safely to base.

A short time after these crews landed back at base at approximately 0300 hrs, an aircraft was heard circling the airfield and, as the weather had deteriorated with visibility down to 100ft, there was much concern for the pilot and crew. Research has revealed that this aircraft was a XV Squadron Lancaster, ED383, that had just returned from a raid to Augsburg and had taken off from its home base at Mildenhall at 2130 hrs. On returning, due to the bad weather, the pilot, F/Sgt J.A. Davis tried to land at Lakenheath instead, but he overshot the runway and, from eyewitness accounts, the Lancaster flipped over onto its back and caught fire. F/Sgt J.A. Davis, Pilot, age 23; Sgt D. Haydock, F/Eng, age 24; F/Sgt J.E. Carrott, Nav, age 21; Sgt W.A. Geraghty, B/A, age 22, were all killed in the crash. Sgt W.E. Harbidge age 19 was trapped in his rear turret and a desperate struggle by the rescue team ensued to free him. Two of the people involved in this rescue were later to be decorated for their efforts and bravery.

Acting Squadron Leader W.R. Pettit, DFC, RCAF and Leading Aircraftsman Joseph Therwell Wray received the MBE and BEM respectively being promulgated in the *London Gazette* on 26th May 1944. Their citation best explains this incident and is printed in full: *"One night in February 1944, Squadron Leader Pettit was the officer in charge of night flying at a Royal Air Force station when an aircraft, whilst attempting an emergency landing, overshot the end of the runway and overturned. The aircraft immediately caught fire. Squadron Leader Pettit rushed to the spot and, with the assistance of the fire party led by Leading Aircraftman Wray, quickly released two members of the crew who had been trapped in the fuselage. Squadron Leader Pettit then found that the rear gunner was seriously injured and trapped upside down in his turret. By this time the aircraft was burning furiously and the petrol tanks had started to explode. In spite of this and of further danger from exploding ammunition and pyrotechnics, Squadron Leader Pettit decided to attempt the extremely difficult task of removing the rear turret completely from the fuselage as all other attempts to reach the trapped gunner had failed. By strenuous efforts he was ultimately able to get into the turret while a party, headed by Leading Aircraftman Wray, wrenched at it from outside. Eventually the gunner was extricated alive and without any addition to the severe injuries which he had sustained in the crash. Squadron Leader Pettit's coolness, courage and initiative and Leading Aircraftman Wray's determination and devotion to duty in dangerous circumstances were of a very high order and were instrumental in saving the lives of three members of the crew of the aircraft".*

Sadly, despite the heroic efforts of everyone involved, Sgt Harbidge died the next day from his injuries. The wireless operator W/O G. Franklin and the mid upper Sgt H. Bysouth were both injured in the crash, but survived.

S/Ldr Pettit's citation for his DFC is recorded earlier on 23rd August 1943. He was to be posted to 620 Squadron after completing two more mining operations with '199' and was killed in action on 'D' Day, 6th June, aged 32 years.

He had been flying Stirling EF295 as 'A' Flight Commander carrying fifteen paratroops of the 591st Parachute Squadron, Royal Engineers, including the officer commanding and two men from HQ RE. Their DZ was an area north east of Caen and all the aircraft were subjected to intense light flak on the run in.

S/Ldr Pettit's Stirling was hit and two engines were knocked out and caught fire and some explosives that were being carried also caught fire, causing serious problems among the troops in the rear fuselage. Four troops parachuted to safety, but the remainder, including the crew, could not reach the exits before the aircraft crashed. S/Ldr Pettit and three of his crew together with one of the dispatchers and eight of the troops, were killed when the Stirling came down at Chateaux de Grangues, fourteen miles ENE of Caen. The remaining crew and troops survived, although some were seriously injured. The rear gunner, Sgt A. Pryce was lucky to receive immediate treatment to his injuries by one of the paratroops, who was a 'medic', which undoubtedly saved his life.

S/Ldr Pettit who came from Brantford, Ontario, Canada was buried in Ranville War Cemetery alongside his comrades in arms who died with him in the crash of EF295.

26th and 27th February 1944

Bad weather prevented any flying.

28th and 29th February 1944

On both days five crews and aircraft were readied for operations, but on each occasion they were cancelled when the weather deteriorated. And so the month ended much as it had begun, with severe weather interfering with operations. These conditions would have a major bearing on events during the month of March.

March

More casualties – another "Home Run"

1st March 1944

Special Operations for four crews were ordered but, by 1800 hrs, three were stood down, leaving only P/O Sturrock, LK385 EX-A ("Phono 10") to take off at 2228 hrs. His mission was successful, being able to deliver his load of fifteen containers and one package to the waiting Resistance group. He landed back at base at 0313 hrs.

P/O Chappell and his six regular crew members received orders that they were to be posted to 190 Squadron, based at RAF Leicester East. This veteran crew were not too pleased with the news, as they had been hoping to get their tour finished. Now they learned that they were to be flying Mk IV Stirlings, towing Gliders, dropping paratroops and dropping supplies to the Resistance fighters.

Worthy of note here is that the bomb aimer of P/O Chappell's crew – Tom Higgins – was another American who had joined the Squadron on 28th August 1943, the other being 2nd Lt Carl Carlson. Having initially joined the Royal Canadian Air Force and given the rank of W/O2, he came to England and was posted to Lakenheath. On joining the Squadron he was given the rank of flight sergeant and given an American rank of technical sergeant towards the end of his posting with '199'. However, just before leaving the Squadron to move to '190', he was again promoted to the American rank of flying officer. F/O Higgins did not complete his tour until August 17 1944, a full thirteen months after setting out on his first operation with 199 Squadron.

2nd March 1944

Two separate sorties were ordered for eight crews. Two were detailed for mining operations in the 'Hyacinth' area off the north west coast of France and six for 'Special Operations' over Europe. The mining sorties were allocated to Sgt Holmes, BK816 EX-R and F/Sgt Allen, EE941 EX-U. Sgt Holmes was unable to locate the target area and reported: *"We were unable to obtain a Gee fix within five miles of the target. The mission was abandoned after spending twenty minutes trying to obtain a fix. All mines brought back to base"*. F/Sgt Allen did find his allotted pinpoint and dropped his mines at 4842N – 0206W, but one hung up. His report stated: *"Owing to one mine sticking up a second run was made to try and release it. This was not successful therefore it was brought back to base"*.

The special operations were carried out by: F/Lt Lumsdaine, LK397 EX-P ("Archdeacon 11A"), P/O Winter, EE943 EX-V ("Bob 149"), F/Lt Craw, LJ480 EX-S ("Tom 43"), F/Lt Guthrie, EF508 EX-G ("Archdeacon 12"), F/Lt Barson, EF192 EX-J ("Bob 114"), and F/Sgt Bowering, EE953 EX-E ("Bob24").

Only two – F/Lt Craw and F/Lt Guthrie had good receptions at their allotted drop zones and delivered their loads of containers and packets. F/Sgt Bowering had reached his DZ and started to prepare to drop the load when the reception lights went out and he was forced to abort his mission.

Ted Coppen. FME: *"I was posted to Lakenheath in November 1943, to 'A' Flight with Sgt Slim Saunders i/c. We were then on Stirlings, first on bombing Ops then on to 'Fruit' (Arms for the Resistance – Canisters). Initially I worked on 'G' George with Johnny Wagstaff, Jimmy Kelly, Vic Greenwood and Sgt Bob Jones. Then I transferred to 'B' Beer with Vic Greenwood, Percy Stell, Harry Foster and Sgt Hartley. I have a photo of 'B' with all the aircrew and ground staff. I also have a photo of Halifax 'J' taken at North Creake. I was known as Ted with a nickname of 'Pickles'. Vic and Perce used to call me 'Ike'. I then went on to 'H' Harry with Cpl Niemen, Jimmy Kelly and Hugh McGrory. Some of us were then left on the station as rear party to repair a Stirling that was in the graveyard prior to moving to North Creake."*

3rd March 1944

The Squadron was detailed for Special Operations and eight crews briefed for the night's missions. Sadly, another of the Stirlings, F/Lt O'Connor, EE957 EX-Q, was to be listed as 'missing', adding to the mounting toll of men and aircraft. The seven remaining all reached the allotted areas, but only four made good pinpoints and dropped their containers. F/Lt O'Connor and his crew's mission was code-named "Bob 107" and he was the last to take off from RAF Lakenheath at 2050 hrs. The Stirling had reached the Dijon area when it was attacked and shot down, at 0058 hrs, by an Me110 flown by Ofw Kunker of 5./NJG4. It appears that the aircraft was at a low altitude ready to drop the container load and crashed between Gemeaux and Is-sur-Tille, France. Due to this low altitude only four of the crew were able to parachute to safety. The four successful crews were F/Lt Button, BF508 EX-G ("Trainer 148"), P/O Sturrock, LK385 EX-A ("Director 55 and 65"). No lights were seen at 65 and only 55 was successful), P/O Cutler, EF161 EX-Z ("Bob 113") and P/O Noble, LJ480 EX-S ("Bob 82").

EE957 EX-Q crew: F/Lt Kevin Bernard O'Connor, Pilot, RNZAF, age 29, from Waipawa, Hawkes Bay, New Zealand, buried in Is-sur-Tille communal cemetery, France; Sgt G.W. Green, F/Eng, RAFVR, POW; P/O R.B. Charters, DFM, Nav, RCAF, evaded; F/O Edward George Brown, B/A, RAFVR, age 21, from North Harrow, Middlesex, buried in Gemeaux communal cemetery; F/Sgt D.A. Chisholm, W/O, RNZAF, POW; Sgt Lawrence Eric Crick, M/U, RAFVR, age 21, from Pirbright, Surrey, buried in Is-sur-Tille communal cemetery; F/O Adam P. Chisholm, R/G, RNZAF, POW.

F/Sgt Green was interned in Stalag Kopernicus and given POW number 2878. He was later promoted to flight sergeant. F/Sgt D.A. Chisholm was also taken to Stalag Kopernicus and given the POW number 3016. He was promoted to the rank of warrant officer during his internment. P/O A.P. Chisholm was taken to Stalag Luft Sagan and Belaria where he was given the number 3602. As with his two comrades he too was promoted, gaining the rank of flying officer.

After extensive research in New Zealand, it was confirmed that the two crew members named Chisholm were not related. Adam Chisholm was traced and contacted and he agreed to write out the following notes on his own experience of this night's operations: *"On the morning of the 3rd of March 43, two days back from leave, we took Q EE957, a Stirling Mk.III of 199 Sqd Lakenheath, our usual aircraft, on an air test as it had been in for its 100 hour inspection, a usual 20 min flight took one hour. The under carriage didn't go down so had to be wound down by hand, then the flaps jammed which meant a shaky over shoot. The next time round we made it but still with stuck flaps, a bit of good flying. We were briefed that afternoon for a drop south of Dijon. These operations by 199 only took place for three or four nights of the full moon period as it was low level map reading by the bomb aimer up front with help from the rear gunner and other crew who had time to look out and verify a map position. The navigator, of course, was busy making sure we were heading in the right direction.*

We took off about 2000 hrs. Our pilot Kevin O'Connor RNZAF, nav: Bob Charters RCAF, bomb aimer Eddy Brown RAF, engineer Gerry Green, RAF, wireless op, Dick Chisholm, RNZAF mid upper gunner Laurie Crick, RAF and rear gunner Adam Chisholm RNZAF. I can still see Kev after he gave the order to climb in and get ready for take-off, he was always first aboard, climb in then step back out and take a long look round the drome, then on in as if he knew it was his last time.

Crew of Stirling EE957 EX-Q, shot down 3rd March 1944.

Back row: W/O Dick Chisholm, RNZAF, W/Op; Sgt Laurie Crick, RAF, Mid Upper; Sgt Gerry Green, RAF, F/Eng; F/O Adam Chisholm, RNZAF, R/G.

Front row: F/O Eddy Brown, RAF, B/A; F/Lt Kevin O'Connor, RNZAF, Pilot; F/O Bob Charters, RCAF, Nav.

Soon after take-off a slight oil leak in the port inner engine caught fire and glowed a little but got no worse, we couldn't put it out, as it didn't affect the engine we carried on, it glowed a little all the way. Nothing else happened till we found our dropping point, which was in a clearing by some woods. We flew over, but no signal light, so we went over a little lower, but still no light. We were only allowed to circle an area for about ten min, so next time, Kev went right down for a close look, but no sign of life among the trees.

We were climbing away to circle for one last look when I saw a ME110 pass under us so close my guns wouldn't depress far enough to catch him. I am sure he never saw us till we dived away; otherwise he would never have come up so close under us without firing. He turned and came in to attack from slightly to port of dead astern. It was almost as light as day and we expected him to open up with cannon out of range of our 303s so we held our fire, maybe he thought we were asleep or he wanted to make sure of putting the rear turret out first burst.

I was giving the usual patter over the intercom regarding the approach of the 110 distance etc and evasive action to take, this was done when the pilot was unable to see, so no wonder, as the 110 got closer, he wanted to know what was wrong that we weren't firing. When he seemed almost on top of us I opened up, at the same instant, he did likewise. Then I heard the mid upper open up, or rather I saw his trace. We were hitting him. He broke away down to port. He didn't seem damaged, but he didn't return to the attack. His cannon shells and tracer were passing above below and to the side of us, but nothing seemed to hit us, I can't understand why.

After Kev had checked everyone and everything was ok, he decided to have one last look at the drop area. The engineer said we had enough fuel for another ten min in the area. On the way back the mid upper and I cleared stoppages in our guns, which had happened during the attack. We did one circuit and the nav gave Kev the course home. There was no sign of life and were climbing away on course from treetop height when we were attacked by a Dornier 217, some of which were being used as night fighters. There was a fighter OTU in this area. This pilot was no novice, not easily scared off.

The fight seemed to last for ages. We were right down on the deck so as he could not attack from below, I remember chimney pots whizzing past, roof tops seemed to scrape the turret bottom. The W/op went forward into the front turret in case of a head on attack; he had just got in and was turning the turret to the side when the whole front was shot out. He managed to climb back out without a scratch. The 217, because of our low level, had to break away up and I, several times, saw our tracer bouncing off the under surface of his wings and belly, armour plated I guess under cockpit and tanks, so much for 303s!

The guns were starting to pack up again with so much constant firing, lost count of the number of attacks. I then noticed something black rushing past the turret. Someone said we had taken a hit in the starboard wing. The mid upper said there was a fire in the wing and the engineer said we were hit in no 7 tank. Kev tried climbing for height and then dived, but couldn't get the height necessary to put it out. The 217 was now flying on the portside out of range, could have been out of ammo or not risking another attack when we were on fire.

Having just come out of a dive, we were very low and Kev was considering a crash landing, but the broken nature of the country forbade that, so he gave the order to fix chutes and be ready to bale out when he gained enough height. He then asked the mid upper how the fire was, Laurie, only a lad, not started shaving, replied in a cool clear voice: "I am afraid the fire is getting fairly extensive skipper". That was the last time I heard his voice. I could hear Kev reading off the height and talking to Queenie as he tried to get enough height to bail out.

At 1000ft he said stand by, so I unplugged my intercom, climbed out plugged in by my escape hatch, which was just outside the turret, clipped on my chute, which I couldn't do in the turret. I then noticed the 217 had moved in closer, so reached in and was able to move the guns enough to give him a burst from the last gun still firing. Next thing a shout from Kev, who's firing. I replied rear gunner skip: "I told you to go" Sorry, skip, must have been unplugged getting out of turret. Kev then called again, hurry I can't hold her much longer. I then heard the B/A ask: "are you ok, Skip?" and the sizzling reply to get out. I heard others report: "away Skip" which we had to do in our training. The B/A opened the front hatch under his mat and left, followed by the NAV, W/O and Skip (pilot); the rear hatch was for the mid upper gunner and engineer.

My hatch (made for a bod without flying gear or chute on!!) was on the starboard side just outside the turret. I jettisoned the door, flames and smoke rushed past, didn't feel like putting my head out so went out feet first and called rear gunner away: "get out we're going down" was the reply. My chute caught in the narrow opening, it seemed ages to get free, and luckily the smoke seemed to have stopped the flames till I was free. I pulled the rip cord, bang the chute opened and crack on my head from my intercom cord which I had in the rush forgotten to pull out of my head phones, the chute had done it for me without stretching my neck, as it can do so we were told in training. I had a brief glimpse of Queenie still flying straight and level going down on fire, but nothing else.

The trees rushed up, crashed through, a sudden stop, my feet a few inches from the ground. Seconds later the plane went in before I was out of my harness, as the tree that broke my fall was on the side of a hill on the edge of a small wood. Lucky for me, if I had missed it I would have hit the ground very hard. Kev didn't make it. He was found not far from the plane, his chute had not had time to open properly. Laurie was found near by. He had no chute on. He may have been flung out on impact. This is what Mr Pepin thought may have happened, as told to Mr and Mrs Brown when they visited after the war. It was on Mr Pepin's farm by his house where the plane landed. All he received for fighting to keep Queenie up till we got out was a headstone in the Parish Cemetery alongside Laurie (who for some unknown reason didn't get out in time) in Is-Sur-Tille, France.

I released my harness and tried to pull my chute out of the tree with no luck, so had to leave it flapping in the breeze about 300 yds up the hill from a road which was starting to be used even at that early hour. I headed into the woods, but hadn't gone far when I saw I still had the D ring, which you pulled to open your chute in my hand. It was bent out of shape, so it must have had a hard pull as it wasn't light metal. Dogs then started barking up ahead, so I stopped to listen as they were in the direction I was heading, as my rather disjointed thoughts were to head in the direction the plane had come from on the chance of finding others of the crew.

It was then I thought I heard Eddy call my name, but nothing more just dogs barking. Years later I found out he was found days later a long way away on the other side of the hill with horrific head injuries still in his harness and now lies in a cemetery in Gemeaux, visited by my wife and I some years ago. What did I hear? To this day I can still hear his voice, but he must have been dead when he hit the ground, having hit his head leaving the aircraft.

I sat for a while to calm down, the dogs kept barking so, as there was about six ins of snow on the ground, footsteps could be followed, so decided to go down to the road before too many were about where my tracks would be lost, then leave at first opportunity.

Halfway down, with no cover, along came a German army car, so much for that bright idea. For you the war is over they said, waving of all things in great delight sten guns, which were things we were dropping. They were old soldiers and quite friendly.

Dick landed on a house roof, frightened the life out of the old couple living there who offered help, but they could have been shot so he walked out just as the soldiers arrived. I didn't meet Dick till the Frankfurt interrogation centre, which was flattened in a night raid on Frankfurt, on the 22nd March. We were marched out next day, 23rd, and went by rail in crowded cattle trucks to separate POW camps, Sagan Stalag Luft 3 for me on 26th and a Sgt camp for Dick, Heydekrug Stalag Luft 6. We did not meet again till back in the UK after the war".

P/O R.B. Charters, DFM, RCAF was fortunate to evade capture and made his way back to England. He later gave a full and detailed account of the night fighter attack on his aircraft and the subsequent results to the "Operational Research Section (BC)" dated 8th May 1944.

The full narrative is reproduced here:

'Report No K.158. Copy: 11.
Target: Special Task. 3rd March 1944

Information from: P/O R.B. Charters, DFM, Navigator on 21 Operation.

1. *The Stirling took off from Lakenheath at about 1730 hours. The enemy coast was crossed at 6,000ft and shortly afterwards a small fire developed in the starboard inner engine air intake. The fire soon went out and after a discussion between the pilot and flight engineer it was decided to continue on the operation. The engine ran rather rough for the rest of the flight, but it was not necessary to feather it.*

2. *The Stirling proceeded across France on the planned course, flying mainly at 2,000ft, but climbing to 3,500ft over the last two legs of the route owing to high ground in the vicinity. The moon was just past the first quarter and horizontal visibility was good, but the view of the ground was obscured by haze which made it necessary to orbit each of the turning points. Nevertheless these were identified successfully and the target area reached without further incident.*

3. *The Navigator announced that the E.T.A. at the target was up and the bomb aimer replied that he could see the target ahead. Almost at the same moment the rear gunner called out to the pilot to prepare to corkscrew to starboard as they were about to be attacked by a Me110. The Stirling was flying at about 1,500 to 2,000ft at the time and probably not more than 500ft above the high ground. The fighter attacked from the starboard quarter and below, keeping to the gullies between the hills. Both aircraft opened fire at extreme range, both the Stirling's gunners firing. The pilot at once started to corkscrew and kept up this manoeuvre throughout the combat, which lasted several minutes. There appeared to be two separate exchanges of fire before the fighter broke away and was not seen again. The navigator heard numerous bullets strike the fuselage of the Stirling and some glass was shattered in the bomb aimer's compartment, but no material damage was sustained. Neither of the gunners made any claim.*

4. *Having shaken off the fighter the pilot and bomb aimer map-read back to the last pinpoint before the target and started a DR run. At the end of this they circled the area twice and started a second dead reckoning run. At the end of this they again circled the area twice but were unable to identify the target. As it was now long past the time planned for the operation it was decided to abandon the mission. The pilot asked for the most direct course home avoiding heavily defended areas and, on receiving this from the navigator, set course for base.*

5. *About five minutes later, the rear gunner reported a fighter approaching from astern and directed the pilot to prepare to corkscrew. The enemy aircraft which both gunners identified as a Me110 came in from the port quarter below and* *opened fire at fairly long range. Both gunners replied to the enemy fire and the pilot kept up a corkscrew manoeuvre, starting to port.*

6. *The Stirling was hit almost at once in the starboard wing in, or close to, No 2 tank. There was no explosion, but the wing caught fire immediately and the flames spread very rapidly. The pilot dived the aircraft slightly in an unsuccessful attempt to extinguish the flames, but as the Stirling was under 2,000ft when attacked he was unable to maintain this manoeuvre. He therefore gave the order to bale out.*

7. *The navigator disconnected his intercom, put on his parachute and placed the pilot's on the 2nd pilot's seat. As he came forward, the wireless operator was standing by the navigator's table and motioned him on, the order to abandon the aircraft having evidently been given. As the navigator descended the steps he saw the bomb aimer bale out. He had not removed the hatch cover and it closed after him. P/O Charters at once attempted to reopen it. In this he had some difficulty, but eventually succeeded with the aid of the wireless operator after losing valuable seconds. He then baled out feet first. The wireless operator was close at hand ready to follow when he left and the pilot appeared to have the Stirling well under control.*

8. *P/O Charters made a comfortable descent, but landed in a tree from which he was suspended. He managed to climb onto a branch and then released his parachute and climbed down the trunk. He landed east of the village of Is-sur-Tille (Cote-d'Or). He saw the Stirling crash to the south of the village with a violent explosion, followed by several smaller ones. On the ground he was later told that two of his crew were taken prisoner and that three were killed and buried locally. 2544/5 BC/S.30270/ORS. 8th May 1944.*

P/O Bob Charters

This section was part of MI9 and interrogated anyone returning from occupied Europe to glean information on escape routes and names and locations of those people who had assisted an evader.

A further report MI9/S/PG-1894 gives a little more information on P/O Charters' evasion and was taken a few days earlier than the previous statement. He was interviewed by IS9 (W) ORS Bomber Command on 2nd May 1944. The narrative is listed as Secret and is written out in full: *"I was a member of the crew of a Stirling Mk.III which took off from Lakenheath (Suffolk) on 3rd March 1944 at about 1730 hrs on a special mission. On the return flight, we were attacked by a night fighter at about 2330 hrs and were ordered to bale out.*

I came down in a wood at France, 1:250,000, Sheet 17, 0 1275. I was suspended by my parachute in a tree about 10ft from the ground, but managed to get over to the trunk, released myself, and scramble to the ground. While I was coming down I saw the explosion of the aircraft, which I heard, later crashed near Is-Sur-Tille (0 0884). I left my parachute in the tree, and having hidden my Mae West and harness in some bushes in the woods, I started walking S.E.

When I reached the next woods I heard people moving about, so I changed direction to N.E. till I reached the Forest of Velours (0 17). I walked along the west edge of this wood for some distance, and then crossed the frozen fields to the main Langres-Dijon road. I by-passed Orville (0 1689) and rejoined the main road. Shortly afterwards I reached a railway crossing where I received help in the early morning of 4th March. I was later put in touch with an organisation, and the rest of my journey was arranged for me. End."

From entries in the forms consulted it would appear that P/O Charters was passed along an escape line that ran through France and over the Pyrenees to Spain and Gibraltar. He is noted as leaving Gibraltar on 1st May 1944 and was then interviewed at Whitechurch on 2nd May 1944.

4th March 1944

A serious incident was to prevent the Squadron from sending all eleven aircraft and crews detailed for further 'Special Operations'.

At 1943 hrs, F/Lt Lumsdaine, LK397 EX-P ("Mongrel 6") led off those assigned to the night's missions followed by F/Lt Guthrie, LK385 EX-A ("Trainer 144"), F/Lt Barson, EF262 EX-D ("John 69"), F/Sgt Bowering, EF455 EX-B ("John 69"), F/Lt Button, EF508 EX-G ("Marksman 17"), and P/O Noble, BK816 EX-R ("Mongrel 3").

At 2210 hrs, P/O Cutler, EE941 EX-U was just about to take off when the Stirling swung and the undercarriage collapsed, with the aircraft coming to rest right on the intersection of the runways. This effectively blocked the remaining aircraft from taking off and those left on the taxiway were returned to their individual dispersal points. Of the six that did get airborne, F/Sgt Bowering returned early with engine trouble and made a force landing at RAF Tangmere at 2220 hrs.

Only two crews – F/Lt Button and P/O Noble located their primary drop zones and F/Lt Barson diverted to "Marksman 18", to complete his mission. The remaining two crews F/Lt Guthrie, LK385 EX-A ("Trainer 144") and F/Lt Lumsdaine, LK397 EX-P ("Mongrel 6") did not locate their DZs and returned with their loads of fifteen containers and one package.

5th March 1944

Special Operations ordered for eleven crews. All took off and reached their target areas, but only eight were able to locate the pinpoints and deliver their containers and packages. The three that were unsuccessful brought their loads back to base.

On this supply operation F/Lt Chilcott, EH930 EX-N ("Trainer 175") and P/O Winter EE943 EX-V ("Trainer 152") had F/Sgt Allen and Sgt Holmes respectively flying as their 2nd pilots.

On the outbound leg of the mission F/Lt Barson, EJ115 EX-C ("Archdeacon 10") was hit by light anti-aircraft fire and the wireless operator Sgt Donaldson was hit by shrapnel in the left leg, but he carried on with his duties without complaint. Taking an exact extract from the Squadron ORB: *"His courage and devotion to duty earned him a well deserved award of the Conspicuous Gallantry Medal"*. His award was officially promulgated on 31st March 1944 and his citation reads: *'1215802 F/Sgt H.A. Donaldson was the wireless operator of an aircraft detailed for an attack on a target in March 1944. Soon after crossing the enemy coast the aircraft was hit by fire from the ground defences. F/Sgt Donaldson was hit in the leg by fragments of shrapnel that lodged against the bone, causing a most painful wound. Despite this, he acted with great promptitude in assisting to extinguish a fire that had commenced in the aircraft. He afterwards set to work to repair his wireless apparatus which had sustained damage. Not until his task was successfully completed did F/Sgt Donaldson report his injury. Later on, the aircraft again came under fire and received further damage. Although in considerable pain, F/Sgt Donaldson made light of his injuries and remained at his post to execute his wireless duties until the sortie was completed. He displayed fortitude, courage and devotion to duty of a high order.'*

6th March 1944

All operations were cancelled at 1800 hrs due to bad weather.

7th March 1944

The weather cleared sufficiently for eight aircraft to take off on SOE supply drops.

P/O Winter, EF459 EX-X ("Wheelwright 67") found the drop zone to be cloud covered and dropped fifteen containers and one package on his alternative DZ at "Wheelwright 75" and the remainder were forced to abort their missions and returned to base. Having checked the times of take-off and landing for all these aircraft, it appears that the crews were airborne for between 8½ to 9 hours flying time and would be approaching the limit of their fuel and endurance when approaching base. It was all the more exhausting for the crews knowing they had made such a long trip and been unable to drop the much needed supplies to the Resistance.

One air sea rescue search was carried out by F/Sgt Allen, EE943 EX-V from 1116 hrs to 1605 hrs, but no record of anything being sighted.

8th and 9th March 1944

No operations were possible for these two days due to very bad weather conditions that prevented all but a few local test flights close to the airfield.

10th March 1944

Fourteen aircraft and crews were detailed for 'Special Operations' and, as the weather cleared, the Stirlings were individually loaded with fifteen containers and one package for the nights sorties.

Just before take-off, one of the Stirlings, EF508, to be flown by F/Lt Button detailed for "Marksman 16" developed problems and was cancelled from the operations. The remaining thirteen aircraft all got away without further trouble, between 1942 hrs and 2005 hrs, and P/O Cutler, EF138 EX-Y ("Marksman 16") carried an extra crew member on board. His normal navigator F/Sgt Dancer was accompanied by F/Sgt Mills, who was flying to gain experience of the complexities and accuracy required on this type of mission.

The bomb aimer's position on BK816 EX-R ("Marksman 16"), captained by P/O Noble, was filled by S/Ldr Bevington, replacing F/Lt Banahan for this sortie.

F/Lt Betts, EF459 EX-X ("Trainer 128") was shot up by a night fighter en route to the DZ and forced to jettison the entire load of fifteen containers, but the internal load of packets were brought back to base (see combat report at end of day's narrative).

The only other crew not to complete their sortie was that of F/Lt Barson, EE943 EX-V ("Trainer128") due to *"no definite reception"*.

The successful crews who completed their supply drops were: P/O Noble, BK816 EX-R ("Marksman 16"), P/O Cutler, EF138 ("Marksman 16"), F/Sgt Cattell, EE910 EX-K ("Marksman 16"), F/Lt Chilcott, EH930 EX-N ("Mongrel 10"), F/Lt Craw, LJ480 EX-S ("Mongrel 10"), P/O Catterall, LK397 EX-P ("Mongrel 10"), F/Lt Eddy, EF262 EX-D ("Mongrel 10"), W/Cdr Bray, LK385 EX-A ("Mongrel 9"), P/O Turner, EE953 EX-E ("Mongrel 9"), P/O Harrison, LJ582 EX-L ("Mongrel 9"), and F/Sgt Bowering, LK501 EX-H ("Mongrel 9").

The returning aircraft began landing at 0315 hrs and F/Lt Barson, who had not been able to deliver his containers, was the last to land at 0420 hrs, after being airborne for over eight hours.

The combat report submitted by F/Lt Betts LJ580 dated 13th March 1944 reads: *On the night of 10/11th March 1944, outward bound to Special Target, at position 4600N 0525E. Time: 2300 hrs. Height: 5,000ft. Course: 110 true. Airspeed: 165. Visibility very good, full moon.*

No searchlights, ground activity or other unusual phenomena was noticed at the time of the attack. Our rear gunner first saw the enemy aircraft attacking from the starboard quarter, fire at a range of 500 yards and recognised it as a Me110. He immediately ordered the pilot to corkscrew starboard, and both our rear gunner and the enemy aircraft opened fire simultaneously as the pilot commenced to corkscrew.

The enemy aircraft crossed over to our port quarter and did a steep turn and came in for a second attack. Our rear gunner continued to fire and the mid upper also opened fire when the enemy aircraft was on the port quarter.

Our aircraft was hit in the port inner engine, bomb bay, bomb aimer's compartment, port fuselage, port wing and port tail plane by cannon shells. Hits severed all the pipe lines to the mid upper turret making it u/s.

Stirling EH930 EX-N

Both gunners observed strikes on the enemy aircraft in the attack. The enemy aircraft broke off onto the port beam up and was not seen again. Shortly after an explosion and fire was seen on the ground in the vicinity where the enemy aircraft disappeared and was reported by three other Stirling crews who were in the area. In view of these facts we claim the enemy aircraft as a probable kill.

Our navigator, F/Sgt Berry, was injured in thirteen places by small steel fragments. The wounds were all superficial and not at all serious.

The rear gunner (Sgt Wilkinson) fired 700 rounds. Mid Upper gunner (P/O Gumbril) fired 150 rounds before turret packed up.

11th March 1944

A change back to the mining role was ordered on the 9th, and crews were put on standby for sectors of the Bay of Biscay and Spanish coasts to be mined.

Weather conditions were far from ideal and P/O Turner, EE910 EX-K, although reaching his target area off the south west coast of France, was unable to find the pinpoint on the northern tip of Lake Hourtin. Although spending some time searching, a visual landmark, could not be found due to very poor visibility, and the mission was abandoned.

Four other crews had been detailed for this same area and P/O Harrison, LK385 EX-A, F/Sgt Bowering, LJ501 EX-H and Sgt Holmes, LK397 EX-P all found their pin-points and dropped their mines. Another loss to the Squadron was suffered on this mission when Sgt Allen, LJ480 EX-S failed to return, but the cause has not been established. The aircraft came down near Lake Hourtin at Naujac-sur-Mer. Details of the crew follow at the end of the day's reports.

Three crews were detailed for the Bayonne area just north of the French Spanish border and an outflow of the River L'Adour. F/Lt Chilcott, EH930 EX-N, P/O Cutler, EF138 EX-Y and F/Lt Button, LJ500 EX-S mined a section of coastline given as 4331N – 0132W. All crews reported 10/10 cloud with tops to 6,000ft and poor visibility. They were forced to drop their mines as low as 1,000ft to avoid the cloud base.

Debriefing after raid on 11th March 1944. F/Lt Bill Betts is talking to one of the station intelligence officers after a successful mission. It was important to get as much information on how a raid went and to pin-point areas of searchlights and flak to be avoided on future missions. Standing behind F/Lt Betts is Sgt K.D. Walker, W/op and sitting nearest to the camera is P/O Berry, Nav.

The remaining Stirling flown by S/Ldr Pettit, EF262 EX-D flew just a little further south and dropped the mines off the coastal town of Saint-Jean-de-Luz, which is right on the French/Spanish border.

LJ480 EX-S crew: F/Sgt Keith Fowler Allen, Pilot, RAAF, age 21, from Dromana, Melbourne, Victoria, Australia; F/Sgt Thomas George David Mills, Nav, RAAF, age 27, from Blackburn, Melbourne, Victoria, Australia, an analytical chemist in civilian life; Sgt William Howell Ebsworth, W/Op, RAFVR, age 34, from Ilford, Essex; Sgt Cecil Reginald West, B/A, RAFVR, from Newcastle-upon-Tyne; Sgt James Clark, M/U, RAFVR, age 20, from Edinburgh; Sgt Reginald Horace Cantwell, R/G, RAFVR; Sgt Alan Tym, F/Eng, RAFVR, age 20, from Edale, Derbyshire. All the crew are buried in Naujac-sur-Mer communal cemetery.

13th March 1944

The previous day's weather had all but curtailed any flying, but as the conditions improved, seven aircraft and crews were detailed for supply drops to the Resistance in France.

Four aircraft were cancelled and of the three remaining, another failed to take off. F/Lt Barson, EE910 EX-K ("Tom 45") and P/O Catterall, EJ161 EX-Z ("Tom 45") cleared the runway at 2340 hrs, but a little over an hour into his mission, F/Lt Barson was forced to return early with engine trouble, landing back at base at 0100 hrs. P/O Catterall and his crew, the only ones to reach their DZ, successfully delivered fourteen containers and one packet, landing back at RAF Lakenheath at 0556 hrs.

15th March 1944

Bomber Command's main target would be Stuttgart, with 863 aircraft, and Amiens and Woippy in France. 199 Squadron was detailed for the Amiens raid, concentrating on the railway yards, and contributed nine Stirlings, loaded with 22 x 500lb high explosive bombs, although just before take-off one aircraft was scrubbed due to a faulty Gee set.

F/Lt Betts, LJ580, EX-X; P/O Turner, LJ582, EX-L; Sgt Holmes, BK816, EX-R; F/Lt Craw, EH930, EX-N; P/O Cutler, EF138, EX-Y; F/Lt Eddy, EF262, EX-D, F/Sgt Cattell, LK385, EX-A and F/Sgt Bowering, EF508, EX-G took off between 1845 hrrs and 1909 hrs and all reached the target area. They encountered patchy cumulus cloud, as seven Stirlings came in to bomb from 12,000ft between 2100 hrs and 2103 hrs in a very concentrated attack. Sgt Holmes for some unknown reason came in late and bombed at 2130 hrs, but being behind the time schedule, was able to see and comment on the fact that the bombing appeared concentrated. Good target marking was mentioned by all the crews, with red TIs in two clusters directly in the centre of the railhead. Overall the raid was claimed to have caused much damage, but few details ever came out of the target area to justify this. Eighteen French civilians were killed. Overall 41 aircraft were lost from the three raids. A new record was set this night with 1,116 sorties flown.

16th March 1944

At 0740 hrs P/O Catterall and his crew took off for a sea search in LJ501, EX-H returning at 1250 hrs having not spotted anything. Upon landing the crew found they were on Ops again that evening.

Two crews detailed for mining operations off the Frisian Islands.

P/O Catterall, EF161 EX-Z and F/Sgt Bowering, EF138 EX-Y took off at 1928 hrs and 1934 hrs and successfully dropped six mines each at 5303N 0435E.

Another raid on Amiens was also laid on and nine crews were placed on the battle order. The bomb loads were to remain as before, each Stirling carrying 22 x 500lb bombs. P/O Sturrock, LK385, EX-A; F/Lt Chilcott EH930, EX-N; Sgt Holmes, BK816, EX-R; W/Cdr Bray, EE508, EX-G; F/Lt Guthrie, LJ501, EX-H; F/Sgt Cattell LJ582, EX-L; P/O Winter, LK397, EX-P; F/Lt Craw, LJ580, EX-X; and F/Lt Eddy, EF262, EX-D, took off shortly after the two mining aircraft and reached the target area at 2200 hrs. By 2209 hrs all crews had delivered their loads and were on their way back to base.

This was another well co-ordinated attack, with P/O Sturrock releasing at 9,500ft and F/Lt Chilcott at 13,000ft. The other crews releasing between these two heights, giving a measure of protection from flak. The red TIs were easily spotted and bomb aimers reported many clusters in the target area, with bombs bursting across them. Some larger explosions were also seen.

In all, 130 aircraft from Bomber Command attacked the target and no aircraft were reported lost, although another eighteen French civilians were killed and fourteen injured.

Of note, 617 Squadron carried out a successful precision attack on the Michelin tyre factory at Clermont-Ferrand in France.

17th March 1944

Extremely bad weather conditions curtailed any operations, although some local training flights were flown and ground crews were able to carry out much needed maintenance work.

18th March 1944

Bomber Command ordered a maximum effort on Frankfurt, with 846 aircraft taking part. It was decided to try and split the German night fighter defences by conducting a diversionary minelaying raid over the Heligoland area and to this end 199 Squadron detailed nine aircraft and crews: Sgt Holmes, BK816 EX-R; P/O Catterall, EF161 EX-Z; P/O Sturrock, EF262 EX-D; P/O Winter, LJ578 EX-S; P/O Cattell, EE910 EX-K; F/Lt Lumsdaine, LK397 EX-P; P/O Turner, LJ582 EX-L; F/Lt Guthrie, LJ501 EX-H; F/Lt Chilcott, EH930 EX-N.

They started to take off at 1852 hrs, with P/O Winters leading the way. He was closely followed by the eight remaining crews, with P/O Sturrock last to leave at 1913 hrs.

The area allotted for the mines was the same for all the aircraft – 5401N 0804E with instructions to drop from 10,500ft. In their debrief all the pilots reported releasing at the given height and area and, with only minutes between each Stirling passing over the drop zone, it called for some extremely proficient flying.

Aircrew and Groundcrew in front of "E" Edward, EE953 EX-E. *Back row*: P/O J. Osborne, Nav; Groundcrew ?; Groundcrew ?; P/O F. Podd, B/A; F/Lt A. Turner, Pilot; Groundcrew ?; Goundcrew ?; Groundcrew ?; W/O T. Corcoran, Special W/Op. *Front row*: F/Sgt L. Smithers, R/G; P/O D. Savegar, M/U; Groundcrew ?; F/Sgt W. Davies, W/Op; Sgt P. Pannichelli, F/Eng; Groundcrew ?; Groundcrew ?; squadron mascot "Winco".

From the ORB it can be seen that the first two aircraft, those of F/Lt Chilcott and P/O Catterall released almost simultaneously at 2058 hrs, the others followed at 2059 hrs, two at 2102 hrs, 2103 hrs, 2104 hrs and 2105 hrs. Again, markers were used to indicate the drop zone and the crews noted that they were clearly seen and on time.

19th and 20th March 1944

Bad weather set in and curtailed all flying, except a few local training and testing flights.

21st March 1944

Six aircraft and crews were detailed for mining operations around the mouth of the Gironde river in the Bay of Biscay and one aircraft and crew for Ile de Ré. One aircraft failed to take off due to engine trouble.

The remaining five consisting of F/Sgt Bowering, EF508 EX-G; P/O Turner, EE953 EX-E; P/O Winter, EE943 EX-V and F/Lt Eddy, EF262 EX-D all took off and were airborne by 1941 hrs. However, 25 minutes into his sortie, P/O Turner was forced to turn back as the Gee set was unserviceable. All his mines were brought back to Lakenheath. The four aircraft left flying the mission reached the DZ and successfully dropped their mines from 5,000ft in their allotted target area.

The Stirling flown by P/O Catterall, LK397 EX-P was also dogged by problems with the Gee set. Having taken off at 1918 hrs, he set course for his target area, but at 2047 hrs was forced to abandon and brought one mine back having jettisoned three safe at 5012N 0218W. He reported visibility was very bad and the Gee set had been unserviceable since passing over Oxford.

23rd March 1944

A raid was planned on Laon in Northern France and thirteen aircraft and crews were detailed to take part. From the records, it appears that railway marshalling yards were again the prime target. In total 143 aircraft from Squadrons of 3, 4, 6 and 8 Groups took part directed by a Master Bomber.

The crews from '199' consisted of: P/O Cutler, EF138 EX-Y; F/Lt Lumsdaine, LK397 EX-P; F/Lt Guthrie, LJ501 EX-H; P/O Cattell, EF161 EX-Z; P/O Noble, BK816 EX-R; F/Lt Betts, LJ580 EX-K; P/O Winter, EE943 EX-V; P/O Sturrock, LK385 EX-A; F/Lt Eddy, LJ582 EX-L; F/Lt Barson, EF192 EX-J; F/Sgt Holmes, EF455 EX-B; P/O Turner, EE953 EX-E; F/Sgt Bowering, EF508 EX-G.

All the aircraft took off between 1915 hrs and 1941 hrs and proceeded to the target without any problems from flak or night fighters, the first (Sgt Cutler) arriving to bomb at 2201 hrs. The Stirlings attacked from almost due north of Laon at between 10,000 to 12,000ft, dropping their bomb loads on green indicators. The weather was reported as being hazy with good visibility, but after 72 aircraft had bombed, the Master Bomber ordered the attack to be stopped. Reports from local sources stated that half the bombs hit the railway yards and the remainder were scattered over a wide area around the town, some falling up to 3km from the target. Some rail lines were cut, but the Germans had them repaired and in use the following day. Seven civilians were killed and nine injured, but the casualties were kept low as most of the people who lived near the railhead moved away from the area at night. Two Halifaxes were lost on this raid.

Again, this raid and other support operations flown by 20 Mosquitoes over Holland, Belgium and France together with 128 aircraft on a diversionary minelaying sortie in the Kiel Bay area helped to split the German defences. A further 22 Mosquitoes flew harassing raids to Berlin, Dortmund, Hanover and Oberhausen to keep the residents awake and the defences wondering where the main attack for the night was to be concentrated. In fact this was a well thought out strategy to cover another maximum effort to Frankfurt by 816 aircraft. One large section of the German night fighter force was drawn off to the minelaying aircraft as it was thought they were going to attack Hanover. Only a small number of fighters found the main bomber stream taking down 33 of them. 199 Squadron were fortunate and did not suffer any casualties, all thirteen aircraft and crews returning safely to Lakenheath, with Sgt Bowering the last to land at 0026 hrs.

24th March 1944

All flying cancelled during the day due to bad weather, and a night flying exercise ordered for two aircraft, also cancelled.

25th March 1944

A mixed bag of sorties for the Squadron. The battle orders were posted during the late morning showing that eight crews were to take part in a raid on Aulnoye, two for mining off the Frisians, two mining off Le Havre and two off Texel Island. However, earlier in the day, two crews had been ordered to kit up and fly an air sea rescue over the North Sea: F/O Harker, EF192 EX-J and F/O Hancock, EF161 EX-Z took off at 1120 hrs, but after a four hour search they returned to base having sighted nothing.

The raid on Aymeries was carried out by: F/O Hancock, EF161 EX-Z; F/Sgt Holmes, EE910 EX-K; F/Lt Eddy, LJ582 EX-L; P/O Turner, EE953 EX-E; F/Lt Guthrie, LJ581 EX-H; P/O Catterall, LJ580 EX-X; F/Lt Lumsdaine, LK397 EX-P; and F/Sgt Dale, EH930 EX-N.

They took off between 1855 hrs and 1907 hrs, reaching the target area in approximately two and a half hours. F/Lt Eddy came in low at 9,000ft and the bomb aimer, P/O Lauritz, RAAF, identified the target by three red and one green indicators. His rear gunner, P/O Nolie, reported seeing a large block of buildings in the light of the photo flash, slightly to port of the red TIs.

The remaining aircraft bombed within minutes of each other, all reporting a good concentration of target indicators, with many bombs bursting in and around them. The crews returned safely to base and landed between 0004 hrs and 0034 hrs. The two crews detailed for the Frisians were P/O Cutler, EF138 EX-Y and F/O Harker, EF192 EX-J. These sorties were successfully completed, with Cutler taking off at 1855 hrs and Harker at 1953 hrs each flying to individual target areas. F/Lt Noble, BK816 EX-R and F/Lt Barson, EF455 EX-B took off for Le Havre at 1910 hrs and laid their mines, according to the operational record book, at 4823N 0449W and 5824N 0449W respectively – I have checked these positions and both are wrong. One is in the Bay of Biscay and the other in the Channel. Obviously an error when the report was typed up. The two Texel aircraft were flown by P/O Bowering, EF508 EX-G and P/O Winter EE943 EX-V. Both reported successful sorties with good weather and fair visibility above a slight ground haze. Their mines were dropped at 5302N 0436 E.

26th March 1944

The target for this raid was the large railway yard at Courtrai, but only four '199' crews were detailed for a force of 109 aircraft from 3, 4, 6 and 8 Groups: P/O Turner, EE953 EX-E; F/Lt Sturrock, LJ582 EX-L; F/Lt Noble, EF262 EX-D; and W/Cdr Bray, DFC, LJ578 EX-S, took off and attacked the target at 2100 hrs from 10,00ft. The target was well marked by the Pathfinders and the crews bombed on the large concentration of red TIs.

Detailed reports show that the bombing was spread over a large area surrounding the railhead and a great many buildings in the town were destroyed, including the jail, where five prisoners were killed. Much of the jail was blown apart enabling prisoners to escape, including a local butcher, who had been imprisoned for assisting Allied airmen to escape.

A total of 252 civilians were killed during the raid, including 79 visitors from other areas, who were attending a religious feast. The next day the Germans press-ganged 1,500 local men to repair the damage to the tracks and the lines were fully functional, with trains running, three days later.

The Squadron was also involved in a large sea mining operation sending three crews to the Bayonne area and five to the "South West Coast of France" that, after checking out the co-ordinates given by the navigators appears to be the mouth of the Gironde River.

The three crews on the Bayonne sortie did not have much success as P/O Hancock, LK397 EX-P took off at 1926 hrs and turned back at 2020 hrs over Halton, due to the Gee set being unserviceable. F/Lt Betts, LJ580 EX-X

W/Cdr Bray's bombing photograph taken during the raid of 26th March.

had lifted off at 1932 hrs and reached a point just north of Woking, from where he returned with failing engine power. Both aircraft returned with their full load of mines. The remaining sortie, flown by F/Lt Guthrie, LJ501 EX-H, took off at 1929 hrs and reached the designated area, dropping four mines from 5,500ft at 4332N 0133W, and returned at 0329 hrs.

Of the five sent to the Gironde Estuary, only four planted their mines.

P/O Cutler, EF138 EX-Y was forced to abandon his mission when the inner starboard engine started to lose power. They had almost reached the French coast, so decided to jettison the mines in the English Channel on their way back to base. Fl/Lt Button, EF455 EX-B; P/O Bowering, EF192 EX-J; F/O Harker, EE910 EX-K and F/Sgt Dale, EH930 EX-N reported no cloud and good visibility over the DZ and flew in at 10,000ft with no opposition.

533 LKH. 26/27-3-44.//NT. B." 10000 → 072° 2242
GIRONDE. C. 4 VEG. 21 SECS. P/O. BOWERING. J. 199.

P/O Bowering's photo taken on the mining sortie.

F/O Harker returned with one mine not released, owing to a technical failure, and F/Sgt Dale also had one mine hang up, but the bomb aimer, Sgt Swadling, was able to release this manually three minutes after the other mines were planted. It was dropped live while still on the original heading.

27th to 29th March 1944

No operations due to very bad weather. On the 29th twelve aircraft and crews had been detailed and were ready for operations, but at 1900 hrs this was cancelled.

30th March 1944

Bad weather continued, but nine aircraft and crews were put on standby to drop supplies to Resistance groups and one crew was detailed for sea mining.

At 1800 hrs, with six crews stood down due to the weather over the drop zones, P/O Bowering, LJ582 EX-L ("John 61"); P/O Catterall, LJ580 EX-X ("Pimento 63") and P/O Winter, EE943 EX-V ("Jockey 24") took off loaded with containers at 2000 hrs.

The ORB states that only one crew was successful in locating the target and dropping their load, but fails to give any other details. Further research has found that P/O Catterall successfully dropped fifteen containers and one package, P/O Winter was unable to find the DZ due to bad visibility and similarly P/O Bowering found thick cloud cover and poor visibility over the target area and was unable to deliver his load.

Sgt Cox, EF192 EX-J had been allocated the sea mining trip and took off at 0222 hrs (31st March) dropping six mines off the Frisian Isles at 0328 hrs. All the parachutes were seen to open by Sgt Farle, the rear gunner.

For Bomber Command, this night was to see the biggest losses suffered throughout the war, when main force was ordered to attack Nuremberg.

Under normal circumstances, much of the bombing operations would have been curtailed due to the moon period, especially on long range targets. According to weather reports, there should have been good high cloud cover to protect the bombers on the outward flight, but a subsequent reconnaissance flight carried out by a Mosquito reported that this was unlikely. The observation report also stated that there would be more of a likelihood of cloud obscuring the target deeper in Germany rather than anywhere on the outbound flight.

For some unaccountable reason, the order to abandon the raid was not given and this decision has caused a huge amount of debate post-war among academics and historians.

From the beginning of the pre-operational briefings to the time that the 782 aircraft left England, many squadron and flight commanders had voiced their dismay that this raid was taking place, but take place it did and as the first wave of bombers reached the Belgian border, they were intercepted by German night fighters. The German controller had somehow not been distracted by the diversionary raids of minelaying in the Heligoland area and spoofs on Aachen, Cologne and Kassel by Mosquitoes. Some reports state he had 300 fighters at his disposal, and most of them were dispersed over two control beacons named "Ida" and "Otto" that were astride the main route of the bombers. The half moon and clear skies illuminated the aircraft and some fighters armed with a new weapon code named "Schrage Musik" tore into the heavily-laden Lancasters and Halifaxes. This new weapon was a pair of upward pointing cannon that had been fitted to the Me110, that enabled the pilot to fly in under a bomber without being seen and fire directly up into the wing tanks and engines.

For over an hour, the German fighters exacted a steady toll on the bombers, and before the target was reached, 82 had been shot down. The weather and poor meteorological forecasts had also played a major part in this catastrophe; strong winds had blown many of the aircraft off course. The forecast expected northerly winds, but, in fact, became strong westerly and caused most of the bombers to lose their direction, and with so many aircraft falling in flames around them, those still flying were unable to plot the new winds with any accuracy and radio them back to England for updated information to be broadcast.

On the last leg of the run in, the lack of cloud now reversed and cloud started to build up beneath the bombers preventing the Pathfinders from marking the target area with any accuracy. With most of the aircraft now well North and east of the planned turning point to Nuremberg, only about 500 made it into the target area with a great many of the Pathfinders actually drifting well east of track. Only a few were equipped with sky markers and these were dropped late, some coming down ten miles east of the target. It appears that at least two Pathfinders dropped their markers on Schweinfurt drawing around 120 aircraft to this city where they dropped their bombs, causing more damage than in Nuremberg. With the thick cloud and adverse winds the Pathfinders marked Nuremberg too far to the east and a creep-back developed, causing most of the bomb loads to fall into open countryside.

There was no damage of any consequence in Nuremberg and the casualties in the city and surrounding area was put at 69 killed. Later, when all the intelligence was gathered, Bomber Command deemed the raid as a complete failure. 96 aircraft were lost and 545 aircrew died, i.e. with more airmen killed in one night than in the entire Battle of Britain.

A Victoria Cross was awarded, posthumously, to Pilot Officer C.J. Barton, pilot of 578 Squadron. He had carried on his mission after being attacked and his aircraft badly damaged that resulted in three of his crew bailing out through a misunderstanding of orders over the intercom. The navigator and wireless operator were among those who left the aircraft, but Barton decided to bomb the target and then try to return to England. One of the engines of the Halifax had been put out of action, but he and the remaining members of his crew managed to set a course and successfully reached the coast. He then encountered strong winds taking him further and further up the North Sea, so he tried to make landfall near Sunderland as the fuel supply was now all but exhausted. With all the engines intermittently cutting out he made a forced landing, but was killed in the crash. However his three remaining crew who had been ordered to take up their crash positions escaped with minor injuries.

31st March 1944

The final operation of the month fell to F/Lt Craw, LJ578 EX-S, who was detailed for a 'Special Mission', dropping containers to the Resistance in occupied Europe. The Squadron records for these sorties are far from helpful and only brief details are available, although the time of take off and landing is usually noted.

F/Lt Craw took off from RAF Lakenheath at 2002 hrs, the DZ was located and the load delivered, but due to adverse weather conditions was forced to land on his return at RAF Tangmere at 0204 hrs.

Helen Storrar, WAAF Cpl, map clerk, intelligence and navigation sections: *"I was posted to Lakenheath in early 1943 and then went with 199 to North Creake when the Americans took over our airfield. I remember the Duke of Gloucester visiting Lakenheath, but one of my most lasting memories is at North Creake during Christmas 1944, when the water was rationed due to the water tower freezing up during the abnormally low temperatures. We had to take our washing on the "boot lorry" to the YMCA in Norwich. I had a dog nicknamed "Snogger" who was born at Lakenheath and went to every station with me until I was demobbed".*

April

Conversion to Radio Countermeasures

The first four days of the month brought very bad weather conditions, curtailing all but local test and training flights. On the 4th, four aircraft and crews were detailed for SOE 'Special Operations', but cancelled at 1200 hrs.

5th April 1944

Eight crews were detailed for SOE sorties and five for mining operations off the south west coast of France. Of those flying the 'Special Missions' five were cancelled and only three took off: P/O Catterall, EE943 EX-V ("Delegate 1") and P/O Cattell, EF262 EX-D ("Paul 71") made successful drops on their appointed DZs. F/Lt Noble, BK816 EX-R ("Paul 74") is reported in the ORB to have made a successful drop, but in the battle order notes his trip was logged at 'not complete'.

The five mining sorties were flown by: F/O Harker, EE910 EX-K; Sgt Cox, EF508 EX-G; P/O Cutler, EF138 EX-Y; F/Sgt Dale, EH930 EX-N; and F/Lt Barson, EF192 EX-J.

The co-ordinates given in the records show that the target area was the mouth of the Gironde River and that all the aircraft reached the DZ and dropped their mines from 5,000ft. F/O Harker reported clear visibility and no cloud and that his aircraft was attacked by a twin engined night fighter at 4520N 0115W, but no damage was sustained. The crews were using Lake Lacanau as a navigational pinpoint and this attack occurred just after crossing the lake on the run in to drop the mines. Sgt Cox, who had also just crossed Lake Lacanau at about 0030 hrs, encountered inaccurate light flak from some ground batteries, but was not hit. Sgt Dale also found conditions very favourable with good visibility and stated that the shoreline could be seen from 10 miles out to sea.

The weather again prevented operations over the next three days.

9th April 1944

Supply drops were on the battle orders again and three crews were detailed.

F/Lt Craw, EE943 EX-V ("Paul 22"), took off at 2140 hrs. P/O Cutler, EF138 EX-Y ("Pimento 86F"), took off at 2200 hrs and P/O Cattell, EE953 EX-E ("Satirist 1"), took off at 2324 hrs. They all – according to the ORB – reached their allotted drop zones and delivered the loads of containers successfully. However, the notes in the battle orders for 9th April are once more at odds with this entry as they state F/Lt Craw and P/O Cutler did not complete their drop. P/O Cutler, who had flown to DZ "Pimento 86F", returned to base after a gruelling nine hour flight, but on the approach at 350ft, the starboard outer failed and Cutler tried to overshoot. With the loss of power, it was impossible to gain height and the Stirling hit rising ground at Lakenheath and, although the crew escaped uninjured, the aircraft was severely damaged and later scrapped. The ORB omits to say that, during the outbound flight, the aircraft received some serious damage from ground fire that had put several large holes in the starboard wing.

10th April 1944

Six crews were detailed for a major air sea rescue duty over the North Sea: F/Sgt Holmes, EF161 EX-Z; F/Lt Chilcott, EH930 EX-N; F/Lt Sturrock, EF262 EX-B; F/O Harker, EF455 EX-B; Sgt Cox, EF192 EX-J; and P/O Winter, LK397 EX-P. They were all airborne just after 0630 hrs and conducted a thorough sweep, but nothing was sighted after a four hour search.

11th April 1944

No flying due to bad weather.

12th April 1944

Another air sea rescue duty with nine crews detailed for a sweep of the North Sea: F/Lt Sturrock, LK385 EX-A; F/O Harker, EF455 EX-B; F/Lt Eddy, EF262 EX-D; P/O Cattell, EE953 EX-E; F/Lt Barson, EF192 EX-J; F/Lt Lumsdaine, LK397 EX-P; F/Lt Guthrie, EJ161 EX-Z; F/Lt Chilcott, EH930 EX-N; and F/Lt Noble, BK816 EX-R, got airborne just after 0700 hrs and conducted a search ranging from three to four hours in duration, but again nothing was sighted.

13th to 18th April 1944

No operations or flying duties, apart from local training flights, ground crews using the days to carry out major maintenance work.

19th April 1944

Nine crews and aircraft detailed for air sea rescue duty over the North Sea: F/Lt Eddy, EF508 EX-G; F/Lt Barson, EF192 EX-J; W/O Robbins, LK385 EX-A; P/O Harrison, LJ501 EX-H; P/O Cattell, EF262 EX-D; F/O Harker, EH930 EX-N; P/O Turner, BK816 EX-R; P/O Catterall, EF141 EX-Z and F/Lt Betts EE941 EX-U.

Nothing was sighted.

21st April 1944

Six crews detailed for air sea rescue duty over the North Sea: W/O Robbins, EF262 EX-D; F/Lt Sturrock, EF192 EX-J; F/Lt Guthrie, LJ501 EX-B; P/O Turner, EE953 EX-E; Sgt Cox, EE943 EX-V and P/O Harrison, EF161 EX-Z, all got airborne just after 0800 hrs.

A four hour sweep with no result.

22nd April 1944

A leaflet drop carried out by two crews over the town of Toulouse in France. F/Sgt Holmes, BK816 EX-R and P/O Winter, LK397 EX-P lifted off at 2126 hrs, but only F/Sgt Holmes completed the flight. He dropped his leaflets at 0015 hrs, flying over the town at 14,000ft. P/O Winter's Gee set became u/s and he landed back at 0030 hrs.

23rd and 24th April

No operations detailed. Maintenance and flying training carried out.

25th April 1944

This was to be the last time the Squadron flew their Stirlings while attached to 3 Group and was another air sea rescue sweep over the North Sea.

The six crews detailed for the duty were: W/O Robbins, LK397 EX-P; P/O Cattell, EF455 EX-B; P/O Turner, EF192 EX-J; F/Lt Guthrie, LJ501 EX-H; Sgt Cox, EE943 EX-V; and F/Lt Eddy, EE941 EX-U.

It was another fruitless search with nothing sighted.

For the remainder of the month, the Squadron was stood down, with minimum flying training and maintenance, as it had been decided by Bomber Command to re-equip the Squadron's Stirlings with new and secret electronic radar jamming sets. This would necessitate a move, and personnel were ordered to start packing and crating stores and equipment in readiness for the impending transfer to their new airfield at RAF North Creake in Norfolk.

The Squadron records show that, during April, P/O R.L. Cutler was awarded the DFC. His citation, published in the *London Gazette* on 9th May 1944, reads: *'Pilot Officer Raymond Llewellyn Cutler, 171393, RAFVR. – In April 1944 this officer was the pilot of an aircraft detailed for a sortie against a target far in enemy territory. On several occasions on the outward flight the aircraft was subjected to heavy fire from the ground defences and was hit in the starboard wing. Nevertheless, Pilot Officer Cutler accomplished his mission successfully. His skill and determination was typical of that which he has shown throughout the many sorties in which he has taken part.'*

'Window'

Due to the ever mounting losses of Bomber Command, several scientists had been employed to create some form of countermeasure to the German radar and night fighter control systems. The ideas were many and varied and are too numerous to be included in this narrative. However, due to the nature of the work to be carried out by 199 Squadron from June 1944 to the end of the war, an explanation of the two systems they would be using to good effect is set out here.

The two systems were known by their code names 'Window' and 'Mandrel', and extremely effective in disrupting German radar, but in themselves, completely different in their structure and the way they came into service. Broadly speaking, 'Window' was the use of bundles of aluminium strips, cut to a specific length, and dropped at a controlled rate and height. Each individual bundle consisted of hundreds of thin strips of a given width and length that corresponded to half the wavelength of the radar signal to be jammed. The resulting effect of a large cloud of strips showed up on German radar as a number of heavy bombers. Initially it was impossible for the German operators to distinguish between a genuine echo and a false one and the reduction in bombers shot down was considerable. Although the idea was thought of before war broke out, its introduction was delayed.

As early as 1937, Dr R.V. Jones had spoken about the possibility of our new secret radar sets being produced at the time, having their signals swamped and unrecognisable by the simple use of a 'dipole' or reflective strip suspended in the air. This put many people against using 'Window' as they feared the Germans would quickly use something similar to blind our own radar system. This argument raged for several years in the highest levels of scientific and political circles. The main thrust of those against the idea was that the scientists should produce a radar set that was almost invulnerable to the effects of a German mounted countermeasure using something similar to our 'Window'.

It is perhaps relevant to explain how the rather unusual name of 'Window' came about. It was during some trials at the Telecommunications Research Establishment in 1941, that the chief superintendent, Mr A.P. Rowe, was visited by Dr Cockburn to discuss a suitable code name for the bundles of metal strips. They decided that the name should have no relation to the material or device, so as not to give the enemy any idea of its purpose. Mr Rowe looked around the room and suggested *"why not call it something like 'Window'"* – and so it was.

Trials using 'Window' carried on unabated into 1942 and it was decided to use the foil, cut to the sizes of propaganda leaflets, and sandwich them in between two sheets of paper, thus disguising their true purpose from the Germans. The smaller leaflet size of 8½" x 5½" was found to be the most effective and a bundle of approximately 250 of this size sheet gave a corresponding echo as large as a Blenheim bomber and would jam the German Wurzburg radar.

A firm called Vanesta was given the order to produce the aluminium foil strips manufactured from the raw material already used to produce radio-condensers. They were also instructed to produce only the foil strips and not to bother with covering them with paper, as it became obvious that the Germans would quickly discover the true nature of the countermeasure.

In March 1942, Bomber Command had planned to launch a 1,000-bomber raid on Cologne and it had been sanctioned to use 'Window' for the first time to cover the operation. However, Sir Charles Portal, the Chief of Air

Staff withdrew his permission at the last moment on the insistence of Sir Sholto Douglas, Commander in Chief, Fighter Command. He again argued that if the Germans were presented with this form of counter measure and used it against our radar network he could not guarantee the effectiveness of our fighter defences. So again Bomber Command was denied the use of a proven and effective tool to disrupt the German radar system and were forced to wait while more experimenting and testing was carried out to satisfy the sceptics.

During May 1942, the arguments raged on, with the scales still tipped in favour of not allowing 'Window' to be used operationally. One of the chief concerns was that, if the Germans defeated the Russians, they would be able to turn all the bombers used in that theatre against Britain. As a consequence of this huge number of aircraft, coupled with their own form of 'Window' thrown against our defences, the German air force could tip the balance, overwhelm our defences, and cause unknown damage to British industrial output.

The Germans were steering an almost parallel course. From German records it appears that they were experimenting in early 1942 with a form of metallic strip they code named 'Duppel'. Their results gave them cause for concern, as it had been shown that this form of jamming was an almost total blinding of the radar units set up along the Baltic Coast. When Reichsmarschal Goering was informed of the devastating effect 'Duppel' was having, especially on the early warning radar, he immediately ordered the withdrawal of any further experiments and stopped development of any countermeasures to the effect of the jamming. He also ordered the destruction of a two page report on the effects of Duppel submitted to him by General Martini, the head of the German Signals Organisation. Nothing, it seems, was to be allowed to fall into British hands that could be used against the German defence systems.

In England, although 'Window' had not been cleared for operational use, several companies had, since as early as 1942, been instructed to acquire the necessary manufacturing machinery and to produce as much of the aluminium foil strips as possible. It was not until June 1943 that the use of 'Window' was finally resolved.

Meetings at the highest level of government and Bomber Command were held and Sir Charles Portal raised the question at a staff conference on the 23rd. Winston Churchill gave it his backing and Sir Arthur Harris was given official instructions to prepare his crews and aircraft for its use. It was noted that at least 400 tons of the aluminium strips would be required each month and this equated to something like 1,000 million individual pieces. Production was increased to meet this demand and stockpiles laid in at various warehouses around the country. Winston Churchill, at a meeting on 15th July 1943, gave his final approval for Bomber Command to begin using 'Window' as soon as was practicable. All other parties who had raised objections in the past now withdrew from the arguments and Sir Arthur Harris ordered his staff to prepare an attack on a suitable target, using their new won radar countermeasure. The short nights of the summer precluded any long-range flights into Germany and, with this in mind, Hamburg was chosen as the initial target, and the date set for 24th July. Records show that 791 aircraft were detailed for this raid and, as a result of using 'Window', only twelve aircraft were lost, representing 1.5% of the force. This figure must be set against previous losses that were usually in the 5.5 to 6.0% range of totals despatched and would have amounted to perhaps 50 aircraft.

In most aircraft, it was the bomb aimers who had been nominated to drop the bundles of foil at one minute intervals and the crews had been given specific instructions as to the correct position and height when they should begin. The resulting cloud of metal strips that began to form reproduced an echo for each bundle similar to a heavy bomber on the German radar screens. From this, it is easy to calculate that the Germans were facing a force of over 1,000 bombers.

Confusion set in and the German night fighter control was unable to give instructions to the waiting pilots and those aircraft that did take off also had their airborne radar sets equally disrupted. Many fighter pilots attacked the clouds of 'Window', thinking they were on the track of a bomber, only to find nothing at all but empty sky.

Another bonus from using 'Window' was that radar controlled flak guns were almost useless. According to some bomber crew reports and also comments later made by the Germans themselves, the blue coloured Master searchlights were following false targets. The flak gunners resorted to firing 'blind' but it is thought they only accounted for three of the bombers shot down.

'Window' was later refined and became integrated into larger and much broader radio countermeasures of which 199 Squadron would play a major role.

The Bruneval Raid
"Operation Biting"
27th to 28th February 1942.

In 1941, Dr R.V. Jones was appointed Principal Scientific Officer, in recognition of his work in defeating the German X-Gerat navigation beams, used by their bombers to locate targets in Britain. He was also heavily involved in understanding the radar used by the Germans and in particular their Wurzburg systems, their latest and most advanced, set up mainly on the coast.

Photographic reconnaissance by low level Spitfires revealed a new radar installation on the cliff tops near the French village of Bruneval which Jones believed to be a Wurzburg installation, and asked for more detailed photographs. This sortie was given to F/Lt Tony Hill, who was one of the best reconnaissance pilots at the time. At extremely low altitude he photographed the site and proved beyond doubt that they were using a parabolic reflector.

Due to the installation's proximity to the sea, a raid could capture components and bring them back for evaluation. This idea went down well with Churchill, who immediately instructed Lord Louis Mountbatten, the Chief of Combined Operations, to set up the raid.

The French Resistance reconnoitred the area and from their findings it was decided a full frontal assault on the beach was out of the question due to strong defences. It was decided that an air dropped raiding party would stand a better chance and, if staged, taking into account the tide times, they could be extracted by the Royal Navy using landing craft from the beach at the foot of the adjacent cliffs.

The planners decided to use twelve RAF Whitley bombers to drop 120 paratroops from C Company of the 2nd Battalion of the 1st Parachute Brigade, drawn from Scottish Regiments, including the Black Watch, Cameron Highlanders, King's Own Scottish Borderers and the Seaforths under the command of Major John Frost. The Royal Navy were to patrol the coast using, six landing craft and MGBs, their firepower stiffened by men of No 12 Commando equipped with Bren guns. One important addition to the raiding party was Flight Sergeant C.W.H. Cox, one of the RAF's best radar technicians, whose responsibility it would be to remove all the important components of the Wurzburg.

Much intense training took place, especially for F/Sgt Cox, who was instructed in the finer arts of jumping from an aircraft by making several drops from tethered balloons at No 4 Parachute Training Squadron, Ringway. Once this was completed, he received further training at Tilshead on Salisbury Plain, with exercises in unarmed combat, weapon training, route marching, PT, and night patrols. All the personnel taking part in the raid had now been brought together at Tilshead under great secrecy and they trained under a strict 'need to know' doctrine. The soldiers were told they had been chosen to put on a display before members of the war cabinet that would demonstrate techniques for raiding a headquarters building behind enemy lines. F/Sgt Cox thought otherwise, he was fairly certain that in a short time he would be making a rather rapid trip abroad.

The RAF's photographic interpretation unit built a scale model of the area around Bruneval, but no details were shown of actual place names; only the function of the buildings were labelled thereby keeping the actual target area secret.

On the 26th February 1942, after a week of frustrating cancellations due to bad weather, the raiding party was finally given the order to be prepared for action at a few hours notice and the following night twelve suitably modified Whitley bombers of 51 Squadron took off for the French coast and Bruneval.

Wing Commander Charles Pickard, an experienced pilot who had already seen considerable action against the enemy, flew the lead aircraft. He was a celebrity, having taken a major role in the RAF film "Target for Tonight", shown in cinemas across the country.

At midnight, the first two aircraft dropped their troops, commanded by Lieutenant Charteris, but they were slightly off track as the RAF crews had mistaken the drop zone. The two sections descended and landed one and a half miles away in the Val aux Chats, not far from the hamlet of L'Enfer. The remainder of the force dropped successfully, dead on target, without alerting the defenders. Major Frost gathered his men and was rather worried that Lt Charteris and his men were missing but decided to press on with the attack and each special section already briefed for a specific task moved off to take up their positions. Some sections were to attack German strong points while others were to give defensive and covering fire for the withdrawal down to the sea.

The section containing F/Sgt Cox and the engineers had been ordered to proceed immediately to the radar installation and begin to dismantle it. German opposition began shortly after the troops started to move into position, but F/Sgt Cox and his party managed to strip out all the important components of the Wurzburg set and load them onto a specially built trolley that had been dropped by parachute along with the supply containers. As it was too large to dismantle, photographs were taken of the large parabolic bowl, but the flash bulbs attracted far too many German bullets, some close enough they were striking the surrounding structure of the bowl itself, so this was quickly abandoned.

The paratroops were now fighting hard to keep the Germans away from F/Sgt Cox and the engineers and in the darkness everything appeared to be confused, with heavy firing all around. However, they managed to make their way to the top of the cliffs and found the path leading down to the beach and it was here that they were caught by accurate fire from a machine gun down on the beach.

Sergeant-Major Strachan was hit and fell with three wounds to his stomach. He was dragged out of harm's way behind a concrete casemate, where field dressings were applied, and a shot of morphia administered. The machine gun on the beach fell silent as the German troops withdrew and F/Sgt Cox and his party scrambled down the icy path hauling the heavily-laden trolley together with all the pieces of the radar unit. It was reported to Major Frost that the German troops were deploying towards the cliff top positions he now occupied and he ordered his troops to counter this by mounting an assault with the heavy section.

As the battle intensified, shooting was heard from the southeast. Charteris, who had unfortunately been dropped away from the DZ, had arrived with his section of men. Their arrival outflanked the enemy's positions, who immediately abandoned their heavy machine guns and departed with some haste into the darkness. By pure coincidence the charge made by Charteris's men came at the same time as the assaults mounted by Frost's troops, and their combined effort was enough to clear the area of the enemy and proceed to the beach.

Charteris realised as soon as he had landed that the two lead aircraft had been way off track and he would have to modify his plans accordingly. Just after landing, he was able to observe the other Whitleys coming in well to the north and this helped to orientate his position to the DZ. He gathered in the containers and distributed the contents among his troops and sent out two scouts to assess the immediate terrain and was informed they were fortunately near the road leading to Bruneval. Setting off at a steady jog they saw other soldiers as they neared the village, but remained unchallenged. One of the German soldiers joined the line of British troops thinking they were his own making their way to the cliff tops and he was immediately killed.

Nearing Bruneval village they came under fire from the Germans and had to shoot their way out of a difficult situation, but managed to avoid any casualties and pressed on towards their objective. This was the gunfire that Frost had heard earlier, leading to some confusion as to who and where it was coming from, but equally it was just as confusing for the German garrison as they knew commandos had landed, but had no idea as to their intended objective. It was about this time that two or three of the party got separated and as a consequence a radio set carried by one of them would not arrive at the beachhead.

Once past Bruneval, Charteris allowed his troops a short respite to gather their bearings and get their breath back and then he led a charge on the Germans with much shouting and pent up anger at being late for the fight.

On the beach two sappers had used their mine detectors to sweep an area down to the water's edge and luckily found nothing, so Frost deployed his men in a defensive ring, although he knew he would not be able to hold out for too long should the Germans attack from above. They had with them two No 18 radio sets to contact the navy, but neither seemed to be working; two signallers with Charteris's party had been reported missing together with their No 18 set, so this compounded the problems further. Contact was tried on the No 38 set, but again, nothing was heard from the boats.

A small secret transmitter beacon, known by the code name of 'Rebecca', was set up by the sappers and switched on and appeared to be working correctly. Its counterpart receiver named 'Eureka' was being carried in one of the landing craft, but there was no way of knowing if the directional signals were getting through. As a last resort, Frost ordered Lt Ross to fire green Very lights from the north and south end of the beach. Reports started to come in that headlights could be seen moving towards them from the east and southeast and it seemed inevitable that the Germans would soon arrive in strength and, if armed with heavy mortars, the waiting troops would have little protection on the open area of shingle at the base of the cliffs.

Under cover of darkness, the navy for their part had made their way unopposed to the co-ordinates given and hove to. But just as they thought they would have a clear run in to the beach, two German destroyers and two E Boats were seen steaming at high speed from north to south and passed within a mile of the tiny flotilla. Fortunately, the enemy did not see the landing craft that slowly made their way closer to the shore, standing off at about 300 yards when the lookouts saw the green Very lights and also a light from a signalling lamp. At the same time, one of the signallers on the beach made contact with the boats on a No 38 set and ordered the boats to land without delay. Frost had not observed any of this going on and heard a soldier shout out 'Sir! The boats are coming in, God bless the ruddy navy'.

It was now that the men on the beach were submitted to a withering fire from the Bren guns mounted on the landing craft as they sent bullets up and down the cliffs. A quick radio message from Frost put an end to this and, to his relief, no one had been hit. After a few tense minutes the boats were loaded. The first to go were the wounded and F/Sgt Cox together with the Royal Engineers and their valuable cargo. The remainder all got away safely and the landing craft were eventually met by motor gun boats who took them in tow. F/Sgt Cox and the German radar components were transferred to MGB312 and made for Portsmouth at over twenty knots. Due to the adverse weather the other boats were making slow progress and by dawn were only fifteen miles from the French coast, but help was at hand as four Free French chasseurs, *Bayonne, Calais, Lamor* and *Le Lavandou* plus two destroyers HMS *Blencathra* and HMS *Fernie* arrived to cover their passage back to England. To ensure complete protection, a squadron of Spitfires was detailed to stay overhead until they reached harbour.

The radio sets were still being manned on the boats and one of the operators received the distressing message that the two signallers missing from Charteris's party had made it to the beach, but had just failed to make it in time to be picked up. They were helped by members of the French Resistance to stay out of the Germans hands, but in March 1942, they were captured and made prisoners of war. The two French people helping them escape, Maurice de la Joie and his wife were also taken at the same time and sentenced to death. Although the death sentence was not carried out, they were sent to Ravensbruck and Buchenwald and survived the war, but as invalids.

Operation 'Biting' was a major success and much was made of it to boost morale throughout the country. There were losses on each side.

British Casualties and Decorations:

Two killed: Pte Alan Scott, age 24, 9th Bn Royal Berkshire Regiment attached to 2nd Bn Parachute Regiment, A.A.C. and Rifleman Hugh McIntyre, age 28, 9th Bn Cameronians (Scottish Rifles) attached to 2nd Bn Parachute Regiment, A.A.C.

One wounded: Company Sergeant Major Strachan – he later made a good recovery from his wounds.

Six reported as missing and all were taken prisoner and survived the war.

Awards:

Major Frost and Lt. Charteris received the Military Cross; F/Sgt Cox, Sgt Grieve and Sgt MacKenzie received the Military Medal; Lt. Peter Young was Mentioned in Despatches; Company Sergeant Major Strachan was awarded the Croix de Guerre.

Major Frost was to later command the 2nd Parachute Battalion at the Battle of Arnhem.

German Casualties:

Army: Two killed. One seriously wounded. Two missing.

Luftwaffe: Three killed. One wounded. Three missing.

Of those reported missing by the Germans, two had been taken prisoner during the raid and were transported back to England for interrogation.

One very important point can be cleared up. A number of paratroops had been ordered to execute F/Sgt Cox should it appear likely he would be captured. Several books dealing with the Bruneval Raid mention that this *may* have been the case. It can be stated categorically that F/Sgt Cox was to be shot to prevent him revealing any knowledge of the British radar system. He was not aware of this when he volunteered for the mission but afterwards learned the truth. This important fact came from F/Sgt Cox himself and was related to his son many years after the war ended, as he would not talk about his experiences to anyone immediately after the event.

The capture of components from the Wurzburg radar set allowed the scientists at TRE (Telecommunication Research Establishment) to evaluate it and how best to jam its signals. It proved that the radar could not be disrupted using normal countermeasures, similar to Mandrel, as it was capable of radiating signals over a broad range of frequencies. The only measure capable of effective jamming, proved to be 'Window' and, as already stated, it would be many months before clearance was given for its use.

Another interesting result of the raid prompted the German High Command to strengthen the defences of all radar stations along the French and Low Countries coastlines. This had a major impact on the areas surrounding these installations as the barbed wire, prevented grazing animals getting at the grass. The sites stood out like sore thumbs making photographing them so much easier, and had an important bearing prior to D Day.

May
RAF North Creake, Norfolk

A change in the Squadron's activities, from bombing missions within 3 Group, to electronic jamming and radar counter measures associated with 100 Group, began on 1st May.

From being in the thick of deep penetration raids over heavily defended targets, the squadron was now called upon to carry out a more subtle and secret role – one rarely mentioned in the annals of Bomber Command. It began with a marching in inspection of the Squadron on movement from RAF Lakenheath to RAF North Creake, situated at Egmere, Wells next the Sea, Norfolk.

100 Group had been set up specifically to operate all aspects of countermeasures against the German radar system, incorporated in their ground and air defence systems. The Group, officially established on 23rd November 1943, would also operate 'Intruder' aircraft, mainly Mosquitoes, to shoot down enemy night fighters over their own territory. One other important role was that of intelligence gathering to provide information on the Germans' progress in developing new forms of radar, so that British countermeasures could keep pace, and to find and plot the locations of the German transmitters, so that they could be taken out before D-Day. This most secret activity within the Group became known as ELINT (Electronic Intelligence) and was mostly carried out by specially equipped Mosquitoes.

After some initial teething troubles and moving from RAF Radlett to RAF West Raynham, the command structure of 100 Group finally found permanent quarters at the Victorian mansion Bylaugh Hall near Dereham, Norfolk, during late December 1943 and remained there until the end of the war.

At RAF North Creake, seventeen ground crew from 199 Squadron were despatched on the 1st May to RAF Foulsham to assist in the modifications needed to convert the Stirlings from front line bomber to the RCM role. This entailed fitting Mandrel jamming equipment, already described, inside the fuselage and all the associated transmitting aerials on the underside of the aircraft together with some extra chutes to dispense the bundles of 'Window'. An extra jammer named 'Shiver' was also fitted, and was in fact, a modified R3003A Mk II IFF (Identification Friend or Foe) set that operated on the Wurzburg 53cm band. This equipment could also be used as a normal IFF set if required.

During the first week of May, there were no Stirlings at North Creake, and all personnel were occupied with moving in stores and equipment from Lakenheath, and allocating the many buildings to various trades. The airfield, built by Taylor Woodrow Ltd, was completely new and came under 3 Group in November 1943, but was handed over to 100 Group on 7th December 1943. Plans were then put forward to lengthen the runways and, accordingly, the station was placed on Care and Maintenance, but this work was eventually cancelled. Consequently the station re-opened during April 1944 and 199 Squadron moved in on May 1st.

The Squadron soon got established and were well prepared for the arrival of the modified Stirlings. Many of the station personnel were also involved in anti aircraft defence training.

The first Stirling arrived around the 10th of May, and over the next two weeks, twelve more arrived. During this time, three more aircraft were modified at RAF Defford, Worcestershire, (TRE) and a further four at RAF Foulsham that was now classed as the BSDU (Bomber Support Development Unit) for 100 Group.

During the remaining days of May, the aircrews were involved in intensive flying training, and ground staff were equally hard at work checking the Stirlings and carrying out any remedial work.

With the Mandrel and Shiver equipment fitted, the Stirling, needed an additional crew member, wireless operator (special). His sole responsibility was to ensure that the jamming equipment was tuned to the frequencies allocated.

RAF North Creake, looking east towards the North Sea in 1944.

As the extra personnel arrived during May, they were allocated to individual crews and immediately began to get to grips with operating the Mandrel sets while airborne. There were some difficulties with this final phase of the training, as it had been decided to hold back the use of the Mandrel screen until D-Day and the invasion of Normandy so as not to alert the Germans prematurely of what was to come. It was therefore necessary not to operate the equipment anywhere near the enemy coast and training flights were confined to keep them as far away from German electronic 'eyes and ears' as possible. All training and maintenance was almost completed by the end of May and final preparations were put in hand for the D-Day invasion of occupied Europe.

W/O M. Stones, station warrant officer: *"I was posted to North Creake on 1st May 1944 as SWO. I had to sign for the RAF buildings from works and bricks, as it was known at the time. The incident of when the American Flying Fortress landed all shot up comes to mind, it was taken over to a corner of the 'drome and rebuilt by a mobile repair unit from the USAAF. As a consequence I had to issue a large number of bicycles to the American airmen. From the outer perimeter of the aerodrome you could free-wheel into Wells-on-Sea but it was a good slog coming back!"*

199 Squadron Flight and Section Leaders, North Creake, 1944. *Front*: F/Lt Doug Halliwell, signals leader; F/Lt George Wilde, navigation leader; F/Lt Lance Smith, squadron adjutant; S/Ldr 'Doc' Gorringe, medical officer. *Back*: F/Lt Bill Knights, 'A' Flight Commander; F/Lt Doug McIlroy, special signals leader; W/Cdr Bev Bevington, commanding officer; F/Lt Ted Teer, engineering leader; S/Ldr Harold Jepson, 'B' flight commander.

199 Squadron flight and section commanders, North Creake. *From left to right*: F/Lt Doug Halliwell, DFC, signals leader; F/Lt H.T. Malloy, gunnery leader; F/Lt Lance Smith, squadron adjutant; F/Lt Doug McIlroy, special signals leader; W/Cdr Bev Bevington, commanding officer; F/Lt Bill Knights, 'A' Flight commander; F/Lt George Wilde, navigation leader; F/Lt Ted Teer, engineering leader; F/Lt W. Doolan, bombing leader; F/Lt A.W. Burley, 'B' flight commander.

June 1944
D-Day – another first for the Squadron – an unsolved mystery

From the 1st to the 4th June all '199' crews were putting the final touches to their training programme and the ground crews double-checked the Stirlings and their essential equipment. Unknown to the troops gathered on the South Coast of England, a great deal rested on the successful jamming and 'spoof' sorties to be flown in their support as they crossed the channel in the largest invasion fleet ever assembled.

The planners of the invasion had held numerous meetings with the Scientific Intelligence Department and other associated departments to prepare a gigantic hoax that would wrong-foot the German coastal defences and hopefully keep vast numbers of their troops away from the actual invasion beaches.

By D-Day, virtually all the enemy coastal radar stations had been located and taken out by bombing or by rocket firing Typhoons, but some were purposely spared from destruction. Dr Cockburn and his team had worked long and hard on perfecting the means to generate two 'phantom fleets' on the remaining German radar screens. This was to be made possible by dropping 'Window' at a very precise rate over just as precise an area of the Channel. Using careful calculations by one of the team, Mrs Joan Curran, it was found that aircraft flying rectangular orbits over a sixteen mile square area dropping 'Window' and getting the square to move forward at eight knots at 3,000ft would produce an echo resembling a large fleet of ships. To further the illusion, the Mandrel sets to be operated by 199 Squadron would be positioned in such a way as to allow the remaining enemy radar installations to see through gaps in the blanket jamming, so these could plot the approach of the phantom fleets.

By late evening on 5th June all the planning was complete. It now remained to put the invasion into motion. The main objectives for the allied landings were the beaches of Normandy and the troops were to be positioned off shore at first light on the 6th.

As the huge armada of ships left the English ports and harbours the jamming war began in earnest and the two ghost fleet aircraft assembled to the north east under the code names of "Glimmer" and "Taxable". They were flown by 617 and 218 Squadrons respectively, with "Glimmer" aimed at Boulogne and "Taxable" at Cap d'Antifer.

With the aid of Gee and G-H navigational equipment they flew their precise courses, dropping 'Window' at the required rate whilst a number of RAF air-sea rescue launches and other small boats towed out barrage balloons with radar reflectors fitted inside. The balloon reflectors amplified any German radar signal, making it appear much larger and stronger than it was and gave a trace that represented a large ship. The Mandrel screen was to be flown between Portland Bill and Littlehampton and 199 Squadron contributed nineteen Stirlings for the sortie, sixteen flying in the jamming role with three as reserves. The USAAF added a further four B17 Flying Fortresses to the screen. Another line of defence was flown along the Somme estuary with ABC and 'Window' aircraft and 214 Squadron, which had converted to the American B17, flew five sorties and were joined by 24 Lancasters of 101 Squadron. These aircraft produced a decoy representing a major attack by a large force of bombers.

As history has shown, the invasion of Europe was successful, but little mention is made of the huge effort mounted in support of the ground troops by the use of countless 'spoof' and decoy raids, nor the use of jamming equipment and the scientists who invented and produced it.

The losses recorded for Operation Overlord are in the region of 10,000 men, from the initial total 155,000 troops sent to the landing beaches. This is a huge number by any account, but how many more would have been lost had it not been for the countermeasures put in place during the sea crossing.

Mandrel Tactics

The Mandrel screen aircraft had to fly a series of precise circuits that became known as the 'Racecourse Pattern' and consisted of flying an oval orbit ten miles long keeping to the Gee lines perpendicular to the enemy coast. Two aircraft formed a 'jamming centre', one on the up leg and one on the down leg each transmitting on a different frequency to fully cover the 68 to 203 Mhz and 78 to 203 Mhz bands. By making accurate turns and allowing for wind speed and direction it was possible to produce a circuit of ten minutes duration. This procedure, of course, called for the highest degree of flying and navigational skills by the '199' crews, who were initially required to fly at the Stirling's maximum altitude of between 15,000 and 19,000ft. Certain modifications to the actual positioning of the Mandrel screen were called for when it was found that it could severely hamper our own communication and radar systems. From mid-June all Mandrel jamming sorties were usually routed out over the North Sea keeping between 70 and 90 miles away from the enemy coastline and later in 1945 the jamming aircraft using Window and Mandrel, accompanied Main Force right through to the targets.

Ken Hartley, radar mechanic: *"One evening, early June 1944, I was enjoying a film in the little cinema in Wells. I can't remember the name of the film or the name of the cinema – too many years have passed by! However, I can remember quite distinctly the film suddenly stopping followed by all the house lights going on. Several RAF Police entered the cinema and ordered all military personnel to return to their bases, whereupon scores of soldiers and airmen left hurriedly. We didn't need to be told why – we all knew – at last it was the invasion of Europe, – D-Day!*

Back at the aerodrome we all went and prepared the aircraft for Ops, but in actual fact everything was suddenly cancelled. Twenty-four hours later it was 'on' again. What we had worked for and waited for was about to happen".

199 Squadron Electronic Countermeasure Jamming Sorties
June 1944 to May 1945

5th and 6th June 1944
D-Day Landings

Sixteen Stirlings and crews were detailed for their first operational missions using Mandrel. Three more aircraft were to be flown in reserve. Because of the top secret nature of this new role, documentation was at first kept to a minimum and consequently the ORB, for this period, has little to offer in the way of detail. The entry for each crew just carries a note "Special Mission", and no crew comments are entered as was usual after a mission, nor are there any indications of problems with the aircraft or the jamming equipment. Much of the following information is taken directly from a separate source of handwritten notes collectively headed "Sortie Records N Creake" that were fortunately found in a Nissen Hut at RAF Quedgely, Gloucestershire:

The sixteen front line crews for Operation Overlord consisted of:

ROUTE	POSITION	PILOT AND AIRCRAFT SERIAL
1	1. 5042N 0023E	F/Sgt Dale, LJ536 EX-P F/Lt Sturrock, LJ510 EX-A
1	2. 5027N 0003E	P/O Holmes, LJ580 EX-X W/O Keen, LJ514 EX-B
1	3. 5023N 0020W	F/Lt Eddy, LJ544 EX-D F/O Hancock, LJ525 EX-R
1	4. 5019N 0043W	F/Lt Chilcott, LJ531 EX-N F/Lt Turner, LJ513 EX-E
1	5. 5023N 0100W	P/O Catterall, LJ520 EX-Z P/O Bowering, LJ542 EX-G
2	6. 5027N 0217W	F/Lt Winter, LJ562 EX-V F/Lt Guthrie, LJ650 EX-H
2	7. 5025N 0229W	Sgt Gilbert, LJ578 EX-S P/O Cattell, LJ518 EX-K
2	8. 5014N 0233W	F/Sgt Milsom, LJ565 EX-Q P/O Harrison, LJ569 EX-C

Reserves:

'A' Flight. F/O Harker, LJ543 EX-J.
'B' Flight. Sgt Lind, LJ557 EX-Y. F/Sgt Cox, LJ538 EX-T.

Route 1: Base – Reading – Littlehampton – 'Racecourse' – Littlehampton – Reading – Base.
Route 2: Base – Reading – Portland Bill – 'Racecourse' – Portland Bill – Reading – Base.
Heights: Base – 12,000ft. Reading – 18,000ft. Operational Height – 18,000ft.

Take-off for all aircraft commenced at 2138 hrs and the last Stirling was airborne by 2154 hrs. (Nineteen aircraft in sixteen minutes).

F/Sgt Milsom reported problems and his aircraft was replaced at position 8 by F/Sgt Cox, LJ538 EX-T.

Position 1:
F/Lt Sturrock, LJ510 EX-A jammed position 1 until 0400 hrs and was then ordered to position 8. Commenced jamming at position 8 at 0428 hrs and completed. F/Sgt Dale, LJ536 EX-P remained at position 1 until 0440 hrs.

Position 2:
P/O Holmes, LJ580 EX-X at position 2 was diverted to position 7 at 2334 hrs and commenced jamming at 0051 hrs. W/O Keen, LJ514 EX-B detailed for position 2, had problems with his aircraft and was ordered to return and forced to land at Langham.

Position 3:
F/Lt Eddy, LJ544 EX-D arrived on station at 2330 hrs. Reported *"Led pattern and visual contact was maintained"*. Left 'A' at 0450 hrs.

Position 5:
P/O Bowering, LJ542 EX-G arrived at 'A' 2338 hrs. Kept station until 0120 hrs. When 'X' returned to base continued on 10 minute periods. Opinion – *"Possible by Nav alone. Three turns to get timing OK"*.

Position 6:
F/Lt Winter, LJ562 EX-V arrived at position 'A' 2330 hrs. After 2 turns, settled down to 30 seconds, done purely on navigation. *"Recommend homing against wind"*. Left area at 0450 hrs. *"Radar trouble coming home"*.

Position 7:
P/O Cattell, LJ518 EX-K on station as ordered, but switched to position 2 at 2330 Hrs. Arrived at position 2 at 2358 hrs. *"Done purely on visual contact until Sgt Gilbert, LJ578 EX-S left pattern short of fuel"*. Left position 'A' – 0450 hrs.

Position 8:
F/Sgt Cox, LJ538 EX-T 1st reserve. *"Position 'A' 2351 hrs. Left 'A' at 0420 hrs short of petrol. Continued jamming until 0435 hrs. Hit position 'A' within 30 seconds each time"*.

F/Sgt Milsom, LJ565 EX-Q. *"Reached position 'A' at 0228 hrs. Switched to position 1. Position 'A' 0340 hrs – Navigation. Left – 0451 hrs"*.

Note: The above transcripts are taken directly 'as written' from the original sortie records.

Because Mandrel jamming impeded the Gee signals used by the navigators, they were forced to use dead reckoning to plot their courses and positions, calling for a very high degree of proficiency to ensure the jamming screen stayed exactly on station.

The average approximate hours flown per crew on this first mission was seven hours, with some aircraft almost running out of fuel before landing back at North Creake.

The invasion was carried out successfully and the Mandrel and 'Window' jamming proved, beyond doubt, its worth to all the Allied forces. From this point the methods and equipment would be improved and refined mostly staying one step ahead of the Germans' attempts to counter the jamming of their radar and communication systems.

Frank Hancock F.M.A. (Flight Mechanic Airframe) recalls an incident just prior to D-Day: *"Ray Varley who was the FMA on Stirling LJ513 EX-E and myself were ordered by a flight sergeant, who will remain nameless, to get some BLACK and WHITE paint from the stores to paint the invasion recognition stripes on the wings and fuselage. We were almost put on a charge for arguing that we only needed WHITE paint".*

Stan Bethel PTI: *"I think I can claim to be the longest serving airman or officer serving at North Creake. I was attached to the station whilst it was being constructed and before it was commissioned to Bomber Command and I was still there when it was put on a 'Care and Maintenance' basis in the autumn of 1945".*

6th June 1944

Twelve crews and aircraft, with four reserves, were detailed for operations but all were cancelled prior to take-off.

7th to 12th June 1944

No operations were carried out, but the Squadron maintained a steady programme of training flights and maintenance with some airfield defence training thrown in for good measure.

13th June 1944

The pattern of cancelled operations continued, with sixteen crews assembling for a mission only to have it scrubbed at the last minute.

14th June 1944

Two crews were ordered to fly an experimental RCM sortie in support of a Bomber Command raid.

F/Lt Barson, LJ543 EX-J and F/Sgt Milsom, LJ557 EX-Y took off at 2120 hrs and 2124 hrs respectively. They proceeded to a point off Beachy Head and flew two minutes behind main force, consisting of 221 Lancasters and 13 Mosquitoes which attacked targets near Le Havre. This was the first daylight raid since May 1943 and was aimed at the E-boats and light naval forces stationed there. These were a direct threat to the shipping supplying the invasion forces on the Normandy beaches and the raid almost erased the risk from this area with most of the German naval craft moored in the harbour destroyed.

The RCM screen experiment was noted as 'completely successful' with both Stirlings returning to North Creake at 2325 hrs.

There are no indications in the Squadron records that show the type of jamming carried out by these two aircraft, but other sources point to the mission being the first flown by the newly formed Special Window Force (SWF) that was officially created on 14th June. The units incorporated in this force were 192, 199 and 214 Squadrons and they would carry out this duty in tandem with the Mandrel jamming. The SWF was equipped and able to drop a higher concentration of 'Window' than their counterparts in Bomber Command, the main difference being Bomber Command dropped one packet of 'Window' per bomber approximately every two minutes whereas SWF could drop ten packets per aircraft every minute. A small number of SWF aircraft could generate the appearance of over a 100 bombers and coupled with the Mandrel screen it was possible to spawn a completely bogus main force attack thus drawing up the German fighters away from the intended target area.

16th June 1944

Bomber Command ordered a raid on the Ruhrchemie synthetic oil plant at Sterkrade-Holten, Oberhausen, north of Duisburg and 199 Squadron despatched sixteen Stirlings to form the first flying Mandrel screen.

Main Force consisted of 321 aircraft – 162 Halifaxes, 147 Lancasters, 12 Mosquitoes and although the weather forecasts were poor, the attack went ahead as German oil production was now becoming more and more a priority target. However, due to the thick cloud cover the bomb aimers were unable to see the marker flares and bombs were dropped haphazardly. The results amounted to very few bombs hitting the oil plant and production was not significantly affected. Although initially covered by the Mandrel screen, the bombers were forced to pass near to Bocholt where the Germans had erected a night fighter beacon and by chance on this occasion the controller had chosen to assemble his force there. 21 bombers were shot down by the night fighters and a further ten by flak.

There follows a breakdown of the 199 Squadron aircraft participating in the raid and it must be remembered that from the co-ordinates given they were only able to protect the bombers in the early stages. The Mandrel screen formed an arc from a few miles off Felixstowe to a point midway in the North Sea between Sheringham and Den Helder on the Dutch coast. Once across the enemy coast the bomber stream was committed to fly towards the Ruhr and the heavy defences surrounding the likes of Essen, Duisburg and Gelsenkirchen.

199 Squadron Bomber Support 16th June 1944

POSITION	A/C	PILOT	NAVIGATOR
8	J. S.	F/Lt Barson	F/O Duckett
		P/O Cutler	P/O Dancer
10	K. Z.	P/O Robbins	F/O Hartwright
		P/O Catterall	P/O Ison
6	G. R.	W/O Keen	F/Sgt Wilkes
		F/Lt Noble	P/O Smith
4	D. N.	F/Lt Guthrie	F/O Marriot
		P/O Dale	P/O Whittleston
2	B. X.	F/Sgt Cox	F/O Maden
		F/Lt Betts	P/O Berry
1	A. P.	F/Lt Sturrock	F/O Wilde
		S/Ldr Lumsdaine	F/O White
12 Reserve	L. Y.	F/O Harker	W/O Russell
		P/O Holmes	F/Sgt Moore
13 Reserve	E. Q.	F/Lt Turner	F/Sgt Osbourne
		F/Sgt Gilbert	Sgt Webber

Positions:
1. A/C, A. P. 5320N 0300E
2. A/C, B. X. 5308N 0255E
4. A/C, D. N. 5245N 0246E
6. A/C, G. R. 5225N 0220E
8. A/C, J. S. 5210N 0154E
10. A/C, K. Z. 5159N 0118E

Routes Positions:
1, 2, 4, 6, 12. Base – Happisburgh – Posn – Happisburgh – Base

Reserves:
12. A/C, L. Y. 5300N 0030E
13. A/C, E. Q. 5220N 0130E

Routes Positions:
8, 10, 13. Base – Posn – Base

Sadly during the operation P/O Dale and his crew, flying LJ531 EX-N, were listed as missing. In the Operational Record Book they are listed as "missing from operations", no other comments are made and none of the other crews saw or heard anyone in difficulties. In the "Sortie Records" a handwritten note beside P/O Dale's entry states "– MISSING – PROBABLY DUE TO COLLISION". For many years this has been a puzzle to me and much thought has gone into the disappearance. With two wireless operators on board why was a distress signal not sent out if the crew had a major problem. It was also standard practise if the W/Op thought the aircraft was in danger especially over the English Channel or North Sea to immediately lock down his Morse key, so sending out a continuous signal that listening posts along the English coast could home onto and give an accurate fix. This does not appear to have happened. There are no reports of any night fighter activity in the ORB but as already mentioned the details of the Mandrel sorties are poorly written up. None of the returning aircraft reported a collision and the twin aircraft flying the same orbit – Stirling LJ544 flown by F/Lt Guthrie and the most likely to be involved in a collision due to its close proximity, did not report anything untoward. LJ544 was flying again the next day. Another mystery is that no air-sea search was ordered the next day. The Stirling and a highly trained crew just vanished on a detailed and known course, (the position this aircraft was flying in racecourse pattern is given in the table on the previous page), and no one thought to see if anyone could still be alive in a dinghy or clinging to wreckage. It is quite clear that before moving to North Craeke '199' was involved in many air-sea searches for other Squadron's missing aircraft but no search was ever conducted for one of their own.

Missing Crew of LJ531, 17th June 1944: P/O Thomas Wilson Dale, Pilot, RNZAF, age 25, from Wellington, New Zealand; P/O Ronald Joffre Whittleston, Navigator, RNZAF, age 28, married to Frances Whittleston, Frankton Junction, Auckland, New Zealand; W/O Francis Charles Brittain, Wireless Operator, RAFVR, age 22, from Kilburn, north London; W/O Frank Lofthouse, Special Wireless Operator, RAFVR, age 23, from Lupset, Yorkshire; F/Sgt Kenneth Matthew Francis Swadling, Bomb Aimer, RAFVR, from Wembley Hill, Middlesex; Sgt John Critchley Higginbottom, Mid Upper Gunner, RAFVR, age 21, from Streatham Hill, London; Sgt William McCreadie Lattimer, Rear Gunner, RAFVR, age 19, from Garlieston, Wigtownshire and Sgt John Martin Watts, Flight Engineer, RAFVR, age 19, from Caxton, Cambridgeshire. All are remembered on the Runnymede Memorial.

Sgt Allen, who flew as flight engineer with P/O Bowering, poignantly remembered the loss of this aircraft and crew. He painted a mural depicting LJ513 EX-N on the wall of the flight office at North Creake and written under the painting the words "RIP 16-6-44".

The paints he used were those normally applied to the outer surfaces of the Stirling's fuselage, black being the predominant colour. The artwork was applied directly to the brickwork of the wall and, by some small miracle, survived the ravages of time right up to 1982 when I was shown it while on a post-war visit to the old airfield. Once seen, I decided to try and save this remarkable piece of history and immediately made enquiries from the then owners of the site, Messrs Seamans. The full story of this project is shared at the end of the book complete with photographs.

Mandrel operations continued throughout June, with nightly sorties averaging fourteen aircraft forming the protective screen.

July
Mandrel sorties reinforced with Window force – diversionary "spoof" raids begin

Mandrel sorties continued into the first week of July, but plans were in place to form a Special Window Force to produce 'spoof' raids to draw off the German night fighters from main force attacks. 199 Squadron adapted their Stirlings to carry large quantities of 'Window' and the crews familiarised themselves with this new tactic. Reports state that the SWF became operational on 14th/15th July, but '199' sortie records show they were operational on the night of 12th July when the first combined Mandrel and Window jamming sorties were flown in conjunction. That the Squadron got the full complement of twenty Stirlings detailed for this mission airborne, speaks volumes for the work put in by the ground crews.

This new type of mission called for very precise planning due to the complexities of routes to be flown and racecourse patterns to be implemented at concise times and positions. There was a constant need to keep refining the way the Mandrel and Window countermeasures were presented to the German operators so that they were always being tested to the limit as to the intentions of Bomber Command and to define if a raid showing on their radar screens was a real one or not.

The Window force was directed to fly from North Creake to Cromer and follow a course 5252N 0200E out to 0410E then back to Cromer – Base. Window was to be dropped from 0200E to 0410E using a gentle weave en route maintaining a speed of 150 knots. The times given for the jamming were – commence at 2300 hrs, cease at 0200 hrs. The sorties flown on 12 June, both Mandrel and the diversionary attack using Window, were classed as completely successful.

Peter Ballard, wireless mechanic: *"I was a wireless mechanic working in the Lakenheath WT section and remained in that section for the first few months after we were posted to North Creake. In due course I was transferred to the special signals section, working on the Mandrel jamming equipment. Eric Nichols was in this section with me and I also remember Sgt Major, known as 'Myth' and Sgt Jones who was i/c the section".*

14th July 1944

The Squadron performed a complete diversionary raid in support of a main force attack on railway yards at Revigny and Villeneuve in France. Also flying bomb sites at Anderbelck and Les Landes received attention as part of the ongoing campaign against this threat. In fact, Bomber Command had singled out this type of target and, over the previous two weeks, dropped many hundreds of tons of HE bombs, destroying not only the launching sites, but storage depots as well. The diversionary raid, consisting of seven aircraft, used a set number of courses to fly, dropping Window at a predetermined rate. Twelve other aircraft flew a normal Mandrel jamming mission covering main force as they approached the enemy coast.

From the course plots logged in the records, it appears that the diversion was aimed at the Ruhr Valley and would have drawn a considerable amount of attention by the German night fighter controllers who were always alert to raids aimed at this particular area. The main railway yards selected as the targets were in the centre of France, not far from the Swiss border, and this raid covered by the Mandrel screen and the 'spoof' raid would have split up the German defences.

15th July to 31st July 1944

The Squadron was called upon almost every day for the remainder of the month, flying moving Mandrel screens and diversionary sorties. As the invasion forces tried to move inland, Bomber Command were called upon to provide attacks on German front line forces, including armoured divisions that were putting up a stiff fight. The other priority targets at this point still remained the V1 sites and railheads, the latter being the main source of German supplies and troop movements to bolster resistance against the Allied armies moving south and east. However, after the breakout of the bridgehead, and with the Allies gaining ground, Bomber Command were able to switch to plants producing synthetic oil. These plants were situated at: Wesseling, just south of Cologne; Buer, east of Osnabruck; Bottrop, north of Essen in the Ruhr and Homberg, midway between Kassel and Stadtallendorf.

Ken Hartley radar mechanic wrote of North Creake: *"What do I remember of North Creake? I have so many vivid memories. Free-wheeling all the way down to Little Walsingham on those rare 'days off' having sometimes stayed in bed until nine o'clock – a rare luxury! Having a late breakfast at a little café there, bacon and egg (a real egg). I can't remember how much it cost but in those dark days it seemed a meal fit for a king. Sometimes wakening at 4 am to go on leave, cycling down to Wells-on-Sea to catch the early morning 'fish train' at about 5 am. Leaving my bike on the station platform and returning 14 days later to find, of course, that it was still there, unlocked, just where I left it. Those were what we called 'the good old days'".*

Bill Hollman, fitter: *"I actually joined the Squadron at Lakenheath as a flight mechanic and went to Blackpool on a fitters course and came back as a fully fledged fitter. We then moved to North Creake and I went on a radar checking flight down to Newmarket and stayed for a few days. While we were there the 1,000 Guineas Race was run and we were allowed to watch. I suppose my fondest memories are of the dances at Holkam Hall and the Catholic Canteen in Walsingham".*

Jack Harris, radar mechanic: *"I can still remember 'Bing' (Cpl Des Bingham) sitting in the Radar section gazing at the screen of a radar set, occasionally thumping the box with a clenched fist and making remarks about its pro-creative abilities".*

20th July 1944

The raid on the synthetic oil plant at Homberg is a good example of the hazards still faced by the bomber stream when flying deep into Germany. Although the RCM support was there at the beginning of the raid with a Mandrel screen and a diversion sortie carried out, the bombers became more at risk the further they flew towards the target. Although the 147 Lancasters detailed were able to drop large amounts of Window as they progressed into Germany, the night fighters caught them and twenty were shot down. This was a particularly bad night for 75 Squadron who had converted from their Stirlings to Lancasters in March; they lost seven out of the 25 despatched on the raid. The oil plant was severely damaged with a significant reduction in aviation fuel being produced. German documents show that, during April, the tonnage being manufactured of this particular fuel stood at something like 6,000 tons per day but after attacks by Bomber Command and the American 8th Air Force this figure was reduced to an average of 500 tons per day.

As the month of July drew to an end the Allied ground forces were still fighting an extremely difficult battle having made slow but steady progress against strong German defences and counter-attacks. Bomber Command continually bolstered the Allied thrust whenever possible by close support. This called for dropping large numbers of bombs onto strong concentrations of enemy troops and armour with the bombs exploding sometimes only a few hundred yards from the advancing British, American and Canadian forces. Many of these attacks were carefully co-ordinated by the use of a Master Bomber who ensured the area to be hit was marked extremely accurately and the bombers given continuous verbal orders as they approached their bomb runs.

Ken Hartley, radar mechanic: *"I was working on an H2S Trainer, which had been installed in a building in North Creake for aircrew training when a visitor arrived to look around. The face seemed familiar, but it was some time before I realised it was Wing Commander Guy Gibson VC, DSO and Bar, DFC. He looked so young and yet he was already a legend in his own lifetime. I can't remember the date – perhaps the Station Log Book will have recorded his visit. It must have been sometime between the 'Dams Raid' on May 16th 1943 and September 19th 1944 when he was killed in action aged 26".*

Eileen Lowery, counter radar: *"I was one of the four WAAFs employed in the W.T/Radar section at North Creake. Some of the names that come to mind are Sgt Ken Hamilton, Norman Reed, Peter Ballard, Sgt 'Miff' Major, Tom Sheering, Denis Bird and Cpl Joe Rowe. The girls were Doreen Read, Joan Naish, Maudie Winfield and myself."*

Eric Nichols, Wireless Telegraphy Section, Mandrel: *"I joined 199 at Blyton in December 1942 and went on to Ingham, Lakenheath and finally North Creake. We didn't have too much time for fraternising between sections but we were next door in the farmyard at Ingham. I can remember these names in the Mandrel (counter radar) section at North Creake; Dick Masters, Ivor Burch, Mike Connolly, 'Dickie' Bird, George Reed, Cpl Joe Rowe, Sgt 'Miff' Major, Pete Ballard, Terry Buckley and Freddie White."*

29th August 1944

Bomber Command launched attacks on Konigsberg and Stettin. 199 Squadron detailed fourteen aircraft and crews to provide a Mandrel screen and a 'Window' diversionary raid. The Mandrel crews for this sortie consisted of: F/Lt Turner, LJ513 EX-E; W/O Townsend, LJ562 EX-V; F/Lt Harrison, LJ532 EX-L; F/Lt Holmes, LJ525 EX-R; F/Lt MacNamara, LJ543 EX-J; F/Lt Wood, LJ578 EX-S; F/Sgt Green, LJ518 EX-K; and F/Sgt Heggison, LJ536 EX-P.

The 'Window' Force was split into two sections:

Section '1' –
F/O Lind, LJ595 EX-N
F/O Briggs, LJ538 EX-T
F/O McColl, LJ520 EX-Z

Section '2' –
W/O Keens, LJ569 EX-C
F/Sgt Reidy, LJ542 EX-G
F/O Robbins, LJ516 EX-H

F/O Robbins, LJ516 EX-H, sustained a puncture on taking off, causing the Stirling to swing, rip off the undercarriage and catch fire. The crew escaped uninjured, except the navigator F/O Hartwright, who was admitted to the RAF General Hospital at Ely suffering from a compound fracture of the left leg.

The two sections were to proceed out on a route to Cromer then to pinpoints: 'A' – 5333N 0310E, and 'B' – 5420N 0600E.

Upon reaching this co-ordinate, the two sections moved slightly apart: Section '1', flew to 'C1' 5356N 0730E, 'D1' – 5423N 0600E, Cromer, Base; Section '2', down to two aircraft, flew to 'C2' 5354N 0724E, 'C2' 5420N 0600E, Cromer, Base.

From the co-ordinates given it would appear that the spoof raid was aimed at Hamburg or Bremerhaven, with the flight being curtailed just short of the German coast north of Wilhelmshaven. Flying at an average height of 16,000ft the crews dispensed two types of 'Window' – Type MB and Type N at anything from four bundles per minute at the beginning, increasing up to fifteen bundles per minute just off the German coastline. The jamming commenced halfway across the North Sea at 5333N 0330E with all the Stirlings weaving gently along their flight path.

The raid on Konigsberg proved to be one of the more successful carried out by 5 Group, even allowing for the fact the target was at extreme range and the 189 Lancasters were forced to carry a lighter bomb load. During the run up to the target the leading Pathfinder aircraft found thick low cloud obscuring the aiming points, so the Master Bomber, W/Cdr J. Woodroffe, held off the marking and postponed the raid for approximately 25 minutes. This delay caused the Lancasters to eat into their precious fuel reserves, but once a few breaks appeared in the clouds, the target was accurately marked and severe damage was caused to 41% of the houses and 20% of the industrial area in the town. Even though the diversionary raid had pulled off many German aircraft, they still managed to mount a substantial defence with many fighters reported by the bomber crews.

A total of fifteen Lancasters were lost.

402 Lancasters and one Mosquito drawn from 1, 3, 6 and 8 Groups carried out the Stettin raid.

Reports from the town indicate that many of the previously undamaged areas were badly hit, with 1,569 houses and 32 industrial sites totally destroyed. Severe damage was caused to a further 565 houses and industrial premises. A large ship, of 2,000 tons, was sunk and several others damaged. 1,033 people were killed and 1,034 injured.

From this larger Bomber force 23 Lancasters were lost.

Betty Price, Clerk: *"My husband was with 199 at Lakenheath; he was an electrician. I was a cockney WAAF on the same camp and worked in the station armoury office; the officer in charge was F/Lt Wolstencroft. It was a bit of an upheaval when we all had to move to North Creake to make way for the Americans. The office where I worked at Lakenheath was very near the path we used to reach the dining hall and looking out of my window I could see the long lines of gliders parked ready for use. Talking of the dining hall reminds me of 'Chiefy' Dines our mess boss and the very good food that he dished up.*

Bill and I were married in August 1944 while at North Creake and a great number from the aerodrome came to the wedding, the ceremony was held in the parish church at Wells-on-Sea. Our best man was Reggie Arrowsmith, known as 'Digby' and another electrician, a big fellow called 'Spud' Murphy gave me away."

Relaxing at the "Crown", Wells next the Sea.

Author's note: Lakenheath airfield was used to store Horsa gliders, from early April 1943 until late April 1944 with many gliders were being ferried in and out, using Whitley and Albemarle bombers converted for the task. Some were requisitioned for the Normandy Landings and others would take part in the Arnhem (Market Garden) operations, while others were towed out by C-47 Dakotas of the USAAF to be utilised in their various campaigns. At any one time there were up to 32 Horsa gliders at Lakenheath, under the care of No.2 Heavy Glider Maintenance Unit.

August
Formation of 171 Squadron from 199 C Flight

September 1944

Mandrel jamming contributes to Bomber Command successes

7th September 1944

This was a significant day in the history of 199 Squadron as an order was received from the Air Ministry via HQ 100 Group for the formation of 171 Squadron. It had been decided that '199' was to be reduced from a three to a two flight Squadron, with 'C' flight becoming the nucleus of 171 Squadron. The orders also contained instructions that '199' continue to administer the flight intended for 171 until all personnel were posted in. This was to be completed by 1st October. In line with the poor upkeep of 199 Squadron's ORB no mention is made of this occurrence. However, '171' did commence an ORB promptly on 8th September 1944 and the changeover recorded accordingly. It has been possible to obtain several relevant facts from this ORB that relate directly to '199' and North Creake. From 17th September until mid October, all '171' squadron operations were recorded in the '199' Sortie Record Book.

9th September 1944

Ten aircraft and crews plus two reserves were detailed for a normal Mandrel RCM sortie to cover the attack on Munchen Gladbach by 113 Lancasters and 24 Mosquitoes of 5 and 8 Groups. This was a highly successful raid with most of the town centre completely destroyed. No aircraft taking part in the raid was lost, however, 199 Squadron did suffer the loss of one Stirling in similar circumstances to that of LJ560 on 29th August. F/Lt Wood was taking off in LJ578 EX-S when it swung violently causing a tyre to burst and the aircraft veered through a hedge. As a result, the undercarriage collapsed and the Stirling caught fire and was subsequently written off. All the crew escaped without any injury.

15th September 1944

A raid was planned for Kiel with 490 aircraft drawn from 1, 4, 6 and 8 Groups taking part and '199' were to support them with a Mandrel screen and a full-scale diversionary spoof raid. Eleven aircraft and crews were to mount the Mandrel screen and six to fly in the diversionary sorties.

The planning and execution of this RCM operation had mixed results, with several aircraft suffering technical problems before and just after take off and also in flight. Of those flying the Mandrel screen F/Sgt Reidy, LJ510 EX-A returned soon after taking off at 2143 hrs with unspecified problems, and F/O Merryful did not take off until 2303 hrs, due to equipment failures, and was diverted to a new position. He reported heavy icing and returned early, landing at 0130 hrs.

The 'Window Force' faired little better with F/Lt Harker, LJ516 EX-H, returning early and F/Lt Coventry not taking off. The remaining WF consisted of P/O Keen, F/Lt Noble, W/O Townsend and F/Lt Cattell. They began dropping 'Window' as they passed over Orfordness at five bundles per minute, increasing to ten after making landfall between Calais and Boulogne and proceeding to a point mid-way between Metz and Strasbourg. The rate then went up to twenty bundles per minute as the aircraft flew a course taking them between Saarbrucken and Mannheim, reducing to ten and then five as they made their way back over Belgium, finally exiting over their initial point of entry.

It can be seen from the planned route it was no easy flight as the spoof raid was to simulate a major attack upon the targets already mentioned plus others such as Stuttgart and Frankfurt all being threatened. The crew's only protection was their good navigational skills, avoiding the heavily defended towns and cities and staying alert to night fighter attacks.

F/Sgt Heggison, LJ536 EX-P failed to return from the Mandrel sortie and no trace of the aircraft was ever found. He was operating at positions (A) 5145N 0300E, (B) 5358N 0448E flying parallel with the Belgian and Dutch coast at a varying distance of between 25 and 50 miles. He was paired with P/O Dickinson who was unaware of the loss of LJ536 and her crew until he returned to base.

From studying the map co-ordinates it shows that F/Sgt Heggison would have been flying initially to position 'A' over the North Sea 20 miles from the Dutch coast at a point near Oostkapelle. His route would then have taken him to position 'B' that placed him directly over Den Helder just south of the Island of Texel and possibly within range of German flak batteries. Texel and the surrounding areas were German strongholds on the coast with the island garrison refusing to lay down their arms, even after the main surrender on May 5th 1945. With this in mind, it is possible F/Sgt Heggison encountered flak and crashed into the sea or alternatively with one crew experiencing heavy icing problems it's just possible that this may have been the cause – we will never know. None of the crew was ever recovered and they have no known grave.

Crew of LJ536: F/Sgt Andrew Dempster Heggison, Pilot, RAFVR, age 23, from Bridge of Dee, Aberdeen; P/O Murray Kesselman, Navigator, RCAF, age 21, from Winnipeg, Manitoba, Canada; Sgt James Birch Sowden, Wireless Operator, RAFVR; W/O David Thomson Hughes, Special Wireless Operator, RAF, age 28, from West Linton, Peeblesshire; P/O Lloyd George Langley, Bomb Aimer, RCAF; P/O James Duncan Campbell, Mid Upper Gunner, RCAF, age 22, from Austin, Manitoba, Canada; P/O Gordon Joshua Dennison, Rear Gunner, RCAF, age 22, from Assiniboia, Saskatchewan, Canada and Sgt Stanley Cunningham Rennie, Flight Engineer, RAFVR, age 20, from Ayr. All are commemorated on the Runnymede Memorial.

PILOT OFFICER
MURRAY KESSELMAN

Pilot Officer Murray Kesselman, J-92274, R.C.A.F., of Winnipeg, was officially presumed dead on August 23, 1945. He was listed as missing following air operations on September 16, 1944.

Pilot Officer Kesselman enlisted in the air force in September, 1942, and received his training at Brandon, Saskatoon and Prince Albert. He graduated as a navigator from No. 5, Air Observer's School at Winnipeg in September, 1943, and went overseas the following month. He was attached to the R.A.F. Pilot Officer Kesselman was awarded his Operational Wing posthumously on January 29, 1947.

Born in Winnipeg on November 29, 1922, Pilot Officer Kesselman was the son of Mr. and Mrs. George Kesselman of 483 Ash Street. He received his education in Winnipeg, graduating from Gordon Bell High School. Before his enlistment he was in the shoe business.

16th September 1944

A reduced number of aircraft were detailed to provide a Mandrel screen for a most important support operation by Bomber Command prior to the Allied landings by British and American troops at Nijmegen and Arnhem the following day (Operation Market Garden).

The 199 ORB and the sortie records are once again at odds with one another. The ORB entry for the 16th states that five aircraft and crew were ordered to fly a support mission and that they all took off and completed the mission and returned safely to base.

However, the sortie records are more accurate and say that 'C' pranged on take-off but the crew were OK. Further investigation revealed that the aircraft was Stirling LJ569 EX-C flown by F/Lt Harker and as it took off at 2017 hrs the starboard tyre burst, followed by the starboard inner engine cutting out, resulting in a swing that ripped off the undercarriage and the starboard wing. The crew consisted of: P/O Russell, Nav; F/O Salter, B/A; F/Sgt Durrell, W/OP; F/O Chessell, W/Op Special; Sgt Pallant, M/U; F/Sgt Sewell, R/G; and Sgt How, F/Eng.

LJ569 EX-C after its 'prang' on take-off.

Canadian Aircrew.

All emerged from the wreckage unscathed. The airframe was dismantled and rebuilt by Sebro (Shorts Repair Organisation, Madingley, Cambridgeshire) as a Mk IV.

The remaining five aircraft supported bombing sorties by 200 Lancasters and 23 Mosquitoes of 1 and 8 Groups attacked airfields near Hopsten, Leeuwarden, Steenwijk and Rheine, 54 Lancasters and five Mosquitoes of 3 and 8 Groups bombed flak positions at Moerdijk.

25th September 1944

German troops were still holding out in the Calais area of France and a large force of 872 aircraft was detailed to bomb their positions. This mission was not successful on account of bad weather and very low cloud. Only about a quarter of the bombers dropped their loads through scattered breaks in the overcast but no aircraft were lost.

199 Squadron detailed three crews to join a 'Window' Force mainly crewed from 171 Squadron and a total of eight aircraft took part assisted by four 199 Squadron Mandrel Stirlings.

Sadly '199' lost a Stirling and crew when P/O Chatwin LJ518 EX-K, returning to RAF North Creake, crashed in bad weather near Saxthorpe, Norfolk. There were no survivors and the aircraft was a write-off. Investigations revealed that the aircraft was descending through low cloud and hit a row of trees on high ground. Chatwin pulled up into a steep climb, stalled and plunged into a field beside the Saxthorpe-Edgefield road. The Stirling disintegrated and burst into flames, scattering wreckage across the road, blocking it. A Civil Defence ambulance and a rescue party were despatched to the crash site, but little could be done for the crew. The next day a search was made to ensure all the crew had been recovered and the wreckage was thoroughly combed for the secret jamming equipment as it was on the Top Secret list.

There was one more tragic aspect of the crash when it was discovered that F/O Barham the special wireless operator lived only five miles from the crash, at Cawston. To this day there are gaps in the hedgerow alongside the road where the Stirling crashed and, in the adjacent field, small fragments of alloy and exploded .303 cartridge cases can be found in the topsoil.

Crew of LJ518 EX-K: P/O Francis Reginald Chatwin, Pilot, RAFVR, age 26, married to Phyllis Chatwin of Bolton, Lancashire, cremated at the Birmingham Municipal Crematorium; F/Sgt Richard Thomas Percival Savage, Navigator, RAAF, age 22, from Tivoli Hill, Queensland, Australia, buried in Grave 15127, Cambridge City Cemetery; Sgt Robert Campbell Saddler, Wireless Operator, RAFVR, age 22, from Hastings, Sussex, buried in Div. O, Sec. A, grave 102, Hastings Cemetery; F/O Leonard Alfred Barham, Special Wireless Operator, RAFVR, age 29, from Cawston, Norfolk, buried in Sec. H, grave 8. Cawston Cemetery, Norfolk; F/Sgt Colin Silkirk Henderson, Bomb Aimer, RNZAF, age 25, from Dunedin, Otago, New Zealand, buried in grave 15327, Cambridge City Cemetery; Sgt Pyrs Owen Roberts, Mid Upper Gunner, RAFVR, age 19, from Nantgwynant, Caernarvonshire, buried in row E, grave 1, Beddgelert New Cemetery, Caernarvonshire; Sgt John William Naylor, Rear Gunner, RAFVR, age 36, married to Ena Naylor of Southall, Middlesex, buried in Holy Trinity Churchyard, Gedney Hill, Lincolnshire; Sgt Ambrose William Loveland, Flight Engineer, RAFVR, age 31, married to Marguerite Loveland of Shirley, Croydon, Surrey, buried in St John The Baptist Churchyard, West Wickham, Kent.

28th September 1944

A further raid on German defences at Calais and surrounding strong points was launched by almost 500 aircraft of Bomber Command as this area had been causing problems with the re-supply of Allied troops. A Mandrel and Window support operation was ordered and sixteen aircraft and crews were detailed, with ten drawn from 199 Squadron and the remaining six from 171 Squadron, who were still under the administration of '199'. The Mandrel RCM was to be flown by four '199' crews and six contributing to the Window force with the remaining six Window Force coming from 171 Squadron.

One Mandrel: F/Lt Jepson and one Window Force aircraft: F/Lt Harrison both of 171 Squadron, failed to take off.

One Mandrel: F/Sgt Broadfield, LJ595 EX-N was an hour late taking off due to technical problems and he also had his main compass topple and found it could not be corrected.

F/Lt Hancock, EX-T, part of the Window force, was forced to return early when a serious oil leak was discovered as they were passing over Cromer. The ORB does not credit him with participating in this mission.

F/Lt Wiseman, LJ520 EX-Z also had a compass topple on take off, but this was rectified and worked satisfactorily for the remainder of the sortie.

F/O Green, LJ510 EX-A was hampered by trouble with the Gee set on his return trip.

A German night fighter attacked F/Sgt Reidy, LJ562 EX-V and, after corkscrewing, found that the DRC (Direct Reading Compass) compass had toppled.

The three Mandrel aircraft took up positions midway between Lowestoft and Velsen Zuid and a line drawn from Boston in Lincolnshire and Den Helden on the Dutch coast. The Window force flew north of the Mandrels flying in over the Frisian Islands feigning a raid towards the industrial targets of Osnabruck, Munster and Hanover.

No bombers were lost on the raid on Calais, but it was only partly successful, with just a small proportion of the aircraft attacking the target, the master bomber being forced to call off the raid due to very thick cloud conditions. Shortly after the attack the Germans in Calais surrendered to the Canadian Army. Much of the port was extensively damaged and a great deal of work was required to get it functioning again, but as time progressed a large amount of badly needed supplies was being unloaded and pushed forward to the advancing troops.

29th September 1944

A spoof raid was launched by '199' and '171' squadrons in support of a raid on Karlsruhe by 40 Mosquitoes. They were ordered to provide only a 'Window' force of six and four Stirlings respectively, no Mandrel aircraft being required. The ten crews were to climb to 15,000ft and proceed to point 'A' 5000N 0428E near Le Nouvion en Thierache in France and to fly an almost due east course to the furthest point 'C' 5007N 0710E east of Mulheim in the Rhineland. This flight path took the force deep into German territory and they were dropping 'Window' at the rate of ten bundles per minute at the commencement (point 'A') increasing to 15 BPM at point 'C' reducing to 5 BPM on the return trip.

There is one discrepancy between the '199' crews listed in the ORB and an entry in the Squadron sortie records. P/O Green is shown in the ORB as flying LJ510 EX-A, but the sortie records show this flight plan allotted to F/Lt Hancock, EX-R. F/O Lampkin, LJ513 EX-E; F/Sgt Walford, LJ543 EX-J; F/Sgt Finnimore, LJ514 EX-B; F/Lt Wiseman, LJ562 EX-V; and F/Sgt Broadfield, LJ580 EX-X, commenced take-off at 0134 hrs and were all airborne by 0145 hrs. The ORB shows P/O Green as taking off at 0134 hrs and returning early at 0225 hrs, and although there is no mention why this happened, it might be safely assumed that F/Lt Hancock was flying as a reserve and immediately took P/O Green's place.

F/Sgt Walford reported spotting a Me210 at 5006N 0610E, but no combat report was filed.

F/Lt Wiseman had one of his engines fail and a note records he returned early.

Even though no major raid was mounted, this type of sortie by a small number of Mosquitoes and an accompanying Mandrel and Window force kept the German defences stretched to the limit and the civilian population awake for most of the night with constant air raid warnings.

October

The "Second battle of the Ruhr" –
"Operation Hurricane" a complete success

5th October 1944

An attack on Saarbrücken was ordered in the support of the American Third Army that was advancing through the area. Situated near the German/French border it was an important rail and road link for German supplies.

531 Lancasters and twenty Mosquitoes from 1, 3 and 8 Groups made an accurate and devastating raid on the town, cutting the rail lines and causing the destruction of 5,882 houses and damaging a further 1,141. The attack was covered by both a 199 Squadron Mandrel screen and a diversionary spoof raid by 199 and 171 Squadrons, the latter still operating under the auspices of '199'.

The Mandrel screen consisted of six '199' aircraft flown by: Sgt Finnimore, LJ513 EX-E; F/Lt Wiseman, LJ557 EX-Y; F/Sgt Walford, LJ514 EX-B; F/O Milsom, LJ538 EX-T; F/O Lampkin, LJ542 EX-G; F/O McColl, LJ520 EX-Z.

Their jamming flight plan took them out over the North Sea, leaving the English coast over Cromer and flying eastward to a point halfway between there and Den Helder on the Dutch coast. Keeping parallel with this coast they then flew north of the Frisian Islands as if covering an attack on Bremen or Hamburg.

The diversionary spoof raid was to be flown by eight '199' and four '171' Stirlings, but F/Lt Hancock's aircraft was found to have technical problems and did not take off. The remaining seven Stirlings were flown by: P/O McNamara, LJ541 EX-K; F/O Lind, LJ595 EX-N; F/Lt Todd, LJ614 EX-S; F/Sgt Reidy, LJ544 EX-D; P/O Green, LJ516 EX-H; P/O Keen, LJ651 EX-C; F/O Marshall, LJ525 EX-R.

Stirling Mk. III, LJ514 EX-B, completed 75 operations that were recorded by painting a beer mug on the port side of the cockpit. 'B' Beer was struck off charge in February 1945.

Taking off between 1755 hrs and 1809 hrs the crews made their initial exit point over the English coast at Beachy Head and made for Le Treport on the French coast. A course was then set for Charleroi, south of Brussels, where Windowing began at a rate of 10 BPM. They continued to a point west of Frankfurt, terminating between the towns of Bullay and Zell, where the bundle rate was increased to twenty per minute. All the aircraft taking part in both missions reported satisfactory results and returned safely to North Creake.

6th October 1944

Bomber Command selected two targets at Dortmund and Bremen, both of which had been attacked on several occasions. Some historians class the raid on Dortmund as the "The Second Battle of the Ruhr".

The Mandrel sortie was flown by six '199' Stirlings: P/O O'Brien, LJ516 EX-H; F/Sgt Currell, LJ520 EX-Z; P/O Keen, LJ651 EX-C; F/O Marshall, LJ557 EX-Y; F/Sgt Reidy, LJ544 EX-D; F/O Lind, LJ536 EX-P, who carried out a normal jamming mission routed out over the North Sea to a point midway between Grimsby and Norden in Germany. The Window force, from the co-ordinates given, appears to have been trying to draw the German fighters south from Dortmund and Bremen as their intended track threatened Stuttgart and Munich.

F/Sgt Ray Lind's crew: Sgt G. Prout, R/G; F/Sgt E. Prout, Nav.; Sgt H. Stenner, F/E; F/Sgt R. Lind, Pilot; F/Sgt P. Payne, B/A; Sgt A. Birchill, M/U; W/O W. Alcock, SWO; W/O J. Strachan, W/Op.

As with most of the positions and tracks given throughout this narrative, they are only a calculated assumption on my part using the routes and positions given for each individual aircraft.

The Window Stirlings were flown by: F/O Lampkin, LJ542 EX-G; F/Sgt Walford, LJ514 EX-B; F/Lt Jepson, LJ525 EX-R; P/O MacNamara, LJ513 EX-E; F/Sgt Broadfield, LJ562 EX-V.

They began by dropping five BPM over Neufchateau in France and flying due east towards Strasbourg increasing the rate to ten and then twenty BPM.

The raid on Dortmund by 523 aircraft was successful and considerable damage was caused to the city, industrial and transport installations being particularly hard hit. The reports from Dortmund listed 191 dead, 38 missing and 418 injured.

Only two Halifaxes, two Lancasters and one Mosquito were lost – less than 1% of the total sent.

Bremen was attacked 246 Lancasters and seven Mosquitoes and this was to be the last major raid on this target for the remainder of the war. Marking was excellent and over 1,000 tons of bombs were dropped on the city, mostly incendiaries. The bomb aimers were presented with a large target in virtually ideal weather conditions and with a three quarter moon, all the aiming points were visible. Large fires was soon started, although a fire storm did not materialise due to the large numbers of burnt out areas already produced in the raid on August 18th.

Figures released from Bremen show that 4,859 houses, five churches, one hospital, eighteen schools and sixteen public and historic buildings were destroyed. Due to the large evacuation ordered for Bremen, casualties were low, with 65 killed, 766 injured and 37,724 bombed out. Transport systems were disrupted and aircraft and heavy electrical factories severely damaged. Having been the target for one of Bomber Commands earlier 1,000 bomber raids and also subjected to 30+ regular attacks through 1943 and 1944 this raid finally put paid to all war efforts within the city.

Five Lancasters were shot down.

7th October 1944

The Squadron was detailed for a purely 'feint' attack on Bremen. No other raids were planned by Bomber Command and this spoof was intended to draw up German fighters so wasting valuable fuel. '199', assisted by 171 Squadron, ordered four Mandrel and ten Window Force Stirlings to carry out the task. Although the German controllers were alerted to this raid they did not commit many fighters to investigate.

No Allied aircraft were lost.

Attacks continued over the next few nights with raids on Bochum, gun batteries on the River Scheldt and the oil refinery at Wanne-Eickel, the raid on Bochum on the 9th October being the only one calling on 199 Squadron for RCM. It would seem that Bomber Command had been preparing for a maximum effort and by sparing aircraft and crews for almost a week was set to launch "Operation Hurricane".

14th October 1944
"Operation Hurricane"

The various governmental and RAF departments responsible for overall planning were keen to show the German High Command just what the RAF and the USAAF could launch against the Ruhr by way of overwhelming numbers of aircraft. The order for the operation was given on the 13th October and ground crews were given the mammoth task of preparing over 1,000 heavy bombers for the next day. The main raid for the RAF, with both day and night operations detailed, was to be aimed at Duisburg with a secondary attack on Brunswick also ordered.

During the early morning of the 14th October the largest number of aircraft ever assembled for one specific target were made ready having been loaded with a mix of high explosive and incendiary bombs. Bomber Command despatched 1,013 Lancasters, Halifaxes and Mosquitoes with Fighter Command providing close escort. The USAAF provided 1,251 heavy bombers escorted by 749 fighters – their main target in the operation being Cologne.

The American losses were relatively light, 5 bombers and 1 fighter were shot down and it appears that no German fighters were seen during the raid. A total of 957 RAF bombers attacked Duisburg in the first raid and dropped a total of 3,574 tons of high explosive and 820 tons of incendiaries.

A total of 14 bombers were lost – 13 Lancasters and 1 Halifax.

During the night 14/15th October, 1,005 RAF bombers returned to Duisburg in two waves about two hours apart, and dropped a further 4,040 tons of high explosives and 500 tons of incendiaries for the loss of 7 aircraft.

By this time RAF Bomber Command was not only able to launch 1,000 bomber raids, but was able to launch secondary raids of considerable size at the same time. During the same night 5 Group attacked Brunswick with 240 bombers and a further 319 aircraft flew on various diversionary and support missions for the main raids. The statistics for the raids as a whole are as follows:

The night operations were flown by a total of 1,572 aircraft, with 10 lost. The combined effort for the 24-hour period was 2,589 sorties flown with 24 aircraft lost that equates to 0.9%. Tonnage of bombs dropped during the 24-hour period – approximately 10,050 tons. These figures were a record for the RAF and would never be bettered during the whole course of the war.

Nearly 9,000 tons of bombs fell on Duisburg in less than 24 hours, but the damage to Duisburg is difficult to assess because much of the documentation including the final report, is not held by the Duisburg state archive. However, the documentation which is available mentions "Very serious property damage. A large number of people buried." At the Thyssen Coal Mines III and IV 8 day's production was lost.

199 Squadron were called upon to provide a maximum 'Window' coverage as part of a diversionary raid for the night element of "Operation Hurricane" with 15 Stirlings and crews placed on the Battle Order. These were split into 'Window Force 1' containing 11 aircraft and 'Window Force 2' made up of the remaining four supplemented by a further five from 171 Squadron.

Force 1: Took off from RAF North Creake, Gravesend, Beachy Head and then to Calais. From here the force penetrated inland crossing the Belgian/German border 20 miles west of Koblenz. The furthest point reached over enemy territory was 0705E near the German town of Idar Oberstein. The return route was flown back over the North Sea making landfall at Orfordness landing back at North Creake.

The operating heights for this operation were between 6,000 and 10,000ft. Windowing rates for the initial stages of the sortie were 20 bundles per minute slowly decreasing to 5 bundles per minute.

Force 1 crews detailed: P/O Green, LJ510 EX-A; F/Sgt Reidy, LJ544 EX-D; F/O Keen, LJ516 EX-H; F/Sgt Finnimore, LJ542 EX-G; P/O MacNamara, LJ562 EX-L; F/Sgt Walford, LJ514 EX-B; F/Lt Dickinson, LJ518 EX-K; F/Lt Holmes, LJ557 EX-Y; F/Lt Hancock, LJ656 EX-Q; F/O Marshall, LJ536 EX-P; and F/O McColl, LJ520 EX-Z.

Of the crews detailed for Force 1 only F/Sgt Finnimore who took off at 2320 hrs encountered any problems and was forced to return early, landing at North Creake at 0016 hrs. The ORB and summaries fail to mention exactly what caused the problem.

Force 2: Took off from North Creake, flew out into the North Sea at Cromer and took up positions between Grimsby and the North Frisian Islands before progressing on track and making for the final pinpoint in the Heligoland Bight over the town of Weselburen in Schleswig – Holstein, Germany.

Force 2 crews detailed: F/O Milsom, LJ538 EX-T; F/Lt Wiseman, LJ525 EX-R; F/Lt Jepson, LJ578 EX-S; and F/Sgt Broadfield, LJ568 EX-V.

The 171 Squadron Stirlings were flown by: F/Lt Sturrock, F/Lt Cattell, W/O Townsend, F/Sgt Austwick and F/O Briggs.

Operating heights were between 5,000 and 14,000ft with Windowing rates varying between an initial 5 bundles per minute up to a maximum of 15 bundles per minute.

F/Lt Jepson took off at 0047 hrs but due to technical problems was forced to abandon the sortie and return early, landing back at North Creake at 0205 hrs.

Roy Richards, Special Wireless Operator: *For my second tour I was posted to North Creake and allocated to S/Ldr Jepson's crew ('B' Flight Commander) as a Special Wireless Operator. Our aircraft as I recall was 'S' for Sugar. The other crew members were Ben Webster, Navigator from Stoke on Trent; Norman Depoe, Bomb Aimer from Canada; Ken Speed, Flight Engineer from Swindon; Ron Berry, Wireless Operator from Rotherham and one of the Gunners was Sgt English from Hunstanton.*

This gives the reader an idea of how a diversionary raid was set up and executed with all aircraft flying precise routes in and out of enemy territory. The Window dropping also had to be carried out exactly as ordered with heights, speeds and rate of discharge closely monitored.

Throughout the remainder of October and to the end of the war the Squadron would fly RCM sorties almost every day in support of Bomber Command. Their efforts much reduced the overall losses.

During the months of October, November and December the Sortie records increasingly refer to the usage of 'Gee' and its effectiveness. It would appear that the transmitters based in England were given code names and these appear with frequent regularity when navigators gave their post Op reports. The three names written in the records are "Reims", "Ruhr" and "Eastern".

Australian air crew, attached to the squadron.

November
Mandrel tactics penetrate deeper into France

2nd November 1944

Six Mandrel and four Window force Stirlings were detailed to cover Bomber Command raids on Dusseldorf. This was the last main raid on the city and, from the 992 aircraft despatched, seventeen were lost. The raid concentrated on the northern part of Dusseldorf and resulted in 5,000 houses being destroyed or damaged. It was reported that 678 people had been killed.

One crew from 199 Squadron on the Window sortie was attacked by a night fighter. The combat report of F/O Gilbert, Stirling LJ543 EX-J reads as follows: *"Enemy aircraft sighted at 500 yards, position 5043N 0413E (south of Halle and 10 miles SSW of Brussels, Belgium) against the dark part of the sky, on the fine port quarter, slightly up, and the skipper was informed. The aircraft came in on a curve of pursuit and the skipper was told to corkscrew port. At 400 yards both gunners (F/Sgt Baker R/G and F/Sgt Pratt M/U) identified the aircraft as a Fw190 and opened fire. At about 200 yards the enemy aircraft opened fire with a short burst that failed to hit the Stirling. The rear gunner's tracer could be seen to enter the belly of the fighter and at 100 yards it broke away to starboard up. Both gunners claim the fighter was damaged. Combat timed at 1952 hrs. Height 9,000ft. Heading 245 mag. Weather clear with moon behind cloud and astern resulting in fair visibility."*

"Rear gunner fired 500 rounds.
Mid upper fired 300 rounds.
No damage to our Stirling."

December
Rail and oil targets given priority –
the Squadron pushes into German airspace

4th December 1944

The towns of Karlsruhe and Heilbronn were selected for this night's raid and '199' provided ten Stirlings and crews for a Mandrel screen.

F/O Van Welie, LJ649 EX-P was one of the first to take off, at 1645 hrs, but was soon forced to return when the W/T went u/s and the starboard inner failed and had to be feathered. He landed safely at 1736 hrs. The remainder of the flight consisted of: P/O Broadfield, LJ617 EX-E, who replaced F/O Van Welie; F/Lt Thurlow, LJ557 EX-Y; F/O Chatterton, LJ614 EX-S; F/Sgt Currell, PW259 EX-V; F/Lt Todd, LJ567 EX-X; F/Sgt Pearce, LJ542 EX-G; F/Lt Keen, LJ651 EX-C; F/Lt Simon, LJ514 EX-B; F/O Gilbert, LJ543 EX-J; and F/O Green, LJ611 EX-A. All the aircraft were airborne by 1650 hrs with the exception of P/O Broadfield, who was ground reserve getting away at 1725 hrs. The route for this sortie was given as: Base, Gravesend, French Coast, Positions 5, 6, 7, 8, 9, French Coast, Gravesend, Base.

The co-ordinates given show that the screen was to operate between 5004N 0510E and 4912N 0520E, putting the aircraft well into French territory west of Bastogne running south to Verdun-sur-Meuse. The Allied advances were still gaining further ground enabling the RCM sorties to fly deeper into France without the threat of German anti-aircraft defences and fighters.

Heilbronn

F/O Green reported heavy jamming of Gee and his special wireless operator Sgt Beamand also had problems with the Mandrel set that eventually stopped working.

The two raids by Main Force were successful, with the Durlacher machine tool factory in Karlsruhe completely destroyed, while in Heilbronn a devastating attack left 82% of the town in ruins following what was thought to have been a genuine firestorm. The latter raid was tasked to 282 Lancasters of 5 Group, who dropped 1,254 tons of mainly incendiaries on the town, completely destroying over 350 acres of housing and causing over 7,000 deaths among the civilian population.

Of those, 5,000 were later buried in mass graves in the *Ehrenfriedhof* (cemetery of honour) in the valley of the Köpfer creek close to the city.

Due to an obstruction on the main runway at RAF North Creake all the returning aircraft were diverted to RAF Woodbridge.

Next day, the crews were able to return to North Creake, but as he was about to land, F/Lt Todd, LJ567 EX-X struck a four-foot high wall in the undershoot area of the runway and damaged the undercarriage. He was forced to overshoot and returned to Woodbridge where he was able to successfully belly land the Stirling with no injuries to his crew.

5th December 1944

The target selected for this raid was Soest, 25 miles east of Dortmund in the Ruhr Valley. Ten aircraft were detailed for a Mandrel screen. Much of the railway sidings and northern suburbs of the town were destroyed including 1,000 houses and other important buildings. Of the 497 bombers despatched only two were lost.

6th December 1944

Bomber Command launched a maximum effort for this night with Leuna, Osnabruck and Giessen selected as the main targets. A total of 42 Mosquitoes also carried out diversionary and nuisance raids on Berlin, Schwerte and Hanau. Leuna was classed as an oil target and was situated 250 miles inside Germany near the large town of Leipzig. Much damage was caused to the synthetic oil plant. The Osnabruck raid was not very successful, with only slight damage caused to the railway installations. However some factories producing munitions were destroyed. The attack on Giessen was divided between the attacking force of 255 Lancasters, with the town centre taking the brunt of the raid and the railway yards also suffering severe damage.

199 Squadron detailed nine aircraft and crews for a Mandrel screen flying over France and Belgium to cover the attacks, but severe icing conditions caused problems for all the crews and forced the early return of F/Lt Thurlow, LJ559 EX-Q. This aircraft, and LJ617 EX-E flown by F/Lt Simon, both landed at RAF Manston, returning later in the day to North Creake.

7th and 8th December 1944

No operations. Crews stood down except for training, maintenance and test flights.

F/Lt Howard Gray, Radar Section: *"Some of my best memories of the radar section relate to the corporals upon whom we relied so heavily. With such support, along with that of the sergeants, it made the job so much more manageable. I recall one older corporal, a former radio man in civvy street, who had not had a radar course but was able to repair a special trainer when nobody else could."*

9th December 1944

No major raids ordered, but 199 detailed nine crews for a standard Mandrel screen as part of Bomber Command's strategy of keeping up the pressure on the German civilian population and their defence organisation. In line with this scheme, 60 Mosquitoes attacked Berlin, eight attacked Koblenz and a further four struck the oil plant at Meiderich.

F/Lt Thurlow, LJ614 EX-S was again forced to return shortly after taking off at 1720 hrs due to the port outer engine failing. His position in the screen was taken by the reserve aircraft, flown by F/O McNamara, LJ544 EX-D. All the Mandrel aircraft completed an average of 5½ hours flying time.

10th and 11th December 1944

All operational flying for the Squadron was cancelled due to unfavourable weather conditions.

12th December 1944

The final night raid on Essen was undertaken by 540 aircraft and resulted in a very accurate and devastating attack on the city. The aiming point was the Krupp works which was hit many times by concentrated sticks of bombs, but 696 houses were destroyed and a further 1,370 damaged. The casualty list included 160 German civilians, 89 prisoners of war, 13 foreign workers and 201 prisoners in the city jail with 39 prisoners 'missing'. Bomber Command lost six aircraft. This attack was covered by a Mandrel screen flown by ten Stirlings of 199 Squadron who flew their patterns over Belgium approaching the German border at Aachen.

F/Sgt Currell, LJ614 EX-S returned early, the port inner engine having failed. On 9th December the port outer on this aircraft had forced F/Lt Thurlow to abandon his mission.

F/Lt Simon, LJ544 EX-D was diverted to RAF Manston, but no reason is given.

13th December 1944

With no operations ordered, some much-needed servicing was carried out by ground crews.

14th December 1944

Ordered to provide a Mandrel screen, but all nine crews subsequently stood down due to adverse weather conditions.

15th December 1944

The weather having improved, orders arrived at North Creake to provide a dual Mandrel and Window operation to cover a raid on Ludwigshafen by 327 Lancasters and fourteen Mosquitoes of 1, 6 and 8 Groups. Also included in this attack was the town of Oppau, where several I.G. Farben chemical factories were situated.

The I.G. Farben installations were almost completely destroyed and one site that was producing synthetic oil was seriously affected and ceased production. Ships and quay facilities on the nearby Rhine also received many direct hits causing damage and dislocation of war material supply and distribution. At least five other large industrial sites were hit by high explosive and incendiary bombs causing large fires that were difficult to control. Post-raid reports by Bomber Command assessed this raid as among one of the most successful of any night attack on a German target. One Lancaster was lost.

The Mandrel force consisted of four aircraft flying out over Gravesend and Dungeness to a point 5020N 0530E (Marche-en-Famenne) near the Belgian-German border. In total they were transmitting from 1720 hrs to 1920 hrs giving good coverage for the entire raid.

Initially the Window force was made up of seven aircraft, but P/O Reidy and F/Sgt Currell had technical problems and did not take off and F/O Marshall returned early when it was found that the oxygen system was u/s.

The remaining four aircraft flew from North Creake, out over Gravesend to positions plotted for Flight A as position 'A' 5000N 0500E, position 'B' 5000N 0600E, position 'C' 5000N 0706E and position 'D' 5024N 0826E.

Flight B flew a parallel track given as position 'A' 4957N 0500E, position 'B' 4957N 0600E, position 'C' 4957N 0709E and position 'D' 5021N 0829E. Both plots put them just inside the Belgian border near Wellin and Libin when they began dropping their Window and ended the sortie twenty miles north of Frankfurt.

16th December 1944

Bad weather again curtailed any operational flying by the Squadron. Nine crews had been briefed but were stood down during the afternoon.

17th December 1944

Three cities, Duisburg, Ulm and Munich were selected for this night's attacks with minor spoof and nuisance raids on Hanau, Munster and Hallendorf. Although the raids were supported by 44 RCM sorties from other Squadrons, '199' crews had to abandon their contribution due to extremely bad weather. The Squadron sortie records and ORB show that eight aircraft took off to carry out a Mandrel screen, but shortly after leaving North Creake, F/O Gilbert and W/O Currell were recalled and the remaining six abandoned due to severe icing conditions.

The main raids went ahead and it is worth mentioning that the attack on Ulm was the first and last made on the city. Situated within the area were two large lorry factories and industrial plants producing war materials. It was fortunate for the local population that they had been warned to evacuate their homes following news of the devastating raid on Heilbronn. The actual evacuation had been delayed, but was then implemented with some urgency on the morning of Sunday 17th and many thousands of people departed by whatever means was available to them.

That night, 317 Lancasters and 13 Mosquitoes from 1 and 8 Groups took part in the raid dropping 1,500 tons of bombs in less than half an hour, completely destroying almost a square mile of the city. The lorry factories and many industrial plants were badly damaged and at least 82% of all the buildings in the city were affected by the attack. Thanks to the timely evacuation, many lives were spared, but the German records show that 606 civilians were killed and 613 injured. 25,000 people were bombed out.

18th December 1944

A long-range attack planned for the Baltic port of Gdynia was carried out by 236 Lancasters of 5 Group. Other minor raids included 40 Mosquitoes attacking Nuremberg and sixteen to Munster. A further fourteen Lancasters of 5 Group were also detailed to lay mines in the Danzig Bay area. A Mandrel screen was detailed to fly in support of these raids and twelve aircraft and crews were detailed.

Although the port of Gdynia is in Poland within the Gulf of Gdansk, the '199' Mandrel screen operated over Belgium, orbiting over Namur situated in the Walloon area of the country. Shortly after taking off W/O Werner, EX-T was informed by his navigator that the Gee set was not functioning and the crew were only able to complete part of the mission. Their position was replaced by one of the airborne reserves, F/O Marshall, EX-Q. S/Ldr Jepson EX-R reported problems with his Gee set, but managed to carry on and complete his sortie. The attack damaged several ships and surrounding facilities. Four Lancasters were shot down.

19th December 1944

Bad weather had set in again causing the cancellation of twelve aircraft ordered for a Mandrel screen.

20th and 21st December 1944

No operations ordered.

22nd December 1944

Rail yards were becoming more of a prime target for main force attacks due to their importance of pushing through supplies for the German Ardennes offensive and two situated at Koblenz and Bingen were selected for this night's raid. 272 Lancasters and Halifaxes from 1 and 4 Groups aided by Pathfinder aircraft attacked both targets with mixed results.

The raid at Koblenz was scattered due to cloud cover and many of the bombs fell in open country or on outlying villages. However, some bombs did fall on the railhead destroying many main line tracks and bridges. Better results were obtained at Bingen where a very accurate attack was carried out and all but a few bombs fell on the marshalling yards and along the banks of the River Rhine where two barges were sunk. No traffic moved through this area after the raid, thereby substantially cutting supplies to the Ardennes front.

A Mandrel screen was ordered to cover the two raids and thirteen aircraft were detailed for a normal Mandrel sortie orbiting over Belgium. Jamming was turned on between 1725 hrs and 1930 hrs with maximum jamming called for between 1735 hrs and 1835 hrs. F/O Milsom and F/O Chatterton both returned early due to their Gee sets becoming unserviceable.

23rd December 1944

German transport facilities again came in for attention, beginning with two daylight raids on the rail yards at Trier and Cologne/Gremberg. These were small in comparison with a normal night attack, with 153 Lancasters being sent to Trier and only 27 Lancasters and three Mosquitoes to Cologne.

The raid on Cologne went badly from the outset when two Lancasters collided over the French coast, with the loss of both crews. The tactics were for these waves of aircraft led by 'Oboe' equipped Lancasters to bomb the target through cloud cover, but the crews found that the cloud had cleared, leaving the approaching bombers vulnerable to ground defences as well as the threat from fighter aircraft. Worthy of mention is the action of the lead pilot S/Ldr R.A.M. Palmer, DFC, who did not receive the message to abandon the straight and level 'Oboe' run in to the target. He continued his 'Oboe' run, although his Lancaster had been damaged by flak, and set two engines on fire. Ignoring the threat of fire and possible explosion he carried on and dropped his bomb load dead on target. His aircraft was then attacked by German fighters and the Lancaster went out of control and crashed. Only the rear gunner survived. S/Ldr Palmer was awarded a posthumous Victoria Cross for his action; he had completed 110 operational sorties by the time he was killed.

An evening attack on the railway yards at Limburg and Seigburg was detailed for 92 Mosquitoes, with a further seven on nuisance flights to Bremen, Hanover, Osnabruck and Munster. 199 Squadron were required to provide a Mandrel screen of ten Stirlings, with two more acting as Window force.

F/Lt Lind, LJ595 EX-N took off at 1610 hrs, but did not complete his sortie, returning early as the rear turret guns would not depress; his aircraft landed at 1718 hrs. From the records it appears that a further three crews encountered engine problems and returned before completing the mission. Again a poorly written ORB fails to give details. The remainder of the Mandrel aircraft kept up a screen over Belgium from 1720 hrs to 1900 hrs and all completed their allotted tasks and returned to base. The two Windowing Stirlings flew almost the same track as the Mandrel sortie, dispensing from 1740 hrs to 1820 hrs.

24th December 1944

Christmas Eve 1944 saw two raids planned for Hangelar Airfield and rail yards at Cologne. Eight RCM sorties were ordered for 199 Squadron to cover the attacks. The attacks on both targets were extremely accurate and at Cologne an ammunition train received a direct hit and blew up. Also, as an added bonus, the airfield at Butzweilerhof was bombed, causing widespread damage. All RCM Stirlings completed their missions except F/Lt Simon, LJ568 EX-L who had problems with the Gee set and returned to North Creake at 1758 hrs; the remaining aircraft returned to base, landing between 1953 hrs and 2029 hrs.

25th December 1944

The station was classed as on "Official Stand Down", everyone hoping this would be the last Christmas Day at war. A programme of entertainment had been formulated over the previous weeks to ensure everyone had a pleasant time and joined in the festive spirit.

No operations ordered for 100 Group. However, due to great improvements in the weather, Bomber Command was able to launch an attack on the German ground forces that had made great inroads on the Allied forces front line in the Ardennes region. This was known as the "Battle of the Bulge" and had been fought during some of the most atrocious weather encountered during the war.

The freezing conditions, snow and fog hampered all Allied aircraft endeavouring to give air support during the initial stages of the battle. The German forces committed 500,000 men and pitted them against 600,000 Americans and 55,000 British who were strung out thinly along the Belgium/Luxembourg border. The total secrecy applied to the planning, movement of troops and the positions to be attacked enabled complete surprise when the German armies struck on 16th December. With the preparations and then the advance made under cover of the Ardennes Forest itself and the bad weather contributing in keeping allied aircraft grounded, the Allies were blinded to the Germans' intentions.

From the 16th to the 23rd strong attacks by German infantry and armour made serious inroads into Allied held territory, but then with improving weather and tough resistance by the American and British troops, the tide was turned and gradually the Germans were forced to retreat, leaving 100,000 casualties killed, wounded or captured.

The battle was declared over on 15th January 1945.

ROYAL AIR FORCE STATION, NORTH CREAKE.

Christmas Day Menu

BREAKFAST.

Cornflakes.   Porridge.
Tea.   Coffee.
Bread and Butter.   Marmalade.
Fried Egg and Bacon.

DINNER.

Hollandaise Soup.
Roast Turkey.   Roast Pork.   Roast Goose.
Chestnut Stuffing.   Bread Sauce.   Apple Sauce.
Roast Potatoes.   Creamed Potatoes.
Brussel Sprouts.   Cauliflower.   Parsnips.
Christmas Pudding.   Brandy Sauce.
Mince Pies.   Cheese Straws.
Apples.   Oranges.   Nuts.   Dates.
Beer.   Minerals.   Cigarettes.

TEA.

Cold Duck and Cold Ham.
Christmas Cake.   Mince Pies.
Tea.   Bread and Butter.   Jam.

Christmas 1944.

CONFIDENTIAL MESSAGE FROM THE STATION COMMANDER.

I should like to wish you all a very happy Christmas at North Creake. I am sorry that it was not possible for you to be with your loved ones at this time and hope with all my heart that before very long you will be restored to those whose thoughts are with you now.

You have all worked very well indeed and your efforts are sincerely and gratefully appreciated. I hope it will make your Christmas all the more enjoyable to know that you have been instrumental in saving the lives of thousands of our gallant crews, and that there is many a household in Britain and the Empire whose present joy would have been turned to sorrow but for the work you have done.

N. A. N. BRAY, G./Capt.,
Christmas, 1944.   Station Commander.

For Security reasons this message should not be despatched from, or communicated to any person outside this Station.

28th December 1944

167 Lancasters of 3 Group were ordered to make a daylight raid on Cologne/Gremberg, with the main marshalling yards selected as the aiming point. An accurate attack was made and much damage caused to the railhead and surrounding buildings. No aircraft were lost.

For the night raids, the two main towns at München-Gladbach and Bonn were selected for attack by a combined force of 348 aircraft from 1, 4 and 8 Groups. Railway yards and associated installations were the prime target, but it appears little damage was caused to these at either location. The bombing being scattered, some falling as far as seven km from München-Gladbach, and the raid on Bonn caused more damage to surrounding buildings and houses than to the railway network. One Lancaster was lost on the Bonn raid.

To cover both morning and night raids, 199 Squadron provided Mandrel screens as follows:

The morning sorties were flown by: F/Sgt Pearce, LJ651 EX-C; F/O Milsom, LJ538 EX-T; F/Lt Spaulding, LJ544 EX-D; F/O Chatterton, LJ??? EX-X; P/O Finnimore, LJ568 EX-L; F/O McColl, LJ520 EX-Z; and W/O Currell, LJ611 EX-A.

W/O Currell appears to have replaced F/O O'Brien who would take part in the later sortie.

Take-off for this mission started at 0319 hrs and all aircraft were airborne by 0328 hrs. Flying out over the English Coast at Gravesend they crossed the French Coast at Abbeville, then on an east track to reach Cambrai. From there they changed course, NNE, to reach a point east of Brussels, where the aircraft commenced jamming at 0520 hrs and continued until 0650 hrs. They all returned safely via Orfordness, landing between 0801 hrs and 0818 hrs.

Right: **F/Sgt H. Broadfield, photographed whilst he was flying 20ft above the Wash. There were four wakes left behind in the water, one for each propellor.**

Below: **Crew of LJ525, "Jolly Roger".**

Eight aircraft jamming with Mandrel covered the night raid on Cologne and Bonn. This force was made up of: S/Ldr Button, LJ651 EX-C; F/O Marshall, LJ649 EX-P; F/O Green, LJ611 EX-A; F/Lt Lind, LJ538 EX-T; F/O O'Brien, LJ544 EX-D; W/O Werner, LJ525 EX-R; P/O MacNamara, LJ568 EX-L; F/O Van Whelie, LJ520 EX-Z. Take-off was between 1544 hrs and 1641 hrs, with a flight pattern almost identical with the morning's operations. It is not possible to give the time the jamming commenced or ended, as this is omitted from the sortie records. All the aircraft returned safely to base, the last landing at 2107 hrs. Lancasters of 5 Group made an attack on a naval target in Oslo Fjord, but no direct hits on any shipping were claimed. Of the 67 bombers and one Mosquito taking part all returned safely.

29th December 1944

Rail yards and oil refineries were placed on the target list and it was decided to attack the oil installation at Scholven/Buer and the marshalling yards located at Troisdorf. The latter raid was a complete failure, with very few bombs hitting the target due to extremely thick cloud cover. The raid on Scholven however, had better results as the accompanying Oboe equipped Mosquito Pathfinders dropped accurate sky-markers and over 300 bombs hit the refinery. Many large and uncontrollable fires were started, causing further oil tanks to rupture. A large number of houses were destroyed in the towns and two nearby coal mines had winding houses and other ancillary buildings damaged. Unfortunately 24 prisoners of war were among the total of 93 people reported killed in the raid. Many unexploded bombs caused much disorder and delays among the fire fighting and rescue services long after the raid had finished. The two attacks were covered this time with a "Moving Mandrel Screen" of eight Stirlings. The outward route followed the normal exit at Gravesend and then to Abbeville in France, taking up the first Mandrel jamming positions flying between 'A' and 'B' at 1800 hrs ESE of Brussels (A) and SSE of Maastricht (B), the pilots were then instructed to all fly to position 'B' at 1850 hrs and continue to transmit until 1930 hrs. Mandrels were to be turned on at 1750 hrs and off at 1940 hrs.

30th December 1944

Rail targets at Cologne/Kalk were attacked by 470 aircraft, resulting in severe damage to the marshalling yards. Train stations were hit and two ammunition trains blew up after direct hits by high explosive bombs, with subsequent collateral damage to a wide area. Roads being used by motorised traffic in and out of the railhead were also badly affected.

The second raid was at Houffalize, twenty miles north of Bastogne in Belgium, that had been reported as a choke point for German transport. This target was in a river valley, but no results are recorded as to the outcome of the attack by 154 Lancasters and twelve Mosquitoes of 5 Group.

The above raids were covered by ten aircraft from 199 Squadron flying a normal Mandrel sortie orbiting at a point ESE of Charleroi in Belgium.

31st December 1944

A daylight raid on the marshalling yards at Vohwinkel was carried out by Lancasters of 5 Group. Much of the bombing was reported to have hit areas well south of the aiming point with some falling in nearby Solingen.

An evening raid by 149 Lancasters and seventeen Mosquitoes on rail yards at Osterfeld was covered by ten RCM Stirlings. The crews on this last Squadron sortie of 1944 were flown by: P/O Finnimore, LJ617 EX-E; P/O Broadfield, LJ525 EX-R; F/Lt Simon, LJ542 EX-G; F/O Milsom, LJ538 EX-T; F/Sgt Pearce, LJ611 EX-A; F/O Marshall, LJ649 EX-P; F/O O'Brien, LJ541 EX-K; F/O Chatterton, LJ567 EX-X; S/Ldr Button, LJ514 EX-B; and W/O Werner, LJ614 EX-S.

And so the year ended, with many people convinced that the war was soon to end. Although the Germans were putting up stiff resistance on the ground, their main attacking force, the Luftwaffe, was now of little consequence. Bombers and fighters were difficult to replace and, equally, finding enough fuel to train new pilots. The latter shortages were a direct result of a policy set out by both Bomber Command and the USAAF that oil targets were to take priority whenever the opportunity arose. This, coupled with attacks on rail and road networks, was slowly starving the German forces of essential supplies.

1945

The Final Act –
conversion to the Halifax and Allied victory in Europe

January
German transport facilities disrupted – industrial targets hit with greater accuracy – 199 Squadron Stirlings accompany the bomber streams to their targets

1st January 1945

The first raids of 1945 were a continuation of plans by Bomber Command to disrupt the German oil and transport systems. Attacks were planned on the Mitteland Canal, rail marshalling yards at Vohwinkel and a synthetic petrol plant situated near Dortmund. A Mandrel screen was provided by eleven Stirlings and crews operating racecourse patterns at points midway between Mablethorpe and Hartingen on the Frisian Islands where jamming commenced at 1705 hrs. At 1745 hrs all the aircraft moved to a point twenty miles off the Frisians and continued jamming until 2000 hrs switching off at 2015 hrs. This was a change to the routine of jamming over Belgium used during the latter part of 1944. One aircraft flown by F/Lt Spaulding developed engine trouble shortly after take-off and, returning to North Creake, was replaced by the reserve. The remaining aircraft all completed their sorties satisfactorily. The raid on Mitteland resulted in some breaches of the canal; no aircraft was lost. Great damage was caused to the railhead at Vohwinkel, with one Lancaster shot down, but the raid on Dortmund was a failure, with no bombs hitting the oil plant. Fortunately no aircraft were lost on the Dortmund raid.

2nd January 1945

Bomber Command was called on for a maximum effort from 1, 3, 4, 6, and 8 Groups. The total sorties flown amounted to 1,069 made up of 389 aircraft assigned to a raid on Ludwigshafen, 514 to Nuremberg and the remainder on minor operations to Berlin, Castrop-Rauxel, Hanue and RCM. The minor operations were carried out by Mosquitoes. Nuremberg had escaped serious damage, but this raid would change that, as the Pathfinders, aided by a full moon, accurately marked the aiming points. The centre of the city received the full brunt of the attack and much of it was completely destroyed. Some other areas, notabley the north eastern and southern sections, also received attention and the M.A.N. works and the Seimens factories were severely damaged. Almost 5,000 houses were destroyed with 1,838 people killed.

The attack on Ludwigshafen was chosen, due to the large I.G. Farben factories that were producing chemicals. Extremely accurate bombing resulted in almost all the bombs falling on the factories with very little damage to surrounding houses. Several other industrial plants were hit and with the electrical power supply cut to all areas the production of chemicals and war related materials was seriously affected.

A total of nine bombers were lost on both raids.

RCM was to be covered by ten aircraft from North Creake, however F/O Milsom, who was flying LJ538 EX-T, did not take off due to the starboard outer engine giving problems. The remaining nine aircraft took off just after 1500 hrs to provide a Mandrel screen, flying out to occupy five positions at 1715 hrs around Montmedy on the French/Belgian border. They only stayed at this point for fifteen minutes and then moved to an area south of Metz where they remained until 2020 hrs. All aircraft returned safely to base, the last landing at 2246 hrs.

3rd and 4th January 1945

No operations due to unfavourable weather conditions.

5th January 1945

It was decided to mount a full-scale attack, with 664 aircraft, against Hanover as it had escaped any large concentration of bombing since October 1943. Also, a smaller force of 131 Lancasters and nine Mosquitoes was to be sent to Houffalize, as much German transport was constricted in this area on its way to supply troops in the Ardennes offensive.

Hanover reported bombs scattered over a wide area of the city, with 493 buildings destroyed and 250 people killed. The raid appears to have been split into two waves, with bombers taking off between 1600 hrs and 1900 hrs.

199 Squadron was detailed to set up a Mandrel screen and ten aircraft began taking off at 1626 hrs and were all airborne by 1647 hrs. F/Lt Spaulding was on the initial battle order, but his Stirling was found to have technical problems and scrubbed from the operation. F/Lt Simon, LJ568 EX-L took off at 1636 hrs, but returned early when the intercom was found to be u/s, landing back at North Creake at 1701 hrs. His place in the screen was taken by the reserve aircraft LJ520 EX-Z flown by P/O Broadfield, who took off at 1723 hrs. Another Stirling, LJ541 EX-K, flown by S/Ldr Button was recalled early when it was found that the Gee set was malfunctioning. He landed at 2028 hrs. The screen was operated over two areas of the North Sea – the first at positions 120 miles east of Grimsby, jamming from 1740 hrs to 1840 hrs. At 1840 hrs all the aircraft moved south to new positions 80 miles east of Cromer orbiting until 2120 hrs.

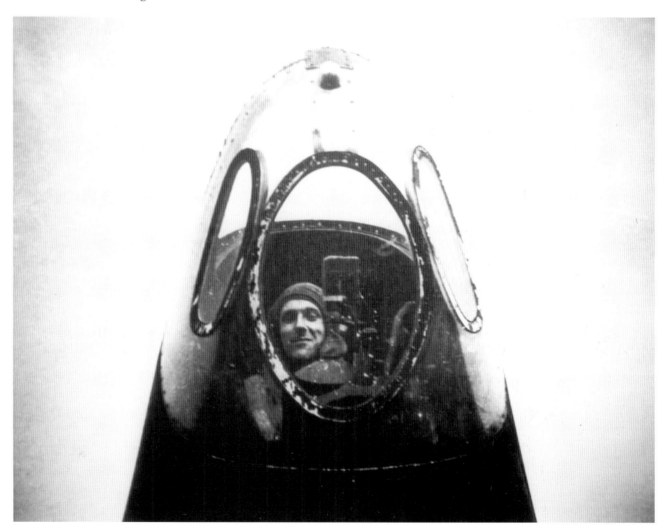

F/Sgt Colin Munro, Bomb Aimer on F/Sgt H. Broadfield's crew.

One other Stirling encountered problems before the sortie was completed. F/O Van Welie, LJ567 EX-X was told by his flight engineer, Sgt Fludder, that the port outer engine was not running smoothly and would have to be shut down. Because of this, the crew left the screen and made an emergency landing at RAF Great Massingham, touching down at 2036 hrs. The remaining aircraft completed their allotted tasks and landed back at North Creake between 2138 hrs and 2206 hrs. Interestingly there are several notes in the sortie records where crews reported 'peculiar' jamming of Gee. In one instance F/Sgt Pearce mentions that the jamming was *"somewhat like a 500 signal steady and continuous for one hour"*. The night's raids were not without heavy casualties. That on Hanover cost 23 Halifaxes and eight Lancasters with German night fighters taking a heavy toll, and two Lancasters were shot down on the Houffalize raid.

6th January 1945

Railway systems continued to be targeted and two in particular at Hanau, east of Frankfurt and Neuss, west of Düsseldorf, were selected to be attacked. The yards and main lines at Hanau, were on a junction serving many parts of central Germany. The raid consisted of 482 Lancasters and Halifaxes backed up by fourteen Oboe Mosquitoes. A small number of bombs hit the railway system selected as the aiming point, but a large number were scattered over the centre of the town and the surrounding area. One German report stated that almost half of the town was destroyed. A similar result was achieved at Neuss, and although the rail target was hit and damaged, much of the bombing fell over the town itself, destroying 1,749 houses, nineteen industrial buildings plus a further nineteen public establishments. 39 people were killed and 91 injured.

In support of these two raids, 199 provided ten aircraft and crews flying a normal Mandrel screen and there were also spoof raids by twenty Mosquitoes on Kassel and six on Castrop-Rauxel. The screen was operated SW of Namur in Belgium jamming from 1735 hrs to 2010 hrs and was supplemented with four Halifaxes from 171 Squadron. P/O Milsom LJ614 EX-S returned early with the starboard outer u/s, but was immediately replaced by the reserve aircraft LJ520 EX-Z flown by F/O Marshall.

7th January 1945

A moving Mandrel screen was ordered to support a raid on Munich by 645 Lancasters and nine Mosquitoes. The Squadron detailed eight Stirlings for this operation, all of which returned safely. The screen was first positioned at a point SE of Montherme in Belgium jamming from 1905 hrs to 1915 hrs, then moved almost due south to a point east of Verdun-sur-Meuse in France. This was the last large scale effort mounted by Bomber Command on Munich. Eleven Lancasters were lost.

8th to 13th January 1945

All operational flying was cancelled due to unfavourable weather conditions.

14th January 1945

Two oil refineries at Leuna and Dulmen, plus a railway target at Grevenbroich, were selected as targets for the night's bombing attacks. In support of these, '199' placed fourteen Stirlings and crews on the battle orders to provide a normal Mandrel screen.

Aircraft began taking off at 1617 hrs with F/Lt Turner, LJ514 EX-B and F/Lt Spaulding, LJ544 EX-D, leading, and all but two were airborne by 1637 hrs. The last to leave were P/O McColl, LJ559 EX-Q who lifted off at 1735 hrs and F/Lt Hancock, LJ595 EX-N at 1800 hrs. No reason is given for these delayed departures; it can only be assumed that some technical problems may have arisen that could be dealt with by the ground crews in time for the aircraft to join the screen. The outward track was over the North Sea, making landfall at Bruges and continuing to a point SW of Bastogne where jamming commenced at 1820 hrs and continued until 2025 hrs.

A one hour pause in jamming was then ordered and the sortie records contain a note where all the aircraft were instructed during this pause to *"do 1hr radius of action towards Amiens during non-jamming period"*. Enemy counter-jamming was again experienced on the Gee sets. F/O McNamara's navigator, P/O Marshall, noted in his report that the Mandrel jamming was also affecting the 'Riems' transmitter, but was not causing problems with those coming from the 'Cologne' transmitter. Other navigators reported fake pulses coming through on the German transmissions, but none of these had any significant effect on the mission. After the one hour pause, jamming recommenced at 2130 hrs and continued to 2255 hrs. This sortie was by all accounts quite extended with jamming taking place for approximately four and a half hours.

The bombing attacks had mixed results. That on the fuel storage depot at Dulmen was not very successful – most of the bombs dropped by the 115 aircraft falling in open countryside, the fuel dump escaping serious damage. The raid on the Leuna synthetic oil plant, on the other hand, was a complete success and one of the most damaging on the German oil industry during the war. Grevenbroich marshalling yards sustained heavy damage after a well co-ordinated attack by 151 aircraft and no aircraft were lost.

Supplementing the Mandrel screen there was a diversionary raid set up to sweep over the North Sea and the usual Mosquito raids on Berlin and other cities kept the German defences and civilian population awake all night. Over 30 Lancasters and Halifaxes went on mining sorties in Norwegian and Baltic waters.

15th January 1945

No operations ordered.

16th January 1945

Four individual targets were selected for attack, with three of them being oil and petrol producing plants at Zeitz near Leipzig in Saxony, Wanne-Eickel, north of Bochum in the Ruhr and Brüx in Western Czechoslovakia. The fourth target was at Magdeburg in Lower Saxony. Apart from oil producing plants Wanne-Eickel was also the location of one of the largest rail marshalling yards in the Ruhr. Overall the raids were very successful, causing major problems to oil production. The raid mounted against Magdeburg destroyed most of the city's built up areas and the official death toll was put at 16,000.

371 aircraft were detailed for the raid on Magdeburg with 17 shot down and from the 697 despatched on oil plant raids 12 were lost.

The Mandrel screen, flown by twelve aircraft of 199 Squadron, was initially centred in the North Sea, 180 miles east of Bridlington. Jamming commenced at 1945 hrs and continued until 2005 hrs, when all the aircraft moved eastward towards the Baltic, the furthest point reached being 5443N 0648 E. The aircraft remained on station until 2030 hrs, before proceeding to position 5400N 0450E, where they remained until 2140 hrs. The Mandrels were switched off at 2150 hrs.

The crews and aircraft on this sortie were: F/Lt Turner, LJ617 EX-E; P/O Broadfield, LJ538 EX-T; F/Lt Green, LJ514 EX-B; F/O McColl, LJ520 EX-Z; F/Lt Simon, LJ516 EX-H; F/Sgt Currell, PW259 EX-V; F/O MacNamara, LJ568 EX-L; F/O Chatterton, LJ614 EX-S; F/Lt Spaulding, LJ544 EX-D; F/O Marshall, LJ649 EX-P; F/Lt Dickinson, LJ541 EX-K; F/Lt Lind, LJ559 EX-Q. The two reserves were F/Lt Keen and F/O Milsom. All crews reported heavy German jamming on the Gee sets, with dummy pulses giving the navigators a difficult time plotting the courses to be flown. The overall comments show that, despite German jamming, the sortie was a complete success.

17th January 1945

Minor operations ordered, with 72 Mosquitoes carrying out attacks on Mannheim, Frankfurt, Koblenz, Cologne, Magdeburg and an oil plant at Ruthen. RCM sorties were flown by nine aircraft orbiting over the Sedan area on the French/Belgian border. They took off from RAF North Creake between 1619 hrs and 1634 hrs and completed their allotted sorties, with the exception of F/O McNamara, LJ568 EX-L who returned early due to the starboard inner engine failing. The remaining aircraft were back at base by 2234 hrs.

18th to 21st January 1945

All operational flying cancelled due to bad weather. Ground crews, many working in the open in freezing conditions, carried out much-needed maintenance work.

22nd January 1945

An attack on the oil producing plant at Bruckhausen was planned and 306 aircraft attacked the target with high explosive bombs. The refinery was badly damaged and bombs that fell outside the area partly destroyed a nearby steelworks. Also on Bomber Command's target list for this night was the town of Gelsenkirchen. The raid, by 152 aircraft, was aimed at residential and industrial areas and appears to have been moderately successful. A Mandrel screen was flown by seven aircraft, but engine problems forced some early returns.

P/O Broadfield had only just taken off, around 1700 hrs, when he experienced problems with an overheating port inner engine. Landing, the crew transferred to a reserve aircraft, LJ514 EX-B and took off at again at 1944 hrs. F/Lt Thurlow, LJ538 EX-T, took off at 1706 hrs, but abandoned his mission and landed back at 1820 hrs, his port outer engine being u/s. The next to experience problems was W/O Currell, PW259 EX-V. He had left base at 1705 hrs, but was forced to return with a dead starboard inner engine. He was replaced by another reserve, LJ516 EX-H flown by F/Lt McNamara.

23rd to 27th January 1945

Severe weather conditions prevented any flying.

28th January 1945

Eight Stirlings were detailed to carry out a combined Mandrel Screen and Window Patrol to cover a raid on Stuttgart by 602 aircraft of 1, 4, 6 and 8 Groups. The night's raids and support sorties were by no means straightforward; the attack on Stuttgart was divided into two parts with a distinct 3 hour gap between them and the Mandrel/Window sorties had very complicated time/position parameters. Just before 1630 hrs seven of the assigned RCM aircraft were preparing to take off but due to technical failures of one sort or another F/O Van Welie was forced to abort his mission. The remaining six Stirlings all got airborne in short time the last lifting off at 1736 hrs; this was F/Lt Lind, LJ516 EX-H who replaced F/O Van Welie. Last to leave at 2044 hrs was F/Lt Thurlow, LJ538 EX-T who had been instructed to form part of a second Mandrel Screen.

The other aircraft were flown by F/Lt Keen, LJ554 EX-D; F/Lt Gilbert, LJ514 EX-B; W/O Werner, LJ595 EX-N; F/Lt McNamara, LJ611 EX-A; W/O Currell, LJ559 EX-Q; and F/Lt Hancock, LJ549 EX-P.

The operation is further complicated by having 'Position A' entered in the Sortie Records for both Mandrel and Mandrel/Window sorties.

Entries are written up as follows: Mandrel Force transmitters turned on: Position 'A' 4900N 0604E (Arnaville, France) 1910 hrs to 2000 hrs.

The combined Mandrel/Windows Force proceeded to:

Position 'A' (Mandrell/Window) 4906N 0650E (Hemilly, France), at 2018 hrs.
Position 'B' (Mandrell/Window) 4914N 0830E (Kuhardt, Germany).
Position 'C' (Window) 4858N 0900E (Ammerbuch, South of Stuttgart, Germany).

Up to position 'B' Mandrels had been turned on but at position 'C' the special wireless operators were instructed to turn their jamming sets off. At the last position mentioned the jamming screen was almost over Stuttgart itself and the Stirlings had completed their longest penetration into German territory flying at 16,000ft using a combination of Mandrel and Window. From the navigators reports it would seem that much of the Gee transmissions were also obliterated by their own Mandrel jamming. This may have been caused by the weakening Gee signals as the aircraft increased the range from the transmitters on the English coast.

The actual raid on Stuttgart was scattered to some degree due to dense cloud cover and sky markers had to be used by the Pathfinders. However, rail yards and the surrounding area in the north of the city received many direct hits causing great disruption with fires burning all night and well into the next day. Some bombs were drawn away from the target by decoy fires and target indicators but the majority hit built up areas and industrial sites.

Four Halifaxes, six Lancasters and one Mosquito were shot down during the attack.

29th to 31st January 1945

Continuing bad weather curtailed all operational flying from RAF North Creake.

February

"Operation Thunderclap" – the bombing of Dresden – conversion to Halifaxes.

1st February 1945

Over 1,000 bombers were detailed for the first raids of the month, targeting Ludwigshafen, Mainz and Siegen, but the weather made accurate bombing almost impossible. Thick cloud obscured the aiming points for much of the attacks and the bomb aimers had to rely on sky markers. Rail yards and industrial sites were the main target in Ludwigshafen and were hit, together with a road bridge over the Rhine. However, the raids on Mainz and Siegen failed to do any significant damage, with most of the bombs falling well outside the target areas. Cloud, strong winds and dummy fires and markers all contributed to make accurate bombing almost impossible.

The eight aircraft sent in support of these attacks were airborne by 1600 hrs, and flew a normal orbiting Mandrel screen over positions twenty miles east of Nancy in the Lorraine district of France.

Minutes after taking off, at 1601 hrs, F/Lt Turner's navigator, F/O Brimson, found the Gee set malfunctioning and immediately returned to North Creake, landing at 1638 hrs. The remaining aircraft completed their sorties, returning between 2217 hrs and 2256 hrs. Also of consequence, and important to mention at this juncture, is the significant contribution made by the squadrons flying Mosquitoes to targets in Germany. On this night, for example, over 100 made the long and difficult trip to Berlin where they bombed specific areas to keep the defences alerted all night and draw off night fighters from the main attacks. Smaller numbers also attacked petrol and oil targets in Bruckhausen and populated areas in Mannheim and Hanover.

To add to the confusion, four Mosquitoes dropped dummy target indicators at Mannheim and Stuttgart to give the impression major raids were to follow. The Mosquito could carry a comprehensive mix of bomb loads, its most useful being the 4,000lb 'Cookie' blast bomb. Equipped with 'Oboe', a highly accurate navigation aid, it was also used extensively by the Pathfinder Force for precision marking of targets. Being fast and manoeuvrable at all altitudes – and especially deadly at low level strikes – this aircraft, and the crews that flew it, served the RAF well.

2nd February 1945

Eight Stirlings and crews were detailed for a Mandrel screen to cover raids on Wiesbaden, Wanne-Eickel and Karlsruhe. F/Lt Gilbert, LJ520 EX-Z. F/Lt Milsom, LJ538 EX-T and F/Lt Hancock, LJ559 EX-Q, failed to take off for technical reasons but were not replaced. The remaining five completed their missions successfully, but P/O Pearce was forced to land at RAF Foulsham on his return; no details are recorded. The raid on Wiesbaden killed 1,000 civilians and injured 350, with widespread damage in the only large attack mounted by Bomber Command on the town. The raids on Wanne-Eickel and Karlsruhe were recorded as complete failures due to the targets being cloud covered, most of the bombs falling on open ground causing little or no damage. Over the three raids 21 aircraft were lost.

3rd February 1945

After several nights of intense activity, Bomber Command reduced the number targets selected. Only two light raids were planned, with 192 Lancasters and eighteen Mosquitoes sent to Bottrop and 149 Lancasters to Dortmund. Both targets were Benzol producing plants, but only the one at Bottrop was damaged to any significant degree. Twelve Lancasters were shot down. RCM support was provided by seven Stirlings orbiting north east of Liege on the Belgian/German border. They provided jamming from 1835 hrs to 2135 hrs flying at 15,000ft. The only problems encountered during the sortie were with the main compasses on three aircraft.

4th February 1945

Bonn, Gelsenkirchen and Osterfeld, where synthetic fuel producing plants were situated, came up on the Battle Orders for aircraft of 4, 6 and 8 Groups. All three raids were unsatisfactory, with most of the bombing falling outside the target areas. Three Lancasters were lost on the Bonn raid.

A normal Mandrel screen was provided by seven Stirlings of 199 Squadron positioned south of Liège in Belgium. The jamming transmissions were used in two phases of the sortie, the first phase starting at 1945 hrs and ending at 2130 hrs. A short break was then ordered during which time all the aircraft were instructed to carry out *"a radius of action"* towards position 5010N 0330E, a point near Le Cateau in France. Jamming recommenced at 2215 hrs for 30 minutes.

5th and 6th February 1945

No operations ordered.

7th February 1945

Two of the three main targets for the night's attack were selected in support of the ground forces advancing into Germany near the Reichswald Forest. The towns of Kleve and Goch had been strongly fortified and most of the civilian population moved to safer districts. The British XXX Corps Commander, Lt. Gen. Brian Horrocks, requested that the towns be bombed with incendiaries to minimise the blocking of main roads and adjacent streets. This, he hoped, would enable his mechanised forces a more speedy passage through the German positions.

The attack on Goch was very accurate, but only 155 of the 464 aircraft despatched to the target were able to drop their loads, due to low cloud and heavy smoke rising from the buildings. Unfortunately, there were many casualties among foreign workers who had been brought in by the Germans to build defences, and more than 150 died.

Kleve was attacked by 295 aircraft. Despite the army's request not to use high explosive bombs, almost 1,500 tons rained down, causing utter destruction. When the ground forces started their attack, a general thaw of the frozen ground coupled with the debris choking the roads in Kleve quickly stopped the advance.

The third target for the night, the Dortmund-Ems Canal, was a failure and reconnaissance aircraft later found that the bombs had fallen well away from the banks of the waterways they should have breached.

Jamming was carried out by '199' in the St Vith area of Belgium, with eight Stirlings using a moving Mandrel screen. The tactics used were that when the aircraft reached their starting points over France NNE of Abbeville they then proceeded to four orbiting points all on the same eastern co-ordinates but spanning from La Roch-en-Ardenne in Belgium down to Mangiennes in France. The Stirlings, in pairs, flew the normal racetrack patterns and started jamming at 1900 hrs. However, they were instructed to move at regular intervals from their first allocated positions to that flown by the next more northerly station. The average height for this sortie was 15,000ft and lasted until 2230 hrs.

8th February 1945

Two synthetic oil plants at Politz and Wanne-Eickel, plus the large railway yards at Krefeld, were attacked with a force of 854 aircraft. The raid on Politz was such a success that it produced no further oil for the German war effort. Those on the other two targets were complete failures, with only light damage to the oil refinery at Wanne-Eickel and no discernible new damage to the rail yards in Krefeld.

The RCM coverage was provided by six 199 Squadron Stirlings, but those flown by F/Lt McNamara and F/Lt Simon were forced to return early, each on three engines.

9th to 12th February 1945

No operations flown due to severe weather conditions.

13 February 1945

Bomber Command mounted a maximum effort raid on the city of Dresden, to which 199 Squadron provided eight Stirlings and crews with two in reserve. They set up the initial Mandrel screen over Bastogne, beginning transmissions at position 'A' at 2335 hrs until 0030 hrs. They then moved eastwards, to Position 'B', east of Beringen on the Belgian border, at 0030 hrs. Jamming continued until 0220 hrs. All the aircraft completed their missions successfully.

Much has been written and debated since this raid took place and after the war many people who were involved in the planning both political and military have tried to distance themselves from the consequences of the destruction and high casualties caused to this city. The arguments still go on to this day about whether or not Dresden should have been attacked. Reports and intelligence gathered during the early part of 1945 showed that Dresden, Leipzig, Chemnitz and Berlin were suitable targets to attack to aid the advancing Russian armies. They were all just within the German border of the eastern front, were vital communications and supply centres and choke points for refugees and wounded fleeing the advancing red army.

The official directive for these raids was issued by the Air Ministry to Bomber Command at the end of January and was codenamed 'Operation Thunderclap'. Churchill took an active part in the planning, although he, like many others, would distance himself from the outcome. At the Yalta conference held on 4th February the Russians asked for the raids to take place and the Americans were also asked to participate to which they agreed.

The first raid was to have been carried out in daylight by the USAAF during the morning of the 13th February, but bad weather prevented this from being implemented. It therefore fell on Bomber Command to mount the first attack during the night of the 13th.

The RAF sent 796 Lancasters and nine Mosquitoes split into two separate raids, dropping a total of 1,478 tons of high explosives and 1,182 tons of incendiaries. In the first wave, 244 aircraft of 5 Group dropped 800 tons of bombs, after marking the area with their low level marking method. This first phase was not very successful, but the second wave of 529 Lancasters that attacked three hours later dropped more than 1,800 tons of bombs with great accuracy.

A consequence of this devastating attack was the creation of a firestorm on the same proportions as that inflicted on Hamburg in July 1943. The exact number of people who died in this raid has never been established, but it is reliably estimated that the figure was near 50,000. Large areas of the city were completely destroyed. The next day the Americans bombed Dresden with 311 B17s, dropping a further 771 tons of bombs and used their long-range Mustang fighters to strafe any transport targets seen on the outlying roads. They also bombed the city again on the 15th February and again on 2nd March.

As well as the raid on Dresden, Bomber Command also detailed an attack by 368 aircraft on the oil facilities at Bohlen near Leipzig. This raid was reported to have been scattered due to 10/10 cloud cover over the target.

The total sorties flown this night amounted to 1,406 with the loss of nine aircraft.

14th February 1945

'Operation Thunderclap' continued with a raid on Chemnitz by 499 Lancasters and Halifaxes of 1, 3, 4, 6 and 8 Groups. This took the same form as the attack on Dresden, with the aircraft bombing in two waves, with a three hour gap. There was a thick blanket of cloud over the aiming point, forcing the Pathfinders to employ only sky markers. Reports show that, although a great deal of damage was caused in the city, much of the bombing fell in open country. A further 224 Lancasters and eight Mosquitoes of 5 Group bombed the oil refinery at Rositz where part of the plant was hit and put out of action.

To draw off German fighters and wrong foot their controllers, an elaborate diversionary plan was put into effect. 95 aircraft from 3 Group and some of the heavy conversion units carried out a spoof sweep into the Heligoland Bight. 46 Mosquitoes raided Berlin and nineteen went to Mainz. A further fourteen went to Dessau, twelve to Duisburg, eleven to Nuremberg and eight to Frankfurt.

As part of the diversions, '199' detailed eight Stirlings to fly a normal Mandrel sortie over exactly the same positions at Bastogne as those of the previous nights operations.

15th to 17th February 1945

No operations due to bad weather.

18th February 1945

Bad weather prevented any major raids, but '199' was able to mount a normal Mandrel operation in support of a number of "Siren Tours" (small air raids carried out to cause alarm, as opposed to damage) over various towns and cities in central Germany. 32 Mosquitoes did make bombing attacks on Mannheim with a further six each to Berlin and Bremen. Six Stirlings and crews of 199 Squadron flew a normal Mandrel screen over the North Sea midway between the Lincolnshire and Dutch coasts.

19th February 1945

No operations ordered.

20th February 1945

A mix of targets with oil production listed as a priority. The Rhenania Ossag oil refineries at Dusseldorf and Monheim were attacked by a total of 301 Halifaxes, Lancasters and Mosquitoes. Both raids were successful and the plants' production ceased completely.

A major attack on Dortmund carried out by 514 Lancasters and fourteen Mosquitoes of 1, 3, 6 and 8 Groups. No reports from the city exist to substantiate Bomber Command's claims that the southern half of Dortmund was destroyed. This was the last major raid on the city. A Mandrel screen was flown by ten Stirlings and diversionary raids were carried out by HCU aircraft flying spoof sweeps over the North Sea.

W/O J.F. Martin rear gunner in F/Lt Keen's crew was awarded the DFC, *Gazetted* on 20th February 1945.

21st February 1945

To cover the night's raids on Duisburg, Worms and the Mittelland Canal it was decided to employ a moving Mandrel screen in conjunction with other tactics. Ten aircraft were detailed from 199 Squadron comprising: F/Lt Green, LJ611 EX-A; F/Lt McNamara, LJ568 EX-L; F/Lt Thurlow, LJ544 EX-D; F/Lt Lind, LJ541 EX-K; F/Lt Sturrock, LJ516 EX-H; F/Lt Harker, LJ649 EX-P; F/O Arkinstall, PN373 EX-Y; F/Lt Burley, LJ595 EX-N; F/O Brooks, PN375 EX-F; F/O King, RG375 EX-R.

The co-ordinates show that the aircraft were jamming in three specific areas – Brecht, Maaseik and Liège covering the Belgian/Dutch border and was maintained for over four hours.

The raid on Duisburg was ordered as an area bombing attack and was successfully carried out by 362 Lancasters and eleven Mosquitoes of 1, 6 and 8 Groups. Seven aircraft were lost. This was Bomber Command's last large raid on Duisburg. The raid on Worms, the only one carried out during the war, comprised 349 aircraft: 288 Halifaxes, 36 Lancasters and 25 Mosquitoes which dropped 1,116 tons of bombs on the town with 64% of the buildings being destroyed or damaged. Much of its industry was put out of action, including the only plant producing war materials, namely drive sprockets for tanks. 239 people were killed and 35,000 bombed out from a population of 58,000. Ten Halifaxes and one Lancaster were lost.

The attack on the Mittelland Canal was to breach its banks and by allowing the water to escape and render it unnavigable. The aiming point selected was Gravenhorst and 165 Lancasters and twelve Mosquitoes of 5 Group carried out a pinpoint attack, breaching the canal. Unfortunately, a high percentage of the attacking bombers were lost, with nine Lancasters shot down and a further four crashing in France and Holland. One of the Lancasters was flown by G/Capt A.C. Evans-Evans DFC, the station commander at RAF Coningsby, home to 83 Squadron. It is worth recounting a few facts relating to this crew – the Lancaster was shot down by a night fighter and crashed in Holland near Gertruda Farm owned by the Ypna family, 12 kms NE of Helmond (liberated). All the crew were killed, except the rear gunner P/O Hansen, RAAF. G/Capt. Evans-Evans was 43 years old and one of the oldest officers to be killed on bomber operations. In contrast, his highly decorated navigator S/Ldr Wishart, DSO, DFC, and Bar was only 22 and the youngest squadron leader killed in the war. Two other crew members had also been decorated – F/Lt Fitch DFC, GM and F/O Ball DFM.

This mission was the first time that modified Halifax bombers were used by 199 Squadron. The first three, F/O King RG375, F/O Arkinstall PN373 and F/O Brooks PN375. RG375 was lost in tragic circumstances on 3rd May 1945.

22nd February 1945

A Mandrel screen was ordered for six aircraft to cover what were classed as minor operations by Mosquitoes to Berlin, Bremen, and Erfurt. These were nuisance raids operated to keep the German defences and civilian populations awake even though there were no raids mounted by Bomber Command. The Mandrel screen was also part of this subterfuge by creating the false impression a major raid was imminent.

The six aircraft taking part were flown by: S/Ldr Button, LJ544 EX-D; F/Lt Keen, LJ541 EX-K; F/Lt Sturrock, LJ611 EX-A; F/Lt Turner, LJ568 EX-L; F/O Reidy, Halifax RG373 EX-T; and F/Lt Burley, Halifax RG375 EX-R.

The Mandrel screen was operated near to Liège on the German-Belgium border.

23rd February 1945

The Squadron detailed eight aircraft to support a major raid on Pforzheim, a large town between Karlsruhe and Stuttgart just inside the Alsace-German border, carried out by 367 Lancasters and thirteen Mosquitoes of 1, 6 and 8 Groups, accompanied by a film unit Lancaster to record the events.

The crews ordered for this sortie were: F/Lt Keen, LJ541 EX-K; F/Lt Green, LJ611 EX-A; S/Ldr Button, LJ516 EX-H; F/Lt McNamara, LJ568 EX-L; F/Lt Turner, LJ542 EX-G; F/Lt Lind, PW259 EX-V; F/O Arkinstall, LJ525 EX-R; P/O Reidy, Halifax, RG372 EX-P.

The aircraft operated over a large area of Belgium flying south of the towns of Charleroi and Liège with average sortie times of six hours.

This was the only Bomber Command attack on this town and the Pathfinder aircraft laid down their markers and TIs with great accuracy from an altitude of only 8,000ft. In a short time, estimated as 22 minutes, 1,825 tons of bombs were dropped in the centre of the town. An area 1½ by 1 mile was engulfed in a huge fire and over 17,000 people were killed in the third heaviest death toll in Germany during the war, following Hamburg and Dresden. Over 80% of the towns buildings were destroyed, and thought to be the greatest proportion in one raid in the war.

The master bomber was Captain Edwin Swales, DFC, a South African serving with 582 Squadron. Over the target area, his Lancaster was attacked by German night fighters on at least two occasions, putting two engines and the rear turret out of action. He carried on directing the attack using all his skill and experience and did not leave until the raid was over. Much of the credit for the accuracy of the attack was due to his coolness and nerve. Although his Lancaster was badly damaged and difficult to fly he set course for base, but ran into turbulence over France. The aircraft became increasingly difficult to fly and he ordered his crew to bale out. The seven left the aircraft, leaving Captain Swales to find a suitable area in which to set the Lancaster down. Unfortunately it hit high tension wires near to Chapelle-aux-Bois, Valenciennes killing him in the crash. His crew, included a second navigator P/O Wheaton RAAF and three others, had been decorated for their previous actions with the Squadron – F/Sgt Bennington DFM, S/Ldr Archer, DSO, DFC, and F/Lt Dodson, DSO, DFC.

Captain Swales was buried in the Leopoldsburg War Cemetery, Belgium and awarded a posthumous Victoria Cross – the last to be awarded to a member of Bomber Command during the war. Twelve aircraft were lost on the Pforzheim raid.

24th February 1945

There were no major operations for the night, but it was decided to mount a diversionary spoof raid over Northern France by various training units, together with a raid on Berlin by 63 Mosquitoes. Other minor raids were detailed for Neuss, Erfurt, Dessau and Halle, to keep the local populations awake and their defences on alert. The diversionary raid by 74 aircraft over France was supported by six 199 Squadron aircraft together with, as was usual, a number from other RCM Squadrons. '199' successfully carried out a normal Mandrel jamming mission over Belgium, all returning safely. However, one RCM unit did not fare well; 469 Squadron lost four Halifaxes MZ447, MZ448, MZ461 and PN429 to flak and fighters, with only five of the 32 crew surviving.

25th February 1945

Limited operations. '199' called on to detail four aircraft for RCM duties. The town of Erfurt was subjected to a raid by 63 Mosquitoes with Berlin, Mainz and Bremen also visited to keep the sirens wailing.

26th February 1945

No operations ordered.

27th February 1945

The main attack for the day was a daylight raid on Mainz by 458 aircraft, but 199 Squadron were not called upon to provide Mandrel support. They were however to provide nine aircraft during the late evening covering a diversionary sweep over the North Sea to draw up German fighters. F/Lt Keen was forced to return early due to the starboard outer engine u/s. The attack on Mainz was the city's worst of the war with 5,660 buildings destroyed, including many industrial sites. Reports gave the number of dead at approximately 1,200, among whom were 41 nuns, killed when their convent received a direct hit. This was the last raid on Mainz.

28th February 1945

During the late evening another diversionary sweep over the North Sea by 98 training aircraft. Mosquito squadrons mounted spoof raids against Berlin, Nuremberg and Munich. '199' detailed eight aircraft and crews to support these sorties, with the following taking part:

Stirlings: F/Lt Gilbert, LJ568 EX-L; F/Lt Keen, LJ544 EX-D; F/Lt Green, LJ617 EX-E.

Halifaxes: F/Lt Harker, RG375 EX-R; F/O King, PN375 EX-F; W/O Sharples, NR244 EX-V; F/O Paddon, RG373 EX-T; W/O Porter, PN373 EX-Y.

As can be seen from the above list, more crews were converting to the Halifax as they gradually replaced the Stirling.

March

Daylight sorties over Germany – Stirlings and Halifaxes form jamming screens – RCM aircraft carry bomb loads to the target area

1st March 1945

Many more attacks on German towns, cities and oil installations were now being carried out during daylight hours due to the continuing advances of the Allied Armies over occupied France and Belgium. This obviously cut down on the amount of flak and fighters encountered. Mannheim was attacked in a daylight raid, for the last time.

During the late evening '199' sent eight aircraft to support minor operations to Berlin and Erfurt. All completed their tasks and returned safely to base. During this sortie all the aircraft were ordered to take part in an experimental 'Window' exercise, dropping bundles of type 'MM' and 'N' at up to twenty bundles per minute. There are no indications in the records if the experiment was a success.

2nd March 1945

The trend continued, with a daylight raid on Cologne by 858 aircraft, consisting of 531 Lancasters, 303 Halifaxes and 24 Mosquitoes. Many buildings were destroyed but the damage reports, if any, did not survive. The city fell to Allied troops four days later.

Night operations produced another sweep over the North Sea – again by training aircraft – to lure German night fighters into the air to further use up their dwindling fuel supplies. Other Mosquitoes paid visits to Kassel and Berlin.

199 Squadron detailed nine aircraft to support these diversions, flying a route to a point over the North Sea midway between Middlesborough and Westerland on the Denmark coast.

3rd March 1945

The oil refinery at Bergkamen was attacked by a force of 234 aircraft, all of which bombed accurately, totally destroying the plant. No further production was possible.

The Dortmund-Ems Canal also came in for attention and 212 Lancasters and ten Mosquitoes attacked one of its aqueducts at Ladbergen, breaching it in two places. The waterway in the immediate area was put out of action, stopping all waterborne traffic. Diversionary sweeps and raids were ordered to support the two major operations.

German fighter tactics changed with their command instructing as many as 200 aircraft to follow the bomber stream back to England. Codenamed 'Gisella' it caught the British defences by surprise, and resulted in the Germans shooting down twenty bombers over England. 199 Squadron provided nine aircraft to cover the raids, but did not suffer any casualties.

5th March 1945

199 Squadron was detailed to mount a maximum effort to support major raids on Chemnitz and Bohlen with minor operations to Berlin, Gelsenkirchen and Hallendorf. For the first time for many weeks the aircraft were to be split into Mandrel and Window forces and the Mandrel force was to have two 'wind velocity finders' flying with them. The Mandrel aircraft were made up of four Stirlings and two Halifaxes flown by:

Stirlings: F/Lt Lind, LJ542 EX-G; F/Lt McNamara, LJ568 EX-L; F/Lt Thurlow, LJ617 EX-E; F/Lt Sturrock, LJ544 EX-D.

Halifaxes: F/O Walford, RG387 EX-B; F/O Reidy, RG376 EX-Z.

The aircraft orbited at points near Malmedy, Belgium, with most sorties lasting over six hours.

The two wind finder aircraft were flown by F/O Brown who was designated "master w/v finder" and F/Sgt Goss "deputy w/v finder".

Window force consisted of six Halifaxes flown by: F/O Arkinstall, RG372 EX-P; S/Ldr Knight, RG381 EX-Q; F/O Ward, PN374 EX-N; W/O Porter, RG388 EX-S; F/O Brooks, RG375 EX-R; F/O King, RG373 EX-T.

Their route took them out over Gravesend and Dungeness to a point on the French coast at Abbeville. Windowing commenced near Thommen in Belgium and was carried on to points at Beho, Morhausen, Gemmersheim and returning NNE of Luxembourg.

W/O Porter landed at RAF Woodbridge.

The Squadron lost F/Lt Thurlow, LJ617 EX-E, and his crew from the Mandrel operation when his Stirling was shot down by an American anti-aircraft battery and crashed at 1930 hrs near Thionville. Seven of the crew baled out, but F/Lt Thurlow was unable to escape and was killed. His body was never recovered. All of the crew reported some injuries, but the causes are unclear. This was the last Stirling to be lost by the Squadron; it had completed 47 operational sorties.

Casualty Details: F/Lt Jack Alvin Thurlow, Pilot, RCAF, age 26, from Woodstock, Ontario, Canada, commemorated on the Runnymede Memorial, panel 278.

Surviving Crew: Sgt A. Plumtree, Flight Engineer; F/O R.G. Noon-Ward, RCAF, Navigator; F/Sgt E.A. Evans, Bomb Aimer; F/O A.A. Twaddle, RNZAF, Wireless Operator; P/O T.R. Nichols, RCAF, Special Wireless Operator; F/Lt F. Fenning, Mid-Upper Gunner; F/Sgt W.J. Phillips, Rear Gunner.

Of the two raids undertaken by Bomber Command that day, the one on Chemnitz did not begin well. Nine aircraft crashed soon after take-off due to severe icing conditions, with one Halifax crashing in York, killing some civilians. The attack on Chemnitz caused severe damage to parts of the central and southern areas of the city, including the complete destruction of the Siegmar factory that produced tank engines. The second target at Bohlen was the synthetic oil refinery which was covered by a thick layer of cloud that prevented any accurate bombing. No results were observed and no local reports recording damage are available. Losses for the night amounted to 52 aircraft through icing, enemy action and collisions.

6th March 1945

The Squadron provided a normal static Mandrel screen to cover attacks by main force bombers on Nuremberg and Wurzburg. Nine Halifaxes took off from RAF North Creake between 1732 hrs and 1740 hrs, taking up stations in the Montmedy area of Belgium, and transmitting from 1945 hrs to 2225 hrs. F/O Finnimore returned early owing to fuel shortage and landed at 2359 hrs. The remaining aircraft completed the mission and were all safely back at RAF North Creake by 0050 hrs.

The attack on Nuremberg was successful, with much damage to the railway station and gas works. Other areas were hit, but there are no records of the damage. The bomber stream was intercepted by German night fighters on its way to the target and most of the 24 Lancasters shot down were attributed to them. This was to be the last major raid on Nuremberg.

The raid on Wurzburg by 225 Lancasters and eleven Mosquitoes was a text book attack with all aircraft bombing the aiming point within seventeen minutes of the TIs going down. 90% of the city was destroyed and up to 5,000 people were killed. There are no detailed reports of specific damage.

7th March 1945

Dessau, Hemmingstedt and Harburg, with rail and oil installations, selected as targets. Dessau was attacked by 526 Lancasters and five Mosquitoes of 1, 3, 6 and 8 Groups resulting in much damage to the town centre and industrial premises. The rail yards were also hit and put out of action. The raid on Hemmingstedt was disappointing as the aiming point on the Deutsche Erdoel refinery was missed by up to three miles by the 256 Halifaxes and 25 Lancasters. The oil refinery at Harburg was severely damaged and a nearby rubber factory was also set on fire. 422 people were killed and of the 99 fires recorded by the German authorities 37 were classed as large. To support these raids, 199 Squadron detailed twelve aircraft and crews to provide a Mandrel screen operating for two hours in a line west of Cologne down to the town of Lutzerath.

W/O Sharples flying Halifax NR254 EX-V took off at 1702 hrs, but was forced to return early due a faulty artificial horizon, landing back at RAF North Creak at 1843 hrs. He was replaced by F/Lt Lind, Stirling, LJ516 EX-H, who was the ground reserve, and having been alerted of W/O Sharples problems, took off at 1738 hrs and joined F/O Brooks on their allotted station.

Having completed the sortie, all returned safely to base. However, the sister 171 Squadron based at North Creake lost a Halifax and crew, only the pilot F/Lt J.M. Stone survived. They had also been providing a Mandrel and 'Window' screen for the raids, but were also loaded with bombs to drop on one of the targets.

8th March 1945

The cities of Hamburg and Kassel were selected for the night's attack, but both were blanketed with cloud and no serious damage was caused to either. 312 aircraft had been detailed for Hamburg and 262 for Kassel. Only four aircraft were lost.

'199' mounted another large Mandrel screen with twelve aircraft (two Stirlings and ten Halifaxes) to support these raids, stretching from Vlissinggen in Zeeland down to Malmedy, 25 miles SSE of Liège covering a line approximately 140 miles long. The crews detailed were:

Stirlings: F/Lt Gilbert, LJ542 EX-G; F/Lt Turner, LJ516 EX-H. F/Lt Turner took off at 1810 hrs, but returned early when his bomb aimer F/Lt Schofield became ill. He landed at 2113 hrs.

Halifaxes: F/O Brown, RG381 EX-Q; F/Lt Van Welie, RG375 EX-R; F/Lt Harker, RG373 EX-T; F/O Ward, PN374 EX-N; F/Lt Chilcott, PN375 EX-F; W/O Sharples, NR244 EX-V; F/O Brooks, RG387 EX-B; F/O Arkinstall, PN373 EX-Y; F/O Reidy, NR243 EX-D; W/O Porter, RG388 EX-S.

F/Lt Harker took off 1740 hrs but returned 'early' with starboard outer engine u/s, landing at 2342 hrs.

F/Lt Van Welie was also forced to abort his sortie with two engines coring. He had lifted off from North Creake at 1744 hrs and landed at 2215 hrs.

The remaining aircraft returned between 0015 hrs and 0036 hrs giving an average of seven-hours for the sortie.

9th March 1945

The Emscher Lippe Benzol plant, at Datteln, was attacked by 159 Lancasters of 3 Group. Cloud was again a problem for the Pathfinders who resorted to using G-H to drop sky markers. No results were observed. An attack was also planned on the Bielefeld Viaduct by 21 Lancasters of 5 Group, but was abandoned due to thick cloud over the area. RCM was to be provided by four Mandrel and three Window force aircraft.

F/Lt Green, LJ542, returned early with oil leaks in all four engines. Of the three Halifaxes assigned to the Window detail, only one took off after it was found that F/O Walford's aircraft had a u/s port inner engine and F/Lt Van Welie's Halifax developed hydraulic problems.

10th March 1945

A very successful daylight raid was carried out by 155 Lancasters of 3 Group on the oil refinery at Scholven. Later in the evening, 60 Mosquitoes attacked Berlin and 199 Squadron provided six aircraft for a Mandrel screen.

Stirlings: F/Lt Button, LJ516 EX-H, and F/Lt McNamara, LJ542 EX-G.

Halifaxes: F/Lt Wills, RG372 EX-P; S/Ldr Knight, PN375 EX-F; F/Lt McColl, NR244 EX-V; F/O Broadfield, PN374 EX-N.

F/O Broadfield was forced to return early when his wireless operator W/O Sinclair reported that his radio equipment was not functioning, and was replaced by W/O Porter, RG388 EX-S.

13th March 1945

199 Squadron entered a new phase of operations within 100 Group when it was ordered that, the Halifax B.III RCM aircraft would not only provide an electronic/window RCM force, but would carry a bomb load and attack designated targets along with main force bombers.

The Squadron had been converting its crews from the Stirling to the Halifax since mid February and this stage of training was almost complete. The Bristol Hercules Mk.XVI 1,615 hp engines, as in the Stirling, powered the new aircraft. For the ground crews, this smoothed the transition. The electronic jammers, wireless equipment and armaments carried were the same as those fitted to the Stirling, enabling the special wireless operators, wireless operators and gunners to carry on seamlessly. The navigators were supplied with Gee sets to assist with precision plotting and, in some cases, aircraft carried the air to ground scanning radar H2S.

Most of 199 Squadron's pilots were experienced on four engined aircraft and their conversion went smoothly. The only large differences encountered were the crew positions – in the Stirling the navigator, wireless operator, special wireless operator and engineer had their normal stations immediately behind the pilot in the main fuselage. Only the engineer and special wireless operator kept to their usual positions on the Halifax, with the navigators' and wireless operators' stations being situated in the nose of the aircraft. A significant difference in the aircraft was the increase in operating altitude. The operating ceiling of the Halifax was 24,000ft as opposed to the 17,000ft for the Stirling. Cruising speed at 20,000ft was 215 mph, but at lower altitudes over 280 mph could be achieved.

Bomber Command launched daylight raids on Wuppertal and Barmen, together with one on the Arnsberg and Bielefeld railway viaducts. Much damage was caused in the towns, but the viaducts were not hit due to bad weather hampering the attack.

During the evening, 195 Lancasters and 35 Mosquitoes from 1 and 8 Groups attacked Benzol plants at Herne (a failure) and Gelsenkirchen (a success). One Lancaster was lost.

199 Squadron detailed one Stirling and eight Halifaxes for Mandrel and Window coverage with four of the Window Halifaxes going on to bomb the target. The Squadron ORB and summary, together with the sortie records all fail to give any details of the actual target, bomb loads carried or results.

The Window/bombing Halifaxes were flown by: F/O Arkinstall, PN373 EX-Y; F/O Paddon, RG376 EX-Z; F/O King, PN376 EX-E; F/Lt Simon, NR243 EX-D.

The remaining Halifax Mandrel jammers were flown by: S/Ldr Knight, PN375 EX-F; F/Lt Van Welie, NR244 EX-V; F/O Ward, RG373 EX-T; F/O Finnimore, RG375 EX-R; F/Lt Chilcott, RG381 EX-Q; F/O Broadfield, RG387 EX-B; F/O Iles, PN385 EX-C.

F/Lt Sturrock flew the only Stirling, LJ516 EX-H.

F/O Iles returned early, but no note was made of the problems he encountered. F/O Reidy, RG388 EX-S took his place. The Mandrel force positions were in the Euskirchen area SSW of Cologne and the main Windowing route was from a point ten miles south of Liege to Bad Homburg north of Frankfurt. They then flew northwards to bomb either Gelsenkirchen or Herne, both of which are five miles north of Bochum.

Ken Hartley, radar mechanic: *"There were not many occasions at North Creake when the lads in the radar section could go out en masse for a booze-up – this sometimes happened when Ops were scrubbed for the night, probably due to adverse weather conditions over the target, and the whole Squadron was put on a stand down. When this did happen several of us would go down to the Edinburgh Hotel in Wells-on-Sea and celebrate a past or future birthday or anniversary, an impending fourteen days leave, an addition to someone's family, any excuse was good enough. We would all cycle down to Wells on our battered service bikes, park them outside the Edinburgh and go to our usual upstairs room. There the mild and bitter would flow, sent up, several flagons at a time on the 'dumb waiter' by mine host down below. On these rare occasions having saved up our pennies we would let ourselves go and have a very enjoyable night out. It wasn't very often we got the opportunity, but when we did we made the most if it. Rank was forgotten – we were all equal and the best of friends. To the young people of today this would seem tame, but to us it was an escape. There was a war on and for once we could get away from it all for a couple of hours.*

Time dims the memory, but among those who did join our merry throng were Johnnie Fisher, Bing. Jack Harris, Reg Hinxman, Brian Coleman, Ray Hudson, Archie McMaster, Alistair MacDonald, and Canadians Joe Latham, 'Jerry' Jerrome and Jack Penzer. On one or two occasions Jack's wife, Marjorie, was also there. During one period Jack lived out in Wells. At closing time we would mount our bikes and wobble back to camp. Fortunately there was no traffic on the way back. We always had a good sing-song but can't repeat the words we sang. I do however remember that one of the songs cast doubts on the parentage of one particular flight sergeant on the camp who was not very popular to say the least.

On one of these evenings out, after a few pints, we were all cycling back up the road from Wells back to the camp. It was a summer's evening, but it was well after closing time and just about dark. There was a whole crowd of us, aircrew as well as ground crew, officers as well as sergeants and other ranks. I don't think anyone had any lights on his bike – you just didn't bother in those days especially as the road back to the drome was closed to normal traffic. Anyway batteries were not easy to find in wartime and they also cost quite a bit of money – of the latter we didn't have much to spare unlike the youth of today.

Suddenly, shadowy figures pounced on us from behind the roadside bushes!! Being rather befuddled at the time we didn't at first realise who they were. Then it dawned on us that the figures that had just sprung up from nowhere were in fact the local coppers, some in uniform and some in plain clothes. Those who were lucky near the front of our cycle procession plus a few others pedalled furiously and were able to escape their clutches. Others like me were stopped, had names and addresses taken and several days later were summoned to appear at the court in Little Walsingham. There we were all fined five shillings (25p) for riding a bike without lights. We all protested vociferously about what we considered to be a petty action by the local police, especially in wartime, but the fines had to be paid, and five bob to us in those days was a lot of money. This was my one and only blot on an otherwise unblemished record.

I just couldn't understand why in those days the police couldn't have found more useful ways to occupy their time, and when I look back on it today, I find it almost unbelievable. The one consolation I had was that among those present in court to pay his five shilling fine was one Flight Sergeant Denman, the discip. sergeant who was not a particularly good friend of mine, our paths having crossed on several previous occasions".

14th March 1945

This would be the last time a Stirling would fly on operations with Bomber Command. The aircraft LJ516 EX-H had been in service with 199 Squadron from 23rd July 1944, and had completed a total of 56 Ops in the RCM role. On this final sortie it was flown by S/Ldr Button who took off at 1704 hrs and landed safely back at North Creake at 2350 hrs.

Bomber Command continued attacks on synthetic oil plants coupled with area bombing on three targets at Lutzkendorf, Zweibrucken and Homberg.

244 Lancasters and eleven Mosquitoes of 5 Group attacked the Wintershall oil refinery at Lutzkendorf. This was a long-range target calling for slightly lighter bomb loads, but reconnaissance photographs later showed an accurate raid with moderate damage to the plant. Eighteen Lancasters were lost.

It was known from intelligence reports that Zweibrücken was an important town and road link through which a large number of German troops and supplies were passing to the nearby front line. The town was attacked by 230 aircraft consisting of 121 Lancasters, 98 Halifaxes and eleven Mosquitoes of 6 and 8 Groups. German reports compiled after the raid show that every public building and approximately 80% of the town's houses were destroyed or damaged. Most of the civilian population had been evacuated, but some of those remaining took shelter in two large caves situated to the north and south of the town. However, those who chose to shelter in the basements of houses mostly perished and 192 was given as the official count of those who died. No bombers were lost on this raid.

The area attack on Homberg was carried out by 161 aircraft – 127 Halifaxes, 23 Lancasters and eleven Mosquitoes of 4 and 8 Groups. No local reports and results were made of the raid but later reconnaissance showed a result similar to that on Zweibrücken. Two Halifaxes were lost.

199 Squadron provided a Mandrel and Window force of nine aircraft to screen these raids with the Mandrel crews flying out as far as Saarbrücken, taking them almost as far as the target at Zweibrücken. The Window/Mandrel bombing force of four Halifaxes released bundles of Window from a point near Thionville in Belgium, then east to the main force target at Zweibrücken and then NNE for their own bombing objective at Weisbaden. These aircraft were ordered to use their H2S, Mandrel and Monica sets from Thionville onwards, but they were to switch off the Mandrel transmitters for one minute in every ten to enable accurate Gee fixes. These sets were to be switched off on the return journey when crossing 0600E apart from Monica. All aircraft returned to base.

15th March 1945

Two attacks were mounted by Bomber Command, one against the Deurag oil refinery at Misburg and an area raid against Hagen. The latter target was bombed by 267 aircraft, causing considerable damage with almost 1,500 extensive fires in the centre and eastern parts of the town. 493 people were killed and between 30,000 and 35,000 people were bombed out. Ten bombers were lost. The raid on the Deurag oil plant was not altogether successful, with the majority of bombs falling well south of the aiming point.

'199' detailed four aircraft to form a normal static Mandrel screen and six to form a moving Mandrel screen and accompany main force to the target at Misburg. The static Mandrel was flown by: F/O Arkinstall, RG373 EX-P; F/O Burley, RG373 EX-T; F/Lt Simon, PN375 EX-F; and W/O Porter, PN373 EX-Y.

The moving screen was to follow a more complicated and intricate course to the target and to illustrate this, the original handwritten sortie record is reproduced below. F/Lt Jepson RG388 EX-S returned early due to a faulty oxygen system but the remaining five crews completed their mission. They were: F/O Reidy, NR243 EX-D; F/O Paddon, NR244 EX-V; F/Lt Chilcott, PN385 EX-C; F/O Walford, RG387 EX-B; and F/O Ward, PN374 EX-N.

F/O Paddon commented at his debrief that the Pathfinder TIs were nine minutes late. Several crews reported a large explosion followed by a huge fire.

17th March 1945

As 199 Squadron was not required for operations, flying training was ordered, at the discretion of individual flight commanders, and much-needed maintenance was carried out on the aircraft.

18th March 1945

Targets at Witten and Hanau were selected for two more intensive area bombing raids. 324 aircraft attacked Witten dropping over 1,000 tons of bombs, destroying 129 acres of the built-up area of the town. Eight aircraft were lost. Hanau was similarly hit by 277 Lancasters, destroying 2,240 houses and 50 industrial sites. 2,000 people are reported to have been killed.

Ten 199 Squadron aircraft provided a moving Mandrel screen for main force and operated from a point SE of Aachen to Wittlich in Germany. F/O Brooks was replaced by F/O Walford NR244 EX-V before take-off. This aircraft was approximately one hour behind the others taking up station. F/Lt Burley RF372 EX-P completed his sortie, but returned on three engines.

15-3-45   MANDREL FORCE "A" (STATIC SCREEN)

Posⁿ A/c Posⁿ A   ROUTE

7	P T	5037N 0620E	BASE - GRAVESEND - DUNGENESS -
8	C Y	5024N 0629E	ABBEVILLE - POS^N - ABBEVILLE - READIN
			- BASE

MANDREL ON 1925 OFF 2244   TIME AT A 1930 - 2230

Tactics

BASE - GRAVESEND	5000	170		A FLIGHT	17000	160
G'END - ABBEVILLE	5/15000	160		B "	17500	160
AB'VILLE - POS^{NS}	18/7000	160		WIND SECTORS		
POS^N - ABBEVILLE	17/12000	200		A BASE - G'END		
AB'VILLE - READING	12/7000	200		B G'END) - AB'VILLE		
RDG - BASE	7/3000	200		C AB'VILLE - 0400E		
				D 0400E - POS^N		

Posⁿ A/c PILOT   NAV   REMARKS

7	P	F/O ARKINSTALL	F/LT WILSON	ON RETURN PH → DR DESYN 180 OK AFTER RESYN
7	T	F/O BURLEY	F/O CLARKE	OK
8	C	F/L SIMON	F/O WHEALING	OK
8	Y	W/O PORTER	F/S MORGAN	RC ON LIGHTS ON GROUND

MANDREL FORCE "C"

ACCOMPANYING MAIN FORCE:- Δ MISBURG 5223N 0951E

	A/c	PILOT		
1ST PR	D	F/O REIDY	AT Δ AT 2100 → MAIN FORCE "H HR	
	V	F/O PADDON		
2ND PR	C	F/L CHILCOTT	" 2103	
	S	S/L JEPSON		
3RD P2	B	F/O WALFORD	" 2106	
	N	F/O WARD		

ROUTE :- BASE - GRAVESEND - DUNGENESS - 5010N 0130E - 5015N 0415E - 5100N 0530E - 5045N 0640E - 5055N 0735E - 5107N 0900E - 5140N 0945E - Δ - 5228N 1000E - 5220N 1012E - 5150N 1015E - 5113N 1000E - 5045N 0810E - 5014N 0705E - 5010N 0130E - READING - BASE

TACTICS :- 7000 ft at READING & HOLD TO 0530E at 170 THEN CLIMB TO 15000 ft by 0640E AT 160. THEN TO 17-20000 by 0900E AT 155 HOLD TO 5200N AT 155 THEN TO Δ 19000 ft 155. AFTER Δ HOLD TO 5220N 1012E AT 170, THEN LOSE HT TO 12/15000 ft by 1000E AT 190. HOLD 12/15000 ft TO 0705E AT 175 THEN DESCEND TO CROSS CONTINENTAL COAST AT 1,9000 ft AT 190. DESCEND TO CROSS ENG COAST 4/7000 ft AT 170 & HOLD TO BASE AT 155

MANDRELS ON AT 0700E OUT AND OFF AT 0700E ON RET

MANDRELS TO BE SWITCHED IF BETWEEN 2035 - 2115

H2S TO BE SWITCHED ON ONLY WHEN MANDRELS ARE ON

D.RAM DIVERSION :- HUNSDEN

19th March 1945

No operations ordered for 199 Squadron.

20th March 1945

Two oil targets were again selected in an effort to starve the Luftwaffe of much needed fuel. The refinery at Bohlen was attacked by 224 Lancasters and eleven Mosquitoes of 5 Group, this being the second attack on the plant, as the first, on 5th March, had not been successful due to thick cloud cover. This time the weather was more favourable and an accurate and devastating attack completely wrecked the refinery which was still inoperable when the Allied forces overran the site a few weeks later. Nine Lancasters were lost on this raid.

A similarly successful raid was carried out on the oil plant at Hemmingstedt by 166 Lancasters of 1, 6 and 8 Groups, with the loss of one Lancaster shot down.

Ten Halifaxes and crews were detailed to support these two attacks and, following the new development of tactics, all were to carry bombs to a specified target as well as operate the Mandrel and Window screen within the bomber stream.

The master wind finder for the raid was F/O Reidy.

The Mandrel/Window force was made up of eight aircraft: S/Ldr Knight, PN385 EX-C; F/Lt Chilcott, LK868 EX-J; F/O Reidy, RG373 EX-T; F/O Walford, NR244 EX-V; F/O Broadfield, RG375 EX-R; F/O Arkinstall, RG372 EX-P; F/O Ward, PN374 EX-N; W/O Sharples, RG381 EX-Q, which left North Creake a few minutes past midnight and returned between 0645 hrs and 0725 hrs. The two Window force aircraft flown by F/Lt Wills PN375 EX-F and F/O Finnimore PN376 EX-E had a longer route to fly and left base at midnight, returning just after 0800 hrs.

The Squadron ORB records for the preceding and subsequent bombing operations are not always written up with details of target, bomb loads or crew comments. This makes it very difficult to make sense of the sortie records, as the co-ordinates given do not always correspond to a main force target. The Mandrel and Window tactics and positions to be used are quite specific, but the important information of place names and targets is not at all clear. For example, in this instance the two Window force aircraft have no target mentioned, but are listed in the ORB as *"Special Mission Window/Bombing Patrol"*. The sortie records specify detailed map co-ordinates and times with Window type and rates of dispensing, but nothing to indicate the actual target to bomb.

After consulting maps of Germany and using the furthest eastward co-ordinate given at 5132N 1159E, it puts the aircraft a few miles north west of the main force target at Bohlen. The crews debrief notes are not included in the ORB, but the pilots' comments do get a scaled down, very brief mention in the sortie records. From these it is possible to glean some basic details of a sortie, but the emphasis must be on the basic aspect.

F/O Finnimore reported that he had to bomb on H2S and that the Loran (an American developed radio navigation system) set was tried. F/Lt Wills stated his H2S set was u/s and his navigator F/Sgt Winterholder obtained four Loran fixes and that the Halifax bomb doors jammed. There is no written account if the bomb doors jammed before or after his bombing run on the target.

The Mandrel/Window Force Sortie Records give the co-ordinates for the eight aircraft as 5001N 0830E. This pinpoint is the town of Anspach, north of Frankfurt and 150 miles from the target at Bohlen. The target at Hemmingstedt can be discounted altogether as it is approximately 250 miles to the north of Bohlen in the Heligoland Bight.

Interestingly, only four of the eight crews are mentioned as to proceed to this co-ordinate at Anspach: F/O Arkinstall and F/O Reidy who were on co-ordinates given as position 3 and F/O Walford and F/O Broadfield who were flying on co-ordinates given as position 4. The remaining four crews do not seem to have any orders to bomb a target. It can be assumed F/O Reidy did drop his bomb load as a brief note states he was two minutes late on target.

21st March 1945

Two oil targets at Hamburg and Bochum were selected for the night's bombing attacks. The Deutsche Erdolwerke refinery near Hamburg was attacked by 151 Lancasters and eight Mosquitoes of 5 Group with very accurate bombing that destroyed twenty large storage tanks and most of the ancillary equipment. The Germans were unable to produce any more fuel from this plant right up to the end of the war. Four Lancasters were lost.

The Benzol plant at Bochum was hit, in a very accurate raid by 131 Lancasters and twelve Mosquitoes of 1 and 8 Groups, but there are no specific results available of the actual damage caused. One Lancaster was lost.

Six Halifaxes and crews were ordered to provide a Window patrol with bombing and four to form a Mandrel/Window support patrol.

The Mandrel/Window Force operated in the Boos, Krefeld and Huckelhoven areas, jamming with Mandrel and dispensing Window. These aircraft were flown by: W/O Porter, PN375 EX-F; F/Lt McColl, RG372 EX-P; F/O Finnimore, RG381 EX-Q; and F/O Broadfield, RG375 EX-R.

The Window/bombing force consisted of: F/Lt Harker, LK868 EX-J; P/O Brown, RG388 EX-S; F/O Reidy, PN374 EX-N; F/Lt Marshall, RG376 EX-Z; F/Lt Burley, RG373 EX-T; and F/Lt Jenkins, PN373 EX-Y.

Their area of operations stretched from the Island of Heligoland in the North Sea to a point ten miles north of Kiel obviously screening the main force raid on Hamburg. From Kiel it can be assumed these six aircraft then turned due south and attacked the target at Hamburg. The master wind finder is listed as F/O Pearson, but there is no mention in the ORB of him taking off.

Bomber Command's policy of continuing attacks against Berlin were highlighted this night with the extra large force of 142 Mosquitoes sent to the city. It appears that some of the crews made two trips during the night and, on further investigation, it was found that this was normal for crews of the Light Night Bombing Force. The Mosquito could carry up to a 4,000lb 'Cookie' in its specially constructed bomb bay, fly at over 400 mph at a ceiling of over 30,000 ft. A statistic worth noting is that the Mosquitoes' bomb load exceeded that of the American B17 Flying Fortress.

22nd March 1945

Bomber Command carried out five daylight raids on the rail yards at Hildesheim, rail and canal targets at Dorsten, rail bridges at Bremen and Nienburg and area bombing of Dolmen. No RCM sorties were flown in support. During the evening and night only minor operations were detailed, mainly Mosquito attacks on Berlin, Paderborn and Bochum. 199 Squadron flew two Mandrel and six Window Force sorties in support of the night operations. This was again to keep all the German defences thinking a major raid was in the offing and preventing them having any respite from their duties. Some crews reported seeing the launching of "V" weapons from the "Dutch Isles"

23rd March 1945

195 Lancasters and 23 Mosquitoes of 5 and 8 Groups mounted the last raid by Bomber Command on the town of Wesel, which claimed to have been bombed more intensively than any other comparable town. By the end of the war its population had fallen from 25,000 to 2,000.

A Mandrel and Window screen was ordered for 199 Squadron, with four crews flying the static Mandrel patrol and six to dispense Window. F/O Finnimore PN376 EX-E took off at 1936 hrs, but returned early from the Mandrel sortie with the port inner engine u/s, landing safely on three engines at 2106 hrs. The Mandrel aircraft were jamming from 2150 hrs to 2320 hrs over the Hilvarenbeek – Eindhoven area of Holland.

The Window force covered a moving front at 2225 hrs from a start point twenty miles west of Mönchengladbach, turning NNW to the target at Wesel 5138N 0635E, then turning west to Goch and returning on a SSW course back to Mönchengladbach. Window discharge rates were given as 'Type MM' 20 BPM and 'Type N' 10 BPM. The crews were instructed not to use H2S on this sortie. Although going directly to the target at Wesel there is no mention in the records of the six aircraft carrying a bomb load.

24th March 1945

Allied Armies were now crossing the River Rhine and advancing into Germany. Airborne British commandos parachuted into Wesel on this day and found the German defences stunned and shocked from the previous night's raid.

Daylight attacks were ordered against railway yards at Sterkrade and Gladbeck, a town near to the new battlefront, both raids were successful. Oil installations were also hit at the Harpenerweg plant at Dortmund and the Mathias Stinnes plant at Bottrop.

Night raids were confined to Mosquito attacks on Berlin, Nordrhein and Magdeburg. The usual Mandrel and Window Force sorties were flown in support of these raids.

25th and 26th March 1945

No operations ordered for 199 Squadron, the days being used for maintenance of the aircraft and training flights. However, on the 26th, Bomber Command directed heavy attacks on Hanover, Munster and Osnabrück, towns on the main supply routes to the German Army defences opposing the Allied advance.

27th March 1945

Support attacks were ordered during daylight hours to support American troops in the Ruhr area and targets in the Paderborn region were hit hard with this old town completely devastated in an attack by 268 Lancasters and eight Mosquitoes. Over 3,000 separate fires were recorded by the local fire brigade and 330 people were killed.

Two oil storage and production plants were also attacked at Hamm and Farge, on the River Weser. The latter target also housed a new, almost completed, U-boat shelter. This shelter was thought by the Germans to be invulnerable as it had a concrete roof 23ft thick. However, they had not reckoned on Barnes Wallis's 22,000lb Grand Slam bomb, two of which were carried by Lancasters of 617 (Dambuster) Squadron. Both bombs were dropped with extreme accuracy and penetrated the roof, bringing down thousands of tons of concrete and steel, completely destroying the facility.

Night operations were limited to raids by Mosquitoes on Berlin (82 aircraft), Bremen (7), Erfurt (4), Hanover (3) and Magdeburg (3). Three aircraft were lost on the Berlin raid.

Again, 199 Squadron participated in the operations with their normal RCM/Window duties and again there are no details recorded in the Squadron ORB. Two crews were also detailed to provide a static Mandrel screen from 2025 hrs to 2210 hrs.

The Window/bombing sorties were flown by: F/Lt Wills, PN385 EX-C; F/Lt Chilcott, PN376 EX-E; F/O Brown, RG381 EX-Q; F/Lt Van Welie, RG372 EX-P; F/O Broadfield, RG375 EX-R; F/Lt Jenkins, RG388 EX-S; and W/O Sharples, NR244 EX-V.

The co-ordinates given in the sortie records do not give a pinpoint for any of the targets allotted to the Mosquito squadrons, the only specific place overflown is given as Bremerhaven. However, Bremen appears to be the closest nominated target so it may have been selected as the aiming point for the '199' crews.

The Mandrel Halifaxes flew a racecourse circuit approximately 40 miles north of the Frisian Islands. These were flown by F/Lt Spaulding NR243 EX-D and F/Lt Burley RG373 EX-T. Both aircraft would have covered the raids mentioned above and also given support to the eight Mosquitoes minelaying in the River Elbe.

28th and 29th March 1945

No operations ordered.

30th March 1945

The final operation of the month for 199 Squadron was to detail six Halifaxes and crews for a Window/bombing patrol to support Mosquito attacks on: Berlin (43 aircraft), Erfurt (43), Nordingen (4), Hamburg (3), and Kiel (3).

The aircraft were flown by: F/Lt Simon, RG388 EX-S; F/O Iles, PN374 EX-N; P/O Pearce, PN376 EX-E; F/O Paddon, RG376 EX-Z; F/O Brooks, RG375 EX-R; and F/Lt Arkinstall, PN373 EX-Y.

Four of the pilots reported that their H2S radar sets were u/s during the operation. From the plots given, the aircraft came in over the North Sea and made landfall at the mouth of the River Weser. They then carried out Windowing, flying a course bringing them to the town of Stade on the River Elbe, a few miles west of Hamburg. The ORB fails to name the target, but it may have been Hamburg due to its close proximity to the final Windowing pinpoint.

31st March 1945

Operations were ordered, but subsequently cancelled. The Squadron ORB gives the following totals and list of awards:

DFCs promulgated on 23 March 1945 and awarded to: F/Lt F.S. Waldren, 50455; F/Lt Coventry, Aus, 410042; F/O Broomhead, 158995.

Bombs Dropped: 108 x 750 CL, 128 x 500 CL, 46 x 500 MC, 36 x 250 TI No.8 Mk.3. Red, and 36 x 250 TI No.8 Mk.3. Green.

From this information it would appear that some 199 Halifaxes were being used to either act as "backers up" to the Pathfinders or they were dropping target indicators as part of a spoof raid to draw the German night fighters away from a main target.

April
A change in tactics – attacks on oil and shipping targets

1st April 1945

No operations ordered.

2nd April 1945

The beginning of April saw a continuation of harassing raids by Mosquitoes on: Berlin (54 aircraft), Magdeburg (50), Luneburg (8), Hamburg (1), and Lubeck (1).

'199' detailed twelve crews to form a static Mandrel screen for the night's operations as follows: F/Lt Harker, PN385 EX-G; F/Lt Ward, RG375 EX-R; F/O Currell, NR244 EX-V; F/Sgt Spaulding, NR243 EX-D; F/O Chatterton, GR376 EX-Z; F/O Pearce, PN375 EX-F; F/O Finnimore, PN376 EX-E; F/Lt Chilcott, PN378 EX-A; F/O Brooks, RG373 EX-T; F/Lt Marshall, RG372 EX-P; S/Ldr Jepson, RG388 EX-S.

F/O Brown did not take off and was replaced by F/Lt Wills H.

The crews flew a regular racecourse pattern centred on 5427N 0711E, approximately 20 miles west of the North Frisian Island of Sylt. F/O Pearce and F/O Finnimore, both flying the lower orbits of the pattern, obtained a good H2S fix on the Island of Heligoland.

3rd April 1945

No operations, but flying training and maintenance carried out as required.

4th April 1945

Oil refineries were again the focus of Bomber Command, with attacks on those at Leuna, Harburg and Lutzkendorf. The raid on Leuna by 327 Lancasters and fourteen Mosquitoes was not a success due to thick cloud coverage and only slight damage was reported. Two Lancasters were lost in a collision and crashed between Waldhof Elgershausen and Greifenthal, four miles south of Sinn.

The 327 Halifaxes, 36 Lancasters and fourteen Mosquitoes that attacked the Rhenania plant at Harburg had better results and much of the refinery was destroyed. One Halifax and two Lancasters were lost. Moderate damage was caused to the refinery at Lutzkendorf by the 258 Lancasters and fourteen Mosquitoes detailed for the raid. 6 Lancasters lost.

Jamming was provided by twelve aircraft over the North Sea in almost the same positions as the previous operation on the 2nd April. Only Mandrel was used on this occasion and, according to the first entry of its kind in the ORB summaries, it was in direct support of the raid on Harburg.

5th to 6th April 1945

No operations ordered.

7th April 1945

Four Halifaxes of 199 Squadron were detailed for a Mandrel jamming and bombing sortie in support of a raid on the oil refinery at Molbis, a town ten miles south of Leipzig. 175 Lancasters and eleven Mosquitoes of 5 Group attacked in clear weather and, according to German reports, the refinery was destroyed and no further production was possible.

The '199' Halifaxes made landfall in France and picked up their first pinpoint between Abbeville and Flixecourt, then flew almost due east to Wiltz in Luxembourg, then to Schwalmtal and Molbis. The Mandrel jammers were switched on when approximately 80 miles west of the target in the area close to Mühlhausen and Erfurt and remained on during the outbound route until passing north of Frankfurt. The crews were instructed to keep the H2S sets turned off to a point 0800E on the outbound leg and after reaching 0930E on the return. Jammers were to be switched on when passing 1030E and turned off on the return journey when passing 0800E.

F/O Iles, PN385 EX-C; F/O Walford, RG387 EX-B; F/O Finnimore, PN376 EX-E; and W/O Porter, NR243 EX-D, took off from RAF North Creake between 1849 hrs and 1852 hrs. Their time on target was 2255 hrs for Walford and Porter and 2302 hrs for Iles and Finnimore. However, the records show that Iles was two minutes late, Walford nine, Finnimore one and Porter four. All the aircraft landed at Juvincourt in France after completing a successful operation. No aircraft was lost.

8th April 1945

The port installation at Hamburg and the oil refinery at Lutzkendorf, that had previously been attacked on 4th April, were selected as targets. 263 Halifaxes, 160 Lancasters and seventeen Mosquitoes of 4, 6 and 8 Groups attacked the dockyards at Hamburg. Due to partial cloud the bombing became scattered and only a small number of bombs fell on the port area itself. However, some parts of the city were hit hard and much serious damage caused with 292 people killed and many injured. This was Bomber Command's last attack on Hamburg. Three Halifaxes and three Lancasters were lost.

The oil refinery at Lutzkendorf had not been badly damaged in the previous raid, but the 231 Lancasters and eleven Mosquitoes of 5 Group soon rectified this and launching a precision attack that left the installation permanently out of commission. RCM was provided by eight Halifaxes and crews divided equally as Mandrel and Mandrel/bombing.

The four Mandrel sorties were flown by: F/Lt Wills PN378 EX-A, F/Lt Arkinstall NR243 EX-P, F/O Brown PN375 EX-F, and F/Lt Harker RG389 EX-H.

They flew racecourse patterns 40 miles west of the Islands of Sylt approximately parallel with the German – Danish border. Jamming commenced at 2110 hrs and continued until 2200 hrs.

The Mandrel/bombing crews were: F/Lt McColl RG375 EX-R, F/Lt Marshall PN374 EX-N, F/Lt Burley RG388 EX-S, and F/O Paddon NR244 EX-V.

Sgt Bob Sewell, Rear Gunner on F/O E. Harker's crew, 1945.

The four aircraft were instructed to maintain radar signal silence at all times and to operate their Mandrel jammers from a point of 0930E on the inbound track and to turn them off at 0800E returning to base. The target co-ordinates are given as 5118N 1152E Lutzkendorf a crude oil refinery east of Mucheln and 30 miles west of Leipzig. The plant also included a hydrogenation unit and specialised equipment to process heavy gasoline from synthesized oil. There are no details of the bomb loads carried by this flight in either the Operational Record Book or the Sortie Records nor are there any details of the bombing crew's de-brief after the raid.

9th April 1945

Tactics changed for the Squadron and they were detailed to provide eight aircraft for a moving Mandrel screen and three for a Window force. No mention is made in the ORB of the crews carrying a bomb load. However, the sortie records show entries and comments relating to crews being early or late 'on target'. The symbol Δ is used in the "Remarks" column to denote a target and is entered specifically in the Window force entries. Later investigations revealed that the three Halifaxes were part of a diversionary raid on Stade, a town 50 miles SSW of Kiel.

The target for this night's raid was Kiel and 591 Lancasters and eight Mosquitoes of 1, 3 and 8 Groups delivered a precision attack on the U-boat yard that was very badly damaged. High explosive bombs hit the pocket battleship *Admiral Scheer* causing it to capsize. Also hit and put out of action were the heavy cruiser *Admiral Hipper* that sustained very heavy damage to its superstructure and the light cruiser *Emden*. The latter was towed with a 15-degree list into the Heikendorfer Bucht and beached. All three yards at Kiel were severely hit, causing much damage to buildings, plant and equipment. The houses in the immediate vicinity were also reduced to rubble and 81 civilians were killed. Three Lancasters were lost. The moving Mandrel screen operated over an area west of the Sylt Islands, jamming from 2125 hrs to 2245 hrs. The Window aircraft carried out their missions and all returned safely.

10th April 1945

To continue supporting the ground forces, railway yards at Plauen and Leipzig were attacked to prevent the movement of German troops and supplies to the battle zones. At Leipzig, the Wahren yards were hit and severely damaged, by 76 Lancasters and nineteen Mosquitoes, with the loss of seven Lancasters. 307 Lancasters and eight Mosquitoes carried out the attack on Plauen, destroying much of the rail network and over half of the town's built-up area. No aircraft was lost.

199 Squadron supported the raid on Plauen (5029N 1207E), with eight Halifaxes flying a moving Mandrel screen and also bombing the rail yards. The records for the first time show in the sortie records the target name complete with co-ordinates. Also details of the bomb loads carried are given. The pilots flying this mission and the bomb loads carried are as follows: F/Lt Wills, PN378 EX-A (2 x 1000lb MC 6 x 500lb GP); F/O Paddon, RG376 EX-Z (10 x 500lb GP); F/Lt Harker, RG389 EX-H (2 x 1000lb MC 6 x 500lb GP); F/Lt Marshall, NR244 EX-V (10 x 500lb GP); F/O Reidy, NR243 EX-E (2 x 1000lb MC 6 x 500lb GP); F/O Chatterton, RG373 EX-T (2 x 1000lb MC 8 x 500lb GP); F/Lt Burley, PN374 EX-N (2 x 1000lb MC 8 x 500lb GP); F/O Iles, PN376 EX-D (2 x 1000lb MC 6 x 500lb GP).

F/O Iles PN376 EX-D replaced F/Lt Spaulding whose aircraft developed a technical fault prior to take off. All the pilots reported that they were between 1 and 3 minutes early over the target, 'H' Hour was 2310 hrs with each pair of Mandrel aircraft given a staggered time from this datum of between –2 to +9 minutes.

The two Window Halifaxes were flown by W/O Porter, PN375 EX-F and F/Lt McColl, RG381 EX-Q, their target given as 'Wessam' in the sortie records. This name cannot be identified, but may indicate a district of Dessau, 40 miles north of Leipzig. Both Halifaxes carried bomb loads, consisting of 4 x 750lb Cluster Incendiaries, 5 x 500lb GP and 1 x 250lb photoflash.

11th April 1945

'199' detailed eleven aircraft for operations, which were subsequently cancelled.

12th April 1945

No operations.

EE948 EX-T crashed at Nutt's Corner, Lakenheath, on 12th April 1945. It had been transferred to 1332 Conversion Unit, but still carried 199 Squadron code.

13th April 1945

Ten RCM Halifaxes detailed for a static Mandrel screen, flying off the North Frisians, and jamming from 2200 hrs to 0045 hrs with the additional order that –

"At 2250 all aircraft will fly to make good a track of 090(T) for 30 NM [nautical miles] or to within 10 NM of the enemy coast whichever is less and remain there till 0015 hrs then return to base".

The above screen was to support another attack on Kiel by 377 Lancasters and 105 Halifaxes. The aiming point was designated as the U-boat pens in the main harbour area, but the raid was scattered and little damage was caused to the naval facilities. Most of the bombs fell in outlying districts including that of Elmschenhagen and a direct hit on an ammunition dump caused a large explosion. Two of the '199' Halifaxes developed problems and were forced to return early. F/Lt Simon had two compasses u/s and F/Lt Murray had problems with the Gee set, making station keeping impossible. Two crews were detailed for Window/Mandrel and bombing, although again there is no information as to the target, or bombing times. Taking plots from the sortie records it appears that these two aircraft attacked targets at Kiel.

14th April 1945

The final raid by Bomber Command on a major city area in Germany was carried out by 500 Lancasters and twelve Mosquitoes, on Potsdam situated SSW of Berlin. Virtually all raids on Berlin and the immediate area had been undertaken by Mosquitoes since March 1944 and this was the first time since then that four-engined heavies had ventured over the formidable defences surrounding the German capital. However, progress in the war on the ground meant a great deal of land that was overflown was in Allied hands and therefore posed no threat. Only one Lancaster was lost possibly to a night fighter.

The attack was aimed at the centre of Potsdam that included important railway yards and a great deal of damage was caused. As the raid progressed, some bombs fell into the northern and eastern districts of Berlin, but no reports are available of the damage caused. There are no official figures for casualties in Potsdam, but some unofficial ones, put forward after the war, report that up to 5,000 people died in the raid.

To support this raid, 24 Lancasters and four Mosquitoes mounted a diversionary raid on Cuxhaven and also in support, 199 Squadron detailed twelve aircraft to fly a Window and Mandrel screen and to mount their own diversion by bombing targets in Juterbog (5159N 1300E), 25 miles south of Potsdam. The Window and Mandrel screen transmitted on the way to the target gave excellent cover to the main force bombers. The crews were instructed to "bomb on best Nav. aids". Windowing rates were high and reached up to 30 bpm for type 'MM' plus 15 bpm for type 'N' with Mandrels switched on once passed 5205N 1000E (Hildesheim) 140 miles west of the target.

Crews were as follows: F/O Brown, PN378 EX-A; F/Lt Murray, PN374 EX-N; F/Lt Chilcott, NR243 EX-D; F/Lt Van Welie, NR244 EX-V; F/O Walford, RG387 EX-B; F/Lt King, RG381 EX-R; F/Lt Simons, RG389 EX-H; F/O Brooks, RG373 EX-T; W/O Porter, PN376 EX-E; S/Ldr Jepson, RG388 EX-S; F/Lt Bleakley, RG375 EX-Q; and P/O Currell, RG372 EX-P.

All the aircraft completed their sorties successfully.

15th April 1945

Only minor operations were ordered and no main force aircraft were detailed. A force of 106 Mosquitoes attacked Berlin and eight bombed Oranienburg Airfield and four Mosquitoes and four '199' Halifaxes hit the airfield at Lechfeld, 15 miles south of Augsburg (4811N 1052E). The '199' aircraft only dispensed Window on this mission – no Mandrel jamming was ordered.

17th April 1945

A Mandrel/Window screen was detailed for eight aircraft covering an attack on the airfield at Ingoldstadt, north of Munich. The main raid was carried out by 43 Mosquitoes with support from the Halifaxes of 199 Squadron. F/O Iles returned early due to his port outer engine u/s. Plots and co-ordinates in the sortie records put all remaining seven aircraft at or very close to the target, but no mention is made if bomb loads were carried.

18th April 1945

Another airfield was on the battle orders, this time Schlessheim (4814N 1125E) situated south of Munich and was attacked by 36 Mosquitoes. A Window/Mandrel force of seven aircraft from '199' was detailed to provide RCM cover. F/Lt Spaulding was unable to take off due to technical problems and his aircraft was replaced by that of F/O Brooks RG388 EX-S. F/Lt Murray PN375 EX-F took off at 0043 hrs but was forced to abort his mission and returned to North Creake, landing at 0136 hrs. No explanation is given as to what was wrong with the aircraft.

The remaining crews all completed their missions successfully.

The main force target for the night was the rail yards at Chomutov in Czechoslovakia. This long range raid was carried out by 114 Lancasters and nine Mosquitoes of 5 Group. The attack was completely successful and no aircraft were lost.

19th April 1945

No night time main force operations detailed. The usual Mosquito raids on Berlin took place and 35 were sent to Wittstock airfield and eight to Schleswig airfield. 199 Squadron provided two separate RCM patrols. The first was a Window/bombing force of four aircraft detailed to also provide Mandrel jamming on the way to the target assigned at Schleswig. The second patrol was a static Mandrel screen operating over the North Sea, ten miles west of Sylt.

The Window force consisted of: F/Lt Spaulding, NR243 EX-D; F/Lt Murray, PN435 EX-L; F/Lt Burley, PN374 EX-N; and S/Ldr Jepson, RG388 EX-S.

It appears from the few notes available regarding the raid on the airfield that only Jepson and Murray were required to bomb the target. No results were logged.

Mandrel aircraft were flown by: F/Lt Dickenson, PN378 EX-A; F/Lt Bleakley, RG372 EX-P; W/O Porter, PN376 EX-E; and F/Lt Van Welie, NR244 EX-V.

20th and 21st April 1945

No operations.

22nd April 1945

Main force attacked the port of Bremen during daylight hours, with 651 Lancasters, 100 Halifaxes and sixteen Mosquitoes of 1, 3, 6 and 8 Groups. Only a small number of the bombers completed their mission due to cloud and smoke.

Night operations continued, with 40 Mosquitoes attacking Bremen and eleven attacking Kiel. Although only a small number of aircraft were actually flying bombing operations, 100 Group sent out a total of 56 RCM sorties to cover these, of which 199 Squadron provided four Mandrel and eight Window/Mandrel patrols. The Mandrel aircraft operated a normal static patrol 60 miles north of the West Frisian Islands and the Window force flew across the North Sea towards the Frisian Islands, almost making landfall at Alte Kirche before turning away and returning to base.

Mandrel aircraft: F/Lt Simon, RG387 EX-B; P/O Sharples, RG372 EX-P; F/Lt Iles, PN385 EX-C; P/O Currell, RG375 EX-R.

Window aircraft: F/Lt Chilcott, PN378 EX-A; W/O Porter, PN375 EX-F; F/O Brooks, RG373 EX-T; F/Lt Dickinson, PN440 EX-G; F/Lt Paddon, RG376 EX-Z; F/O King, RG381 EX-Q; F/Lt Ward, PN374 EX-N; F/O Finnimore, PN376 EX-E.

All aircraft returned safely to base.

23rd April 1945

60 Mosquitoes attacked Kiel, 38 to Rendsburg, 32 to Travemunde and eight to Schleissheim Airfield. '199', according to the operational record book detailed eleven aircraft and crews to support the Mosquito squadrons, but this record is at odds with the sortie record book that lists only 10 crews and these names do not correspond correctly with those in the ORB. The list of aircraft and crews that follows is taken from the ORB:

Mandrel: F/Lt Wills, RG389 EX-H; F/Lt Jenkins, RG388 EX-S; F/Lt Spaulding, PN375 EX-F; F/Lt Arkinstall, RG375 EX-R; F/Lt Iles, PN435 EX-L; F/Lt Ward, RG373 EX-T; F/O Finnimore, RG387 EX-B; P/O Sharples, RG372 EX-P.

Window: S/Ldr Knight, PN440 EX-G; F/O Pearce, LJ617 EX-E; F/O King, RG381 EX-Q.

24th April 1945

Bomber Command attacked rail targets in a daylight raid on Bad Oldesloe situated between Hamburg and Lubeck. From German reports it appears that the air raid precautions were far from satisfactory and 700 people were killed and 300 injured when bombs fell wide of the aiming point in the railway yards.

The night's activities were limited to Mosquitoes dropping leaflets over eight P.O.W. camps in Germany, informing the British troops of their impending release from captivity and how they should prepare themselves. Also dropped at the Neubrandenburg camp near Berlin were much-needed medical supplies.

According to the records, 199 detailed six crews and Halifaxes for a Window/Mandrel force sortie to Munich. The plots given place the final co-ordinate (4818N 1139E) at Neufahrn Bei Freising, a town about five miles north of Munich. There are no details regarding any bombing of Munich, nor are there any notes as to why this trip was necessary; after all no other aircraft were within miles of the city. All aircraft returned safely to base.

25th April 1945

No operations ordered.

26th April 1945

Seventeen aircraft and crews were called upon for a maximum Squadron effort, but operations were subsequently cancelled due to unfavourable weather conditions.

27th to 30th April 1945

All operations cancelled.

At the end of the month, three more decorations were awarded to Squadron personnel: DFC awarded to S/Ldr John Jeffrey Mervyn Button, RAAF, 414464, promulgated 13th April 1945; DFM awarded to F/Sgt (Promoted to P/O) Philip Charles Branson, RAFVR, 1808484, promulgated 13th April 1945; DFC awarded to P/O Wilfrid Morris Jones, RAFVR, 183943.

The End of the War in Europe

May

A collision over Kiel – "Cook's Tours" for ground staff

1st May 1945

Bad weather continued to prevent any operations.

2nd May 1945

The last operation carried out by the Squadron in the European War, with 21 aircraft taking part in 3 separate missions to Kiel, Schleswig and a diversionary raid to the North Frisian Islands. This was by far and away the largest number of aircraft and crews placed on the Battle Orders since moving to North Creake in mid 1944 and it would seem that every serviceable Halifax on the Squadron was used in this last show of the Squadron's strength. It must have been an awe inspiring sight to have seen so many four engined bombers starting up, taxiing round the long North Creake perimeter tracks and then finally taking off into the darkness. From this large force leaving base only one aircraft P/O Brown, PN378 EX-A returned early with compass problems.

The Mandrel Force was in the van and the first to lift off was F/Lt King, RG381 EX-Q at 2030 hrs followed by F/Lt Burley, PN374 EX-N, 2032 hrs; P/O Parsons, RG389 EX-H, 2034 hrs; P/O Brown, PN378 EX-A, 2040 hrs returned early landed 2315 hrs and F/Lt Short, PN385 EX-C, 2104 hrs. F/Lt Short and his crew were in fact attached to 171 Squadron. The remaining aircraft designated to the Mandrel Screen was that of F/O Werner, NA275 EX-W who was late taking off at 2130 hrs due to technical problems.

The Halifaxes of the Kiel bombing force was next away. Each individual aircraft carried 8 x 500lb Medium Capacity bombs. P/O Porter, PN375 EX-F, 2045 hrs; F/O Finnimore, RG378 EX-X, 2047 hrs; F/Lt Paddon, RG376 EX-Z, 2048 hrs; F/Lt Murray, PN435 EX-L, 2049 hrs; F/Lt Brooks, RG373 EX-T, 2050 hrs; F/O Pearce, NR243 EX-D, 2051 hrs; F/Lt Dickinson, PN440 EX-G, 2052 hrs; F/Lt Arkinstall, RG372 EX-P, 2053 hrs; F/O Currell, RG375 EX-R, 2054 hrs; F/Lt Clifton, NA640 EX-O, 2103 hrs.

Finally the Schleswig flight lifted off carrying the same bomb loads as the Kiel flight – 8 x 500lb MC. F/Lt Ward, PN373 EX-Y, 2046 hrs; F/Lt Van Welie, NR244 EX-V, 2051 hrs; F/Lt Wills, PN541 EX-K, 2102 hrs; F/Lt Jenkins, RG388 EX-S, 2108 hrs and last to leave on this historical night was S/Ldr Knight, RG387 EX-B who lifted off from the main runway at 2110.

In something like 40 minutes 21 aircraft had taken off and formed up into their 3 separate flights. Of all the crews now getting airborne nor anyone left on the ground waving them off had any idea that this final night was to end with tragic results.

The Mandrel aircraft took up their two initial allotted positions at 5430N 0754E and 5445 N 0802E NNW and NNE of Heligoland and then moved eastwards to 5420N 0824E and 5428N 0826E that brought them to the coast of Jutland at Ording 30 miles north of Cuxhaven. The time given to reach the first positions was 2230 hrs staying there orbiting until 2305 hrs and the Mandrel sets were switched on, together with dropping bundles of RTDI Window at 20 bmp (bundles per minute),and N3 Window at 10 bpm. At 2305 hrs the aircraft moved to the second position, dropping Window at the same rate leaving at 2340 hrs. All the aircraft were operating at 17,000ft.

The central Window Force flying to Schleswig was also required to transmit on the Mandrel equipment. Time given to arrive at position 'A' was 2258 hrs and an average plot for all the aircraft is 5420N 0700E, north of Heligoland, RTD Window was then dropped at a rate of 10 bpm and N3 at 5 bpm flying towards position 'B' at 5420N 0833E a midpoint between Heligoland and Sank Peter-Ording in Denmark.

However once a point at 0800E was reached the Window rates were stepped up to 20 and 10 bpm respectively until reaching the target at 5428N 0931E. After reaching and bombing the target at Schleswig, approximately 40 miles west of Kiel, the aircraft returned on a reciprocal course dropping Window at the reduced rate of 5 bpm for both types until reaching 0800E. Mandrels were not switched off until reaching 0700E.

The Southern Window Force detailed to attack Kiel was to reach an average plot position 'A' 5420N 0700E west of Heligoland between 2245 hrs and 2248 hrs. They then commenced dropping RTDI Window at 10 bpm and N3 at 5 bpm until reaching a point at 0800E when the rate was increased to 20 and 20 bpm up to the target. The second co-ordinate given is position 'B' 5420N 0833E, which was the same position as the Mandrel force, and the third position 'C' 5420N 0950E 20 miles due west of Kiel. The actual Kiel target co-ordinates are given as 5420N 1010E. After bombing the target the aircraft returned on a reciprocal course continuing Windowing at 5 and 5 bpm until reaching 0800E when it was stopped. Mandrels were turned off at 0700E.

The aircraft began returning to North Creake and the first to land was F/Lt Burley at 0010 hrs closely followed by F/Lt King 0016 hrs and P/O Parsons 0018 hrs. F/Lt Short of 171 Squadron touched down at 0053 hrs but the last aircraft of the flight, that of F/O Werner did not land until 0206 hrs.

The Halifaxes of the bombing flights landed soon after and looking at the time intervals it must have been a very hectic period for the personnel in Flying Control.

F/Lt Van Welie landed at 0120 hrs while most of other crews were being stacked above North Creake waiting their turn. The remaining crews were soon on finals and landed in the following order; F/Lt Jenkins 0122 hrs, F/O Pearce 0125 hrs, F/Lt Paddon 0129 hrs, F/Lt Dickinson 0132 hrs, P/O Porter 0138 hrs, F/Lt Wills 0139 hrs, S/Ldr Knight 0146 hrs, F/Lt Ward 0150 hrs, F/Lt Clifton 0151 hrs, F/Lt Murray 0153 hrs, F/O Finnimore 0155 hrs and finally F/Lt Arkinstall 0213 hrs.

To land such a high number of 4 engine heavy bombers in the time frame shown was a credit to both air and ground personnel.

As can clearly be seen from the above list two aircraft were missing, those of F/O Currell and F/Lt Brooks. At first there was not too much concern as aircraft often arrived back late due to a multitude of reasons, engines u/s, fuel shortage causing the aircraft to land at another airfield, bad weather etc. The Watch Office would have worked out from the fuel loads the endurance of the two aircraft and a time written on the Ops board. This was the time, when reached, that neither Halifax could continue flying as all the petrol would have been used up. Telephone calls would have been made to other airfields to enquire if the missing aircraft had made emergency landings, but in this case it was to no avail. The high moral felt among the crews before and on returning safely to base was slowly eroded away as it became ever clearer that two of their much-respected crews were to be officially listed as 'Missing'. It was hoped that the crews were safe, perhaps they had been unfortunate and had been shot down but managed to escape by parachute. No news was received and it was to be many months before the families learned of the true fate of the crews.

Casualties:

Halifax RG373 EX-T: F/Lt William Ernest Brooks, Pilot, RAFVR; W/O William Frederick Bolton, Flight Engineer, RAFVR, age 23, married to Edith Bolton of Plaistow, Essex; F/Sgt John Roger Lewis, Navigator, RAFVR, age 21, from Much Wenlock, Shropshire; W/O Keith Alexander Cameron Munro Gavin, Bomb Aimer, RAFVR, age 22, from Strichen, Aberdeenshire; F/O Kenneth Norman Joseph Croft, Wireless Operator, RAFVR, age 22, married to Irene Croft of Kingstanding, Birmingham; F/Sgt Douglas Wilson, Special Wireless Operator, RAFVR; F/O Alfred Samuel John Holder, DFC, Mid Upper Gunner, RAFVR, age 43, from Miserden, Gloucestershire. All buried in Kiel War Cemetery. P/O K.N. Crane, Rear Gunner, survived, evaded capture. F/O Holder at 43 was among the oldest serving Officers killed on Bomber Ops in the second world war.

Halifax RG375 EX-R: Sgt William Henry Vesey Mackay, Flight Engineer, RAFVR, age 29, from Glenageary, Co Dublin, Ireland, he held a BA Degree (Dublin) Trinity College; F/Sgt Arthur Andrew Bradley, Navigator, RAFVR, age 23, from Wilmslow, Cheshire; Sgt Francis Thomas Chambers, Bomb Aimer, RAFVR, age 29, married to Beryl

Mary Chambers of Redditch, Worcestershire; F/Sgt Joseph Loth, Wireless Operator, RAFVR, age 21, from Bitterne, Southampton; W/O Reginald Henry Alfred Pool, Special Wireless Operator, RAFVR; F/Sgt Desmond Greenwood, Mid Upper Gunner, RAFVR, age 20, from Middlesbrough, Yorkshire. All buried in Kiel War Cemetery. F/Sgt R. Hunter, Rear Gunner, prisoner of war. F/Lt Leslie Herman Currell, Pilot, RAAF, 427703, age 34, married to Elsie Currell, evaded capture.

In November 1945 the wife of W/O Bolton, still unsure of the fate of her husband, received a photograph from a family friend serving in the British Army in Germany showing the location of the 13 graves of the missing airmen. On one of the wooden crosses was the name of her husband confirming he had been killed.

Of the three crew who survived only P/O Crane appears to have recorded any details of this fateful night. He later wrote, "*I have no immediate recollection of what happened when the two aircraft collided and I cannot remember leaving my turret. My first memory of the incident was of falling earthwards and, by sheer instinct, pulling the 'D' ring of my parachute and this in built instinct saved my life. I reached the ground safe and unharmed. I was found by a Dutchman whom I discovered was married to a German lady and they lived in Kiel. I was taken to their apartment and hidden away from prying eyes, particularly those of the authorities. Later we heard a commotion outside their building and when my host had questioned the crowd he was told there was an abandoned train in a nearby railway siding containing Red Cross parcels. The Dutchman joined the rush outside making their way towards the train in the hope that they could lay their hands on some of the packages. Much later he returned laden with food parcels, which he and his wife proceeded to open as soon as they got them indoors. Among the usual things such as tea, sugar and chocolate they came across a strange white powder, of which they had no knowledge and were baffled by my explanation as to its purpose. For the first time in their lives they had encountered 'powdered milk' and for the rest of the night and well into the early hours of the next morning we spent our time reconstituting the dried powder into milk for themselves and their neighbours benefit*".

After bidding farewell to his saviours P/O Crane was taken by the British 21st Army Group to Luneburg. From there he was flown to Down Ampney and eventual release from the RAF. He believes the other two survivors of the crash had similar experiences.

The official MI9 report filed after P.O Crane was interviewed on 17 September 1945 reads almost the same as his personal account. It gives the following details:

"*We took off from North Creake in a Halifax aircraft at 2045 hours on 2 May 1945 to bomb Kiel. We bombed the target but as we were turning for base I believe we collided with another aircraft as I was suddenly shot through the gun turret and found myself in mid-air. I pulled the ripcord and parachuted down.*

I landed in open country at about 0100 hours (3 May) about two miles south of Kiel. I hid in the fields till 0530 hours when I was picked up by a Dutch slave worker. He took me to the home of a German merchant service man who sheltered me till 2200 hours when the Dutchman fetched me and took me to his house. I remained there till 1543 hours on 6 May when I reported to the British Army who had by that time entered Kiel.

I was sent to Wensen and then to Luneburg. I flew to the UK on 9 May 1945."

Further research into the survivors of the crew resulted in contact being made with relatives of F/Lt Currell in Australia who informed me that he had died. However it was possible to ascertain that when he did return home he went back to his job working for the West Australian Government Railways as a car and wagon builder. Later he became a train examiner. He was a very good cabinetmaker and made a lot of his own furniture some of which is still being put to good use within his immediate family. In the late 1950's he changed his job once again and took up fishing mainly for crayfish (lobsters) he owned his own boat and carried on this profession until he retired.

Two days after the crash on May 4 1945 the German surrender of all their forces in Northwest Germany was signed on Luneburg Heath. On May 7 General Eisenhower and representatives from Britain, Russia and France accepted the unconditional surrender of all German forces to take effect from 9 May 1945.

On 7 May 1945 seven aircraft and crews were detailed to take members of the ground staff on a sightseeing flight over the Ruhr. This was carried out and completed successfully.

Crew of Halifax RG375 EX-R, one of two crews lost on the last raid of the war 2nd May 1945. Their aircraft and Halifax RG373 collided over Kiel with the loss of 13 crew. *Left to right*: F/Sgt R. 'Jock' Hunter, Rear Gunner; Sgt Frank Chambers, Bomb Aimer; F/Sgt Arthur Bradley, Navigator; F/Lt Les Currell, Pilot; F/Sgt D. Greenwood, Mid Upper Gunner and F/Sgt Joe Loth, Wireless Operator.

8th May 1945, VE Day

On 8th May the Squadron was stood down for Victory in Europe Day and similarly on the 9th May VE Plus 1 everyone was stood down from general duties.

F/Lt Howard Gray, radar section: *"Near the end of the war, Group Captain Bray had a big party to ensure the supply of spirits built up in the mess would not pass to other hands. A tent was pitched to handle the overflow of people from the officers mess. I was selected as orderly officer on VE Day, which passed a lot more quietly than we expected."*

11th May 1945

Flying training for crews was carried out.

12th May 1945

Training flights only.

13th May 1945

Training flights only.

14th May 1945

Night cross countries and fighter affiliation.

15th and 16th May 1945

No flying carried out.

17th May to end of Month 1945

Local flying and "Cook's Tours" for ground staff.

Three more awards were made to members of the Squadron. Promulgated on 22nd May 1945: F/Lt N.T. Keen, 55951, DFC; F/Lt D.H. Halliwell, 169406, DFC; F/O A.E. Wood, 142341, DFC.

June and July
Fate deals a cruel blow on the Norfolk coast –
disbandment of the Squadron and closure of RAF North Creake

This month was to see only local flying interspersed with fighter affiliation exercises and continuing "Cooks Tours" to the Rhur. However, one last large exercise was planned to take place at the end of the month, named Exercise Post Mortem that was used to test the British and German countermeasures used during the war. Unfortunately, bad weather prevented the Squadron from participating and the whole operation was postponed.

An unfortunate accident occurred on 25th of the month. W/O Ian Dent, flying an air test, was approaching the Norfolk coast at Cromer when his Halifax NA259 hit the cliffs, resulting in the total loss of the aircraft and crew. Local eyewitnesses to the crash stated that, at about 1510 hrs, the Halifax was seen flying low over the sea and turned towards the beach at Cromer, Norfolk. It was too low and crashed at the foot of the cliffs and burst into flames. The crew of four were killed. Two people sitting on the beach had a miraculous escape. Sgt Gleddening, USAAF, and his wife were relaxing by the sea and were a mere 40 feet away from the point of impact. They both suffered minor burns and shock, but after treatment at the Cromer hospital, were allowed home. The local fire brigade attended the crash scene, but found that the aircraft wreckage was inaccessible and fire fighters had to be lowered down the cliff face on ropes to enable them to tackle the burning remains of the Halifax. It took over an hour to bring the flames under control and start to recover the bodies of the crew.

Crew of Halifax NA259: W/O Ian Wilshire Dent, Pilot, RAAF, age 23, from Strathfield, New South Wales, Australia, buried in Cambridge City Cemetery; Sgt William Way, Navigator, RAFVR, age 23, from Morden, buried in Morden Cemetery; Sgt Raymond Ernest George Seymour, Flight Engineer, RAFVR, buried in Henley Road Cemetery, Reading; Sgt Andrew Mill Adams, Rear Gunner, RAFVR, age 21, buried in Wells-Next-The-Sea Cemetery.

1st July 1945

Ten aircraft and crews were detailed to take part in Exercise Post Mortem (an evaluation of German counter measures). This was carried out successfully.

2nd July 1945

Fourteen aircraft and crews detailed for Exercise Post Mortem but bad weather intervened and it had to be cancelled.

3rd July 1945

Fourteen aircraft and crew took part in Exercise Post Mortem that was completed successfully.

4th July 1945

Eighteen aircraft and crews took part in Exercise Post Mortem. All carried out successful sorties.

5th July 1945

Seventeen aircraft and crews took part in Exercise Post Mortem. All carried out successful sorties.

5th to 11th July 1945

Local air tests.

12th July 1945

Seven crews posted to ORTU matching for duties with 38 Group. This was the first indication to personnel on the base that the Squadron was to be disbanded.

13th July 1945

Two more "Cook's Tours" for ground staff.

14th July 1945

Eight crews were selected for posting to 192 Squadron to form the nucleus of a new Radar Warfare Squadron.

17th July 1945

The Squadron was officially informed at a station commander's conference that 199 Squadron was to be disbanded on 29th July 1945. Over the next few days all flight and section commanders began to clear outstanding inventories and make preparations for the disbandment. The first batch of postings of redundant personnel was also received and was seen to indicate that many aircrews were to take over sedentary occupations in catering, equipment and intelligence.

23rd July 1945

The group redundancy board paid its final visit to the Squadron. All redundant personnel had by this time been interviewed and they were now awaiting postings.

25th July 1945

Seven more redundant officers received their postings to new units.

27th July 1945

It appears from the records that only two effective pilots were left on the Station and carried out local air tests.

28th July 1945

All remaining aircrew were stood down on the penultimate day in the life of the Squadron.

Three awards were made to aircrew, promulgated on 17th July 1945: F/Lt H. Green, 182398, DFC; F/Lt R.E. Lind, 179076, DFC; F/Lt Gilbert, 178882, DFC.

29th July 1945

No. 199 Squadron was officially disbanded. It had been operational for 2½ years and had carried out many and varied types of operation, including night bombing raids on Germany and occupied countries, sea mining, dropping supplies to the French Resistance and finally, acting as a bomber support squadron combating enemy radar defences.

Initially equipped with Wellington III aircraft, it converted to Stirling Mk.III and finally to the Halifax Mk.III. During their service they despatched 2,941 sorties for the loss of 34 aircraft. In the words of the Squadron diarist *"We conclude the summary of the life of No.199 Squadron, which though short has contributed in no small measure to the overwhelming success of that splendid organisation "Bomber Command" which played such a great part in absolute and final victory over Germany".*

The final act was a disbandment parade and service for 199 and 171 Squadron, with many local dignitaries and civilians as guests. The programme began with a lunch, followed by a parade and march past, the salute taken by Air-Vice Marshall E.B. Addison, CB, CBE. For the occasion the Bomber Command band was in attendance. A valedictory service was held in No.1 hangar, with the lesson read by The Earl of Leicester and after hymns and prayers, The Lord Bishop of Norwich, The Right Reverend P.M. Herbert, DD, gave an address. The final hymn *"Lord dismiss us with Thy blessing"* was sung and the parade ended with the Benediction.

With the official parade over, everyone made for the NAFFI, where tea was served. In the evening, No.1 hangar was opened once again and a grand dance was held with music from the station dance band.

Bill Peters, chaplain: *"North Creake was my first posting after initial training at Cranwell. I was not there very long, but greatly enjoyed the time I spent with everyone on the aerodrome. At the end of the war I arranged and conducted the disbandment service, and I have a pack of photographs (RAF) of the event."*

Harry Lofts, armourer: *"On the occasion of the disbandment, a service was held in No.1 Hangar with the Earl of Leicester reading the lesson, and an address was given by The Lord Bishop of Norwich. In the evening a dance was held in the hangar with plenty of activity. My best friend on the camp, who was a cabinet maker in civvy street, made a beautiful model in perspex of a Halifax which was won in a raffle by one of our aircrew.*

Two vivid memories come to mind of my time at North Creake. One was when the C.O. invited all ranks to see the 1945 Derby run at Newmarket when everyone, myself included, had a great day out. I backed three winners at the meeting, but not Dante, the Derby winner. The second and perhaps the most stirring memory was being invited by the C.O. of our Squadron to go for a flight a few days after the war ended. We went over the flying bomb sites in France, flying low to see the saturation of bomb craters and then we flew over Cologne in Germany where the cathedral appeared to be untouched amid the surrounding devastation. Then we flew along the Rhine ending a day never to be forgotten. All during the flight I had a bird's eye view as we were allowed to stand just behind the pilot."

F/Lt Howard Grey, radar section: *"The role of 100 Group was unique and I often thought that a book should have been written on its special contribution to the war. The nearest to it so far is a book published by my old friend Wing Commander Cordingly, who was one of the pioneers in the radar field in the early days of the war. It was published in 1988 and covers his career before the war, right through to the early days of radar. Quite a lot is said about his experience with 100 Group so that it was intensely interesting to me. It is called 'From a Cat's Whisker Beginning', printed by Anthony Rowe Ltd."*

North Creake was taken over as a storage depot for out of service Mosquito aircraft and where many were broken up. The RAF was now phasing out propeller-driven fighters as the jet age came along, with Meteors and Vampires.

The RAF relinquished North Creake in the autumn of 1947, when it returned to agricultural use. The runways were removed and the hardcore used in the construction of new roads in the Norfolk area. The technical site buildings and hangars are still used by an animal feedstuff company and the control tower has been converted into a house.

199 Squadron was by no means finished. On 16th July 1951 it was reformed in No.90 Signals Group based at Watton, equipped with Lincoln Bombers and a few Mosquitoes that had escaped the breaker's yard. These aircraft were again fitted out with a range of radio countermeasure sets capable of jamming enemy radar and radio communications. In mid April 1952, the Squadron moved to Hemswell and transferred to Bomber

Command and then re-equipped with Canberra B.2 medium jet bombers during July 1954. During May 1957, 199 Squadron joined the nuclear age when it was alloted a flight of Valiant B.1 bombers although it still retained some of its Lincolns. In October 1957 the Squadron moved yet again, this time to Honington, although the Lincoln element stayed at Hemswell to form No.1321 Flt. On 17th December 1958, 199 Squadron was finally disbanded and the main element of the unit was renumbered as No.18 Squadron based at Finningly.

The disbandment parade at North Creake on 29th July 1945 with 199 and 171 Squadrons drawn up on parade. Forming a backdrop are Halifax bombers that served in the RCM role. In the foreground can be seen local people who were invited to join in the celebrations.

Left: The Right Reverend P.M. Herbert, Lord Bishop of Norwich (1942-1959), on the left, gave an address during the valedictory service.

Right: The final disbandment service held in one of the T2 hangers.

Appendix 1: Abbreviations and Terms

A.A. . . . . Anti-Aircraft (ground or shipboard artillery defence against aircraft).
A.F.D.U. . . . . Air Fighting Development Unit.
A.O.C. . . . . Air Officer Commanding.
A.P. . . . . Armour Piercing. (Bomb).
A.S. . . . . Anti-Submarine. (Bomb).
A.S.R. . . . . Air Sea Rescue.
B.D.U. . . . . Bomber Development Unit.
Bf. . . . . Bayerische Flugzeugwerke (successor to Messerschmitt).
Boozer.   A passive aerial device fitted under a bomber's rear turret to detect the radar pulses emitted
                       by German night fighters.
C.A.S. . . . . Chief of Air Staff.
Circus. . . . . Fighter escorted and covered daylight raid.
C.U. . . . . Conversion Unit.
D/F. . . . . Direction Finding.
Do. . . . . Dornier. Type number prefix. (German aircraft manufacturer).
D.R. . . . . Dead Reckoning. (Navigational).
D.Z. . . . . Dropping Zone.
Cat. E . . . . Write-off of an aircraft.
E.T.A. . . . . Estimated Time of Arrival.
F/O. . . . . Flying Officer.
F/Lt. . . . . Flight Lieutenant.
F/Sgt. . . . . Flight Sergeant.
F.N. . . . . Frazer-Nash. (Gun turret with type number prefix).
F.S. . . . . Full Supercharger.
G.C.A. . . . . Ground Control Approach.
Gee, Gee H. . . . . . . Radio and Radar navigational aids.
G/Cpt. . . . . Group Captain.
G.P. . . . . General Purpose Bomb.
H.C. . . . . High Capacity Bomb.
H.C.U. . . . . Heavy Conversion Unit.
H2S. . . . . Radar Navigational Aid.
I.A.S. . . . . Indicated Airspeed.
JG. . . . . Jagdgeschwader. (German Day Fighter Wing).
Ju. . . . . Junkers. (German aircraft manufacturer).
L.C. . . . . Light Case Bomb.
L.F.S. . . . . Lancaster Finishing School.
                       The Lancaster Finishing Schools were divided into the following units:
                       No. 1. Based at RAF Hemswell near Gainsborough, Lincolnshire.
                       No. 2. Based at Feltwell, Norfolk.
                       No. 3. Based at Syerston near Flintham, Newark, Notts.
L.Z. . . . . Landing Zone.
Mae West. . . . . . . Life Jacket.
Mandrel. . . . . Radar Jamming Equipment.
M.C. . . . . Medium Capacity Bomb.
Me. . . . . Messerschmitt (correct type number prefix being Bf – Bayerische Flugzeugwerke).
MG. . . . . German Machine Gun.
M.U. . . . . Maintenance Unit.
NJG. . . . . Nachtjagdgeschwader (German Night Fighter Wing).
Noball. . . . . Attack on Flying Bomb (V-1) site.
Oboe. . . . . Radio navigational aid.
O.T.U. . . . . Operational Training Unit.
P.F.F. . . . . Path Finder Force.

P/O. . . . . Pilot Officer.
Ramrod. . . . . Fighter escorted bomber operations against a specific target.
R.D.X. . . . . Type of High Explosive.
Rebecca. . . . . Radio Navigational Aid.
R/T. . . . . Radio Telephony.
R.T.O. . . . . Resident Technical Officer.
S.A.P. . . . . Semi-Armour Piercing. (Bomb).
S.A.S. . . . . Special Air Service.
Satellite. . . . . Airfield close to main base.
S.B.C. . . . . Small Bomb Container. (For Incendiaries).
Shaker. . . . . Main Force attack incorporating O.T.U. aircraft.
S.O.E. . . . . Special Operations Executive.
S/Ldr. . . . . Squadron Leader.
T.A.S. . . . . True Air Speed.
Tinsel. . . . . Radar jamming device.
T.R.E. . . . . Telecommunications Research Establishment.
Trinity. . . . . Radar navigational aid.
W/Cdr. . . . . Wing Commander.
Window. . . . . Metal foil strips dropped to give false image on enemy radar.
W/O. . . . . Warrant Officer.
W/T. . . . . Wireless Telegraphy.

Photo Flash.
A pyrotechnic device, conataining a mixture of powdered magnesium and aluminium, dropped via the flare chute from a bomber after the main bomb load had detonated. Ignited by a delay fuse, the photo flash produced a burst of light in the region of 800,000 candlepower, illuminating the bombed area, enabling a photograph to be taken of the target using a fixed automatically triggered camera.

Fighter Affiliation.
At the beginning of the war a new unit called the Bomber Defence Training Flight and The Central Gunnery School was formed and based at RAF Sutton Bridge in Lincolnshire. The trainee crews mainly flew Wellington bombers over the Wash and were subjected to simulated attacks by Spitfires and Hurricanes, thus gaining valuable experience in avoiding enemy fighters.

PFF Pathfinder Force.
In the early years of the war it was found that a large amount of bombs were failing to hit designated targets. The main problems were poor navigation and lack of suitable equipment. To overcome the many difficulties a new force (PFF) was formed in August 1942, consisting of some of the most experienced pilots in Bomber Command Groups. These crews, using the latest navigational aids and technology, flew ahead of the Main Force, marking the route and the target with special coloured flares known as Target Indicators.

Stirling flare chutes. Jim Hallas instructing RAF fitters at the Austin Aero Works, 1942.

Bullseye Exercise.
Exercises to assess the flying and navigational skills of new and, experienced crews. The main test was to fly to predetermined map references covering a track of several hundred miles, logging in detail the natural features and towns and villages along the route. At a later stage, a load of practise bombs would be dropped on a designated bombing range, usually the Wash off the Lincolnshire coast.

Gee.
Initially designed as a short range blind landing system this device was further developed into a long range navigation system. It used a series of transmitters, based in England, sending out precisely timed signals. Using an oscilloscope, the navigator could work out his exact position.

Oboe.
Developed as an aerial blind bombing targeting system. Introduced in December 1941 it become one of the main devices used by the PFF to locate and mark specific targets. It was modefied and improved to such an extent that an aircraft could be signalled from England when to drop its markers or bombs, on an exact co-ordinates for the target.

H2S.
An airbourne radar unit mounted under the rear fuselage of bombers. Used initially by the Pathfinders it was later fitted to many Main Force aircraft. Using micro waves generated by a cavity magnetron, the pulses were transmitted on a 10cm wavelength and the resulting echo, from buildings, rivers and coastline, displayed on a cathode ray tube, in the navigator's station. Using calibrated range markings on the CRT screen and an overlay map, the navigator could work out his precise location.

Appendix 2: Aircraft Types

The Vickers Wellington Medium Bomber.
The Wellington was designed by Vickers Chief Designer Reginald Kirshaw 'Rex' Pierson (1891-1948), using a method of fuselage construction devised by Barnes Wallis which formed an extremely strong structure of metal lattice members known as geodetic. Between 1936 and 1945, 11,461 Wellington bombers were produced. Vickers-Armstrong Ltd had factories at: Brooklands, Weybridge, Surrey; Broughton near Chester, North Wales; and Blackpool (Squires Gate), Lancashire.

199 Squadron used two variants of the Wellington – the Mk.III and Mk.X between November 1942 and July 1943 while flying from RAF Blyton and RAF Ingham.

Wellington B Mk.III.
This aircraft featured some of the major improvements over previous varients including the installation of the more powerful 1,375hp Bristol Hercules Mk.III and Mk.XI engines. A modified rear turret was installed with four machine guns as opposed to a two gun configuration. Vickers produced a total of 1,519 Mk.IIIs.

Wellington Mk.X.
Similar in design to the Mk.III, Vickers produced 3,804 Mk.Xs, the only difference being the higher rated 1,675hp Hercules VI or XVI engines and minor changes to the fuselage construction.

Short Stirling Heavy Bomber.
Built to a design produced by Sir Arthur Gouge (1890-1962), Short Bros. chief designer, the Stirling was the first four engine heavy bomber produced for the RAF and made its official entry into service with 7 Squadron on 3rd August 1940. Following modification a Mk.I Stirling flew its first operational sortie on the night of 10/11 February 1941. A total of 2,383, in various marks, were built and flown throughout the war.

The aircraft was produced in factories situated at: Short & Harland Ltd, Queens Island, Belfast; Short Brothers (Rochester & Bedford Ltd), on the river Medway, Kent; and Austin Motors, Longbridge, Birmingham.

A formation of MK.I Stirlings.

199 Squadron flew two variants of the Stirling. The Mk.III, bomber version, and the modified Mk.III RCM version, fitted with Mandrel radar countermeasures equipment. The Mk.III was powered by four Bristol Hercules 1,635hp Mk.VI or Mk.XVI radial engines.

Handley Page Halifax.
Designed by George Volkert, of Handley Page, the Halifax was produced in many marks and variants with production beginning at Cricklewood in N.W. London and Radlett in Hertfordshire. Production continued for a short time after the war bringing the total produced to 6,178.

The Halifax was a modular build involving many disperse factories and then brought together for assembly. So dispersed was the production it is only possible to mention a few locations where the various sections were made and assembled. Cricklewood, North West London (the main Handley Page factory), and Rdlett, Hertfordshire. London Aircraft Production Group (LAPG) that was governed by London Transport (LPTB) and comprising the following: Park Royal Coach Works, London; Express Motor and Body Works; Chrysler Motors; Duples; and LPTB Works at Aldenham, Chiswick and White City. Outside London Halifaxes were built at English Electric, Strand Road, Preston; Rootes Securities, Speke; and Fairey Aviation at Stockport.

During February 1945 199 Squadron was equipped with the B.Mk.III Halifax powered by four Bristol Hercules Mk.XVI 1,650hp radial enginesw. At least 22 aircraft were taken on charge and modified along the lines of the Stirling to enable the aircraft to carry out RCM sorties. In addition to this role the aircraft also carried a substantial bomb load.

Hercules engine isntallation, Elmdon 1942. RAF fitters being instructed by Harry Priest (centre) and Bill Maynard, Flight Shed Supervisor (right).

Appendix 3:
Record of 199 Squadron Stirling Aircraft with dates of service

All dates are noted as accurately as possible. During WWII a large number of Stirlings were allocated to a specific Squadron on a particular date but were often transferred to another Unit within a day or so and never served operationally with the initial designated Squadron. This has sometimes caused problems in sorting out the dates, code letters and final fate of a particular aircraft. Also movement and accident cards are sometimes at odds with the Squadron ORBs. The available data has been researched and the following table compiled from the information available but there may be discrepancies beyond the author's control.

Abbreviations:

Cat E. F/A – Write Off: Flying Accident.
Cat E. F/B – Write Off: Flying Battle Damage.
SEBRO: Short Brothers Repair Organisation. Based at Madingley Road, Cambridge.

Serial No.	Code	Dates of Service
BK762	EX-C	07/07/43 – 19/01/43. Battle damage. Repaired in works, SEBRO.
BK772	EX-A	06/07/43 – 27/08/44. Flying accident. Cat E. F/A.
BK806	EX-S	02/08/43 – 28/08/43. Nuremburg. Failed to return.
EE910	EX-Q	19/07/43 – 22/04/44. Flying accident. Cat E. F/A.
EE911	EX-G	08/07/43 – 03/09/43. Mining La Pallice. Failed to return.
EE913	EX-F	19/07/43 – 27/08/43. Nuremberg. Failed to return.
EE917	EX-L	06/07/43 – 30/08/43. Remscheid. Failed to return.
EE940	EX	11/07/43 – 19/07/43. Transferred to XV Sqd. No code allocated.
EE943	EX-X	06/07/43 – 18/11/43. Coded X. Recoded V 20/11/43 – 25/04/44.
EE946	EX-P	05/07/43 – 31/08/43. Berlin. Failed to return.
EE947	EX–D	05/07/43 – 25/09/43. Battle damage. Cat E. F/B.
EE948	EX-G	07/07/43 – 24/08/43. Battle damage. Repaired & recoded T 01/10/43 – 20/11/43.
EE953	EX-E	11/07/43 – 21/04/44. Transferred to 149 Sqd.
EE954	EX	11/07/43 – 19/07/43. No Ops flown. No code. Transferred to XV Sqd.
EF118	EX-O	17/08/43 – 27/09/43. Hanover. Failed to return.
EF138	EX-S	02/09/43 – 11/02/44. Recoded Y 07/03/44 – 09/04/44. Battle damege. Cat E. F/B.
EF153	EX-D	26/09/43 – 11/02/44. Crashed Lakenheath. Cat E. F/A.
EF154	EX-V	05/10/43 – 01/12/43. Mining Kattegat. Failed to return.
EF161	EX-Z	20/12/43 – 21/04/44. Transferred to 149 Sqd.
EF192	EX-J	30/09/43 – 25/04/44. Transferred to 149 Sqd.

Serial No.	Code	Dates of Service
EF300	EX	27/12/43 – 30/12/43. No code. Transferred to 1653 CU.
EF301	EX	27/12/43 – 30/12/43. No code. Transferred to 1653 CU.
EF304	EX	27/12/43 – 30/12/43. No code. Transferred to 1653 CU.
EF450	EX-N	06/07/43 – 18/11/43. Mannheim. Battle damage. Cat E. F/B.
EF453	EX-F	24/07/43 – 04/11/43. Mining Kattegat. Failed to return.
EF455	EX-B	05/06/43 – 25/04/44. Transferred to 1651 CU.
EF459	EX-X	13/01/44 – 10/03/44. Battle damage. Repaired, recoded P 12/05/44 – 17/07/44.
EF505	EX-K	30/08/43 – 23/09/43. Battle damage. Cat E. F/B. Repaired, recoded R 09/10/43 – 28/01/44
EF508	EX-G	29/08/43 – 06/05/44. Transferred to 1653 CU.
EF514	EX	17/03/44 – 09/05/44. Transferred to 1651 CU. No code.
EH926	EX-T	05/07/43 – 07/02/44. Transferred to 1654 CU.
EH927	EX-E	06/07/43 – 23/08/43. Berlin. Failed to return.
EH930	EX-N	27/12/43 – 06/05/44. Transferred to 1651 CU.
EH934	EX-K	29/07/43 – 23/08/43. Berlin. Failed to return.
EH995	EX-L	25/08/43 – 04/01/44. Recoded H 14/01/44 – 04/02/44.
EJ111	EX-P	11/09/43 – 23/11/43. Ground accident. Cat E. F/A.
EJ115	EX-H	01/10/43 – 06/01/44. Battle damage. Repaired, recoded C 02/02/44 – 27/04/44.
LJ510	EX-A	22/04/44 – 24/10/44. Battle damage. Repaired in works, SEBRO.
LJ513	EX-E	22/04/44 – 10/11/44. Transferred to 171 Sqd.
LJ514	EX-B	03/05/44 – 24/02/45. Struck off charge at end of war.
LJ516	EX-H	23/07/44 – 17/04/45. Struck off charge at end of war.
LJ518	EX-K	26/04/44 – 25/09/44. Written off Cat E. F/B.
LJ520	EX-Z	08/05/44 – 24/02/45. Struck off charge at end of war.
LJ525	EX-R	27/04/44 – 31/01/45. Struck off charge at end of war.
LJ531	EX-N	26/04/44 – 17/06/44. Sterkrade. Failed to return.
LJ536	EX-P	24/04/44 – 16/09/44. Site unknown. Failed to return.
LJ538	EX-T	19/05/44 – 21/02/45. Struck off charge at end of war.
LJ541	EX-K	10/07/44 – 17/07/44. No code. Transferred to 171 Sqd. 17/07/44 – 02/10/44. Reallocated to 199 Sqd coded K 02/10/44 – 06/03/45.
LJ542	EX-G	28/04/44 – 31/01/45. Struck off charge at end of war.
LJ543	EX-J	23/05/44 – 31/02/45. Struck off charge at end of war.
LJ544	EX-D	25/04/44 – 06/12/44. Transferred to 171 Sqd.
LJ557	EX-Y	16/05/44 – 31/01/45. Struck off charge at the end of war.
LJ560	EX-H	27/04/44 – 29/08/44. Flying accident. Cat E. F/A.
LJ562	EX-V	03/05/44 – 10/11/44. Transferred to 171 Sqd.
LJ565	EX-Q	11/05/44 – 10/11/44. Transferred to 171 Sqd 10/11/44 – 17/11/44. Reallocated to 199 Sqd coded J 17/1/44 – 22/02/45.
LJ567	EX	29/08/44 – 17/09/44. Transferred to 171 Sqd. No code.
LJ568	EX-L	29/08/44 – 17/09/44. Transferred to 171 Sqd 17/09/44 – 10/11/44. Reallocated to 199 Sqd coded L 10/11/44 – 06/04/45.

Serial No.	Code	Dates of Service
LJ569	EX-C	09/05/44 – 16/09/44. Flying accident. Cat E. F/A.
LJ578	EX-S	29/02/44 – 10/09/44. Battle damage. Written off. Cat E. F/B.
LJ580	EX-X	05/03/44 – 31/01/45. Struck off charge at end of war.
LJ582	EX-L	05/03/44 – 10/11/44. Transferred to 171 Sqd.
LJ595	EX-N	04/07/44 – 22/02/45. Struck off charge at end of war.
LJ611	EX-A	29/08/44 – 17/09/44. No code. Transferred to 171 Sqd 17/09/44 – 26/10/44. Reallocated to 199 Sqd coded A 26/10/44 – 06/03/45.
LJ614	EX-S	28/08/44 – 06/03/45. Struck off charge at end of war.
LJ617	EX-E	28/08/44 – 17/09/44. No code. Transferred to 171Sqd 17/09/44 – 10/11/44. Reallocated to 199 Sqd coded E 10/11/44 – 05/03/45. Shot down by American AA.
LJ649	EX-P	28/08/44 – 17/09/44. No code. Transferred to 171 Sqd 17/09/44 – 02/10/44. Reallocated to 199 Sqd coded P 02/10/44 – 24/04/45.
LJ651	EX-C	28/08/44 – 17/09/44. No code. Transferred to 171. Reallocated to 199 Sqd coded C 02/10/44 – 06/06/45.
LJ670	EX	29/09/44 – 02/10/44. Transferred to 171 Sqd.
LK381	EX-Z	01/10/43 – 31/12/43. Abbeville. Flak damage, Cat E. F/B.
LK385	EX-A	05/11/43 – 27/04/44. Transferred to 149 Sqd.
LK397	EX-P	05/11/43 – 27/04/44. Transferred to 149 Sqd.
PW256	EX	25/09/44 – 02/10/44. No code. Transferred to 171 Sqd 02/10/44 – 27/11/44. Reallocated to 199 Sqd. No code. 07/12/44 – 31/03/45.
PW258	EX	30/09/44 – 02/10/44. No code. Transferred to 171 Sqd.
PW259	EX-V	13/09/44 – 17/09/44. No code. Transferred to 171 Sqd 17/09/44 – 10/11/44. Reallocated to 199 coded V 10/11/44 – 24/04/45.

Appendix 4:
Some Crew Members

1.

2.

3.

4.

5.

6.

7.

8.

9.

10.

11.

12.

1. P/O Ray Davies, M/U.
2. F/O George Cubby, W/Op.
3. P/O Roy Smith, Nav.
4. Jeff Riley, Station photographer.

5. Johnny Russell, W/Op.
6. P/O Norman Pettie, Nav.
7. F/Lt Lance Smith, Squadron Adjutant
8. F/Lt Ernie Harker, Pilot.

9. Sgt Harry Durrell, W/Op.
10. Johnny Russell, W/Op.
11. Sgt Bernie Howe, F/Eng.
12. Sgt Stan Pallant, M/U.

Appendix 5:

Squadron Air Crew

The list contains names of Wellington, Stirling and Halifax crew members. A few names have the initials missing due to them being omitted from the Squadron records and although a thorough search of other material has been conducted it has been impossible to trace them.

A

Adam, R., Sgt, Nav.
Albiston, A., Sgt, M/U.
Alcock, W., W/O, SWO.
Albinston, A., F/Sgt, M/U.
Alcorn, W., W/O, SWO.
Aldritt, J., W/O, Nav.
Allen, C., Sgt, F/E.
Allson, A., Sgt, Pilot.
Anadell, J., Sgt, R/G.
Anderson, J., W/O, SWO.
Andrews, C., Sgt, Pilot.
Andrews, L., Sgt, B/A.
Andrews, V., Sgt, F/E.
Angus, T., Sgt, M/U.
Ansdall, G., F/Sgt, R/G.
Arben, D., Sgt, B/A.
Archer, G., F/O, Pilot.
Arkinstall, C., F/O, Pilot.
Ashton, D., F/O, B/A.
Aspinall, S., Sgt, W/Op.
Atkinson, J., Sgt, R/G.
Austin, T., F/Sgt, Pilot.

B

Bagshaw, ?, Sgt, B/A.
Bailey, P., Sgt, M/U.
Bailey, R., F/Sgt, B/A.
Baker, R., Sgt, R/G.
Baker, V., Sgt, R/G.
Bainbridge, A., F/Sgt, B/A.
Baldwin, D., F/Sgt, B/A.
Baldwin, H., Sgt, SWO.
Ball, F., Sgt, F/E.
Banahan, P., F/Lt, B/A.
Baras, M., Sgt, B/A.
Barham, L., F/O, SWO.
Baringer, G., F/Sgt, R/G.
Barkwell, J., Sgt, R/G.
Barnard, M., Sgt, Pilot.
Barrie, F., Sgt, F/E.
Barrow, L., Sgt, R/G.
Barson, P., F/Lt, Pilot.
Barter, F., F/O, Nav.
Bartlett, W., Sgt, F/E.
Barton, B., Sgt, W/Op.
Bassant, C., Sgt, R/G.

Bateman, H., F/Sgt, M/U.
Bater, R., Sgt, R/G.
Battishill, C., Sgt, R/G.
Beagley, P., Sgt, M/U.
Beethroyd, J., Sgt, R/G.
Bell, ?, Sgt, B/A.
Bell, J., P/O, Pilot.
Bell, J., Sgt, M/U.
Bell, S., Sgt, W/Op.
Bellhouse, W., Sgt, Nav.
Benfell, I., Sgt, R/G.
Bennett, ?, F/Sgt, M/U.
Bennett, H., Sgt, Pilot.
Bennett, H., Sgt, Nav.
Berry, F., P/O, Nav.
Berry, R., F/Sgt, W/Op.
Betts, W., F/Lt, Pilot.
Bevington, P., F/O, B/A.
Biffin, N., F/Sgt, W/Op.
Birchill, A., Sgt, M/U.
Binnie, J., Sgt, W/Op.
Binns, S., F/O, SWO.
Birch, G., Sgt, M/U.
Bird, P., Sgt, Pilot.
Bissett, J., F/Sgt, M/U.
Blackmore, C., Sgt, W/Op.
Blake, E., Sgt, M/U.
Blaker, L., F/Sgt, M/U.
Bleakley, C., F/Lt, Pilot.
Blinke, F., F/Sgt, W/Op.
Blumson, L., Sgt, W/Op.
Bolger, J., Sgt, Nav.
Bolton, W., F/Sgt, F/E.
Boniwell, R., F/O, B/A.
Bonnett, H., P/O, Pilot.
Boston, W., F/Sgt, R/G.
Bourgeois, B., F/O, SWO.
Bowering, P., P/O, Pilot.
Boyden, W., Sgt, R/G.
Bradley, C., Sgt, M/U.
Bradley, C., Sgt, R/G.
Branson, P., Sgt, F/E.
Bray, N., W/Cdr, Pilot.
Briggs, P., F/O, Pilot.
Brigham, J., F/O, Nav.
Brimson, J., F/O, Nav.
Brittain, D., Sgt, Nav.

Brittain, F., W/O, W/Op.
Broadfield, H., F/Sgt, Pilot.
Brooke, C., Sgt, F/E.
Brooks, G., F/O, M/U.
Brooks, W., F/O, Pilot.
Brooks, S., Sgt, M/U.
Broomfield, R., F/O, SWO.
Broomhead, A., F/O, SWO.
Bourgeois, B., F/O, SWO.
Bourne, D., F/O, SWO.
Bradley, A., F/Sgt, Nav.
Brown, D., Sgt, W/Op.
Brown, E., F/O, B/A.
Brown, G., Sgt, F/E.
Brown, J., F/O, B/A.
Brown, O., Sgt, W/Op.
Brown, P., P/O, Pilot.
Brown, R., F/O, F/E.
Brown, W., Sgt, M/U.
Browne, D., F/Sgt, B/A.
Browne, W., P/O, R/G.
Bryant, C., W/O, R/G.
Bryce, J., F/Sgt, M/U.
Buchan, H., F/Sgt, B/A.
Bullock, E., Sgt, R/G.
Burch, G., Sgt, R/G.
Burch, G., Sgt, R/G.
Burley, A., F/Lt, Pilot.
Bunce, H., F/Sgt, R/G.
Burnett, A., F/Sgt, F/E.
Burnside, H., F/Sgt, R/G.
Burr, T., F/O, SWO.
Burton, B., Sgt, W/Op.
Burton, E., Sgt, Nav.
Burton, J., Sgt, Pilot.
Burton, P., Sgt, R/G.
Busher, S., W/O, Nav.
Butterworth, D., F/Sgt, SWO.
Button, J., F/Lt, Pilot.
Byerley, M., P/O, M/U.
Byers, M., Sgt, M/U.

C

Caddy, A., F/Sgt, SWO.
Caine, G., Sgt, B/A.
Calcraft, N., Sgt, M/U.
Campbell, J., Sgt, M/U.

Canning, H., F/Sgt, R/G.
Cardall, J., F/Sgt, B/A.
Carlson, C., 2nd Lt, Nav.
Carr, T., Sgt, F/E.
Cattell, E., P/O, Pilot.
Catterall, R., P/O, Pilot.
Challener, R., Sgt, F/E.
Challis, R., F/Sgt, M/U.
Chambers, F., Sgt, B/A.
Champion, L., Sgt, R/G.
Chapman, D., F/Sgt, W/Op.
Chapman, F., F/O, R/G.
Chapman, R., P/O, W/Op.
Chappell, W., Sgt, Pilot.
Charters, R., F/Sgt, Nav.
Chatterton, G., Sgt, F/E.
Chatterton, J., F/O, Pilot.
Chatwin, P., P/O, Pilot.
Cheese, A., F/Sgt, B/A.
Chessell, H., Sgt, R/G.
Chessell, L., F/O, SWO.
Chilcott, P., F/Lt, Pilot.
Child, R., F/Sgt, R/G.
Chisholm, A., Sgt, R/G.
Chisholm, D., F/Sgt, W/Op.
Christie, W., F/Sgt, M/U.
Christopher, P., Sgt, W/Op.
Churchward, H., P/O, M/U.
Clarke, A., F/O, Nav.
Clarke, C., F/O, M/U.
Clarke, S., F/Sgt, W/Op.
Clarkson, J., Sgt, R/G.
Cleghorn, W., Sgt, R/G.
Clever, D., Sgt, W/Op.
Clifford, D., Sgt, Pilot.
Clifton, P., F/Lt, Pilot.
Collins, T., Sgt, F/E.
Conn, L., Sgt, B/A.
Conry, K., F/Sgt, Nav.
Cook, R., P/O, W/Op.
Cooper, A., F/O, SWO.
Copper, D., F/Sgt, W/Op.
Cooper, W., Sgt, W/Op.
Cooper, W., Sgt, R/G.
Corcoran, T., W/O, SWO.
Cormack, A., Sgt, R/G.
Cornick, R., Sgt, M/U.
Coup, H., Sgt, B/A.
Coupar, A., Sgt, Pilot.
Court, T., P/O, B/A.
Couzins, W., P/O, B/A.
Cox, G., F/Sgt, Pilot.
Craig, J., F/O, Nav.
Craigie, E., F/O, W/Op.
Crane, K., F/Sgt, R/G.

Craw, R., F/Lt, Pilot.
Crawford, J., Sgt, M/U.
Crawford, W., Sgt, F/E.
Cresswell, J., Sgt, B/A.
Crick, L., Sgt, M/U.
Crofts, K., P/O, W/Op.
Croker, C., F/Sgt, Nav.
Crossland, C., F/Sgt, W/Op.
Crossman, L., Sgt, Nav.
Cruickshank, W., P/O, W/Op.
Cubby, G., F/O, W/Op.
Cuff, E., Sgt, W/Op.
Cunningham, C., Sgt, W/Op.
Currell, L., F/O, Pilot.
Currie, R., F/O, DFM, F/E.
Currie, R., F/O, Nav.
Curtis, W., W/O, SWO.
Cutler, R., P/O, Pilot.
Cutting, R., F/Sgt, F/E.

D
Daborn, C., F/O, SWO.
Dale, T., P/O, Pilot.
Dalsall, W., Sgt, Nav.
Dammerall, M., Sgt, M/U.
Dancer, S., P/O, Nav.
Dane, H., Sgt, M/U.
Darling, ?, P/O, Nav.
Dater, R., Sgt, R/G.
Davey, A., F/Sgt, Pilot.
Davey, F., W/O, SWO.
Davies, D., S/Ldr, Pilot.
Davies, L., Sgt, B/A.
Davies, W., P/O, M/U.
Davies, W., Sgt, W/Op.
Davis, L., P/O, R/G.
Davy, H., Sgt, B/A.
Dawes, J., W/O, Nav.
De'Ath, W, Sgt, SWO.
Deed, L., Sgt, B/A.
Delaroche, F/O, SWO.
Dennis, R., Sgt, Pilot.
Dennison, G., Sgt, R/G.
Depoe, N., F/O, B/A.
Derbyshire, S., F/Sgt, Pilot.
Dewar, A., Sgt, R/G.
Dick, R., W/O, Nav.
Dickerson, A., Sgt, Nav.
Dickinson, G., F/Lt, Pilot.
Dodsworth, W., F/Sgt, Pilot.
Donaldson, H., F/Sgt, W/Op.
Donaldson, W., Sgt, W/Op.
Donnahay, W., Sgt, R/G.
Doolan, H., F/O, B/A.
Double, R., Sgt, B/A

Douglas, ?, P/O, B/A.
Drayton, V., Sgt, Pilot.
Duckett, A., F/O, Nav.
Duffy, J., F/Sgt, R/G.
Dunkley, W., Sgt, R/G.
Duroe, W., Sgt, F/E.
Durrell, H., Sgt, W/Op.

E
Earle, A., Sgt, Nav.
Earle, W., Sgt, Nav.
Easey, G., Sgt, R/G.
Eaton, E., Sgt, W/Op.
Eddy, K., F/Lt, Pilot.
Edgar, J., Sgt, B/A.
Edwards, B., Sgt, R/G.
Edwards, I., Sgt, B/A.
Edwards, R., Sgt, R/G.
Elesley, H., F/Sgt, R/G.
Eley, A., Sgt, B/A.
Ellis, R., Sgt, M/U.
English, F., Sgt, M/U.
Ereaut, J., Sgt, M/U.
Erickson, A., Sgt, Pilot.
Evans, J., P/O, W/Op.
Ezard, G., Sgt, M/U.

F
Farlie, C., Sgt, R/G.
Farmer, H., Sgt, B/A.
Faulder, E., F/O, B/A.
Fawcett, S., Sgt, R/G.
Fawsitt, R., F/Sgt, R/G.
Fenning, P., F/O, M/U.
Fenwick, F., F/Sgt, R/G.
Fenwick, S., Sgt, F/E.
Ferguson, F., Sgt, SWO.
Fields, J., Sgt, M/U.
Finlaysen, A., W/O, R/G.
Finnimore, M., Sgt, Pilot.
Fisher, J., F/O, W/Op.
Fisher, R., Sgt, Pilot.
Fitch, A., Sgt, F/E.
Fitchett, H., Sgt, W/Op.
Fletcher, W., P/O, Nav.
Fludder, F., Sgt, F/E.
Forbes, R., Sgt, M/U.
Forsythe, J., Sgt, F/E.
Fortin, J., F/O, SWO.
Fowler, L., F/O, Nav.
Fowler, R., Sgt, W/Op.
Fox, B., Sgt, M/U.
Fraser, A., Sgt, M/U.
Francis, L., F/O, B/A.
Freestone, S., F/Sgt, Pilot.

Freeman-Fielding, C., Sgt, R/G.
French, W., Sgt, W/Op.
Fuller, A., Sgt, F/E.
Fuller, K., F/Lt, R/G.
Fuller, W., F/Sgt, B/A.

G

Gandee, G., F/Sgt, W/Op.
Gartland, G., F/Sgt, R/G.
Gavin, K., W/O, B/A.
Gee, F., F/Sgt, W/Op.
George, R., Sgt, F/E.
Ghigi, W., Sgt, R/G.
Gibbons, J., Sgt, W/Op.
Gibson, G., F/O, B/A.
Gibson, J., F/Sgt, W/Op.
Gilbert, R., P/O, Pilot.
Giles, S., W/O, SWO.
Gilpin, J., F/Sgt, M/U.
Gilsen, D., F/O, Nav.
Goldplatt, J., F/Sgt, B/A.
Glossop, C., P/O, Nav.
Gordon, M., F/O, Nav.
Gore, K., Sgt, R/G.
Goss, D., Sgt, Nav.
Goulding, H., Sgt, M/U.
Goulding, J., Sgt, Nav.
Goulding, F., P/O, Nav.
Graham, J., Sgt, R/G.
Green, G., Sgt, F/E.
Green, H., F/Sgt, Pilot.
Green, J., Sgt, Nav.
Green, J., Sgt, R/G.
Greenhalgh, T., Sgt, W/Op.
Greenwood, D., F/Sgt, M/U.
Gregory, C., F/Sgt, F/E.
Gregson, N., Sgt, M/U.
Grimwood, P., Sgt, M/U.
Grout, J., Sgt, F/E.
Gumbril, M., P/O, M/U.
Guthrie, E., F/Lt, Pilot.
Guy, I., Sgt, Nav.
Gyles, A., Sgt, B/A.

H

Hagues, C., F/O, Pilot.
Hales, R., F/O, B/A.
Hall, C., F/O, B/A.
Hallbrooks, K., F/Sgt, W/Op.
Halliwell, D., F/O, SWO.
Hamilton, D., P/O, F/E.
Hamilton, G., F/Sgt, Nav.
Hammond, D., F/Sgt, F/E.
Hancock, W., F/O, Pilot.
Hankins, M., F/Lt, Pilot.

Hanna, A., Sgt, B/A.
Hardacre, D., F/O, B/A.
Hardie, A., F/O, B/A.
Hardin, A., P/O, W/Op.
Hardman, J., Sgt, M/U.
Harker, E., F/O, Pilot.
Harlem, A., F/Sgt, Pilot.
Harpur, R., Sgt, R/G.
Harris, E., Sgt, R/G.
Harris, M., F/Sgt, SWO.
Harrison, H., P/O, Pilot.
Hart, T., Sgt, F/E.
Hartwright, F., Sgt, Nav.
Harvey, E., Sgt, M/U.
Hastings, J., F/Sgt, F/E.
Hathaway, H., Sgt, B/A.
Hawkseworth, J., Sgt, F/E.
Haylett, G., Sgt, W/Op.
Hazlett, K., W/O, W/Op.
Heath, G., Sgt, Nav.
Hedley, D., Sgt, F/E.
Heigon, G., Sgt, SWO.
Henderson, C., F/Sgt, B/A.
Henderson, R., Sgt, F/E.
Hide, R., Sgt, W/Op.
Hiddlestone, A., Sgt, B/A.
Higginbottom, J., Sgt, M/U.
Higgins, T., Sgt, B/A.
Higginson, A., F/Sgt, Pilot.
Higginson, D., F/Sgt, Nav.
Hill, H., P/O, Nav.
Hilton, F., Sgt, W/Op.
Hiscott, W., F/O, B/A.
Hockley, T., Sgt, Pilot.
Hodgson, J., F/O, SWO.
Hodgson, M., Sgt, Pilot.
Holder, A., F/O, M/U.
Hollingsworth, A., Sgt, W/Op.
Holmes, J., W/O, W/Op.
Holmes, J., W/O, SWO.
Holmes, N., P/O, Pilot.
Holmes, W., Sgt, Pilot.
Holt, P., Sgt, Pilot.
Honeyman, H., P/O, Nav.
Hooper, L., F/O, W/Op.
Horton, D., Sgt, M/U.
Horton, G., F/Sgt, W/Op.
Howe, B., Sgt, F/E.
Howe, H., P/O, F/E.
Howard, L., W/Cdr, Pilot.
Hudson, S., Sgt, R/G.
Hughes, H., P/O, B/A.
Hughes, C., F/Sgt, R/G.
Hughes, D., W/O, SWO.
Hughes, H., F/Sgt, B/A.

Hughes, J., Sgt, F/E.
Hughes, R., Sgt, Nav.
Hulme, B., Sgt, Nav.
Humby, K., S/Ldr, DFC, Pilot.
Humphries, W., Sgt, Pilot.
Hunt, E., Sgt, R/G.
Hunter, L., F/Sgt, B/A.
Hunter, R., F/Sgt, R/G.
Hutton, C., Sgt, M/U.
Hyde, S., F/O, R/G.
Hyde, S., F/Sgt, W/Op.

I

Ignatiuk, F., F/Sgt, M/U.
Iles, R., F/O, Pilot.
Inkley, J., P/O, F/E.
Irvine, R., W/O, W/Op.
Ison, J., P/O, Nav.
Ivory, J., F/Sgt, Pilot.

J

Jackson, J., P/O, M/U.
Jackson, W., Sgt, W/Op.
Jenkins, J., F/Lt, Pilot.
Jeffries, A., Sgt, R/G.
Jepson, H., F/Lt, Pilot.
Johnson, H., Sgt, Nav.
Johnson, R., F/Sgt, Nav.
Jones, E., Sgt, B/A.
Jones, W., Sgt, W/Op.
Jones, W., W/O, SWO.
Jones, W., Sgt, B/A.
Jordan, A., Sgt, M/U.
Judkins, E., Sgt, W/Op.
Julian, W., Sgt, Nav.

K

Keen, N., W/O, Pilot.
Kelly, E., Sgt, F/E.
Kelly, M., Sgt, F/E.
Kemp, J., Sgt, W/Op.
Kemp, R., Sgt, M/U.
Kendall, N., F/Sgt, Nav.
Kennall, B., Sgt, B/A.
Kennedy, I., Sgt, F/Eng.
Kennedy, R., F/Sgt, B/A.
Kenning, L., Sgt, F/E.
Kerr, J., P/O, W/Op.
Kesselman, M., F/Sgt, Nav.
Kettle, P., Sgt, B/A.
Kettles, W., P/O, Nav.
Keyes, R., P/O, W/Op.
Kidd, J., Sgt, F.E.
Killin, J., Sgt, R/G.
King, A., F/Lt, Pilot.

King, C., F/O, Pilot.
King, H., Sgt, M/U.
Kirkbright, R., Sgt, B/A.
Kitson, C., P/O, Nav.
Knight, S., Sgt, B/A.
Knight, W., S/Ldr, Pilot.
Knights, R., Sgt, M/U.
Knowles, A., F/Sgt, Pilot.
Kyle, T., F/Sgt, Pilot.
Kynaston, E., F/O, Nav.

L

Laird, R., F/O, B/A.
Lambert, A., Sgt, R/G.
Lambert, L., F/Sgt, F/E.
Lamberts, L., Sgt, F/E.
Lambourne, H., F/Sgt, W/Op.
Lampkin, H., F/O, Pilot.
Lane, C., W/O, W/Op.
Lane, W., F/O, SWO.
Langley, W., F/Sgt, B/A.
Lattimer, W., Sgt, R/G.
Laurence, L., Sgt, B/A.
Lauritz, B., F/O, B/A.
Lawrence, ?, P/O, F/E.
Lawton, D., F/O, SWO.
Leibson, C., F/Sgt, B/A.
Lemon, F., Sgt, F/E.
Lewis, E., Sgt, F/E.
Lewis, L., P/O, R/G.
Levers, R., Sgt, Nav.
Leveridge, B., P/O, W/Op.
Lind, R., Sgt, Pilot.
Little, A., F/O, SWO.
Little, E., F/O, SWO.
Littler, A., P/O, SWO.
Livingstone, J., Sgt, W/Op.
Loak, A., Sgt, R/G.
Lockett, D., F/Sgt, R/G.
Lofthouse, F., W/O, SWO.
Loth, J., F/Sgt, W/Op.
Loveland, A., Sgt, F/E.
Lowe, C., Sgt, R/G.
Lowry, J., F/Sgt, W/Op.
Lucas, D., Sgt, F/E.
Lumsdaine, L., S/Ldr, Pilot.
Lunt, S., F/Sgt, W/Op.
Lywood, C., Sgt, B/A.

M

Mackenzie-Ross, G., Sgt, W/Op.
Maden, F., F/O, Nav.
Makey, F., F/Sgt, R/G.
Makey, W., Sgt, F/E.
Makin, D., F/O, Pilot.

Malthouse, W., W/O, W/Op.
Marriot, D., F/O, Nav.
Marshall, A., Sgt, Nav.
Marshall, F., W/O, SWO.
Marshall, K., F/O, Pilot.
Marshall, R., P/O, W/Op.
Mathieson, D., F/Sgt, Nav.
Martin, B., P/O, M/U.
Martin, G., Sgt, W/Op.
Martin, J., W/O, R/G.
Matthews, A., Sgt, Nav.
Matthews, W., P/O, B/A.
Maw, C., Sgt, B/A.
Mayfield, P., Sgt, M/U.
Mazolletti, R., F/Sgt, W/Op.
Meekins, A., Sgt, W/Op.
Melhuish, R., Sgt, F/E.
Mellor, J., F/Sgt, W/Op.
Menere, D., F/Sgt, M/U.
Merry, P., Sgt, B/A.
Merryfull, C., F/O, Pilot.
Meson, E., P/O, B/A.
McAllister, D., Sgt, R/G.
McCall, T., Sgt, F/E.
McCann, J., F/O, B/A.
McColl, K., F/O, Pilot.
McCorkindale, J., F/Lt, R/G.
McDonnall, H., F/Sgt, B/A.
McFadyen, K., Sgt, W/Op.
McGarrigle, S., Sgt, F/E.
McGregor, D., Sgt, W/Op.
McIlroy, D., F/O, SWO.
McKenzie, L., F/O, B/A.
McKenzie-Ross, C., Sgt, W/Op.
McLaren, L., F/Sgt, B/A.
McLaughlin, P., F/Sgt, B/A.
McLeod, R., F/Sgt, R/G.
McMillan, E., F/O, M/U.
McNamara, E., F/O, Pilot.
McNicol, B., Sgt, B/A.
McPherson, E., Sgt, M/U.
McVeigh, H., Sgt, R/G.
Middle, T., F/Sgt, B/A.
Miles, R., Sgt, Nav.
Miller, J., P/O, Nav.
Milsom, G., F/Sgt, Pilot.
Minns, M., F/O, Nav.
Mison, D., Sgt, M/U.
Mitchell, L., Sgt, F/E.
Mitchell, R., W/O, M/U.
Mitchell, W., W/O, Nav.
Moignard, ?, Sgt, W/Op.
Molloy, M., F/Lt, R/G.
Monk, P., Sgt, R/G.
Moore, C., F/Sgt, W/Op.

Moore, D., F/Sgt, Pilot.
Moore, D., Sgt, M/U.
Moore, J., F/Sgt, Nav.
Morall, R., F/Sgt, Nav.
Morgan, B., F/Sgt, Nav.
Morgan, C., Sgt, R/G.
Morgan, E., Sgt, M/U.
Morgan, G., Sgt, R/G.
Morgan, R., Sgt, M/U.
Morris, D., Sgt, M/U.
Moses, P., Sgt, Pilot.
Mossie, R., P/O, Nav.
Moverley, J., Sgt, B/A.
Munro, C., F/Sgt, B/A.
Murphy, J., Sgt, B/A.
Murra, A., Sgt, F/E.
Murray, G., W/O, R/G.
Murray, G., F/Sgt, Nav.
Murray, J., F/Lt, Pilot.

N

Nairn, C., F/Sgt, B/A.
Nayes, W., Sgt, W/Op.
Naylor, J., Sgt, R/G.
Naylor, T., F/O, B/A.
Newcombe, K., Sgt, Nav.
Newsome, H., P/O, R/G.
Newton, A., Sgt, R/G.
Nichols, T., P/O, SWO.
Night, S., R/G.
Nightingale, J., F/O, SWO.
Nixon, A., Sgt, R/G.
Nixon, G., Sgt, R/G.
Noble, G., F/Lt, Pilot.
Nolde, E., P/O, M/U.
Noon-Ward, R., F/O, Nav.
Norgate, M., Sgt, Nav.
Norman, J., F/O, SWO.
Norton, R., Sgt, F/E.
Noyes, W., Sgt, W/Op.

O

Oakley, A., F/Sgt, W/Op.
O'Connell, J., Sgt, R/G.
O'Conner, K., F/O, Pilot.
O'Dell, E., P/O, Nav.
Odgers, T., Sgt, Pilot.
Oliver, T., Sgt, F/E.
Oram, A., F/O, SWO.
Osbourne, J., Sgt, Nav.
Overbury, W., Sgt, Nav.
Owen, F., F/Sgt, Nav.
Owen, J., Sgt, F/E.
Owen, R., W/O, SWO.
Oxley, D., Sgt, F/E.

P

Pacholka, W., F/O, B/A.
Paddon, M., F/O, Pilot.
Pallant, S., Sgt, M/U.
Palmer, C., W/O, Pilot.
Palumbo, G., P/O, B/A.
Panichelli, P., F/Sgt, F/E.
Panton, S., Sgt, W/Op.
Paradis, J., F/O, SWO.
Park, C., Sgt, SWO.
Parker, B., Sgt, R/G.
Parkinson, C., Sgt, F/E.
Parsons, H., Sgt, F/E.
Parsons, J., P/O, Pilot.
Parsons, W., P/O, SWO.
Partner, R., F/O, B/A.
Pask, O., Sgt, F/E.
Patton, A., F/Sgt, B/A.
Paquin, J., Sgt, W/Op.
Payne, C., Sgt, M/U.
Payne, P., F/Sgt, B/A.
Pearce, J., F/Sgt, M/U.
Pearce, P., P/O, Pilot.
Pearse, L., Sgt, R/G.
Peckham, J., F/O, F/E.
Pesslar, S., F/Lt, B/A.
Pettie, N., P/O, Nav.
Pennycock, D., Sgt, B/A.
Perry, J., F/O, B/A.
Perkins, L., F/Sgt, R/G.
Pettit, W., F/O, Pilot.
Phillips, L., F/Sgt, R/G.
Phipps, J., F/Sgt, R/G.
Pimlott, G., Sgt, F/E.
Pinchin, K., Sgt, Pilot.
Plaster, E., Sgt, B/A.
Plumtree, A., Sgt, F/E.
Plunkett, R., F/O, Nav.
Podd, F., P/O, B/A.
Polichek, V., F/Sgt, R/G.
Pool, R., W/O, SWO.
Porter, W., W/O, Pilot.
Potts, J., F/Sgt, F/E.
Poutney, D., Sgt, R/G.
Powell, D., F/Sgt, SWO.
Powell, K., P/O, Pilot.
Powrie, A., F/O, SWO.
Prangle, V., Sgt, Pilot.
Pratt, H., Sgt, M/U.
Prince, W., F/Sgt, Nav.
Prout, E., F/Sgt, Nav.
Prout, G., Sgt, R/G.
Pullee, L., Sgt, W/Op
Purkis, T., W/O, W/Op.
Pym, F., Sgt, Nav.

Q

Quar, A., Sgt, M/U.

R

Rawlings, F., Sgt, F/E.
Read, F., F/Sgt, M/U.
Read, H., Sgt, R/G.
Reade, F., P/O, Nav.
Rees, R., F/Sgt, Nav.
Reeves, R., F/Sgt, B/A.
Reidy, J., F/Sgt, Pilot.
Renne, J., Sgt, B/A.
Rennie, S., Sgt, F/E.
Reynolds, C., W/O, W/Op.
Rice, K., Sgt, F/E.
Richards, H., W/O, SWO.
Richardson, J., Sgt, W/Op.
Richmond, A., Sgt, W/Op.
Rickwood, F/Sgt, M/U.
Riggs, B., Sgt, W/Op.
Roberts, G., F/Sgt, Nav.
Roberts, J., Sgt, R/G.
Roberts, J., Sgt, Nav.
Roberts, P., Sgt, Nav.
Roberts, P., Sgt, M/U.
Robertson, L., F/Sgt, Pilot.
Robertson, R., Sgt, SWO.
Robbins, S., W/O, Pilot.
Robinson, K., F/Sgt, Pilot.
Robinson, S., P/O, B/A.
Robotham, K., Sgt, R/G.
Rodgers, G., F/O, W/Op.
Rourke, T., F/O, B/A.
Rouse, F., P/O, SWO.
Rowe, F., F/Sgt, SWO.
Rudge, A., W/O, R/G.
Russell, J., W/O, Nav.
Russell, J., P/O, F/E.

S

Saddler, R., Sgt, W/Op.
Sage, R., F/Sgt, R/G.
Salter, A., F/O, B/A.
Sanders, A., Sgt, M/U.
Sanderson, R., Sgt, B/A.
Sartain, C., Sgt, M/U.
Saunders, R., W/O, SWO.
Savage, R., F/Sgt, Nav.
Savegar, D., Sgt, M/U.
Sawdy, T., P/O, Pilot.
Seddon, W., Sgt, R/G.
Segal, M., F/O, B/A.
Sellers, P., Sgt, W/Op.
Serjeant, J., Sgt, W/Op.
Sewell, H., Sgt, R/G.

Scarpa, E., Sgt, Nav.
Schofield, E., F/O, B/A.
Scopes, A., F/O, SWO.
Scott, D., Sgt, M/U.
Scott, T., Sgt, R/G.
Scottie, ?, F/Sgt, M/U.
Sharples, W., W/O, Pilot.
Shaw, G., F/Sgt, W/Op.
Sheldrick, K., W/O, B/A.
Shelly, P., F/Sgt, Nav.
Shepherd, A., Sgt, M/U.
Sherwin, R., F/Sgt, Nav.
Shields, A., Sgt, F/E.
Shields, F., Sgt, M/U.
Short, L., F/Sgt, W/Op.
Short, W., F/Lt, Pilot.
Short, W., Sgt, F/E.
Shortens, A., Sgt, W/Op.
Shorttle, J., Sgt, Pilot.
Simon, G., F/Lt, Pilot.
Simpson, N., F/O, B/A.
Sinclair, A., F/Sgt, W/Op.
Sinclair, P. Sgt, Pilot.
Simmons, V., F/Sgt, W/Op.
Skinner, B., Sgt, F/E.
Slade, B., P/O, M/U.
Sleven, A., Sgt, M/U.
Sloan, J., W/O, W/Op.
Smith, A., Sgt, Nav.
Smith, D., Sgt, M/U.
Smith, F., Sgt, R/G.
Smith, G., Sgt, Nav.
Smith, H., F/Sgt, Nav.
Smith, H., F/O, Nav.
Smith, J., Sgt, F/E.
Smith, N., F/O, Nav.
Smith, P., F/Sgt, W/Op.
Smith, R., P/O, Nav.
Smith, R., Sgt, W/Op.
Smith, R., F/O, SWO.
Smither, L., F/Sgt, R/G.
Sneddon, W., Sgt, F/E.
Snowball, J., Sgt, SWO.
Snowdon, J., P/O, M/U.
Southgate, V., Sgt, F/E.
Sowden, J., Sgt, W/Op.
Spaulding, A., F/Lt, Pilot.
Speed, K., Sgt, F/E.
Spring, J., Sgt, Pilot.
Stallard, R., Sgt, R/G.
Stanley, P., Sgt, W/Op.
Stanten, F., Sgt, W/Op.
Staples, M., F/Sgt, R/G.
Stead, J., F/O, Nav.
Stearman, E., Sgt, M/U.

Stenner, H., Sgt, F/E.
Stevens, J., Sgt, R/G.
Stevenson, P., Sgt, Pilot.
Stevenson, T., Sgt, F/E.
Steward, F/Sgt, Nav.
Stimpson, M., F/O, B/A.
Stock, N., F/Lt, B/A.
Stockwell, C., Sgt, B/A.
Stokes, C., P/O, R/G.
Stokes, R., F/Sgt, R/G.
Stokes, R., F/O, M/U.
Stokie, J., Sgt, R/G.
Strachan, J., F/Sgt, W/Op.
Street, K., F/Sgt, DFM, R/G
Stringer, G., Sgt, R/G.
Stubbings, R., Sgt, Nav.
Sturrock, H., F/Lt, Pilot.
Sullivan, A., W/O, W/Op.
Sullivan, C., Sgt, W/Op.
Summers, H., F/O, B/A.
Sutton, B., W/O, SWO.
Swadling, K., F/Sgt, B/A.
Sweeney, W., P/O, B/A.
Switzer, L., Sgt, W/Op.

T
Tapper, D., W/O, B/A.
Tate, R., F/Sgt, Nav.
Taylor, F., F/Sgt, M/U.
Taylor, H., Sgt, B/A.
Taylor, J., F/Lt, R/G.
Taylor, J., Sgt, F/E.
Taylor, L., P/O, SWO.
Thomas, R., Sgt, Nav.
Thomas, R. Sgt, B/A.
Thompson, A., Sgt, M/U.
Thompson, K., P/O, Nav.
Thompson, R., F/Sgt, Nav.
Thompson, W., Sgt, W/Op.
Thorneycroft, F., F/Sgt, Nav.
Thurlow, J., F/Lt, Pilot.
Tilley, G., F/Sgt, W/Op.
Todd, M., Sgt, Nav.
Todd, R., F/Lt, Pilot.
Tolmei, D., F/O, B/A.
Tomlinson, H., F/O, W/Op.
Townsend, L., P/O, Nav.
Townsend, S., Sgt, W/Op.
Townsend, T., Sgt, B/A.
Townshend, J., P/O, W/Op.
Trafford, R., Sgt, B/A.
Trezise, H., F/Sgt, R/G.
Trussell, J., Sgt, R/G.
Turner, A., F/Lt, Pilot.
Turner, D., Sgt, B/A.

Turner, W., Sgt, M/U.
Twaddle, A., F/O, W/Op.
Tye, G., W/O, M/U.
Tyrell, E., W/O, W/Op.

V
Van-Fleet, D., F/Sgt, M/U.
Van-Welie, A., F/Lt, Pilot.
Vaughan, L., Sgt, B/A.
Voce, S., W/O, SWO.

W
Wain, E., F/Sgt, W/Op.
Wake, T., Sgt, F/E.
Wakeling, A., Sgt, W/Op.
Waldorf, L., Sgt, Pilot.
Walford, T., F/Sgt, Pilot.
Walker, A., F/Lt, R/G.
Walker, D., P/O, SWO.
Walker, K., Sgt, W/Op.
Waller, J., Sgt, Pilot.
Ward, A., P/O, Pilot.
Ward, A., Sgt, B/A.
Warden, T., Sgt, F/E.
Waterfield, J., F/O, Pilot.
Watson, P., Sgt, R/G.
Wattie, C., P/O, Nav.
Watts, F., Sgt, W/Op.
Watts, J., Sgt, F/E.
Weatherill, E., Sgt, R/G.
Webber, D., Sgt, Nav.
Webster, B., Sgt, Nav.
Webster, W., Sgt, W/Op.
Weeks, F., Sgt, W/Op.
Weeks, R., F/Sgt, W/Op.
Welch, B., P/O, Nav.
Weller, D., Sgt, B/A.
Wells, T., Sgt, R/G.
Werner, S., W/O, Pilot.
Weston, A., Sgt, F/E.
Wharmby, T., Sgt, R/G.
Whealing, A., F/O, Nav.
Wheeler, D., F/Sgt, W/Op.
Wheeler, E., P/O, Nav.
Wheeker, L., F/O, Nav.
Whimpenny, A., Sgt, R/G.
Whitbread, L., Sgt, M/U.
White, C., Sgt, W/Op.
White, J., F/Sgt, M/U.
White, M., F/O, Nav.
Whitehouse, B., Sgt, M/U.
Whitmarsh, F., Sgt, Nav.
Whittington, L., F/Sgt, B/A.
Whittleston, R., P/O, Nav.
Whitton, J., F/O, Nav.

Whitworth, C., Sgt, F/E.
Widdecombe, R., P/O, Pilot.
Wightman, G., Sgt, SWO.
Wilde, A., Sgt, F/E.
Wilde, G., F/O, Nav.
Wilkes, A., F/Sgt, W/Op.
Wilkes, K., F/Sgt, R/G.
Wilkes, T., F/Sgt, Nav.
Wilkes, T., Sgt, M/U.
Wilkinson, R., Sgt, R/G.???
Wilkinson, K., Sgt, R/G.???
Wills, A., F/Lt, Pilot.
Williams, C., Sgt, F/E.
Williams, G., F/O, Nav.
Williams, J., Sgt, F/E.
Williams, L., Sgt, F/E.
Williams, R., Sgt, F/E.
Wilson, D., Sgt, SWO.
Wilson, D., F/Sgt, B/A.
Wilson, G., F/Sgt, B/A.
Wilson, H., F/O, Nav.
Wilson, J., Sgt, B/A.
Wingood, A., F/O, Pilot.
Wingrove, F., Sgt, F/E.
Wingrove, T., Sgt, F/E.
Winter, C., F/Lt, Pilot.
Winterhalder, R, F/Sgt, Nav.
Winterton, L., Sgt, W/Op.
Wiseman, A., P/O, SWO.
Wiseman, E., F/Lt, Pilot.
Witney, G., Sgt, R/G.
Wolf, L., P/O, Nav.
Wood, A., F/O, Nav.
Wood, D., Sgt, W/Op.
Wood, K., F/Sgt, R/G.
Wood, S., F/Sgt, W/Op.
Woods, C., P/O, B/A.
Woods, F., F/O, B/A.
Woods, R., F/Sgt, W/Op.
Woodruff, H., Sgt, B/A
Wray, ?, G/Cpt, Pilot.
Wright, G., Sgt, M/U.
Wright, H., F/Sgt, B/A.
Wright, L., F/Sgt, F/E.
Wynne-Powell, G., S/Ldr, Pilot.

Y
Yates, G., F/O, B/A.
Young, A., F/O, R/G.

Appendix 6:
Squadron Roll of Honour

A.

Adam, Russell Edwin, F/Sgt, (27 yrs), RCAF. 31 August 1943. Berlin 1939-45 War Cemetery, 5.A.32-37.

Adams, Andrew Mill, Sgt, (21 yrs), RAFVR. 25 June 1945. Wells-next-the-Sea Cemetery, Norfolk, Grave 376.

Allen, Keith Fowler, F/Sgt, (21 yrs), RAAF. 12 March 1944. Naujac-sur-Mer Communal Cemetery, France, D.6 Coll Grave 2.

Allson, Alan Ernest, F/Lt, (21 yrs), RAFVR. 10 February 1944. Lyminge (SS Mary & Ethelburga) Churchyard, Kent.

Andrews, Clifford Richard, F/Sgt, RCAF. 12 June 1943. Runnymede Memorial, Panel 181.

Atherton, Cyril, Sgt, (31 yrs), RAFVR. 28 January 1944. Esbjerg (Fourfelt) Cemetery, Denmark, A.8.22.

Austin, Horace William, Sgt, (20 yrs), RAFVR. 24 May 1943. Uden War Cemetery, Netherlands, 4.F.13.

B.

Baker, Ronald Valentine, Sgt, (21 yrs), RAFVR. 7 February 1943. Guidel Communal Cemetery, France, Row 3, Grave 18.

Barham, Leonard Alfred, F/O, (29 yrs), RAFVR. 25 September 1944. Cawston Cemetery, Norfolk, Sec H, Grave 8.

Barras, Mark Sidney, Sgt, (19 yrs), RAFVR. 24 August 1943. Runnymede Memorial, Panel 141.

Barrie, Frederick William, Sgt, (22 yrs). RAFVR. 1 December 1943. Runnymede Memorial, Panel 141.

Barrow, Leonard Richard, Sgt, (21 yrs), RAFVR. 12 June 1943. Runnymede Memorial, Panel 141.

Barton, Benjamin Joseph, Sgt, (23 yrs), RAFVR. 28 August 1943. Durnbach War Cemetery, Germany, 9.B.15.

Bell, Claude Stephen, Sgt, (35 yrs), RAFVR. 14 June 1943. Guidel Communal Cemetery, France, Row 5, Grave 45-46.

Bell, John Morling, F/O, RAFVR . 13 February 1943. Guidel Communal Cemetery, France, Row 5, Grave 4.

Bellhouse, William Henry, Sgt, RAFVR. 12 June 1943. Runnymede Memorial, Panel 142.

Bolton, William Frederick, W/O, (23 yrs), RAFVR. 3 May 1945. Kiel War Cemetery, Germany, 2.E.6.

Bottomley, Ronald, LAC, (21 yrs), 7 August 1943. Leeds (Harehills) Cemetery, Yorkshire, Sec.G Coll Grave 21.

Boyden, William Henry, Sgt, (33 yrs), RAFVR. 27 September 1943. Hanover War Cemetery, Germany, 6.F.4.

Bradley, Arthur Andrew, F/Sgt, (23 yrs), RAFVR. 3 May 1945. Kiel War Cemetery, Germany, 2.E.8-1.

Brittain, Francis Charles, W/O, (22 yrs), RAFVR. 17 June 1944. Runnymede Memorial, Panel 213.

Brooks, William Ernest, F/Lt, RAFVR. 3 May 1945. Kiel War Cemetery, Germany. 2.E.16.

Brown, Edward George, F/O, (age 21), RAFVR. 4 March 1944. Gemeaux Communal Cemetery, Cotes d'Or, France.

Burton, Edward, Sgt, (22 yrs), RAFVR. 14 June 1943. Guidel Communal Cemetery, France, Row 5, Grave 45-46.

C.

Caine, Gerrard, Sgt, (22 yrs), RAFVR. 16 February 1944. Mazargues War Cemetery, Marseilles, France, 3.D.Coll.5-6.

Calcraft, Norman James, Sgt, RAFVR. 24 August 1943. Berlin 1939-45 War Cemetery, 4.E.17.

Campbell, James Duncan, P/O, (22 yrs), RCAF. 16 September 1944. Runnymede Memorial, Panel 249.

Cantwell, Reginald Horace, Sgt, RAFVR. 12 March 1944. Naujac-sur-Mer Communal Cemetery, France, D.6 Coll Grave 2.

Carlson, Carl, 2Lt, US Army. 1 December 1943. Ardennes American Cemetery, Neupre, Belguim, B.39.8.

Chambers, Francis Thomas, Sgt, (29 yrs), RAFVR. 3 May 1945. Kiel War Cemetery, Germany, 2.E.8-13.

Chatwin, Francis Reginald, P/O, (26 yrs), RAFVR. 25 September 1944. Birmingham Municipal Crematorium.

Clifford, Dennis John, Sgt, (20 yrs), RAFVR. 13 March 1943. Runnymede Memorial, Panel 145.

Clark, James, Sgt, (20 yrs), RAFVR. 12 March 1944. Naujac-sur-Mer Communal Cemetery, France, D.6 Coll Grave 2.

Clay, Leonard Douglas, F/O, (26 yrs), RAFVR. 27 September 1943. Hanover War Cemetery, Germany, 6.F.1-3.

Clifton, Charles, P/O, (22 yrs), RAFVR. 28 January 1944. Kirkeby Cemetery, Denmark, Coll.911-913.

Cook, Ronald Hermond Downes, F/O, (30 yrs), RAFVR. 13 May 1943. Harderwijk General Cemetery, Netherlands, Plot 2, Grave 32.

Cormack, Archibald McKay, Sgt, RAFVR. 13 March 1943. Glasgow (Sandymount) Cemetery, Section T, Grave 2513.

Costello, Ralph Matthew, W/O, (25 yrs), RCAF. 24 May 1943. Uden War Cemetery, Netherlands, 4.F.12.

Coupe, Harold, F/S, (29 yrs), RAFVR. 28 May 1943. Reichswald Forest War Cemetery, Germany, Grave 15F.5-8.

Cowie, Arthur, F/L, DFM, (25 yrs), RAFVR. 13 February 1943. Guidel Communal Cemetery, France, Row 5, Grave 3.

Crawford, William Arthur, Sgt, (19 yrs), RAFVR. 31 August 1943. Berlin 1939-45 War Cemetery, 5.A.32-37.

Crick, Lawrence Eric, Sgt, (21 yrs), RAFVR. 4 March 1944. Is-sur-Tille Communal Cemetery, Cotes d'Or, France.

Croft, Kenneth Norman John, F/O, (22 yrs), RAFVR. 3 May 1945. Kiel War Cemetery, Germany, 2.E.14.

Cuff, Edward Harold, Sgt, (20 yrs), RAFVR. 24 August 1943. Berlin 1939-45 War Cemetery, Joint Grave 5.A.4-5.

Cunningham, Gordan Strachan, F/Sgt, RAFVR. 1 December 1943. Runnymede Memorial, Panel 136.

D.

Dale, Thomas Wilson, P/O, (25 yrs), RNZAF. 17 June 1944. Runnymede Memorial, Panel 263.

Dalzell, William Madine, Sgt, (20 yrs), RAF. 28 August 1943. Durnbach War Cemetery, Germany, 2.A.15.

Davey, Alan John, F/Sgt, (24 yrs), RAAF. 31 August 1943. Berlin 1939-45 War Cemetery, 5.A.32-37.

Davies, Lancelot Walter, Sgt, (28 yrs), RAFVR. 21 August 1943. Durnbach War Cemetery, Germany, 9.B.14.

Dawe, Harry Victor, Sgt, RAFVR. 1 December 1943. Runnymede Memorial, Panel 147.

Dennison, Gordon Joshua, P/O, (22 years), RCAF. 16 September 1944. Runnymede Memorial, Panel 249.

Dent, Ian Wilshire, W/O, (23 yrs), RAAF. 25 June 1945. Cambridge City Cemetery, Grave 15706.

Douglas, Ronald Thomas, F/O, (23 yrs), RAFVR. 26 May 1943. Jonkerbos War Cemetery, Nijmegen, Netherlands, 20.A.3.

Drayton, Victor Alfred, Sgt, (33 yrs), RAFVR. 28 August 1943. Durnbach War Cemetery, Germany, 2.A.17-19.

E.

Easey, George, Sgt, (20 yrs), RAFVR. 13 February 1943. Guidel Communal Cemetery, France, Row 5 Grave 1.

Ebsworth, William Howell, Sgt, (34 yrs), RAFVR. 12 March 1944. Naujac-sur-Mer Communal Cemetery, France, D.6 Coll Grave 2.

Edwards, Russell Irwin, F/Sgt, RCAF. 13 March 1943. Bergen General Cemetery, Netherlands, Plot 2 Row C Grave 10.

Ellis, Royston Hazeldine George, Sgt, (27 yrs), RAFVR. 31 August 1943. Eindhoven (Woensel) General Cemetery, Netherlands, EE.103

Elphick, Harry Eli, Sgt, (34 yrs), RAFVR. 31 August 1943. Eindhoven (Woensel) General Cemetery, Netherlands, EE.107.

Elsley, Henry Cecil, F/Sgt, (26 yrs), RAAF. 24 August 1943. Berlin 1939-45 War Cemetery, 5.A.3.

Ezard, George, Sgt, (31 yrs), RAFVR. 3 September 1943. Pornic War Cemetery, Loire Atlantique, France. 1.AB.11.

F.

Finlayson, Alexander Douglas, W/O, DFM, (29 yrs), RAAF. 31 August 1943. Eindhoven (Woensel) General Cemetery, Netherlands, EE.108.

Fisher, Russell Gardiner, F/O, (29 yrs), RAAF. 24 August 1943. Berlin 1939-45 War Cemetery, 5.A.1.

Forbes, Robert George Cameron, Sgt, (23 years), RAFVR. Berlin 1939-45 War Cemetery, Joint Grave 5.A.4-5.

G.

Gavin, Keith Alexander Cameron Munro, W/O, (22 yrs), RAFVR. 3 May 1945. Kiel War Cemetery, Germany, 2.E.17.

Gee, Frank Ernest, F/Sgt, (25 yrs), RAAF. 31 August 1943. Eindhoven (Woensel) General Cemetery, Netherlands, EE.106.

George, Herbert Royston, Sgt, (20 yrs), RAFVR. 10 February 1944. Cambridge City Cemetery, Grave 13714.

Gilbert, Reginald Campbell, F/O, RCAF. 3 September 1943. Pornic War Cemetery, Loire Atlantique, 1.AB.7.

Glover, Davis William, Sgt, (22 yrs), RAFVR. 28 May 1943. Reichswald Forest War Cemetery, Germany, Grave 15F.5-8.

Green, James William, Sgt, (22 yrs), RAFVR. 9 April 1943. Guidel Communal Cemetery, France, Row 5, Grave 30.

Greenwood, Desmond, F/Sgt, (20 yrs), RAFVR. 3 May 1945. Kiel War Cemetery, Germany, 2.E.8-13.

Gordon, Macdonald Stuart, F/O, (23 yrs), RCAF. 3 September 1943. Runnymede Memorial, Panel 173

Gregory, Cyril Elvett, F/Sgt, (20 yrs), RAF. 28 August 1943. Durnbach War Cemetery, Germany, 9.B.16.

Guy, Ronald Stevens, Sgt, (29 yrs), RAFVR. 6 February 1943. Runnymede Memorial, Panel 151.

H.

Harlem, Athol Asher, F/Sgt, (21 yrs), RAAF. 31 August 1943. Eindhoven (Woensel) General Cemetery, Netherlands, EE.104.

Hathaway, Herbert Thomas, Sgt, (19 yrs), RAFVR. 28 August 1943. Durnbach War Cemetery, Germany, Coll Grave 2.A.17-19.

Heggison, Andrew Dempster, F/Sgt, (23 yrs), RAFVR. 16 September 1944. Runnymede Memorial, Panel 218.

Herbert, Arthur, Sgt, (22 yrs), RAFVR. 24 May 1943. Uden War Cemetery, Netherlands, 4.F.11.

Henderson, Colin Silkirk, F/Sgt, (age 25), RNZAF. 25 September 1944. Cambridge City Cemetery, Grave 15327.

Higginbottom, John Critchley, Sgt, (21 yrs), RAFVR. 17 June 1944. Runnymede Memorial, Panel 231.

Higginson, Brian Purdy, F/Sgt, (22 yrs), RNZAF. 27 September 1943. Hanover War Cemetery, Germany, 6.F.6.

Hockley, Terence Frederick, Sgt, (26 yrs), RAFVR. 13 March 1943. Barkingside Cemetery, Ilford, Essex, Grave 1753.

Hodson, Maurice Albert Nicholas, P/O, (21 yrs), RAFVR. 27 September 1943. Hanover War Cemetery, Germany, 6.F.7.

Holder, Alfred Samuel John, F/O, DFC, (43 yrs), RAFVR. 3 May 1945. Kiel War Cemetery, Germany, 2.E.15.

Hudson, Richard Taylor Anthony, Sgt, (20 yrs), RAFVR. 28 May 1943. Reichswald Forest War Cemetery, Germany, Grave 18G.17.

Hughes, David Thomson, W/O, (28 yrs), RAF. 16 September 1944. Runnymede Memorial, Panel 214.

Hughes, Ronald, Sgt, (20 yrs), RAFVR. 13 May 1943. Harderwijk General Cemetery, Netherlands, Plot 2 Grave 26-30.

J.

Jackson, James Alexander, P/O, RAFVR. 16 February 1944. Mazargues War Cemetery, Marseilles, France, 3.D.Coll.5-6.

Jackson, William Edward, Sgt, (20 yrs), RAFVR. 12 June 1943. Runnymede Memorial, Panel 154.

Johnston, Andrew, Sgt, (20 yrs), RAFVR. 28 January 1944. Kirkeby Cemetery, Denmark, Coll.911-913.

Joisce, Leslie, Sgt, (24 yrs), RAF. 13 March 1943. Bedlington (Netherton Lane) Cemetery. Sec F Grave 1614C.

Jones, Elwyn Knowles, Sgt, (29 yrs), RAFVR. 13 February 1943. Guidel Communal Cemetery, Brittany, France, Row 5 Grave 2.

Jones, Leslie Morgan, Sgt, RAFVR. 12 March 1943. Runnymede Memorial, Panel 155.

Jones, Walter, Sgt, (20 yrs), RAFVR. 5 November 1943. Runnymede Memorial, Panel 155.

Julian, William Bailes, F/Sgt, (21 yrs), RAFVR. 31 August 1943. Eindhoven (Woensel) General Cemetery, Netherlands, EE.109

K.

Keeton, Anthony Edward, Sgt, (20 yrs), RAFVR. 7 February 1943. Guidel Communal Cemetery, Brittany, France, Row 3 Grave 17.

Kemp, John Leigh, Sgt, (20 yrs), RAFVR. 28 August 1943. Durnbach War Cemetery, Germany, Coll Grave 2.A.17-19.

Kendall, Norman, F/Sgt, (24 yrs), RAFVR. 24 August 1943. Berlin 1939-45 War Cemetery, 5.A.7.

Kennell, Brian James, Sgt, (21 yrs), RAF. 31 August 1943. Berlin 1939-45 War Cemetery, 5.A.32-37.

Kesselman, Murray, P/O, (21 yrs), RCAF. 16 September 1944. Runnymede Memorial, Panel 251.

Keyes, Robert Joseph, F/O, (24 yrs), RCAF. 13 February 1943. Guidel Communal Cemetery, Brittany, France, Row 5 Grave 6.

King, William John, F/Lt, RAF. 13 March 1943. Runnymede Memorial, Panel 119.

Knowles, John Alfred, F/Sgt, MID, (23 yrs), RAF. 1 December 1943. Frederikshavn Cemetery, Denmark, Grave 58.

L.

Lambert, Raymond, Sgt, (19 yrs), RAFVR. 13 March 1943. Runnymede Memorial ,Panel 156.

Lambourne, Henry Edward, F/Sgt, (21 yrs), RAAF. 16 February 1944. Mazargues War Cemetery, Marseilles, France, 3.D.Coll.5-6.

Langley, Lloyd George, P/O, RCAF. 16 September 1944. Runnymede Memorial, Panel 251.

Latimer, William McCreadie, Sgt, (19 yrs), RAFVR. 17 June 1944. Runnymede Memorial Panel 233.

Lewis, John Roger, F/Sgt, (21 yrs), RAFVR. 3 May 1945. Kiel War Cemetery, Germany, 2.E.18.

Lofthouse, Frank, W/O, (23), RAFVR. 17 June 1944. Runnymede Memorial, Panel 214.

Loth, Joseph, F/Sgt, (21 yrs), RAFVR. 3 May 1945. Kiel War Cemetery, Germany, 2.E.8-13.

Loveland, Ambrose William, Sgt, (31 yrs), RAFVR. 25 September 1944. West Wickham (St John the Baptist) Churchyard, Kent.

M.

Mackay, William Henry Vesey, P/O, (29 yrs), RAFVR. 3 May 1945. Kiel War Cemetery, Germany, 2.E.8-13

Makin, Dennis, F/O, (29 yrs), RAFVR. 26 May 1943. Jonkerbos War Cemetery, Netherlands, 20.A.4.

Massie, Robert John, F/O, (24 yrs), RAFVR. 24 August 1943. Runnymede Memorial, Panel 126.

Maw, Clifford Charles, F/Sgt, RCAF. 3 September 1943. Runnymede Memorial, Panel 185.

McLaren, Ian Nichol, F/Sgt, (24 yrs), RAFVR. 31 August 1943. Eindhoven (Woensel) General Cemetery, Netherlands, EE.105.

Menere, Douglas, F/Sgt, (20 yrs), RAAF. 5 November 1943. Runnymede Memorial, Panel 193.

Merry, Patrick Edward Kevin Daly, Sgt, (21 yrs), RAFVR. 12 June 1943. Runnymede Memorial, Panel 159.

Miles, Bertram William, P/O, (22 yrs), RAFVR. 10 February 1944. Walton & Weybridge (Weybridge) Cemetery, Grave 3991.

Mills, Thomas George David, F/Sgt, (27 yrs), RAAF. 12 March 1944. Naujac-sur-Mer Communal Cemetery, Bordeaux, France, D.6 Coll Grave 2.

Mitchell, William Connell, Sgt, RAFVR. 3 September 1943. Yves Communal Cemetery, Charente Maritime, France, Grave 7.

Morrison, William Hugh, F/Sgt, (31 yrs), RAAF. 24 September 1943. St John's Churchyard, Beck Row, Suffolk.

Moore, Donald Francis, P/O, (26 yrs), RAAF. 5 November 1943. Runnymede Memorial, Panel 191.

Moses, George, Sgt, (30 yrs), RAFVR. 6 February 1943. Runnymede Memorial, Panel 159.

Murray, Hugh George, W/O, (23 yrs), RAAF. 22 October 1943. Cambridge City Cemeter, Grave 13723.

N.

Nairn, Clifford Morton, P/O, (22 yrs), RAAF. 24 August 1943. Berlin 1939-45 War Cemetery, 5.A.6.

Naylor, John William, Sgt, (36 yrs), RAFVR. 25 September 1944. Gedney Hill (Holy Trinity) Churchyard, Lincolnshire.

Newman, Walter, Sgt, RAFVR. 22 January 1944. Kirkeby Cemetery, Denmark, Grave 910.

Newton, Arthur Thomas, Sgt, RAFVR. 3 September 1943. Runnymede Memorial, Panel 160.

Norgate, Morris John, Sgt, (22 yrs), RAFVR. 7 February 1943. Guidel Communal Cemetery, Brittany, France, Row 3 Grave 22.

Nunn, Douglas Arthur, Sgt, (21 yrs), RAFVR. 13 March 1943. Runnymede Memorial, Panel 160.

O.

O'Connor, Kevin Bernard, F/Lt, (29 yrs), RNZAF. 4 March 1944. Is-sur-Tille Communal Cemetery, Cotes d'Or, France.

Odgers, Thomas Rex, P/O, (29 yrs), RAAF. 28 August 1943. Durnbach War Cemetery, Germany, 9.B.12.

Ord, Thomas Edward, P/O, RAF. 28 January 1944. Kirkeby Cemetery, Denmark, Coll.911-913.

P.

Parker, Barton Thomas Eric, F/Sgt, (30 yrs), RNZAF. 28 August 1943. Durnbach War Cemetery, Germany, 9.B.18

Parkinson, Jeffrey Cyril Bert, Sgt, RAFVR. 24 August 1943. Berlin 1939-45 War Cemetery, 5.A.2.

Paquin, Joseph Hector, W/O, (33 yrs), RCAF. 9 April 1943. Runnymede Memorial, Panel 180.

Pennycook, David Coventry, Sgt, (21 yrs), RAFVR. 7 February 1943. Guidel Communal Cemetery, Brittany, France, Row 3 Grave 20.

Pinchin, Kenneth Albert, Sgt, (20 yrs), RAFVR. 9 April 1943. Runnymede Memorial, Panel 161.

Pool, Reginald Henry Alfred, W/O, RAFVR. 3 May 1945. Kiel War Cemetery, Germany, 2.E.8-13.

Powell, Kenneth, F/Lt, (24 yrs), RAFVR. 7 February 1943. Guidel Communal Cemetery, Brittany, France, Row 3, Grave 21.

Pym, Frederick Reginald, Sgt, RAFVR. 28 May 1943 Reichswald Forest War Cemetery, Germany, Grave 15.F.5-8.

Q.

Quar, Alfred John, Sgt, (21 yrs), RAFVR. 27 September 1943. Hanover War Cemetery, Germany, 6.F.5.

R.

Read, Howard Jack, Sgt, (22 yrs), RAFVR. 6 February 1943. Runnymede Memorial, Panel 162.

Rees, Ronald Ernest James, F/Sgt, (35 yrs), RAFVR. 28 August 1943. Durnbach War Cemetery, Germany, 9.B.13.

Rennie, Stanley Cunningham, Sgt, (20 yrs), RAFVR. 16 September 1944. Runnymede Memorial, Panel 236.

Richmond, Arthur, Sgt, (20 years), RAFVR. 5 November 1943. Runnymede Memorial, Panel 163.

Richardson, Jack Graydon, W/O, (20 yrs), RCAF. 12 March 1943. Runnymede Memorial, Panel 180.

Roberts, Prys Owen, Sgt, (19 yrs), RAFVR. 25 September 1944. Beddgelert New Cemetery, Row E Grave 1.

Robinson, Kevin Alphonsus, F/O, (21 yrs), RAAF. 16 February 1944. Mazargues War Cemetery, Marseilles, France, 3.D.Coll.5-6.

Robinson, Stuart Quentin, F/O, (22 years), RAFVR. 14 June 1943. Guidel Communal Cemetery, Brittany, France, Row 6 Grave 1.

Robotham, Kenneth James, Sgt, RAFVR. 1 December 1943. Frederikshavn Cemetery, Denmark, Grave 57.

Richmond, Arthur, Sgt, (20 yrs), RAFVR. 5 November 1943. Runnymede Memorial, Panel 173.

Royston, George Herbert, Sgt, (20 years), RAFVR. 10 February 1943. Cambridge City, Grave 13714.

Rush, Leslie Gordon, Sgt, RAFVR. 28 January 1944. Kirkeby Cemetery, Denmark, Grave 914.

S.

Saddler, Robert Campbell, Sgt, (22 yrs), RAFVR. 25 September 1944. Hastings Cemetery, Div O, Sec A Grave 102.

Salkeld, Robert, LAC, (20 yrs), RAF. 7 August 1943. Cathcart Cemetery (Linn Extension), Glasgow, Compt.2B Grave 686.

Sanderson, Robert Louis, P/O, (21 yrs), RCAF. 10 February 1944. Cambridge City Cemetery, Grave 13715.

Savage, Richard Thomas Percival, F/Sgt, (22 yrs), RAAF. 25 September 1944. Cambridge City Cemetery, Grave 15127.

Sawdy, William Ernest, F/O, RAFVR. 14 June 1943. Guidel Communal Cemetery, Britanny, France, Row 6 Grave 2.

Scott, David, F/Sgt, (20 yrs), RCAF. 31 August 1943. Berlin 1939-45 War Cemetery, 5.A.32-37.

Scott, Thomas Mackie, Sgt, (20 yrs), RAFVR. 26 May 1943. Jonkerbos War Cemetery, Netherlands, 20.A.2.

Sealy, Albert Edward, F/Sgt, RCAF. 28 January 1944. Kirkeby Churchyard, Collective Grave 911-913.

Seymour, Raymond Ernest George, Sgt, RAFVR. 25 June 1945. Reading (Henley Road) Cemetery Block 5 Grave 9694.

Shepherd, Eric George, Sgt, RAFVR. 28 August 1943. Durnbach War Cemetery 2.A.16.

Short, Leslie Edwin, F/Sgt, (age 21), RAFVR. 31 August 1943. Berlin 1939-45 War Cemetery 5.A.32-37.

Shorten, Albert George, W/O, (age 20), RCAF. 13 March 1943. Lincoln (Newport) Cem Sec H Grave 293 South.

Skinner, David, Sgt, (age 20), RAFVR. 28 August 1943. Durnbach War Cemetery 2.A.14.

Smith, John Thomas, Sgt, (age 27), RAFVR. 31 August 1943. Eindhoven (Woensel) General Cemetery EE.102.

Southgate, Victor Jack, Sgt, (21 years), RAFVR. 5 November 1943. Runnymede Memorial, Panel 165.

Sowden, James Birch, Sgt, RAFVR. 16 September 1944. Runnymede Memorial, Panel 238.

Stanley, Philip Francis, F/Sgt, RAFVR. 24 August 1943. Berlin 1939-45 War Cemetery, 4.E.18.

Stevens, John Charles William, Sgt, (22 years), RAFVR. 14 June 1943. Guidel Communal Cemetery, Britanny, France, Row 5 Grave 44.

Stockwell, Charles Stanley, Sgt, (27 years), RAFVR. 1 December 1943. Runnymede Memorial, Panel 166.

Strachan, Gordon, F/Sgt, RAFVR. 1 December 1943. Runnymede Memorial, Panel 136.

Stubbings, Ronald, Sgt, (20 years), RAFVR. 16 February 1944. Mazargues War Cemetery, Marseilles, 3.D.Coll.5-6.

Sullivan, Charles Barry, F/Sgt, (21 years), RAFVR. 7 February 1943. Guidel Communal Cemetery, Britanny, France, Row 3 Grave 19.

Swadling, Kenneth Matthew Francis, F/Sgt, RAFVR. 17 June 1944. Runnymede Memorial, Panel 222.

Sweitzer, Leonard James, W/O, (21 years), RCAF. 6 February 1943. Runnymede Memorial, Panel 180.

T.

Taylor, Jack, Sgt, (19 years), RAFVR. 27 September 1943. Hanover War Cemetery, 6.F.1-3.

Thomson, William Henry, Sgt, (32 years), RAFVR. 26 May 1943. Jonkerbos War Cemetery, Netherlands, 20.A.1.

Thurlow, Jack Alvin, F/Lt, (26 years), RCAF. 5 March 1945. Runnymede Memorial, Panel 278.

Townsend, Charles Richard, Sgt, (24 years), RAFVR. 13 March 1943. Runnymede Memorial, Panel 197.

Townsend, Leslie Robert, P/O, (24 years), RCAF. 9 April 1943. Runnymede Memorial, Panel 178.

Turner, Derek Wilfred, Sgt, (20 years), RAFVR. 6 February 1943. Runnymede Memorial, Panel 167.

Tym, Alan, Sgt, (20 years), RAFVR. 12 March 1944. Naujac-sur-Mer Communal Cemetery, France, D.6 Coll Grave 2.

V.

Vaughan, Leonard George, Sgt, (29 years), RAFVR. 13 March 1943. Barking Rippleside Cemetery, London, Sec K Grave 343.

W.

Waldorf, Leonard, Sgt, (20 years), RAFVR. 13 May 1943. Harderwijk General Cemetery, Netherlands, Plot 2 Grave 26-30.

Waller, John Roland Smith, Sgt, (21 years), RAFVR. 28 May 1943. Reichswald Forest War Cemetery, Germany, Grave 15F.5-8

Watson, Peter, F/Sgt, RCAF. 5 November 1943. Runnymede Memorial, Panel 186.

Watts, Francis William, Sgt, (21 years), RAFVR. 3 September 1943. Runnymede Memorial, Panel 169.

Watts, John Martin, Sgt, (19 years), RAFVR. 17 June 1944. Runnymede Memorial, Panel 240.

Way, William, Sgt, (23 years), RAFVR. 25 June 1945. Battersea (Morden) Cemetery, London, Section R, Grave 811.

Welch, Douglas Clement, F/O, (20 years), RAFVR. 5 November 1943. Runnymede Memorial, Panel 130.

West, Cecil Reginald, Sgt, RAFVR. 12 March 1944. Naujac-sur-Mer Communal Cemetery, France, D.6 Coll Grave 2.

Wharmby, Tom, Sgt, (age 21), RAFVR. 13 May 1943. Harderwijk General Cemetery, Netherlands, Plot 2 Grave 34.

Wheeker, Lionel Cottrell, F/O, RAFVR. 9 April 1943. Runnymede Memorial, Panel 130.

White, Cyril Frank, Sgt, (22 years), RAFVR. 13 March 1943. Runnymede Memorial, Panel 169.

Whimpenney, Arnold, Sgt, (21 years), RAFVR. 16 February 1944. Mazargues War Cemetery, Marseilles, 3.D.Coll.5-6.

Whittleston, Ronald Joffre, P/O, (28 years), RNZAF. 17 June 1944. Runnymede Memorial, Panel 263.

Widdecombe, Ronald James, F/O, (22 years), RAFVR. 24 August 1943. Runnymede Memorial, Panel 130.

Wilkes, Kevin John, F/Sgt, (20 years), RAAF. 31 August 1943. Berlin 1939-45 War Cemetery, 5.A.31.

Wilkes, Thomas William Albert, Sgt, (19 years), RAFVR. 28 August 1943. Durnbach War Cemetery, Germany, 9.B.17.

Williams, Ivor George, Sgt, RAFVR. 24 August 1943. Runnymede Memorial, Panel 170.

Williams, Reginald Alfred, Sgt, (28 years), RAF. 16 February 1944. Mazargues War Cemetery, Marseilles 3.D.Coll.5-6.

Wilson, Douglas, F/Sgt, RAFVR. 3 May 1945. Kiel War Cemetery, Germany, 2.E.7.

Wilson, John Guyie, Sgt, RAFVR. 13 May 1943. Harderwijk General Cemetery, Netherlands, Plot 2 Grave 26-30.

Wood, Dugald Gillies, Sgt, (23 years), RAFVR. 27 September 1943. Hanover War Cemetery, Germany, 6.F.1-3.

Woodruff, Harold Eunson, Sgt, (26 years), RAFVR. 13 February 1943. Guidel Communal Cemetery, Britanny, France, Row 5 Grave 5.

The Ely Cathedral Book of Remembrance includes those who served and died with 199 Squadron and is on display within the cathedral. Access to view a particular entry can be arranged by contacting the cathedral in advance of your visit.

Appendix 7: Squadron Awards

DSO (Distinguished Service Order): Usually awarded to Officers for commendable or distinguished service during wartime while in combat conditions with the enemy.

DFC (Distinguished Flying Cross): During WWII this medal was awarded to Officers and Warrant Officers serving in the RAF for an act of courage, valour or devotion to duty while flying on active operations against the enemy.

DFM (Distinguished Flying Medal): Awarded to RAF personnel below the rank of Warrant Officer and was the 'ordinary ranks' equivalent to the DFC with the same criteria applying to an award being made.

CGM (Conspicuous Gallantry Medal): This medal was the 'ordinary ranks' equivalent to the DSO when awarded for bravery while flying on operations against the enemy.

OBE ((Officer) The Order of the British Empire): This honour was bestowed for acts of gallantry and bravery not necessarily in the face of the enemy.

BEM ((Military Division, Non Commissioned Officers) British Empire Medal): Awarded for gallantry and acts of bravery not necessarily in the face of the enemy but worthy of recognition by the Crown.

Dates given are those of publication in the London Gazette. Rank of airmen listed is that at time of promulgation of the award.

1943:

16th April 1943. DFM: Sgt Alexander James Coupar, 1107348.

16th April 1943. DFM: F/Sgt Robert Burns Charters, Can/R. 115419.

4th June 1943. DFM: Sgt Alexander Douglas Finlayson, Aus. 408569.

11th June 1943. DFM : F/Sgt Peter Cyril Lewis Bird, 1376709.

15th June 1943. DFM: Sgt Peter Holt, 1147370.

13th August 1943. DFC: F/Lt Alan John Wingwood, 116081.

17th August 1943. DFM: Sgt Robert Leonard Double, 1336489.

31st August 1943. DFC: F/O Geoffrey Ernest Charles Archer, 124410.

10th September 1943. DFM: F/Sgt John Edwin Burton, 656247.

14th September 1943. DFM: Sgt Roy Dennis, 1137807.

14th September 1943. DFM: Sgt Joseph Malpas Shorttle, 656926.

17th September 1943. DFM: Sgt Robert Currie, 991058.

15th October 1943. DFC: F/Lt Wilmot Reginald Pettit, Can/J. 15517.

15th October 1943. DFC: S/Ldr Maurice Henry Hankins, 42602.

12th November 1943. DFM: F/Sgt William James Earle, 1293866.

12th November 1943. DFM: F/Sgt Ronald Arthur Levers, 1387970.

16th November 1943. DFC: P/O Wilfred Humphries, 156091.

16th November 1943. DFC: P/O Stanley Norman Freestone, 156092.

30th November 1943. DSO: S/Ldr Kenna Humby, DFC, 81059.

7th December 1943. DFC: F/Lt John Henry Waterfield, 124811.

10th December 1943. DFC: P/O Percy Frederick Christopher, 156784.

17th December 1943. DFM: F/Sgt William Dodsworth, Aus. 414342.

1944:

21st January 1944. DFC: P/O Leonard Jack Lawrence, 157491.

15th February 1944. DFC: W/O Burney Edgar Whitehouse, 1200847.

22nd February 1944. DFM: F/Sgt Harry Todd, 1392067.

31st March 1944. CGM: F/Sgt Herbert Allison Donaldson, 1215802.

23rd May 1944. DFC: P/O William Robert Samuel Noyes, Can/J. 18461.

26th May 1944. DFC: F/Lt Ewen John Campbell Guthrie. Nz. 417052.

26th May 1944. BEM (Military Division): LAC Joseph Therwell Wray, 944525.

26th May 1944. OBE (Military Division): S/Ldr Wilmot Reginald Pettit, DFC, Can/J. 15517.*

30th June 1944. DFC: P/O Robert Catterall, 53904.

13th October 1944. DFC: George Allen Noble, Aus. 409214.

13th October 1944. DFC: Edward Comlmey Little, 143475.

13th October 1944. DFC: Douglas Victor Long, 135575.

14th November 1944. DFC: F/Lt Michael Docherty, 155099.

8th December 1944. DFC: F/Lt Arthur Turner, 168844.

8th December 1944. DFC: F/Lt Philip James Bowering, Aus. 416924.

1945:

16th January 1945. DFC: F/Lt Norman Philip Holmes, 174021.

16th January 1945. DFC: F/Lt Edwin Wiseman, 160172.

16th January 1945. DFC: F/O Peter Barson, Aus. 409651.

16th February 1945. DFC: F/Lt George Wilde, 142373.

16th February 1945. DFC: F/Lt Will Hancock, 151660.

23rd March 1945. DFC: Hugh Norman Coventry, Aus. 410042.

13th April 1945. DFM: F/Sgt Philip Charles Branson, 1808484.

17th April 1945. DFC: P/O Wilfred Morris Jones, 183943.

22nd May 1945. DFC: F/Lt Norman Thomas Keen, 55951.

25th May 1945. DFC: Douglas Harold Halliwell, 169406.

25th May 1945. DFC: F/O Alan Edward Wood, 142341.

17th July 1945. DFC: F/Lt Ronald Gilbert, 178882.

17th July 1945. DFC: F/Lt Harry Green, 182398.

17th July 1945. DFC: F/Lt Raymond Edmond Lind, 170076.

1946:

1st January 1946. OBE: S/Ldr Charles Joseph Merryfull, Aus. 424778. With effect from 7th July 1945.**

Author's Note.

    * S/Ldr Pettit was transferred from 199 to 190 Squadron 4th April 1944 but was quickly reassinged to 620 Squadron on 13th April 1944 and made 'A' Flight Commander. He was killed flying in support of the D-Day landings 'Operation Tonga' (Caen, France) on 5th/6th June 1944. Hihs orders were to drop 15 paratroops of 591 Parachute Squadron Royal Engineers and two from HQ Royal Engineers. The Stirling S/Ldr Pettit was flying EF295 QS-J sustained serious damage when hit by flak and crashed in flames at Chateau de Grangues 14 miles ENE of Caen. Of the Stirling crew four were killed plus the two dispatchers. Some of the paratroops managed to bale out but those who survived the crash were soon captured and taken prisoner. Later in the day seven paratroop prisoners and a glider pilot had tried to escape and in doing so were shot and wounded by a guard. They were taken away by a number of German Military Police and shot.

    ** S/Ldr Merryfull was decorated for his contribution to designing and producing the Automatic Window Dispencer used by 199 Squadron in the later steages of WWII. He was killed a short time after the war endedon 8th July 1945 when testing a modified dispenser that had been fitted to a Mosquito. The aircraft broke up shortly after take off from RAF Docking and S/Ldr Merryfull and his passengers LAC Francis Gray both perished.

Appendix 8: Cyril 'Bill' Whitworth

Cyril Whitworth
Service No. 2212936

Born in Bury, Lancashire in May 1925, Cyril was educated at the town's Grammar School, and joined the RAFVR in December 1943. He was sent to No. 4 School of Technical Training at RAF St Athan, Vale of Glamorgan, in November 1944 on a flight engineer's course (Halifax III) and graduated with the rank of sergeant.

He was posted to 199 Squadon and his log book shows that his first flight – 'familiarisation, circuits and landings' – was with F/Lt. Reynolds in the Halifax EX-C on 1st February 1945.

His first sortie, on 7th March 1945, was with F/Lt Chilcott (EX-F) on a 'Bomber Command Radio Countermeasures' flight to Aachen – many more would follow.

With the war in Europe over he served in India (Calcutta and Bombay) from November 1945 until April 1947 when he was demobbed.

He died at Radstock, Somerset on 20th February 1976.

Time carried forward :— 26 HR 10 · 6 6 HR 05 MIN

Date	Hour	Aircraft Type and No.	Pilot	Duty	REMARKS (including results of bombing, gunnery, exercises, etc.)	Flying Times Day	Night
27·3·45	19·15	HALIFAX "E"	F/LT. CHILCOTT	ENGINEER	"OPS" WINDOW·BOMBING·BREMERHAVEN.		4 HR 25
29·3·45	16·10	"J"	F/LT. CHILCOTT	ENGINEER.	FERRYING A/CRAFT TO SWANTON MORLEY	0 HR 20	
					SUMMARY FOR MARCH 1945		
					199 SQUADRON		
					DAY NIGHT		
A/CRAFT TYPE HALIFAX					2 HR 5 MIN 63 HRS 25 MIN		
					31st March 1945 - C Whitworth		
					WDW Knight S/L		
					Officer Commanding "A" FLT.		
2·4·45	20·40	"A"	F/LT. CHILCOTT	ENGINEER.	"OPS" B·C·R·C·M. — HELIGOLAND.		5 HR 0
4·4·45	14·30	B	F/LT CHILCOTT	ENGINEER	COMPASS SWING	1·20	
4·4·45	19·40	"B"	F/LT. CHILCOTT	ENGINEER	"OPS" B·C·R·C·M HELIGOLAND		4 HR 15
14·4·45	18·25	"D"	F/LT CHILCOTT	ENGINEER	"OPS" B·C·R·C·M BERLIN		8 HR 35
17·4·45	21·48	"E"	F/LT CHILCOTT	ENGINEER	"OPS" B·C·R·C·M INGLESTADT		6 HR 10

TOTAL TIME ...

R.A.F. Form 2520/11

ROYAL AIR FORCE
CERTIFICATE OF SERVICE AND RELEASE

SERVICE PARTICULARS

Service Number } 2212936. Rank SERGEANT.
FLIGHT ENGINEER

Air Crew Category and/or R.A.F. trade AIR MOVEMENTS ASSISTANT

Air Crew Badges awarded (if any) FLIGHT ENGINEER.
INDIA COMMAND

Overseas Service FROM. 10·11·45 TO 8-4-47

R.A.F. Character VG (see notes on back of certificate on opposite page)

Proficiency A SAT (" ")

" B _____ (" ")

Decorations, Medals, Clasps, Mention in Despatches, Commendations, etc. 1939/45 STAR,
FRANCE & GERMANY STAR, DEFENCE & WAR MEDAL

Educational and Vocational Training Courses and Results. ALSO: BURMA STAR

DESCRIPTION

Date of Birth 23·5·25 Height 5'5"

Marks and Scars _____
Specimen Signature of Airman _C Whitworth_

of C. WHITWORTH
(Block Letters)

The above-named airman served in the R.A.F.V.R.
on full-time service.

from 13TH DECEMBER 1943 to 8-4-47

(Last day of service in unit before leaving for release and release leave).

Particulars of his Service are shown in the margin of this Certificate.

Brief statement of any special aptitudes or qualities or any special types of employment for which recommended :—

A reasonable and efficient airman - He should be quite satisfactory as a railway clerk.

Ashton

Date 3·4·47 _Wing Commander_
Signature of Officer Commanding

Appendix 9: Richard Masters

Corporal Richard Masters
Service No. 1875938

A native of Welwyn Garden City, nineteen year old Richard Masters was conscripted into the Royal Air Force on 15th April 1943, and although flying duty would have been his preference, his initial medical examination diverted him to ground duties as a leading aircraftman. Of course, noting his civilian employer was Standard Telephones and Cables, the service may have recognised skilss it could use.

After basic training at Skegness – square bashing, bayonet drill and target practice – he went to Woolwich Polytechnic, in July 1943, for basic electrical engineering and to Bolton Technical College, for radio theory, in autumn.

After a succession of postings, he was with 199 Squadron at North Creake in May 1944, joining the wireless telegraphy and radar section. The work ranged from changing light bulbs to repairing and installing radio sets, radar equipment and Mandrel units.

The two accompanying photographs show the whole staff of the unit in July 1945, shortly before it was broken up.

After de-mobbed Richard returned to STC with a spell at Marconi – penning handbooks and manuals on electrical tools and equipment – before his appointment as editor of the trade weekly *Electrical Review*.

Wireless telegraphy section outside workshop at North Creake, shortly before its dibandment in July 1945.

Back row: **Richard Masters, Bosworth, Aldworth, Ivor Burch, Mike Conolly, Dennis Bird, Hugh Dunthorne, Duggie Breed.** *Middle row*: **George Reade, Nicholas, Joe Rowe, Sgt 'Miff' Major, Len Boxall, unknown, unknown.** *Front row*: **Charlie Mason, Alec Wyat, Johnny Cosgrove, Peter Ballard, Terry Buckley, Fred White, Les Tutt.**

Workshop at North Creake, July 1945.

Back row: George Groom, Eric Mosley, Smith, Norman Reed, Fred Partington. *Middle row*: unknown, unknown, 'Nobby' Clarke, unknown, Ron Rowe, unknown, unknown, unknown. *Front row*: Ella, unknown, unknown, Flt Sgt Matthews, Bob Huthinson, Joan.

Appendix 10: The Stirling Mural

In 1982 I mentioned to a friend that I had been reading about old airfields around Norfolk and how some of them still retained buildings and runways. He told me of North Creake and that he had visited the site on several occasions. I joined him on a visit and we spent an hour or two exploring, the domestic site, the bomb dump and taxiways.

As we were leaving, my friend recalled a painting in one of the buildings and asked if I would like to see it. Time was pressing but something made me feel it was worth taking a look.

Upon entering the building, I was amazed to see a large mural of a Stirling bomber, about six feet by four feet, in remarkable condition for its age. I saw the code letters EX-N on the fuselage and underneath the inscription '16-6-44 R.I.P.' I noted this down with the intention of following it up.

The flight office at North Creake.

My good intentions lapsed until seeing an article about the mural in the East Anglian newspaper *The Eastern Daily Press*.

My interest was re-kindled and I resolved to save this piece of historic artwork. The challenge was – how? I was unsure of a course of action. I could find no record of previous attempts to save such a large section of a brick wall bearing a painting, so there was nothing on the technicalities. Consulting the Fenland Aircraft Preservation Society, highlighted two obstacles. First, permission to remove the mural and second, finding it a new home.

When the RAF left North Creake in 1947 it was taken over by Seamans, the animal feedstuff company, and many of the buildings were utilised as offices and production areas. Some of the buildings abutting the main road were converted to houses for employees. The original flight office was now a storehouse and home to the mural.

The original mural painted on the wall of the Flight Office at North Creake.

Removal and Preservation

I telephoned Mr Maurice Hood, the manager (Aug 2009) of Seamans Animal Feeds Ltd (now ABN Ltd (animal feeds)) at North Creake, who was most enthusiastic to the idea of saving the Mural, and suggested I contact Mr Ward-Walters, a director of the company, for his approval. Mr Ward-Walters was as enthusiastic as Maurice Hood and agreed that the wall could be cut out, provided the brickwork was replaced with new.

To find a home for the mural, I contacted the Royal Air Force Museum at Hendon, London and spoke to Mr Tony Harrold. He agreed to put the problem to the museum committee, and a few weeks later he wrote to confirm that the museum would accept the mural as an exhibit in the Bomber Command Museum.

Consulting my brother, Dave Reid, then Contracts Manager to the Wisbech building firm, Colemans Ltd, as to the best method of removing the wall, brought an offer from Michael Coleman, the firm's proprietor to sponsor the task by providing the scaffolding, disc cutters, transport, and the sand, cement, and bricks, to restore the wall.

The mural had small areas of flaking, so next was the question of conservation. The Museums Service for South East England gave me the name of Miss Pauline Plummer, who specialised in the preservation of wall art and frescoes. She went to North Creake and spent the best part of a day (funded by the RAF Museum) re-affixing individual flakes of paint on to the wall and applying a coat of synthetic resin. The result was a credit to her expertise.

The safe removal of the brickwork and its transportation was achieved by clamping it in a purpose-made frame.

Ongoing research work was to identify the aircraft, the significance of the date, and the artist. With the help of Bill Welbourne, Chairman of the Fenland Preservation Society, and Mr Bill Slater of Caxton, Cambridge, who coincidentally was researching a crew of 199 Squadron who went missing on 16-6-44, it was possible to answer all these questions. We eventually identified the aircraft as Stirling LJ531 EX-N, lost without trace on the night of 16 June 1944.

The artist was identified as Flight Sergeant 'Ted' Allen, Flight Engineer, who flew in Flight Sergeant Phil Bowering's crew. He was also credited with the nose art of "The Gremlin Teaser" on LJ542 and also "B-Beer" on LJ514.

Preparation work on the clamps and frame for the mural's transportation was completed, with assistance from the Wisbech firms J. Lane Engineering and Seadyke Freight Systems, who supplied much of the materials and the machine tools needed.

The painting covered with a thick plastic sheet to protect it.

Saturday 29th October 1983 was set for the removal of the mural and everyone connected with the initial cutting and clamping work assembled at North Creake.

Protected with heavy gauge plastic sheeting. Dave Reid and Rod Lyons undertook the difficult task of cutting out the brickwork along the bottom of the mural. This done, a scaffold was erected in the room at the rear of the mural, as it was decided that this was the way the wall would come out. The course above the painting was now removed and the clamping bars and timbers fitted back and front.

Next came the dusty job of disc cutting three vertical slots right through the wall to free the section on which the mural was painted.

Next morning, a larger team assembled to lift out the mural and its brickwork. No lifting equipment could be used as the roof beams were too weak to stand an all-up weight of around 5 cwt (255 kg). The wall was inched until it was skewed around sideways and eased into the back room and slowly lowered onto the waiting scaffold. Boards were removed in stages to allow the wall to descend to ground level. Scraped knuckles and the odd blackened fingernail were quickly forgotten when the mural finally rested on the floor.

The final lift onto the lorry was achieved without incident and bracings put in place to secure it for transit. Dave Reid and Rod Lyons filled the hole with new brickwork, removed the scaffolding and tidied the site. The journey back to Wisbech was uneventful, as was the manhandling of it into my garage.

Arrangements were made with the RAF museum for the final transportation of the mural. They were preparing a suitable frame with captions and photographs to illustrate the work involved, and the crew of EX-N. This work would take some time.

Bill Welbourne traced 'Ted' Allen's (the artist) address to Witchford, Cambs, but sadly he had recently passed away. His wife was informed of the work in progress and she invited myself and Bill to visit her. After explaining the aims of the project, we invited Mrs Allen to attend the memorial dedication and unveil the mural. She agreed, saying she was pleased her husband's painting had been saved and would be preserved.

Next, was to track down any family of the crew of EX-N and this work was also delegated to Bill Welbourne and Bill Slater. Small pieces of information gave leads to many people, some in New Zealand, and gradually relatives were located and informed of the proposed dedication.

In parallel with these investigations, I was working closely with Wing Commander W.G. Wood and Group Captain Bill Randle MBE, AFC, DFM, Director of Appeals at the Bomber Command Museum, to formulate an Order of Service and fix a date for the dedication. He also suggested we contact Padre Schofield, the officiating chaplain at Hendon Museum, to ask if he would conduct the dedication service, who accepted our invitation. A date was then fixed for Sunday 17 June 1984 – another coincidence as this was the exact 40th anniversary of the date the crew went missing. I was beginning to get the feeling that someone on a higher plane was having a hand in these proceedings.

Now news reached me that the frame was ready in the museum, so I organised the transportation of the mural to Hendon. A friend and co-member of the Aviation Society Peter Russell worked at a local firm, Burralls Printers Ltd, and he was able to acquire the use of one of their large delivery vans to take the painting to London. They also provided all the fuel required for the trip. Arrangements were made to have extra staff on hand at the museum should we need any assistance.

The mural was loaded up on 4 December 1983 and, after a rather long and nerve-racking journey, we arrived at Hendon. I spent the whole of the three hour trip in the back of the vehicle checking nothing moved. A surprise was in store for us as we were met by some members of 199 Squadron who were keen to see their picture once more. We unloaded the mural, still with three horizontal clamps in place and left it in the capable hands of Mr Chris Elliot and Mr Tony Harrold and members of the museum staff to place in the prepared frame. The Squadron members in attendance spent some time looking at the mural and talking about their role with 199 and most of those there said they were also eager to attend the unveiling and dedication service. Before leaving the museum, I took one last look at the mural, as I had become quite attached to it by now, and then gathered our small band of helpers for the return journey home.

Jim Newman, John Reid, Bill Welbourne, Ken Peplar, Fred Cubberley, Pete Russell, Peter Gunn, John Welbourne, Paul Reid, Henry Wagner, Dave Reid, Rod Lyons.

 There was still much to be done. The most important item on the agenda now was to arrange the unveiling and dedication and to inform everybody of dates, times and location.

On Sunday 17 June 1984 members of the Aviation Society accompanied by relatives and friends travelled by chartered coach to Hendon.

Arriving at the Bomber Command Museum we saw that the mural had been fitted into its exhibition frame and was covered with the Royal Air Force Standard. Group Captain Randle welcomed the very large gathering of people attending the ceremony. Among whom were family members of the Pilot of EX-N, P/O Dale, a cousin of P/O Whittlestone, a cousin of Sgt Watts, Flight Engineer, brother and sisters of W/O Lofthouse, Special Wireless Operator and relatives of Sgt Latimer, Rear Gunner, who had journeyed from Scotland.

As two of the crew lost on EX-N came from New Zealand I had also contacted their High Commission in London and invited a representative to attend the dedication. We were pleased that Mr B. Lockstone, the First Secretary at the High Commission and Miss Rosemary Banks, attended.

F/Sgt Ted Allen who painted the Mural.

Many ex-members of 199 Squadron were present, along with wives and family and also Mrs Dorothy Allen (May 2014; now 88 years of age) accompanied by two of her three sons, Ian and Peter, and her brother in law Mr Fred Allen, the artist's brother.

After his welcome Group Captain Randle went on to say: *"At this point the museum is as yet unfinished and lacks a human factor. In this mural we have the first reference in the museum to the fact that someone gave their life in Bomber Command. This is the first reference we have to the fact that 56,000 were killed in Bomber Command during the offensive against Germany. This is the beginning of the act of Remembrance that will develop in this museum. The museum has lacked any reference to the Stirling, the aircraft was all but forgotten. In the mural was something which represented the value and history of a great aircraft".*

Mrs Allen unveiled the mural and I handed over the parchment scroll to Group Captain Randle transferring the mural into the safe-keeping of the museum.

A service of dedication was conducted by Padre Schofield, who read out the names of the missing crew and said prayers in memory, and all the other members of crews who gave their lives during their service. He then dedicated the mural as a lasting memorial to them all. Finally, Lance Smith, the ex Adjutant of 199 Squadron, gave a speech, thanking the Fenland Aircraft Preservation Society for *"their keenness, ingenuity and determination in moving the mural".*

It was with a very deep sense of pride that we all came away from the museum. A piece of history had been preserved; many people had been brought together, new friendships struck, old acquaintances reunited. Many brave men who gave their lives have, at last, a fitting memorial and their relatives something with which to relate.

Almost 30 years later, in August 2012, I returned to North Creake, on the invitation of Claire Nugent and Nigel Morter who have made the old control tower their home, before converting it back to its original state. The conversion is being carried out sympathetically and much of the inside and outside will look as it did in 1944. They will run it as a themed B&B and tea room. I took with me all the 199 Squadron and North Creake material that could be easily copied and Claire and Nigel will use this in a small museum room outlining the history of North Creake during the Second World War.

There were a few surprises in store. The old flight office from where the mural had been removed, had been bricked round, given a new roof and now formed the annex to a bungalow. Quite a lot of the original runway and peri-track are still there and used by the agricultural vehicles. I also visited some of the old buildings including the three original hangars, two of which are part of the animal feed business whilst the other is a farm store building.

The last surprise was when I was taken down the Wells road to 'The Real Ale Shop' which stocks a range of Norfolk breweries beers. There was a shelf of bottles of beer brewed by the Beeston Brewery and, to my amazement, a selection called "Stirling" depicting a coloured picture of the North Creake Mural. This malty masterpiece is brewed using barley grown on the farm that surrounds the North Creake Airfield.

My last call upon leaving was to the memorial erected on the site in memory of all those who served at North Creake.

Left: **W/O F. Lofthouse, Special Wireless Operator.**

Above, crew of LJ531 EX-N: **Pilot Officer T.W. Dale, Pilot, RNZAF; Pilot Officer R.J. Whittleston, Navigator, RNZAF; Warrant Officer F.C. Brittain, Wireless Operator; Warrant Officer F. Lofthouse, Special Wireless Operator (not in photograph); Flight Sergeant Sgt K.K. Swadling, B/A; Sergeant J. Higginbottom, Mid Upper Gunner; Sergeant W. Lattimer 'Jock', Rear Gunner; Sergeant J. Watts 'Flap', Flight Engineer.**